Understanding Faith

ST ANDREWS STUDIES IN PHILOSOPHY AND PUBLIC AFFAIRS

Founding and General Editor:
John Haldane, University of St Andrews

Values, Education and the Human World
edited by John Haldane

Philosophy and its Public Role
edited by William Aiken and John Haldane

Relativism and the Foundations of Liberalism
by Graham Long

Human Life, Action and Ethics: Essays by G.E.M. Anscombe
edited by Mary Geach and Luke Gormally

The Institution of Intellectual Values: Realism and Idealism in Higher Education
by Gordon Graham

Ethics, Society and Culture
by John Haldane

Life, Liberty and the Pursuit of Utility
by Anthony Kenny and Charles Kenny

Distributing Healthcare: Principles, Practices and Politics
edited by Niall Maclean

Liberalism, Education and Schooling: Essays by T.M. Mclaughlin
edited by David Carr, Mark Halstead and Richard Pring

The Landscape of Humanity: Art, Culture & Society
by Anthony O'Hear

Faith in a Hard Ground: Essays on Religion, Philosophy and Ethics by G.E.M. Anscombe
edited by Mary Geach and Luke Gormally

Subjectivity and Being Somebody
by Grant Gillett

Understanding Faith: Religious Belief and Its Place in Society
by Stephen R.L. Clark

Profit, Prudence and Virtue: Essays in Ethics, Business and Management
edited by Samuel Gregg and James Stoner

Understanding Faith

Religious Belief and Its Place in Society

Stephen R.L. Clark

St Andrews Studies in Philosophy and Public Affairs

IMPRINT ACADEMIC

Published in the UK by Imprint Academic
PO Box 200, Exeter EX5 5YX, UK

Published in the USA by Imprint Academic
Philosophy Documentation Center
PO Box 7147, Charlottesville, VA 22906-7147, USA

ISBN 9781845401542 (paperback)
ISBN 9781845401559 (cloth)

A CIP catalogue record for this book is available from the British Library and US Library of Congress

Cover Photograph:
St Salvator's Quadrangle, St Andrews by Peter Adamson
from the University of St Andrews collection

Contents

Preface 1

1. **Devils and Mental Microbes** **5**
   - Protestants and Atheists against the Idols 5
   - A Defence of Faith 7
   - Devils and Mental Microbes 16
   - Other Worlds 22

2. **Projects, Conjectures, Refutations** **30**
   - Dogmas and Disagreements 30
   - Science and Story 34
   - Truth and Imagination 44
   - Metaphysics 50
   - Prayer. 55

3. **Understanding Scripture** **61**
   - Reading Scripture 61
   - Hermeneutical Traditions 65
   - Explanations, Therapies and Demons 72
   - Uncovering Evil 79

4. **The Abolition of Man.** **87**
   - The Paradox of Objective Value 87
   - The Anthropocentric Synthesis 88
   - De-Moralizing Nature 91
   - Plato and the Book of Genesis 96
   - The Choice before 'Environmentalists' 100
   - Stripping Away Significance 103

5. **Can Animals be our Friends?.** **110**
   - Pythagoras and the Eternal Self 110
   - Common Sense about Friends and Animals 112
   - Words and the Wordless 118

6. What's Wrong with Darwinian Evolution? 125
Social Darwinism 125
Some Problems with Scientific Darwinism 134
The Gradual and the Catastrophic 140
Darwin's Doubt 145
Intelligence and Natural Norms 148

7. Waking Up 158
Morals in the Dream of Life 158
Waking from the Dream 162
Scientific Enlightenment 165

8. What is God? 172
Understanding Words and Pictures 172
Gods and the Wow Factor 175
The God of Atheists 182
Orthodox Argument 187

9. World Orders, World Religions 195
World Order and the Secularist Illusion 195
The Clash of Civilizations 203
The World Beast and Apocalypse 209
Enmity, Liberty and Solidarity within the State 214

10. More Local Problems 227
Honour, 'Indoctrination' and Faith Schools 227
Two Sorts of Slavishness 239
Sex and Sacred Violence 248
Pleonexia, Health and Achievement 258

11. Considering the End 262

Index 270

Preface

I began this book in a fit of exasperation. My original intention was merely to write a paper on the 'religious' zeal and doctrinaire ignorance, as I saw it, of certain modern atheistical writers, and to point out how often their manner mirrored that of more traditional believers. I soon saw that there would be many incidental references that required or deserved expansion, and began instead to conceive the whole as a fairly lengthy monograph. At this point I was approached by John Haldane, with an invitation to contribute something to this series, and I chose to interpret the suggestion as a sort of external endorsement. Since then, the project has continued to expand, and I have persuaded myself at any rate that my initial insight was correct. Militant atheists, though they will of course disdain the suggestion, are preaching what is in effect a religion, and one that can be seen as a sort of Christian heresy. Like other such heresies it contains and builds upon some truths which are worth recalling, and as such it does a real service, if only to offer a contrast to some *other* heresies (for example, theism as this is often understood), and to require some clarification of the central doctrines especially of Abrahamic faith.

I write as a philosopher with a preference, most of the time, for hermeneutical rather than merely critical examination even of doctrines that I am sure that I reject. The chief flaw in current atheistical discourse is a refusal even to *try* to understand what is meant by 'faith', 'God', 'sin', 'salvation' and the rest. Some atheists will of course reply—it is a constantly repeated theme on Amazon—that there is no need to examine in any detail a doctrine which is absurd from the beginning. But the problem is not that they don't bother with the minutiae of faith, but that they don't understand the bare minimum of the doctrine or the practice they disdain. Obviously (to any believer), if 'God' and 'belief in God' meant what atheists imagine then a belief in God would be—if not absurd—at any rate both dangerous and foolish. It ought to occur to any honest enquirer that there is at least a chance that it doesn't.

I also write, unavoidably, as an Anglican Christian, though one with much more interest in and love of 'animals' than has been the mainstream attitude in most Christian churches. My understanding of the faith has been shaped by this, and by my Neo-Platonic leanings. I have learnt much from non-Christian sources, including Jewish and Islamic writings, and even from non-Abrahamic sources, including Buddhists and pagan Greeks (both philosophical and poetic pagans). It is probably necessary to add—in the light of the routine abuse that has been directed at anyone who doubts some elements of mainstream evolutionary theory, especially as that has been presented to the wider public—that I have no principled objection to the notion that all terrestrial life is genealogically related, that we are all—humans, birds, termites, sea-slugs and archaebacteria—descended from some one ancestor. On the contrary, I take that claim more seriously and draw more comfort from it than most mainstream scientists. But one of the most annoying features of current militant atheism is the habit of equating evolutionary theory solely with the most atheistical form of Neo-Darwinism. I can dismiss the latter—as I do, for philosophical reasons as much as for religious ones—without needing to dismiss the former. I am sure that this will not prevent a host of Amazon and other reviewers naming me as a hypocritical 'creationist', without bothering to understand even what *creation* is. It is also, on the other hand, annoying to find that some American Protestants—and strangely enough, some Muslims—imagine that any benevolent interest in non-human animals, any insistence that we are all 'God's creatures', is a sign of Satanic influence. The only (bad) excuse for this is ignorance.

As a philosopher and as an Anglican Christian I am confident of some things, not of others. I am convinced that there really is a truth which is not dependent on our wishes or our reasonings, and that this truth is nonetheless attainable—in part—by those who follow the right way. Those who say there is no truth are liars; those who deny that we can ever find it out admit they have no reason for what they say. I am also confident that I have friends and family, that there are very many souls within the world, that we are never quite alone. Christian doctrine, it seems to me, supports those claims, and Christian practice is vindicated in the clumsy attempt to live by it. But there are also many things of which I am not confident, and need not be. As a philosopher and an Anglican Christian I reserve the right to speculate, to explore the possibilities, without entirely giving myself to any.

So to summarize: in the opening chapter I consider how militant atheists often seem to echo the hostility that traditional believers have felt for other creeds, and even blame those other creeds on mental parasites. More casual atheists and liberal believers are readier to accommodate individual choice, and may even acknowledge that 'faith' is genuinely valuable (faith, that is, in the possibilities of reconciliation and survival), and that it needs support, but have sometimes forgotten that some creeds are actually evil (as it were, the work of devils or the effect of mental microbes). There have been different strategies for resisting such parasites, including rationalistic scepticism (which self-destructs): the better solution is to acknowledge the real authority of the simple demand 'to do justice, love mercy, and walk humbly with our God'. Religion is very dangerous (like sex, science, family feeling, war and other powerful abstracts): *true* religion is the attempt to live in beauty.

In later chapters I add more detail to the analysis, considering such topics as the alleged openness of 'scientists' compared with the 'dogmatism' of 'believers'; the difficulty of reading 'scripture' outside 'the community of faith' that has selected and elaborated it; the problems of moral realism (and the problem with abandoning it); why Darwinian and neo-Darwinian Theory has been unpopular with some believers, and what if anything can still be affirmed from it; what can be learnt from modern biology (especially) about our relations with other creatures; the nature of God; the metaphor of 'waking up' as applied to our hopes of heaven; the varieties of possible world orders founded on differing religious schemata (including some atheistical ones); and the place of religion in the State. I conclude, appropriately, with some remarks about the End.

I should add that this work is in part an attempt to sum up and clarify arguments and ideas that I have been exploring over the last forty years, and also, in part, an attempt to work myself out of post-operative depression (after a tumour and half my colon were removed), while also suffering considerable family anxiety. My debt to my family (my wife, my children) is enormous. I also acknowledge a comparable debt to my colleagues, my readers, my employers—and of course the militant atheists who so exasperate me. Most of those debts I have no way of repaying, except by gratitude.

Perhaps that will serve: giving thanks, as both Chesterton and Heidegger have observed, is the highest form of thinking.[1]

Stephen R.L. Clark
Liverpool, January 2009

[1] G.K. Chesterton *A Short History of England* (Chatto & Windus: London 1917), p. 59; Martin Heidegger *What is Called Thinking?*, trans. F.D. Wieck & J. Glenn Gray (Harper & Row: New York 1968; original published 1954), pp. 138ff.

1

Devils and Mental Microbes

Protestants and Atheists against the Idols

Casual atheists are merely those who have lost interest in the thought of gods. Militant atheists wish to eradicate such thoughts, whether by making speeches or, if they have the power, outlawing everything they think 'religious'. To those not caught up in their rhetoric, they will often seem to bear a comic resemblance to Inquisitors, devoted to discovering the truth, denouncing harmful heresy and branding their opponents fools or knaves. It is hardly a new form: George Berkeley, back in the 18th century, referred to gentlemen (self-styled 'freethinkers') who 'did not think themselves obliged to prove all they said, or else proved their assertions, by saying or swearing they were all fools that believed the contrary'.[1] Their rhetoric, indeed, often owes a lot to older, openly religious talk. Idolatry, after all, is the worship of false gods, things manufactured by kings and priests and poets to serve their worldly ends. As Nicholas Lash observes

> The ancient traditions of devotion and reflection, of worship and enquiry, have seen themselves as *schools.* Christianity and Vedantic Hinduism, Judaism and Buddhism and Islam are schools... whose pedagogy has the twofold purpose—however differently conceived and executed in the different traditions—of weaning us from our idolatry and purifying our desire.[2]

---

[1] George Berkeley Guardian Essay 'On the Pineal Gland', *Works*, eds. T.E. Jessop & A.A. Luce, vol. 7 (Thomas Nelson: Edinburgh, 1955), p. 191.

[2] Nicholas Lash, *The Beginning and the End of 'Religion'* (Cambridge University Press: Cambridge, 1996), p. 21. See also Moses Maimonides, *The Guide of the Perplexed,* trans. Chaim Rabin, ed. Julius Guttman (Hackett: Indianapolis 1995; original version 1190), Bk. 3, ch. 29: p178: 'the first purpose of the whole law is to remove idolatry and to wipe out its traces and all that belongs to it, even in

From Isaiah to Foxe's *Book of Martyrs*,[3] iconoclasts have insisted that we must not imagine God in our own image, and that 'religious' feeling is often a mask for sin. Most missionaries, at least in the days of empire, have assumed that 'native religions' amount to devil-worship. A few have tried to locate at least *some* elements of truth in what was believed before, but only by allegorizing or moralizing the old rites and stories. Even if the one true God is acknowledged *somewhere* in the 'native religion', His messages have been distorted and mostly forgotten, whether by merely human indolence or by demonic influence.

The missionaries denounced all 'other' gods as false: figments or real devils. Militant atheists denounce *all* gods as false, but are like the missionaries in thinking both that their *own* state of mind is obviously right, that these religions are not harmless fancies, and that they are caused by parasites, now often known as 'memes'. This latter term is only a more modern version of D.G. Ritchie's 'mental microbes',[4] which spread by strict Darwinian rules through vulnerable minds. If we are ever to have peace from them we must construct sound immune systems, inoculate ourselves, and hold on only to the *truth* conveyed by—well, by missionaries for the newer creed. It is 'the religious', now, that are the dupes of evil, rather than mere idolaters, heathens, heretics, Papists or Anabaptists.

Casual atheists are usually bemused by this, finding no universal evil in the fancies of their fellows, and preferring to live and let live rather than impose yet another creed on all. The long experiment of Soviet Socialism, after all, never actually eliminated Christianity, but was responsible for considerable pain—and evil—in the attempt. Better let the creeds dissolve under the weight of their presumed absurdity than bother to denounce them. Put up with them if they don't. Militant atheists, like missionaries (since they *are*), are much more sensitive to evil. Even if they have not yet the power to *outlaw* any religion, they have, at least in the United Kingdom, made it difficult for any 'religious' person to hold high office, unless she is willing to ignore her own beliefs. Those who confess to 'praying' are

---

memory'. The idea is discussed by Jan Assman in, *Moses the Egyptian* (Harvard University Press: Cambridge, MA, 1997), p. 58.

[3] John Foxe (1517–87), *Actes and Monuments of these Latter and Perillous Days, touching Matters of the Church* (John Day, 1563, with many reprints and revised editions to follow; see *The Variorum Edition*, (hriOnline, Sheffield, 2004), available from: http://www. hrionline.shef.ac.uk/foxe/. [Accessed: 25. 12. 2007]).

[4] D.G. Ritchie, *Darwinism and Politics* (Swan Sonnenschein & Co: London, 1891), p. 22.

easily portrayed as would-be prophets and cult-leaders (and of course some of them may be), unless they can instead be reckoned hypocrites (and of course some of them may be).

A Defence of Faith

Liberal believers in some familiar faith are also often bemused by these hostilities. Old-fashioned missionaries, they will say, saw only evil and the work of devils in 'native religions', or in such variants of their own faiths as they disliked. Better educated believers will instead suggest that all such faiths, all such 'religions', offer some aspect of the truth, some outlet for a proper 'religious faith'. The Prince of Wales may have been a little pompous in hoping to be a 'Defender of Faith' rather than a Defender of *the* Faith, in 1994, but his intent was good: he was thereby declaring that he did not see himself as the enemy of faiths other than the Anglican,[5] and so agreeing with the liberal consensus—one only recently shaken by the rise of a more militant Islam or a more self-righteous Protestant fundamentalism. 'The Prince of Wales has, over many years, made clear that, as a committed Christian with a strong personal faith, he believes very strongly that the world in which we live can only become a safer and more united place if we all make the effort to tolerate, accept and understand cultures, beliefs and faiths different from our own.'[6] Quite why this policy should be mocked (as it has been) is unclear—except that anything he says is axiomatically, for some, ridiculous. Even liberals, of course, have never really believed that *every* faith as such is worth defending, but they have usually reckoned it safer to 'live and let live', like the casual atheist. What is defended is the right of everyone to tell her own story about the world, engage in whatever ritual, as long as this is within the law. And that last caveat only requires that we do no harm to others, and either fulfil our civic duties or peacefully endure the lawful penalty for disobedience. Those who believe that they are messengers of the divine, or of the Galactic Empire, are free to do so. Even if they believe that the world is run by the Illuminati, lizards in disguise, or devils, they must be free to do so—after all, their beliefs are not so

[5] For the record, the title 'Defensor Fidei' was originally awarded to Henry VIII by Pope Leo X in 1521 for his reasoned replies to Martin Luther, but is maintained as one of the British monarch's titles by Act of a Protestant Parliament in 1544, naming Edward VI and his heirs as defenders of the *Anglican* consensus. The present Prince made the suggestion in a BBC television interview.

[6] Taken from the Prince of Wales's website, http://www. princeofwales.gov. uk/faqs/what_religion_do_the_prince_and_the_duchess_practice__173958182 4. html, accessed 8th December 2007.

different from other, tamer conspiracy theories (that the world is run by an international cartel, the Mafia, or the CIA). When conspiracy theorists start suspecting that the world is run by *Jews*, even liberals may get restive: we have, after all, clear evidence of what such theorists do. Their beliefs are not so harmless.

And neither are any strong beliefs (including the beliefs, of course, of militant atheists). If I truly believe that p then I must also believe that anyone who thinks otherwise is *wrong*, and really ought to be enlightened. The right to be mistaken, even ridiculously mistaken, is the root of civil liberty and true religion—and one that it is horribly easy to deconstruct. The claim that everyone has a 'right' to her opinions, however foolish or ill-supported, is really very strange—but also very important. Others may be entitled to try and prove her wrong, but not to silence her. So the primary liberal model of civic tolerance is one that I shall not contest: call it the secular model, and one that can be endorsed by most believers, simply because we realize the dangers of any more substantive national creed. 'Anglicanism' was once a firmly Protestant rejection of Romish Error, especially the belief that 'this realm of England' could be subject to a foreign power, the Pope, but also such beliefs as seemed to lessen personal responsibility or increase ecclesiastical power.[7] Anglicans once endorsed particular beliefs in opposition to those errors, but have learned (that is, the institution has concluded, perhaps mistakenly) that most theological disputes, however real, don't really *matter*. Or at least they matter less than the fundamental creed: that we should somehow love each other, that we should, somehow, recognize 'the Divine' in each of us. After all, if *no-one* really understands the nature of God, of sin, or of salvation, it is unnecessarily picky to insist that those with an apparently different understanding of these things are *wrong* (or wrong enough to matter).[8] It's hardly a new problem. In 384 AD Symmachus, as prefect of the city, pleaded with the emperor to allow the ancient *Ara Pacis* to remain in the Roman Senate:

> The divine Mind has distributed different guardians and different cults to different cities. As souls are separately given to

[7] The Anglican *Articles of Religion* that were agreed in 1562, for example, remark that the doctrine of Predestination (which may well be required in logic) is a 'dangerous downfall' for 'curious and carnal persons', and so not to be adopted as a doctrine of the Church (*Article 17*). That 'the Bishop of Rome hath no jurisdiction in this realm of *England*' is declared formally in *Article 37*.

[8] See David B. Burrell, 'Some Requisites for Interfaith Dialogue', *New Blackfriars*, 89 (2008), pp. 300–10.

> infants as they are born, so to peoples the genius of their destiny. We ask, then, for peace for the gods of our fathers and of our country. It is just that all worship should be considered as one. We look on the same stars, the sky is common, the same world surrounds us. What difference does it make by what pains each seeks the truth? We cannot attain to so great a secret by one road (*uno itinere non potest perveniri ad tam grande secretum*).[9]

The merely secular, tolerant understanding of the liberal believer is not the whole story (as may already be evident from the preceding paragraphs). When Charles declared himself a would-be 'Defender of Faith' he was also imputing particular value, exactly, to *Faith*. The thought was not only, or at any rate need not only have been, that it was important for the monarch of the United Kingdom, as a symbol of its strange unity, simply to defend the freedom of every citizen to believe as she prefers (within the law). *Faith*, perhaps, is something to be valued—and not every citizen will think this true. Militant atheists, for example, will contend that 'faith' is mere credulity, susceptibility to dangerous mental microbes. *Faith* is the very thing we shouldn't have (they say).

In opposition to 'faith' we are often encouraged to believe all and only what can be 'rationally established'—and this is usually equated with some particular creed. According to the British Humanist Association, 'Humanism is the belief that we can live good lives without religious or superstitious beliefs. Humanists make sense of the world using reason, experience and shared human values. We seek to make the best of the one life we have by creating meaning and purpose for ourselves. We take responsibility for our actions and work with others for the common good'.[10] Some spokesmen for that Association apparently relish the idea that the European Union Unfair Commercial Practices Directive (which became law in the United Kingdom in 2008) might enable 'spiritualistic

---

[9] Symmachus *Relation* 3, ch. 10: taken from http://www.ucalgary.ca/~vandersp/Courses/texts/sym-amb/symrel3f.html (accessed 1 January 2008). It is perhaps worth adding that the aphorism is greater than its author. James O'Donnell remarks, after prolonged reading of Symmachus's letters, that 'rarely do we get so comprehensive a literary portrait surviving from antiquity of so thoroughly wearisome, fatuous, and pompous an individual. The letters are simply as preposterous as their author was' (James J. O'Donnell, 'The Demise of Paganism': *Traditio*, 35 (1979), pp. 45–88). Symmachus's plea for tolerance was a plea for ancestral privilege.

[10] http://www.humanism.org.uk/site/cms/contentChapterView.asp?chapter=309 (accessed 26th May 2008). It is not clear that any of the terms wildly deployed in this declaration have any uncontested meaning.

mediums'—and by extension any preacher of some doctrine that they consider dubious—to be required to defend their practices in court. Such humanists consider *themselves* entirely rational (though every one of their doctrines is disputable). Whether they would really wish their own beliefs to be put on trial in a court not of their making seems unlikely.

Those who credulously believe whatever they read in the tabloids or overhear in pubs would indeed be well advised to ask for *evidence*, or at least *some* good reason to believe. So would those who credulously believe what they read in books on the history of science and religion, or websites about the Prince of Wales, when these are written by people with a known agenda! They would often also be well advised to ask not only for the *evidence*, but even for the *meaning* of what they read or hear. Can anyone, after all, be seriously advocating bare credulity, believing anything that anybody says? And if not, what is it that is *meant* by a defence of 'faith'? What, for that matter, actually *are* 'science' and 'religion', 'evidence' and 'good reason'? What are 'shared human values' or 'the common good'? How do we know that we have one life alone? How, above all, are we to *prove* the principle that we should believe all and only what can be 'rationally established'. And if we cannot, why should we believe it? Actually, it has been obvious for over two thousand years that we *cannot* believe all and only what can be proved by 'reason', since fundamental truths of logic, as well as fundamental truths of sane existence, cannot be proved by 'reasoning' from other and better established truths (there are none). In G.K. Chesterton's words:[11]

(a) Every sane man believes that the world around him and the people in it are real, and not his own delusion or dream. No man starts burning London in the belief that his servant will soon wake him for breakfast. But that I, at any given moment, am not in a dream, is unproved and unprovable. That anything exists except myself is unproved and unprovable.

(b) All sane men believe that this world not only exists, but matters. Every man believes there is a sort of obligation on us to interest ourselves in this vision or panorama of life. He would think a man wrong who said, 'I did not ask for this farce and it bores me. I am aware that an old lady is being murdered

[11] 'Philosophy for the Schoolroom', in *Daily News*, June 22, 1907 (reprinted in Alan Maycock ed, *The Man who was Orthodox: A Selection from the Uncollected Writings of GK Chesterton* (Dobson: London, 1963), pp. 92f): a reference I owe to Martin Ward (http://www.cse.dmu.ac.uk/~mward/gkc/books/philosophy.html: accessed 8th December 2007).

downstairs, but I am going to sleep.' That there is any such duty to improve the things we did not make is a thing unproved and unprovable.

(c) All sane men believe that there is such a thing as a self, or ego, which is continuous. There is no inch of my brain matter the same as it was ten years ago. But if I have saved a man in battle ten years ago, I am proud; if I have run away, I am ashamed. That there is such a paramount 'I' is unproved and unprovable. But it is more than unproved and unprovable; it is definitely disputed by many metaphysicians.

(d) Lastly, most sane men believe, and all sane men in practice assume, that they have a power of choice and responsibility for action.

Faith, in this context, is continued adherence to the maxims of a sane life—including, most probably other ones than these.[12] These maxims—call them 'dogmas'—aren't unquestionable, nor unquestioned. What exactly they mean requires careful thought. But they can't be proved in advance of our accepting them. There may be many occasions, for example, in both our personal and our national life, when we need to believe that there will be a happy outcome, that it is really *possible* to live in peace and charity with our neighbours, that justice can be done. We have no *proof* of these convictions or proposals—or none, at any rate, that we could obtain without just carrying on 'in faith'. Even if there were good reason to believe the opposite (as there was clearly good reason in 1940, for example, to believe that Hitler would win the war) it may count as virtue that our forefathers did not. Anyone who is liable to acute depression can also reasonably be encouraged by therapists offering a detailed course of exercises and meditations as follows:

> As best you can, simply trust in your fundamental capacity for learning, growing and healing as we go along through this process—and engage in the practices as if your life depended on them, which in many ways, literally and metaphorically, it surely does.[13]

---

[12] See, for example, Plotinus, *Ennead*, VI.5.1 (A.H. Armstrong, *Plotinus*, vol. 6 (Loeb Classical Library, Heinemann: London, 1988), p. 327): 'All men are naturally and spontaneously moved to speak of the god who is in each one of us one and the same'.

[13] Mark Williams, John Teasdale, Zindel Segal & Jon Kabat-Zinn, *The Mindful Way through Depression: freeing yourself from chronic unhappiness* (Guildford Press: New York, 2007), p. 8.

The patient has no *proof* at that point in time that this, or anything else, will work, but her only hope is to *believe* that it may, and act accordingly.

> Where faith in a fact can help create the fact, that would be an insane logic which should say that faith running ahead of scientific evidence is 'the lowest kind of immorality' into which a thinking being can fall.[14]

Even in less political or practical debates it may be necessary just to ignore our doubts. Science (and any other academic discipline) progresses (maybe) because we strive to refute each other's theories, but it would be simply feeble for a theory's advocates to surrender at the very first 'refutation' (which might turn out not to be) or satirical redescription. It is not true that scientists or anyone else only believe, or should only believe, those propositions for which there is absolutely incontrovertible evidence (such that no 'rational and well-informed' person would dispute it).[15] Above all, scientists have to believe that there are truths that we can understand: giving up in the face of mystery isn't well regarded!

Unfortunately, it isn't obviously true that we should *not* give up. 'Darwin's Doubt', for example, was that it was hardly likely that creatures evolved like us could have the cognitive abilities we need to comprehend 'the world'.[16] The only world we are likely to comprehend is ours: that is, the particular environment, the *Umwelt*, that selected us and which we in turn select. 'It is an act of faith to assert

[14] William James, *The Will to Believe* (Longmans, Green: New York, 1919), p. 25.

[15] As Michael Hand apparently supposes in an attempt to 'prove' that 'faith schools' are bound to be trying to 'indoctrinate' their pupils, that is to persuade them of propositions for which there is no absolutely compelling evidence: Michael Hand, 'A Philosophical Objection to Faith Schools' in *Theory and Research in Education*, 1, 2003, pp. 89–99; see also 'The problem with faith schools: a reply to my critics' in *Theory and Research in Education*, 2, 2004, pp. 343–53.

[16] Charles Darwin wrote as follows in a letter to William Graham, July 3rd, 1881: 'With me, the horrid doubt always arises whether the convictions of man's mind, which has been developed from the mind of the lower animals, are of any value or at all trustworthy. Would any one trust in the convictions of a monkey's mind, if there are any convictions in such a mind?' See Alvin Plantinga, *Warrant and Proper Function* (Oxford University Press: New York, 1993) and his 1994 paper 'Naturalism Defeated: evolutionary arguments against Naturalism' (http://www.calvin.edu/academic/philosophy/virtual_library/articles/plan tinga_alvin/naturalism_defeated. pdf: accessed 2 Dec 2007). For further examination of this argument see. James Beilby, ed., *Naturalism Defeated? Essays on Plantinga's Evolutionary Argument Against Naturalism* (Cornell University Press: Ithaca, NY, 2002). The common response, for example by William Ramsey in that latter volume, that 'reliable' equipment would be selected by Darwinian processes, is irrelevant, in that local reliability is not the same as global truth.

that our thoughts have any relation to reality at all. If you are merely a sceptic, you must sooner or later ask yourself the question, "Why should anything go right; even observation and deduction? Why should good logic not be as misleading as bad logic? They are both movements in the brain of a bewildered ape."' [17]

The more firmly we believe that we are accidental products of Darwinian or neo-Darwinian evolution, the more that Nietzsche's commentary seems apt:

> Once upon a time, in some out of the way corner of that universe which is dispersed into numberless twinkling solar systems, there was a star upon which clever beasts invented knowing. That was the most arrogant and mendacious minute of 'world history,' but nevertheless, it was only a minute. After nature had drawn a few breaths, the star cooled and congealed, and the clever beasts had to die. One might invent such a fable, and yet he still would not have adequately illustrated how miserable, how shadowy and transient, how aimless and arbitrary the human intellect looks within nature. There were eternities during which it did not exist. And when it is all over with the human intellect, nothing will have happened.[18]

It is of course comforting to think that our beliefs receive some confirmation as we continue to rely on them: 'truths' discovered in one area of life or by one approved method, do turn out to be compatible, at least, with 'truths' discovered otherwise (or else they don't, but we can still hope they will).[19] But exactly this consistency of outcome is also observed in other 'faiths', including the explicitly religious. And those latter at least have the advantage that their creeds make it more likely that we could find things out. It is not only

---

[17] G.K. Chesterton, *Orthodoxy* (House of Stratus: Thirsk, 2001; 1st published 1908), p. 20.

[18] F. Nietzsche, *On Truth and Lies in an Extra-Moral Sense* (1873), compiled from translations by Walter Kaufmann and Daniel Breazeale: http://www.geocities.com/ thenietzschechannel/tls.htm (accessed 3 Dec 2007). See also John Wilmot, Earl of Rochester, 'Our Sphere of action, is life's happiness, and he who thinks Beyond, thinks like an Ass' in *Satires* ,64. 96–7, *Rochester's Poems,* ed. V. de Sola Pinto (Routledge & Kegan Paul: London, 1964), p. 119.

[19] See Eugen Wigner, 'The Unreasonable Effectiveness of Mathematics in the Natural Sciences', *Communications on Pure and Applied Mathematics,* 13(1):1–14(1960), (accessible at http://www.dartmouth. edu/~matc/Math Drama/reading/Wigner. html, 17th April 2008): 'It is difficult to avoid the impression that a miracle confronts us here, quite comparable in its striking nature to the miracle that the human mind can string a thousand arguments together without getting itself into contradictions, or to the two miracles of laws of nature and of the human mind's capacity to divine them.'

historically but *conceptually* true that theism is a more secure foundation for scientific enquiry than is atheism.

The faith I myself hold is a familiar one—described by Lovejoy as 'the inexpugnable faith of humankind': that there really is a truth which is not dependent on our wishes or our reasonings, and that this truth is nonetheless attainable—in part—by those who follow the right way.[20]

So what would defending 'faith' or 'sanity' amount to? Faith, though it clearly involves belief, is not just the same as 'believing'. Someone may *believe*, like Rorty, that Lovejoy's faith is ridiculous, but he does not have *faith* in that opinion. Someone else may *believe* in devils (or mental microbes) but he does not have *faith* in them. To have faith, at its simplest, is to believe in something that we may also *hope* for, to rely on something that supports us in our trials. Obviously enough there are some conditions, personal or national, where such faith is very difficult. Some saints or heroes or pig-headed simpletons may somehow carry on, but most of us require at least a little confirmation from day to day that we are not all doomed. 'Defending Faith' then amounts to seeking to maintain or encourage those conditions in which faith is easier—with the sad risk that the easier it is the less people will think they need it. After all, in peaceful and in prosperous times it's easy to think that this is how the world *must* be, and that anyone who fails to see this is deranged. Militant atheists repeatedly assert that science isn't based on *faith*, but on reason and repeated experimental confirmation (simply ignoring the patent fallacies in this proposal). Unfortunately, peace and prosperity aren't *necessary* things, and neither is experimental confirmation. We need the example of those saints and heroes (and pig-headed simpletons) to remind us that peace has its costs—the costlier, the more faith do we need.

There is also a role in this for rituals, including the repetition or enactment of inspiring stories. Even crowning a constitutional king (which might reasonably be considered an entirely pointless act) may remind us of our beleaguered history, and be a strange commitment for the future. Even imagining a more *magical* universe than we have absolutely compelling reason to believe is real may be important. 'Religion is the sigh of the oppressed creature, the heart of a heartless world, and the soul of soulless conditions. It is the opium of

[20] See A. O. Lovejoy, *The Revolt against Dualism* (La Salle, Illinois, 1930), p. 14. R.M. Rorty rejected both ideas as absurd, in *Philosophy and the Mirror of Nature* (Oxford: Blackwell, 1980), p. 52n. How anyone could sanely believe him I do not understand.

the people'[21] — not because it is soporific, and reconciles the people to their condition, but because it helps them dream. Without those dreams, without the unproven conviction that things can be better, they probably never will be. 'Faith in a fact can help create the fact', and 'religious' language is sometimes consciously 'poetic' (that is, it seeks to bring about the truth that it proclaims[22]).

Faith is also a matter of *keeping* faith, remaining loyal to chosen, universal or accidental bonds. This will often be inconvenient. It will be especially so if we have abandoned any rationale for the belief that all our bonds, and all our values, are in the end compatible. We are often, as we suppose, confronted by a challenge. Shall we betray our country, or our friends? Shall we honour our friends' opinion or the truth? Have we the right to do whatever seems 'best' to us or even what 'feels really good', regardless of our promises, our duties, and the rights of others? Shall we be 'true' to our spouse, or to 'our own self' (whatever that may be)? An older ethic insists that we should not do wrong, even if we are threatened or offered bribes, and that such virtue will 'in the end' be vindicated. But holding to that duty, in the face of threats and bribes, demands a greater integrity, a greater courage and self-possession than most of us can easily imagine, let alone enact. Such virtues amount to *faith* (and may be displayed by militant atheists as well as more traditional believers, even if they have no rationale for this). And such faith, of course, cannot be compelled: everyone must be permitted or enabled to live by and to keep what faith they can. 'Liberty of conscience was born, not of indifference, not of skepticism, not of mere open-mindedness, but of faith'.[23] If faith were *not* important then people could without harm be compelled at least to a show of believing what the ruling powers prefer. Loyalty — though there are real limits to this claim — is a good thing even if the presumed object of that loyalty is not entirely worthy. Its *real* object is not, perhaps, entirely what it seems.

---

[21] Karl Marx, 'Introduction', in *The Critique of Hegel's 'Philosophy of Right'* (1843–4), trans. Annette Jolin, trans. and ed. Joseph O'Malley (Cambridge University Press: Cambridge, 2000), p. 131.

[22] *Poesis,* from which we derive the word 'poetic', is the ancient Greek for *making*.

[23] John Plamenatz, *Man and Society*, vol. 1 (Longman: London, 1963), p. 50, cited by Jonathan Sacks, *The Dignity of Difference* (Continuum: London, 2003; 2nd edn.), p. 199.

Devils and Mental Microbes

Good liberals, in short, will hope to live and to let live within a stable liberal society, one that makes it easier to have faith in the future, and even, most of the time, to *keep* faith with our fellows, and the past. Militants, of whatever breed, are much more sensitive to evil. There are some creeds, they think, that are perversions that get in the way of civil peace, of honest faith in the future, of proper respect for others. People who start by saying that they have no obligations to the heathen, or that *they* know infallibly what outcome is the best, are hardly to be trusted. Unfortunately, this usually also applies to militants! Those who struggle with monsters sometimes themselves grow monstrous.[24] In identifying 'the religious' as stereotypical bigots who *deserve* to be insulted or even outlawed, militant atheists act out one of the oldest human projects, 'scapegoating' (on which I shall have more to say below).

Are liberal believers and casual atheists both too optimistic? It is more comfortable to believe that there are no monsters, or no more than a few. It is comforting to believe that everyone, or almost everyone, really only has 'faith' in the senses that I described before: just enough integrity to carry on their lives, guided by familiar values. It will be easy enough to keep the peace if most people can obtain their homely pleasures and avoid or at least delay most pains. There will always be other people, of course, who much prefer 'achievements' and the honour that goes with them, and their cooperation also is most easily assured by providing grand occasions when they can be seen to win. A few more people value truth (which is always dangerous), but they can be appeased by making their researches possible. Those 'three lives', identified long since by Pythagoras,[25] can be woven into a peaceful state by statesmen with some knowledge of psychology. But even this ideal (which was, at some point, Plato's) depends on exiling dangerous fantasists and their tales of gods and heroes who care nothing for the peace.

Are there stories that are really dangerous? Are there forms of devotion that would destroy the peace? At what point, if any, must we denounce what seems to be really evil? As I remarked before, even liberals don't really endorse or tolerate just *any* faith, even if they would rather not denounce them (in reasonable reaction against older habits). The usual claim is that it is only 'really absurd'

[24] 'Whoever fights monsters should see to it that in the process he does not become a monster': F. Nietzsche, *Beyond Good and Evil* (1st published 1886), aphorism 146.

[25] Diogenes Laertius, *Lives of the Philosophers*, 8.8.

and 'really dangerous' creeds that cannot be tolerated, 'intolerant' ones and violent ones and ones that 'just anyone' not infected by that creed would consider beyond the pale. Unfortunately, it is not so easy to disentangle the things that we think absurd or dangerous from those that 'really' are. As Chesterton remarked:

> The average agnostic of recent times has really had no notion of what he meant by religious liberty and equality. He took his own ethics as self-evident and enforced them; such as decency or the error of the Adamite heresy. Then he was horribly shocked if he heard of anybody else, Moslem or Christian, taking *his* ethics as self-evident and enforcing them; such as reverence or the error of the Atheist heresy.[26]

Should we only enforce such creeds as we entirely *know* are right? Even the pragmatic rule, that we should live and let live, so as to keep the peace, rests on an unargued assumption, that *peace* is loved by all. It may seem evident that it must be: peace, we can say, is the condition under which everyone can live the lives they wish (so long as they allow others the same liberty). But who are these 'others'? Many stable societies of the past (and even present) have taken it for granted that it is only *adult males* (or even *adult free-born males*) that count. Children are very rarely allowed the lives they *wish*, because we 'know' that their adult selves (once educated) will prefer that they were not. Women have also often been reckoned irresponsible. Does 'live and let live' apply to families and communities, or to 'free individuals'? By deciding which, we have already chosen to enforce *one* ethic amongst many. 'Universal humanism', with its talk of individual human rights, is one creed amongst many. Is it *obviously* irrational to defend the rights of cows or monkeys just as well as the rights of humans? If the law is to be invoked only to prevent harm to 'others', who are the others? If the law is built round property rights (as some would say) what counts as property? In the United States (before the civil war) escaped slaves were reckoned property even in those states whose constitution did not acknowledge slavery. In the United Kingdom escaped slaves were free. What do we say of escaped cattle? The point here is not to argue (as I have often done) for the absurdity of denying 'rights' to 'animals' on no better basis than their 'species' (a concept that no longer has the force assigned it in an earlier biological synthesis). It is enough for now to point out that there is radical disagreement, and the *present* laws enforce a par-

[26] G.K. Chesterton, *St Francis of Assisi* (Hodder & Stoughton: London, 1996; 1st published 1923), p. 144f.

ticular ethic, against 'the errors of the Animalist heresy', so to speak! Liberal laws enforce particular morals, and are tolerant only of things that the law-makers don't mind about (and in this they are hardly different from illiberal laws).

Again, what counts as 'harm'? Is clitoridectomy a harm? Is circumcision? Is daily incarceration (in a school) a harm, or else (conversely) exclusion from 'unsuitable' education? Is it harmful to be taught that there is no objective justice? Richard Dawkins, for example, apparently believes that it is 'child abuse' to bring one's child up Christian (or in any other creed that he despises). We may reject that particular claim, but we are all likely to reckon *some* such practices abusive (Satanism, Social Darwinism ...). Physical damage may be easily assessed, mental damage much less so. Is it harmful to shield children from all risk, at the cost of denying them childish pleasures of a kind that every other generation has enjoyed? What of 'spiritual' damage? Is hard-core porn harmful? Portrayals of violent assault? Advertisements that encourage various forms of greed and *pleonexia* (which is, dissatisfaction with what one happens to have, and an especially damaging vice for ancient moralists)? Ignorant and insulting mockery of all 'religious' principle? The Millian principle, to do no 'harm' to 'others', expressly disallows paternalistic laws to save us from ourselves—but most mental and spiritual harms will also damage others in the end. And aren't some people in need of an authority? Even liberals—or maybe especially liberals—have strong views about the best way to bring up children, and the best public environment for all of us. Even (or especially) *secular* authorities have thought it right to remove children from their parents so that they can be 'socialized' in properly 'secular' ways (and how long will it be before they declare it 'child abuse' to rear a child 'religiously'?). Even liberals are unwilling to use the law to enforce just any voluntary contract: prostitution, though not literally illegal in the United Kingdom, is still 'outside the law', and school careers advisers don't acknowledge it as an available profession. For how long will they be allowed to mention ecclesiastical office?

The point is not to debate these issues here (I shall return to the rights and wrongs of schooling in a later chapter), but only to observe that any settled society will enforce a particular ethic, even if it pays lip service to the liberal rule. It is difficult to see a viable alternative. But in that case we must face the probability that there will be (there are) societies whose ethic is, by some account, immensely evil. Most of its members, probably, will have been infected, and will barely be brought to see that anyone could find their behaviour vile. Even those most abused by their society will often find it difficult to disown it (for that will make their own past suffering quite pointless). It would be comforting to think that they 'only need to be educated' (which is, usually, to be informed of the 'obvious benefits' to be had by changing what they do). But the point precisely is that benefits *aren't* obvious. We cannot simultaneously say that there is no objective, rationally obligatory way of life and thought, that 'right and wrong' are only 'social constructions', and that *our* way of life and thought is obviously right! Or rather (since this is exactly what so many people say) we cannot say this without self-contradiction.

> In this twilight of the twentieth century, we need urgently to understand how little the destructiveness of gods and demons is diminished by denying their existence or by clothing them in 'secular' and hence (supposedly) more innocuous descriptions.[27]

Some people are infected by mental microbes. They believe, to take an extreme example, that they have been appointed as the messengers of gods or Galactic saviours, to reveal that our world is in the grip of psychopathic lizards masquerading as mere people. If this were so, of course, the lizards would be taking special care to defuse the allegation, and prevent our sudden maturity (so it's no surprise that the envoys are widely considered crazy). Is the situation any different if this craziness infects a population? Whole populations have believed that they are chosen, and that the world around them is in the grip of devils. Most probably, most readers of this work will feel immensely smug that they are uninfected! But exactly the same pattern can be seen in 'Brights',[28] self-identified as really knowing the truth, and knowing that the world around is in the grip of mental microbes, 'memes'. Of course, they have got 'reason' on their side—but so says every other population and crazed prophet!

A Bright, we are told, 'is a person who has a naturalistic world-view, ... free of supernatural and mystical elements, [whose] ethics and actions ... are based on a naturalistic world-view' (a description taken from their website). Whether most people who fit this definition actually self-identify as 'Bright', or even as having anything much in common with any other such, is moot—partly because it is not clear what words like 'naturalistic', 'supernatural',

[27] Lash, op. cit., p. 200.

[28] A term initially invented by Daniel C. Dennett in *New York Times*, July 12, 2003, and gladly embraced by others: see http://www.the-brights.net/ (accessed 6th December 2007).

'mystical' really mean. Most of those who so identify themselves probably suppose that they are disagreeing with 'religious' people, but at least one poster to the Bright website can say 'I am a Hindu-Buddhist Bright, meaning I follow a proper subset of Hindu-Buddhist teachings that are consistent with the naturalist, non-dogmatic view of the world and more importantly of the self. Peace. Om Shanti.'[29] Many who self-identify as Abrahamic theists might also think their world-view 'naturalistic', and point out that 'modern science' had its beginnings among theistic thinkers.[30] 'Believing in God' is nothing like believing in a yeti, or a Galactic envoy, or a ghost, and much more like believing (as above) that our intellects can reach out to 'the way things are', and that our ethic is founded upon fellow feeling. But this is for a later chapter! It is enough for now to note that what matters for Brights, as for many other cultists, is to identify with a supportive group, to read appropriate scriptures and to think that non-believers are deranged. This is not to say that 'Brightism' is a 'religion': that term too is ill-defined. It is only to point to a common human pattern, an infection (sometimes called 'conceit'). 'To expel religion is a religious gesture.'[31]

And what is it that we are infected by? The usual modern term, displacing the older one, is 'memes'. But there is another neologism that may catch the thing more aptly: 'macrobes'. 'Macrobes', so C.S. Lewis feigned in his careful fantasy *That Hideous Strength*,[32] is the name given to what once were devils by naturalistic scientists unwilling to acknowledge what they're dealing with. What difference between memes and macrobes? The former, oddly, are *less* natural beings, since they have no physical substrate, no clear criteria of

---

[29] http://www.the-brights.net/people/comments/comments15.html: signed 'Janak, USA'. Whether more mainstream Hindus and Buddhists would recognize this strange conflation, seems, at least, unlikely.

[30] Cornelius G. Hunter, *Science's Blind Spot: the unseen religion of scientific naturalism* (Brazos Press: Grand Rapids, 2007) points out that naturalism, the thesis that the cosmos works according to its own internal rules without being constantly reset or interfered with by the transcendent creator, was a *theological* doctrine in its beginnings, and that there is no way of *proving* that it is true by an empirical enquiry.

[31] René Girard, in René Girard, Jean-Michel Oughourian & Guy Lefort, *Things Hidden Since the Foundation of the World*, trans. Stephen Bann & Michael Metteer (Continuum: London, 2003; originally published 1978), p. 32. Girard's identification of 'scapegoating' as the origin and permanent disease of civil society will concern me later.

[32] C.S. Lewis, *That Hideous Strength* (Bodley Head: London, 1945), a dramatic representation of the argument of *The Abolition of Man* (Collins: London, 1943). Eric Frank Russell devised a similar creature to prey on all of us in his *Sinister Barrier* (Dobson: London 1939).

identity, and exist only in the imagination of thinking things like us. Macrobes are, in a way, corporeal, real 'powers of air and darkness'.[33] Memes have, we must presume, no wills or meanings of their own, and take life only in the imaginations they infect,[34] whereas macrobes (devils) have their own biographies. Maybe this is to reify too much: as far as psychological experience goes the devils are simply inmates of our minds, fragmentary moods and motives that we can personify and—in a way—converse with.[35] The thought of 'macrobes' is in a way *more* dangerous, as any attempt to *argue* with the thoughts they bring is likely to reinforce them (no doubt this is why Dawkins and other such militants are so disinclined actually to *reason* with either theologians or educated believers: they seek instead to follow Thomas More's advice, that 'the devil, that proud spirit, cannot endure to be mocked').[36] But the notion does have this one serious advantage: the devils are, as it were, 'fallen angels'. There is a way of dealing with them that at once denies them any authority and can, eventually, learn from them, rather as though they were irritating strangers seeking company (which is, in effect, what I am doing in this book). To find this out we need to remember ourselves, to remember 'reason'.

But what is reason? Are we even entitled to suppose that we 'have minds' that are independent of the memes? At least some philosophers, including Brights, deny it. Our 'minds', they say, are mere ensembles. Our very 'selves' are stories.[37] Our name is Legion

---

[33] Walter Wink, *Naming the Powers: the language of power in the New Testament* (Fortress Press: Philadelphia, 1984), p. 84: 'these constitute "the powers of the air", the invisible but palpable environment of opinions, beliefs, propaganda, convictions, prejudices, hatreds, racial and class biases, taboos and loyalties that condition our perception of the world long before we reach the age of choice'. See also Frank J. Tipler, *The Physics of Christianity* (Doubleday: New York, 2007), p. 136: 'demons exist, but they should be thought of as forms of computer viruses running on the computer that is the human brain'.

[34] Eric Frank Russell also imagined *this* scenario, in *Three to Conquer* (Dobson: London, 1957): though his invaders, being sentient bacteria, do have a physical presence, they have no thoughts of their own outside infected brains.

[35] Carers find it very easy to think that anorexics, for example, are possessed, and professional therapists will also often suggest that their patient should *talk* to the disease, as if to a separate creature.

[36] See also Martin Luther:The best way to drive out the Devil, if he will not yield to the texts of scripture [aka such books as Richard Dawkins' own], is to JEER and FLOUT him, for he cannot bear scorn'. Both these aphorisms, Luther's and More's, are cited at the beginning of C.S. Lewis, *The Screwtape Letters* (Bles: London, 1942): I have not been able to locate their origins.

[37] Daniel Dennett, *Consciousness Explained* (Allen Lane: London, 1992), for example. See my 'Minds, Memes and Rhetoric': *Inquiry*, 36 (1993), pp. 3–16.

(because we are many).[38] This makes another strange connection. If memes are to be resisted, what's the *non-infected* condition we aspire to? Presumably this is a form of No-Self Doctrine, *Anatta*. Enlightenment will dawn when there is no-one there, when there is no reason to insist that 'individual persons' are real in a way that 'day-selves' or 'individual families' or 'clans of the like-minded' aren't. I may as well consider myself identical with my maternal grandfather as with the seven-year old I once thought I was. All statements of identity, of sameness, are internal to a particular discourse, to a story. The naturalistic story that began by emphasising individual responsibility and private conscience now dissolves. This is only another epic, easily replaced by transmigrating souls, by family honour, or by a rigorous *Anatta*. Maybe the self-styled Bright who spoke from within a Hindu-Buddhist mélange had a point.

Or maybe all this is yet another devil-sponsored delusion.

Other Worlds

We only have a right to distinguish *our* belief from others, if there is a *right* way to believe and live. Otherwise we are all infected, more or less—and the most vociferous and violent will probably win the day.[39]. There can be a *right* way to believe and live, and one that we can achieve, only if there is indeed something 'Divine' in us and in the world. The last words, we are told, of the third-century Platonist, Plotinus, were 'Try to bring back the god in you to the Divine in the All'.[40] Without that Divine the enterprise is vain. Those who deny it, even in good conscience and for what seem to them good reasons, are really denying Reason, and reducing all disputes to power politics, to war.

So a robust 'defence of faith' is likely to go beyond the mere defence of those conditions and beliefs that enable us to continue living peaceably together. We also need to be able to believe in the possibility of finding out the truth, and therefore—it at least seems probable—to believe that the world has more secure foundations than naturalists can provide.[41] 'Faith is the substance of things

[38] See *Mark* 5.9.

[39] Unless our Lord was right to say that it is the *meek* who will inherit: *Matthew* 5.5

[40] Porphyry *Life of Plotinus*, ch. 2: A. H. Armstrong, trans., *Plotinus*, vol. 1 (Loeb Classical Library, Heinemann: London, 1978), p. 7.

[41] See Steve Fuller, *Dissent Over Descent: Evolution's 500–year War on Intelligent Design* (Icon Books: London, 2008).

hoped for, the evidence of things not seen.'[42] We all know very well—and even naturalists must know—that there are things we do not and now cannot see: it *might* be true that those things are entirely hostile to all humane values[43]—but if that were so, we could never come to know it, or anything much else, nor find it possible to live together.

Orthodox Abrahamists (Jews, Christians, Muslims) rarely doubted that 'religion' was immensely dangerous, at least as dangerous as curiosity and sex. 'Religion', after all, was founded in human sin, and often involved traditions, in effect, of devil-worship. Religious devotion may have unworthy ends as easily as erotic infatuation, and may last longer. All human tribes have tried to channel it into convenient ways, and recognized the possibilities of pride, delusion, violence and greed. Hellenic Paganism also recognized, equivalently, that the gods were immortal powers who rarely cared for us: Sex, War, Curiosity and Humour (to give them their abstract titles) are powers we have to deal with. Maybe we can conceive that Zeus, the bright and overarching sky (sometimes concealed in

[42] *Hebrews* 11.1.

[43] So Bertrand Russell, in a fine piece of fine but fundamentally incoherent rhetoric: 'That Man is the product of causes which had no prevision of the end they were achieving; that his origin, his growth, his hopes and fears, his loves and his beliefs, are but the outcome of accidental collocations of atoms; that no fire, no heroism, no intensity of thought and feeling, can preserve an individual life beyond the grave; that all the labours of the ages, all the devotion, all the inspiration, all the noonday brightness of human genius, are destined to extinction in the vast death of the solar system, and that the whole temple of Man's achievement must inevitably be buried beneath the debris of a universe in ruins—all these things, if not quite beyond dispute, are yet so nearly certain, that no philosophy which rejects them can hope to stand. Only within the scaffolding of these truths, only on the firm foundation of unyielding despair, can the soul's habitation henceforth be safely built. .... Brief and powerless is Man's life; on him and all his race the slow, sure doom falls pitiless and dark. Blind to good and evil, reckless of destruction, omnipotent matter rolls on its relentless way; for Man, condemned to-day to lose his dearest, to-morrow himself to pass through the gate of darkness, it remains only to cherish, ere yet the blow falls, the lofty thoughts that ennoble his little day; disdaining the coward terrors of the slave of Fate, to worship at the shrine that his own hands have built; undismayed by the empire of chance, to preserve a mind free from the wanton tyranny that rules his outward life; proudly defiant of the irresistible forces that tolerate, for a moment, his knowledge and his condemnation, to sustain alone, a weary but unyielding Atlas, the world that his own ideals have fashioned despite the trampling march of unconscious power': 'The Free Man's Worship' (1903), *Mysticism and Logic* (Allen & Unwin: London, 1918), pp. 46–57, taken from http://users. drew. edu/~jlenz/fmw. html (accessed 9th December 2007). Gosh.

cloud), can somehow contain and master all of them.[44] Olympian religion served many ends, providing rituals to unite or purify the city and the soul, and allegories to intimate that there is one world, one justice. Those who had a different devotion, to the God of Abraham, preferred to think the Olympians themselves were devils or (equivalently) the embodiment of adolescent dreams. They were as literal-minded in their mockery as militant atheists nowadays, and very nearly as ignorant. Over in India a similar plot played out: the Hindu gods provided ceremonial to unite and purify the nations and the soul, and allegories to suggest that all things come from Brahman, the unknown absolute. Buddhist missionaries taught that even the gods were bound upon the wheel of time, and that escape was by Enlightenment, by giving up the stories and finding Nothing there (or was there Something after all, an Indestructible?). *Organized* religion is at once the effort to contain and harness gods (or at least religious devotion to those gods), and itself a dangerous and fissiparous institution (as fissiparous indeed as nationalism). If we are fortunate some seed of charity and proper devotion will survive the many dreadful forms religion takes, but it is absurd to suppose that *disorganized* religion has any better promise! Sex too is immensely dangerous (though some moderns apparently think this claim is almost blasphemous[45]), and some attempts to harness it are also harmful, but no-one can seriously imagine that we should therefore all both seek and do what sex we please! Nor that we should all abandon it.

It is worth remembering Chesterton's defence of fairy stories against those who suggested that they were too alarming, too brutal, for tender minds and hearts:

> Fairy tales are not responsible for producing in children fear, or any of the shapes of fear; fairy tales do not give the child the idea of the evil or the ugly; that is in the child already, because it is in the world already. Fairy tales do not give the child his first idea of bogey. What fairy tales give the child is his first clear idea of the possible defeat of bogey. The baby has known the dragon inti-

---

[44] For an empathetic account of Olympian religion see W.F. Otto, *The Homeric Gods: the spiritual significance of Greek religion*, trans. M. Hadas (Thames & Hudson: Londo,n 1954; 1st published as *Die Götter Griechenlands* in 1929).

[45] To blaspheme is to offer public insult to something or someone that others hold in honour, and to do so precisely *because* they hold it in honour. It is probably better that there should be no *legal* offence of blasphemy, but those who say so most vehemently sometimes forget what they themselves find most offensive.

> mately ever since he had an imagination. What the fairy tale provides for him is a St. George to kill the dragon. [46]

It is similarly true that it is not 'religion' that produces the impulses of rage, greed, guilt, terror and conceit that plague humanity.[47] 'Religion' is the name we give to the systems which seek to control, to regulate, even to eradicate those impulses—and militant atheism, in its various forms, is just such another effort. Unfortunately, like the more usual forms, it may rather serve to promote or at least excuse them.

So far, although I have pointed to some standard difficulties with merely 'naturalistic' modes of thought alike for epistemology and for ethics (without specifying exactly what 'naturalism' really is), and although I have intimated that there are personal and social uses for stories about 'gods' and 'demons', I have offered no clear account of 'supernaturalism' (which is what many militant atheists now commonly attack). The attacks are doubtfully coherent: apparently it is supposed that 'gods' must simultaneously be entities much like ourselves and also immune to 'natural law'. This is not an adequate account of 'gods' in any ordinarily polytheistic story: gods, as above, are deathless presences, powers discoverable in human life and in the 'natural world'. It is still less adequate as an account of the God of Abraham. Whatever that God may be it is clearly *not* a being that requires (as all of *us* require) a world in which to live, a physiology, a 'natural history', a biography. 'Believing in God' is nothing like believing in Martians or in Super-Yeti. But maybe it is, in some sense, believing 'in the supernatural': believing, that is, that there is something unconstrained by any 'natural law', including such axioms as the conservation of mass/energy, or entropy, or even (though this is more controversial) ordinary 'laws of logic'. 'Naturalism', in one of its many senses, is the conviction that everything is always as it must be, that there's no escape from fate (and in that sense, of course, the ancient Stoics were, like Spinoza, both theists, of a sort, and naturalists). 'Supernaturalism', conversely, is the hope that not all things are

[46] G.K. Chesterton, *Tremendous Trifles* (Methuen: London, 1904), p. 102.

[47] Pascal Boyer, 'Religion: Bound to Believe?', *Nature*, 455 (23 October 2008), pp. 1038–9 proposes that 'religious thoughts seem to be an emergent property of our standard cognitive capacities': that is, certain sorts of story appeal to us even if they aren't the stories that our conscious mind endorses. He doesn't add, but surely could, that even atheists, if they aren't careful, end by speaking and acting the same way. Or to put the point differently, organized religion is a way of managing or even seeking escape from the devils and lesser spirits that surround us.

necessary, that there really is an escape from fate, that even expected futures aren't entirely certain, and that the 'dead hand of the past' can be avoided. Things don't have to be the way they are. Faith in 'the supernatural', in this sense at least, is faith in the possibility of new beginnings. And why should this be regretted?

One strand in 'religion' does advocate something like Stoic resignation: *this* is the way things are, and nothing can happen that is not required 'by God' (that is, by the single unifying principle that animates and orders all things). We are not required to *like* it, but may come to worship at least its elegance, and submit (after all, we haven't much choice about that!). 'Will the pot contend with the potter, or the earthenware with the hand that shapes it?'[48] Oddly, most militant atheists, though they often themselves display a Stoic or Spinozistic reverence for the cosmos, and especially for its most elegant and complex products, living things, are especially outraged by what they take to be a fatalistic submission to 'the will of God'. Ethically, they would have more sympathy with the 'supernaturalist' strand,[49] and perhaps especially its Christian version, in which God can be described as 'the last lost giant, even God, risen against the world'.[50]

'Supernaturalism' may have at least one other meaning, namely that (*pace* Chesterton's defence of sanity, quoted earlier) this world, the world of our everyday concerns and theoretical imaginings, is indeed—as another Stoic, Marcus Aurelius, said—'a dream and a delusion' (though it is not only *mine*).[51] The *real* world, to which we might occasionally awaken, shows all our ordinary concerns to be trivial or ridiculous, our ordinary theories dreams. *True* religion, so far from being another dream, is an awakening—as militant atheists suppose their own enlightenment to be.

Such enlightenments, or alleged awakenings, can be treated 'ethically', as a description of a change of life, a way of prioritizing one view over another, of realizing that our older lives were wrong. But maybe they are more than that. It is another oddity of modern

---

[48] *Isaiah* 45.10; see also *Jeremiah* 18.6.

[49] So Richard Dawkins, earlier in his career, concluded *The Selfish Gene* with a rousing appeal to defy our makers, whether selfish genes or memes, though he offered no plausible story about how such defiance was even possible, let alone practical.

[50] G.K. Chesterton, *The Ballad of the White Horse*, bk4: the full verse is 'Follow a light that leaps and spins, Follow the fire unfurled!/ For riseth up against realm and rod,/ A thing forgotten, a thing downtrod,/ The last lost giant, even God,/ Is risen against the world.'

[51] Marcus Aurelius, *Meditations*, Bk. 2: he proposes that Philosophy is our only hope (which is to say, keeping the god-in-us inviolate).

thought that we are now far *more* inclined than our 'religious' forebears to contrast *reality* and ordinary waking life. Once upon a time we might reasonably suppose that the sun 'rose and set', that the world we travelled through was placed between two hemispheres of light and dark, that Here and Now were 'real' in a way that There and Then were not. Awakening, exactly, to a *modern* view, we know that the earth turns, that it is in motion around the sun and around the Galactic Core, that 'Here' and 'Now' no more identify a single thing than 'I', that there are no privileged places or times or scales or points of view. Of course, we mostly forget these truisms, but occasional awakenings still mould our lives. 'It is as if people who slept through their life thought the things in their dreams were reliable and obvious, but, if someone woke them up, disbelieved in what they saw with their eyes open and went to sleep again'.[52]

We can go still further: it has even been argued, wittily but not absurdly, that we have reason to suspect that all our present experience is no more than a Virtual Reality, an entertainment or educational tape (as it were) enjoyed by the sometime residents of a society technologically some way advanced from the world we *think* we live in.[53] Whatever laws or customs rule the *real* world need not be the ones determined for this world here—though it would be rude to ignore *these* rules while we enjoy the tape! In effect, Reality is Supernature, but recalling this is something that we need to manage carefully. Forgetting it entirely is to forget our real self; remembering it too insistently is to spoil the game (or whatever far more serious cause our real selves have for taking the virtual route).

Seeking *evidence* of an ordinarily empirical kind for this hypothesis is futile (as futile as an attempt to locate the 'other worlds' of speculative cosmology[54]). Do we have any reason to imagine so extreme a system? One reason, the Kantian, remains compelling. On the one hand, we are impelled to believe in a single, coherent world in which

---

[52] Plotinus, *Enneads*, V.5.11: Armstrong, op. cit., vol. 5, p. 189. I shall have more to say below on *how* this happens.

[53] See Nick Bostrom, *Anthropic Bias: Observation Selection Effects in Science and Philosophy* (Routledge: London, 2002).

[54] One non-theistic answer to the puzzle posed by the 'fine-tuning' of the universe we inhabit (such that very slight alterations in values of the cosmic constants would make our kind of life impossible) is to suppose that all possible versions of those values are embodied 'somewhere' or 'somewhen', and that it is no surprise that *we* inhabit the version that makes us possible. As an explanatory device this is, to put it mildly, strange, since it imagines wholly inaccessible worlds into existence, and—by saying that everything *possible* exists—makes all explanation otiose.

'our actions and beliefs' are as much required 'by law' as chemical reactions or the clash of billiard balls. On the other, we are bound to conceive ourselves as bound by *moral* laws that require our freedom, bound to conceive that we *could* have believed and acted otherwise (militant atheists must believe this no less than theists, or they could have no ground for complaint that others believe what *they* do not, nor any right to speak of their moral failings). Kant concluded, in line with a long Platonized tradition, that we choose 'para-temporally' or 'in eternity' the whole lives that are woven into the 'natural' world we now experience.[55] Precisely because, in a way, *this* world is a merely virtual reality, we are duty-bound to live in it as if it really mattered! If it were all that really existed, it could not really matter. It would indeed be 'a tale told by an idiot, full of sound and fury, signifying nothing'.[56]

Religious devotion, faith, remembrance, is not *essentially* and *absolutely* good (any more than sex, parental love, science, humour, art or war). There is a route away from danger that lies through real scepticism (which is not to say, the materialist or rationalist dogmatism that is only another creed), through banishing the stories, memes or devils from our souls and cities, banishing idolatry. But what is left when we have done as much? The 'Western' tradition, so to call it, whether in pagan or Abrahamic guise, has told us that we will find ourselves when we at last acknowledge a divine demand: not a demand for sacrifice or ritual purity.

> I cannot tolerate your new moons and your festivals; they have become a burden to me. ... When you lift up your hands outspread in prayer, I will hide my eyes from you. Though you offer countless prayers, I will not listen. There is blood on your hands; wash yourself and be clean.... Cease to do evil and learn to do right, pursue justice and champion the oppressed; give the orphan his rights, plead the widow's cause.[57]

The 'Eastern', Buddhist, tradition has only occasionally emphasized the pursuit of justice, but is as concerned as the Western to transcend ritual purity, to recognize that 'to the pure all things are pure',[58] that there are still devils among us, wishing us no good, but that there is also something of the Divine, something that demands

[55] On the background to Kant's endeavours see Philip Merlan, *From Platonism to Neoplatonism* (Nijhoff: The Hague, 1953).

[56] William Shakespeare, *Macbeth* Act 5, scene 5 (Macbeth speaks).

[57] *Isaiah* 1.14–17.

[58] *Titus* 1.15

and deserves our love, in us all. Really to give up this faith is a descent more dreadful than we now easily imagine.

Religion is very dangerous. And perhaps it was for that reason that one of the very first commandments of the God of Abraham was simply not to take His name in vain:[59] which is not to say 'Don't use His name as a casual curse', but rather 'Don't claim divine authority for what you want to do (or to see done)'! The prophets tell us that God's commands are simple: 'to do justly, and to love mercy, and to walk humbly with your God'.[60]

Another way of expressing the same thing is the Buddhist aphorism: 'Before Enlightenment, chop wood, carry water; after Enlightenment, chop wood, carry water.' The 'enlightened' attend to what they are doing, and do it with a sense of the action's beauty, and the world's. 'Who sweeps a room as for Thy laws, makes that and the action fine.'[61] Saints, heroes and pig-headed simpletons may manage this no matter what. Defending Faith—and therefore resisting unbelief—is to try and make this easier for us all.

---

[59] *Exodus* 20.7; see also *Matthew* 15. 8f on those who use the literal sense of scripture to subvert its spirit, teaching 'as doctrines the commandments of men'. Protestant Christians have maintained the importance of *Biblical* writings against later ecclesiastical custom, and some Muslims have similarly criticised reliance on the *Hadith*, the reported sayings of the Prophet and his companions, and urged a return to the 'revealed truth' of the Koran. There is a problem with both programmes, in that it is in both cases the community of believers that has identified the true scriptures and the proper mode of reading them. On which see a later chapter.

[60] *Micah* 6.8. See also *James* 1.27: 'the kind of religion which is without stain or fault in the sight of God our Father is this: to go to the help of orphans and widows in their distress and keep oneself untarnished by the world.'

[61] George Herbert, 'The Elixir' (1633), *The Poems of George Herbert* (Oxford University Press: London, 1961), p. 175

2

Projects, Conjectures, Refutations

Dogmas and Disagreements

One of the commonest charges against 'religious believers' is that they accept their doctrines 'uncritically' and 'on authority', whereas the proper 'scientific' approach is to question all authority, and rather attempt to *refute* hypotheses than confirm them. 'Faith', as above, is interpreted as 'credulity', and only 'science' supports, or else relies upon, rational incredulity.

The news that only 'scientists' question their hypotheses, or seek out counter-evidence as well as confirmation, is likely enough to irritate scholars, even unbelievers, in other disciplines. Those who speak for 'science' sometimes seem to know very little of any work done in 'the humanities' (which include history, philosophy, linguistics, and textual analysis). When they intrude upon the province of these disciplines it is often to deploy some startling theory which, they say, 'humanities scholars' would never have considered (perhaps because it cannot be supported from existing records). Their 'fresh look' at the evidence may require an almost endearing ignorance of the actual state of scholarship.[1] This is especially true when they intrude upon the study of 'religious texts': each Christmas someone somewhere will be attempting a novel diagnosis of 'the Star of Bethlehem'[2] or considering some natural form of parthenogenesis, as though there must be some 'natural fact' behind the scrip-

[1] I must except Colin J. Humphreys & W.G. Waddington, whose 'Dating the Crucifixion', *Nature*, 306 (22/29 December 1983), pp. 743–6) is a model for scientists and scholars alike (the date was 3rd April 33 AD).

[2] I should acknowledge that there is at least a *case* for identifying the Star with Jupiter, in a series of conjunctions, first with Regulus and then with Venus, in 3/2 BC: see Frederick A. Larson, *The Star of Bethlehem*, at http://www.bethlehemstar.net/ (accessed 9th February 2008). The fact that I have no particular wish for this to be true is perhaps some reason to suspect that it may be.

tural description. Meanwhile Bible scholars are more likely to be acknowledging that 'the Christmas story' was devised to represent the *significance* of the event, and that there need have been no comet, no supernova, no unusual conjunction or conception, nor even any stable or 'wise men from the East' on the actual occasion of Messiah's birth. Other theologians, regarded as less 'modern' in their sympathies, may suggest that it would not be surprising if 'odd' events attended such a divine incursion, but would probably acknowledge that the chief reason for believing that they did will be *theological* (rather as the chief reason for believing in Darwinian evolution is atheological!). Some of the intruders perhaps believe that they are doing no more than offer frivolous accounts of the difficulties faced by Santa Claus. Others really seem to think that they are uncovering 'historical realities'.

One syndrome that may lie behind these efforts is the habit of taking texts as reporting literal truths, such that only their *interpretation* need be squabbled over. Scholars in the humanities are more conscious that texts have many functions—and only a few of them are offered as 'literal' or 'historical truths'. Some may even be outright fictions, and yet still, in their way, be well worth reading for what they show us of the human condition, or at least of their authors' conditions. I shall address the question, how to read 'holy scripture' (and how not), in my next chapter. My object here is to consider what truth, if any, there might be in the claim of militant atheists that 'science' is questioning and critical, and 'religion' credulous and dogmatic.

The claim is likely to puzzle most ordinary believers, and most scholars of 'religion' (whichever religion that may be).[3] The history of every religious tradition, after all, is packed with abusive argument, schism and reinterpretation. All Buddhists claim allegiance, in some sense or other, to the reported experience and sermons of Gautama, but this has not prevented them from disagreeing, often acrimoniously, about what that experience was, what sermons he preached, and what their implications are. All Abrahamists (taking

---

[3] See Victoria S. Harrison, 'Scientific and religious worldviews: Antagonism, Non-Antagonistic Incommensurability and Complementarity', *Heythrop Journal*, 47 (2006), pp. 349–366, for a brief and helpful account of the three main accounts of the relation of 'science' and 'religion'. My only quarrel with her version is that neither 'science' nor 'religion' is clearly defined—but that is not her fault!

that taxon to be of the same rank as 'Buddhists'[4]) acknowledge the formative event of 'Abraham's call' to leave the city and gods of his fathers, but squabble—apparently unendingly—over the significance of that call, and how best to respond to the God that it revealed. All Christians, in some way, preach the 'gospel of the Lord Jesus Christ', but even the mainstream churches do not quite agree on the nature of the gospel, or His lordship, even when they recite the very same creeds.

That there are creeds to recite is hardly surprising, nor that there are some limits to what, say, self-styled Christians can believe without being 'excommunicated' by their sometime co-religionists. What exactly the limits are may be disputed, and different churches, different sects, are more or less restrictive, but *some* restrictions are unavoidable. There are similar limits on what self-styled *scientists* can believe without being 'excommunicated'. Maybe only the most militant of atheists will deny the status of 'scientist' to such of their colleagues as profess religious belief: it would be odd, for example, to insist that Abdus Salam[5] was no scientist merely because he was a devout Ahmadiyya Muslim. On the other hand, he was a physicist. Biologists willing to consider the claims of 'Intelligent Design' theorists may find their careers cut short, even if they carefully (and correctly) disclaim any 'religious' significance to the theories.[6] Even without the force of excommunication it is possible to hinder the

---

[4] See my *The Mysteries of Religion* (Blackwell: Oxford, 1986), drawing on the work of Wilfred Cantwell Smith, *The Meaning and End of Religion* (Harper: San Francisco, 1976).

[5] 1926–96. He was awarded the Nobel Prize in 1979 for his Electro-Weak theory. The prize was shared with Steven Weinberg and Sheldon Glashow, who arrived at the same theory independently. I acknowledge that he was, by mainstream Muslim standards, a heretic. Tipler, op. cit., pp. 113–6, has argued that the conviction, reinforced by al-Ghazali, that God can do just anything, as not being bound by any 'laws of nature', prevented any serious Islamic science. It can also be argued that the conviction that we can *deduce* the laws of nature from rational first principles known to us without further enquiry is also the bane of science (as Tipler remarks in connection with notions like super-symmetry and string theory: *Ibid.*, pp. 126–7). Al-Ghazali, like Descartes and like Urban VIII in conversation with Galileo, reckoned that God could produce the same effects by many different mechanisms, and that it was therefore impossible to be sure that the mechanism *we* had thought of was the real one. Stanley Jaki has argued, in *Science and Creation* (Scottish Academic Press: Edinburgh, 1974) and elsewhere, that what enabled Christendom to engage in a proper empirically grounded, yet still rational, science, was its careful memory of both these principles.

[6] Though Francis Crick (1916–2004; one of the discoverers of DNA) attacked 'Creation Science', which he equated with Intelligent Design Theory, as the mere product of a 'slavish adherence to religious dogmas' (*The Astonishing Hypothesis:*

research of theorists too far removed from orthodoxy: no official funding body is likely, for example, to support an effort to explain astronomical phenomena as the effect of stellar engineering projects (however plausible, in the abstract, it may be to suppose that there are ancient star-travelling civilizations). Nor will any respectable funding body provide funds to investigate whether we might be living in a computer simulation (however plausible the probabilistic arguments for saying that we *might* be). Medical and other biological experimentalists who are inclined to question the right of scientists to experiment on animals—at least until very recently (and in some countries)—will find their scientific credentials questioned. *Nowadays*, those who suggest that there are genetically determined differences in intelligence and general character between distinct human populations (races) had better have private means and a thick skin[7] (though a few decades ago exactly this claim was orthodox). And any who are found to have forged or falsified experimental results, of course, will be forced to resign their posts and give up any honours. In brief, scientists can expect to be held to particular behaviours, particular research projects, particular ethical views, quite as firmly as 'religious believers' are held to the norms of their particular sects. Rather more so, in fact, since there usually aren't *other* scientific sects (with their own professional rules, funding arrangements, and career structures) for them to join! Religious believers, like John Henry Newman, can be moved by intellectual argument to give up their status in one church in order to join another. They can even, depending on the tolerance of their sect, give up all or most of the sect's defining beliefs and practices and still, with little or no hypocrisy, consider themselves 'believers'. Scientists who re-introduce final causes or Pythagorean numerology, or insist on checking and double-checking every reported physical or chemical datum before they will believe it, or appeal to revelation, or denounce their colleagues as pawns of the Illuminati, have nowhere else to go.

But of course the bizarre hypotheses and methodologies I have just reported or invented are indeed ridiculous, and it is quite sensi-

---

The Scientific Search for the Soul (Scribner: New York, 1994)), he had himself considered that 'directed panspermia' was a reasonable solution to the origin of terrestrial life (*Life Itself* (Simon & Schuster: New York, 1981). That is, he was prepared to consider the influence of 'design'—but he was also very ready to abandon it as soon as an alternative was offered, as though 'design' were automatically less plausible than any other suggestion: why?

[7] As, for example, James Watson, another, along with Crick and Maurice Wilkins (and Rosalind Franklin), of DNA's discoverers.

ble for 'scientists' and funding councils to ignore them all? We ought perhaps to be a little more cautious even about that: after all, many bizarre hypotheses of the past have turned out to be respectable ('some of my ancestors were fish'; 'the earth is revolving on its axis, and orbiting the sun'; 'light travels at a finite speed, which is the same for all observers, and sometimes bends round corners'). Even less bizarre hypotheses than these may not get funding, nor procure promotion. But it is indeed not quite absurd to insist that there are *some* dogmas that define true science, and that those who deny or even question them can't have such privileges as we accord 'true scientists'. In an amusing parallel to the past behaviour of established Christian Churches scientists have even appealed to 'secular authority' (that is, the courts) to determine that Intelligent Design Theory is not 'science'.[8] Even completely lunatic hypotheses (that I am an alien lizard from Betelgeuse 14) *might* turn out to be true, and even those who believe them *might* have other beliefs and practices that are worth pursuing[9]—but public bodies charged with supporting and defending 'scientists' will still, at the very least, be cautious.

Science and Story

The idea that all scientists are curious, open-minded and willing to accept that they were wrong, and that all religious believers are complacent, prejudiced, credulous of ecclesiastical authority, and incorrigibly ignorant, is too silly to require detailed refutation (especially as the classes overlap).[10] But perhaps that is not the real issue. Whatever the character of individuals, there is—perhaps—a real distinc-

[8] Why, in that case, is SETI (the Search for Extra-Terrestrial Intelligence) allowed to be 'scientific', despite depending on the axiom that it is possible to distinguish phenomena that are more probably 'designed' from those that aren't?

[9] Oliver Lodge (1851–1940) was not necessarily a bad physicist (he was involved in the development of 'wireless telegraphy') merely because he was also a socialist and a rather credulous spiritualist. Even if he had adopted some physical hypotheses on the suggestion of a spirit medium, what would have mattered would be the helpfulness of the hypotheses and not their ridiculous origin.

[10] Michael J. Mahoney & Bobby G. DeMonbreun, 'Psychology of the scientist: An analysis of problem-solving bias', *Cognitive Therapy and Research*, 1, 1977, pp. 229–38 report that 'the problem-solving skills of 30 PhD scientists were compared to those of 15 conservative Protestant ministers. Of particular interest was the frequency with which these groups generated confirmatory (rather than disconfirmatory) experiments to test their hypotheses. Experimental results showed that—contrary to a popular assumption—the reasoning skills of the scientists were not significantly different from those of nonscientists. In this study, the ministers showed a longer latency to speculation and generated more experiments per hypothesis than did the scientists'. The ministers, that is, were

tion between the social institutions, 'science' and 'religion' (or rather, the different scientific and religious institutions: colleges, professional bodies; sects and churches). Individual scientists may be as hooked on their own theories as Savonarola, and as disinclined to agree that they were ever wrong. This is not even, necessarily, a scientific sin: scientific debates require that all the parties to the exchanges do their very best—within the rules—to maintain their own positions (or refutation would be far too easy). It is the *institution* of science that is founded on the requirement that results (especially unexpected or bizarre results) are checked, in different laboratories by different people (and preferably by people with their own axes to grind). Theories that cannot be checked, however elegant and even promising they are, are widely considered 'non-scientific' (though since the currently most popular cosmological hypothesis, superstring theory, is in this position, the case is clearly not proven). Theories that are inconsistent with accepted theory may still, of course, eventually win out: it is not necessary for the institution's honour that they be immediately forgotten. As Paul Feyerabend pointed out, 'after Aristotle and Ptolemy, the idea that the earth moves—that strange, ancient and "entirely ridiculous", Pythagorean view—was thrown on the rubbish heap of history, only to be revived by Copernicus and to be forged by him into a weapon for the defeat of its defeaters.'[11] What other utterly ridiculous views will be reforged by our successors we simply cannot tell. But they probably won't get funding just at present, and ambitious researchers will probably go elsewhere.[12] Quite *how* the theories are to be checked will vary between sub-disciplines of science, and the checks will often, in practice, depend on the word of experienced practitioners.[13]

---

slower to assume that they knew what was going on, though neither group was sufficiently alert to seek out *disconfirmatory* evidence. Maybe both groups are by now a little more self-conscious, and aware of the need to *test* the spirits!

[11] Paul Feyerabend, *Against Method* (NLB: London, 1975), p. 49

[12] It is worth noting that, *pace* popular accounts, Darwinism was almost moribund until it was revived and revised in the 1930s, and not because of any supposed 'religious' objections to the theory. It was nearly moribund because there was no plausible mechanism to make it work. It was sustained in the popular imagination by the attractions of *Social* Darwinism—and by outright fraud. See Peter J. Bowler, *The Eclipse of Darwinism: anti-Darwinian evolution theories in the decades around 1900* (John Hopkins University Press: Baltimore & London, 1983), and a later chapter. Wegener's theory of continental drift was rejected for much the same reason: that no-one could see how continents *could* drift.

[13] Consider the problem faced by a surgeon needing to show his patient that the X-ray in front of them confirms the existence of a tumour: it may be wholly

Nonetheless, there is widespread acceptance of the rule that theories need to be supported by 'empirical evidence', that they need to make predictions in addition to the evidence on which they are first based, and that such predictions need to be more accurate than any currently alternative theory. String Theory, as I remarked before, does not, at the moment, meet this stern criterion, but is still sufficiently elegant to attract researchers willing to bet their careers and reputations that someday it will make testable predictions. Whether Neo-Darwinian Theory meets the criterion is a matter for debate.

By contrast, we are told, 'religious institutions' have no generally accepted rule by which internal disagreements can be resolved, even potentially. Speculative theology, so to speak, depends entirely on the tastes and loyalties of particular theologians. The difficulty is not that they are all 'dogmatic', 'set in their ways', 'slavishly obedient to what they have been told before' and utterly incurious about the further implications of their theories. This is simply not true. The problem is rather that it is rarely or never clear what *are* the further implications, nor whether they are ones that can be easily confirmed or contradicted. There is no 'theological method', it seems, as there is a 'scientific method'. There are, allegedly, no research projects in religion, or none that can specify what outcomes would confirm, what disconfirm, the theories. There is, at least in principle, a *scientific* route between believing all and only what the Professor says, on the one hand, and asserting every individual fancy on the other. But can there be a *religious* route between accepting the Church's *magisterium* (or the Imam's) and proclaiming one's own individual, unchallengeable faith? Once Luther and other Protestant heroes broke away from Rome, the story goes, there could be no way of preventing still greater fissiparation: if the Pope had no authority, how could Luther? And how, for that matter, could one's own self? 'Complete self-confidence is not merely a sin; complete self-confidence is a weakness. Believing utterly in one's self is a hysterical and superstitious belief like believing in Joanna Southcott'.[14]

The solution that some have offered—namely that the Bible is the final authority for Christians or the Koran for Muslims—is one that I

---

obvious to the surgeon, while the patient can at best see a faint shadow whose significance she has to take on trust (even if she demands a second opinion, the problem does not go away). A sufficiently paranoid patient, I suppose, would continue to doubt the diagnosis even after very many expert witnesses have commented on the X-rays, on the blood tests, on the tissue samples and so on. But by then she would also, probably, be dead.

[14] Chesterton, *Orthodoxy*, op. cit., p. 5.

shall seek to address in my next chapter. Briefly, it doesn't work, if every reader must interpret it for herself, and find there all and only what she wills to believe. But perhaps there is a solution, nonetheless, and the gap between Science and Religion is not actually so wide. At least, in both cases, we must retain the possibility that we are sometimes *wrong*, that there is something against which our thoughts and practices are to be measured, somehow. And we may also have to retain our determination to carry on inquiring: science too rests on *faith*, on the conviction that things must eventually make sense (but more on this below).

One popular solution, nowadays, is to compare theology with literary studies: even scientific theories, after all, are only widely believed if, somehow, they can be turned into significant stories. Their 'literal truth' matters less than their significance: witness the efforts that popularizing scientists make to draw out morals from their theories. We are told, for example, that all human civilization occupies only a tiny fragment of world-history: 'if the story of terrestrial life were compressed into a calendar year, humankind would turn up in the last three seconds' (or whatever). Or else we are told the universe is Very Big, or that Nature is Red in Tooth and Claw, or that we are robots built by 'selfish genes' (and so on). A merely literal response (for example, that till there were time-binding, story-telling creatures such as us, time was neither short nor long, and that bits of DNA aren't selfish, or even philoprogenitive) would miss the point just as absurdly as most literalistic commentary on 'religious' stories. We are built up of *stories* as well as cells, and stories can be judged *imaginatively* and *ethically*, as well as for precise 'historical' truth.

Even 'historical' truth is not entirely literal or empirical. Stories about the Reformation, or the Glorious Revolution, or the Fall of the Third Reich, must aim to be 'historically accurate', but they inevitably employ concepts and evaluations that cannot be fully quantified, nor made the basis of controlled experiments. They are *better* stories, better history, if they help us to 'make sense' of what has happened., help us to understand and judge and point to better times. Theology is a story about God, or else a study of stories about God or the gods or Heaven. Good literary critics show us things we hadn't noticed about the stories they discuss—not always things we're glad to know. Good critics are distinct from *snobbish* critics: the latter are persuaded that *their* taste is king, and that merely *popular* fiction appeals to baser tastes and stupid people. The former may also make critical judgements, even of an unpopular sort, but start from the assumption that neither popular art nor 'highbrow' art is entirely without value, and that the appeal of either need not be merely specious. Even 'the Christmas Story', wildly expanded from the Gospel narratives, appeals to people well outside the Christian circle, because it speaks to us of new beginnings, comfort in the midst of horror (very much as the escape of a simple family from Death, in Bergman's *The Seventh Seal*, is a sufficient achievement by the disillusioned knight). Saying that 'it isn't true' may serve more purposes than truth: it may be taken as a cynical denial that there are ever such fresh beginnings, or that anyone is ever saved. Even less comforting stories (less comforting at any rate to the comfortable classes), such as the coming of 'the great and terrible day of the Lord', when the crooked shall be made straight, and the rough places plane,[15] have a significance beyond their 'literal' truth. 'Believing' them may be much more like being a fan of *Star Trek* than like forecasting the weather, or the likely rise in interest rates (or else those latter, in their turn, are somewhat more like being a fan of *Star Trek* than professionals admit). Religion, remember, may be 'the opium of the people' without therefore being bad. As Death explains (in capitals) in one of Terry Pratchett's stories:

> 'All right,' said Susan, 'I'm not stupid. You're saying humans need ... *fantasies* to make life bearable.'
>
> ... NO. HUMANS NEED FANTASY TO BE HUMAN. TO BE THE PLACE WHERE THE FALLING ANGEL MEETS THE RISING APE.
>
> 'Tooth fairies? Hogfathers?'
>
> YES. AS PRACTICE. YOU HAVE TO START OUT LEARNING TO BELIEVE THE *LITTLE* LIES.
>
> 'So we can believe the big ones?'
>
> YES. JUSTICE. MERCY. DUTY. THAT SORT OF THING.'
>
> They're not the same at all!'
>
> TAKE THE UNIVERSE AND GRIND IT DOWN TO THE FINEST POWDER AND SIEVE IT THROUGH WITH THE FINEST SIEVE AND THEN SHOW ME ONE ATOM OF JUSTICE, ONE MOLECULE OF MERCY. AND YET YOU ACT AS IF THERE WERE SOME SORT OF *RIGHTNESS* IN THE UNIVERSE BY WHICH IT MAY BE JUDGED.

---

[15] *Isaiah* 40.4; see also *Malachi* 4.1–6, *Acts* 2.20

'Yes. But people have got to believe that or what's the *point* —.'

MY POINT EXACTLY.[16]

That justice and mercy can't be found amongst the ultimate atomic bits is hardly news: neither can personal identity, causality, temporal succession, or even Darwinian Theory.

Considered simply as stories, 'religious stories' must be judged, more or less, on literary terms. There is a limited stock of such stories, as there is a limited stock even of more general plots. It is not surprising that, in most times and places, we find stories about some young woman beloved of the gods, a child of glorious promise, his enemies, and his eventual, strangely uplifting death and apotheosis. If some particular culture does *not* admit such stories, we can reasonably ask for some particular explanation of their absence. It does not follow that the stories are all false: on the contrary, we carry on telling them because they are, in essence, true.

'True in essence', perhaps: but might they also, sometimes, be exactly and significantly true of some particular case? Are such stories, told because they embody our own deepest sympathies and fears, ever fully realized in 'historical reality'? Or is the question rather: might some particular 'historical' story lie behind the many different versions, and how could we tell that this was so?

In some cases, it may well be true that there was a first occasion for some happening or other, and that all later occasions (judged to be occasions of that sort precisely because the 'first occasion' was so memorable, and structures later experience) do no more than repeat or embellish that event. This may be true within our own personal existence. There is always a 'first time' for everything, whether it be 'first word', 'first day at school', 'first love', 'first failure' or 'first thought of death'. It isn't as clear now as perhaps it was that there was ever a 'first human couple' (though I shall return to that idea), and so there may never have been a 'first human word' or 'first human birth'. Even if there was a first time such a thing was *noticed,* it would have been noticed as something that had already happened many times before. And even in our personal experience it may be that we cannot actually *experience* any event unless it's recognizable as something that we've known before (and not realized we knew).

16] Terry Pratchett, *Hogfather* (Gollancz: London 1996), pp. 422–3. John Cornwell, *Darwin's Angel: an angelic riposte to The God Delusion* (Profile Books: London, 2007 p. 35), points out that Richard Dawkins was once prepared to admit the importance of such 'fictions' in our revolt against our 'selfish creators' in his first book, *The Selfish Gene* (Oxford University Press: Oxford, 1976).

'First love' is only possible because it's felt to be a revival of some earlier emotion: we *recognize* the beloved as now embodying something we've 'always' known and loved. So stories about the young mother and the child of promise have been with us 'forever', since before our kind was human, and so have stories about the enemy.

> Fairy tales [and the same is true of openly *religious* stories] are not responsible for producing in children fear, or any of the shapes of fear; fairy tales do not give the child the idea of the evil or the ugly; that is in the child already, because it is in the world already. Fairy tales do not give the child his first idea of bogey. What fairy tales give the child is his first clear idea of the possible defeat of bogey. The baby has known the dragon intimately ever since he had an imagination. What the fairy tale provides for him is a St. George to kill the dragon.[17]

We recognize the old stories when they are acted out in front of us, and some re-enactments influence all later ages. 'Falling in love' has never been the same since Dante encountered Beatrice. All births participate in Bethlehem. The ideal form of Socrates is embedded in Philosophy.

But are all stories worth telling, or living by? Obviously, both militant atheists and 'religious believers' would reject some stories. The problem is not just that some are badly told or boring, but that some are, simply, bad. Stories, after all, are just the sort of mental microbes that may be destructive demons, in the self and in society. Those suffering from depression or 'low self-esteem' are very familiar with the voices that tell and re-tell all their past sins and errors, and cause them to experience all new occasions as repeated failures.[18] We all know how easily our neighbours can be cast as enemies, vile creatures whom 'the one true Lord' desires us to drive out or kill. 'Religious' people are often perceived as both arrogant and judgemental.[19] It is unfortunately, miserably, true that people have sometimes been badly influenced by a corrupt interpretation of Bible stories: 'our first Planters', said George Berkeley, 'imagined they had a right to

[17] G.K. Chesterton, 'The Red Angel', in *Tremendous Trifles*, op. cit., p. 102.

[18] See Walter Wink, *Unmasking the Powers: the invisible forces that determine human existence* (Fortress Press: Philadelphia, 1986), p. 27, speaking of the experience we label 'Satan' or 'satanic', the accuser.

[19] Cf. *Matthew* 7.1–5.

treat Indians on the foot of Canaanites or Amalekites'.[20] It is also, it should be noted, miserably true that people influenced by Social Darwinism did just the same (on which more below).

> How will the New Republic treat the inferior races? How will it deal with the black? How will it deal with the yellow man? How will it deal with that alleged termite in the civilized woodwork, the Jew? ... If the Jew has a certain incurable tendency to social parasitism, and we make social parasitism impossible, we shall abolish the Jew; and if he has not, there is no need to abolish the Jew. ... The Jew will probably lose much of his particularism, intermarry with Gentiles and cease to be a physically distinct element in human affairs in a century or so. ... And for the rest—those swarms of black and brown and yellow people who do not come into the new needs of efficiency? Well, the world is not a charitable institution, and I take it that they will have to go.[21]

This judgement rested on Wells's ready belief in the Evolutionary Story as told by Social Darwinists (and sometimes by Charles Darwin).

> The insoluble problems of pain and death, gaunt, incomprehensible facts as they were, fall into place in the gigantic order that evolution unfolds. All things are integral in the mighty scheme, the slain builds up the slayer, the wolf grooms the horse into swiftness, and the tiger calls for wisdom and courage out of man. All things are integral, but it has been left for men to be consciously integral, to take, at last, a share in the process, to have wills that have caught a harmony with the universal will, as sand grains flash into splendour under the blaze of the sun. .... The old ethical principles, the principle of equivalents or justice, the principle of self-sacrifice, the various vague and arbitrary ideas of purity, chastity and sexual 'sin', came like rays out of the theological and philosophical lanterns men carried in the darkness. ... But now there has come a new view of man's place in the scheme

20] SPG Anniversary Sermon: Berkeley, *Works*, op. cit., vol. 7, p. 122; see Regina M. Schwartz, *The Curse of Cain: the violent legacy of monotheism* (University of Chicago Press: Chicago, 1997). There is a serious issue about the way the actual Canaanites were treated (see, for example, *Numbers* 25), which I shall try to address later.

21] H.G. Wells, *Anticipations* (1901), ch. 9: in *Anticipations and Other Papers* (Fisher Unwin: London, 1924), p. 272. *Anticipations* is also available at Project Gutenberg http:// www.gutenberg. org/etext/19229.

of time and space, a new illumination, dawn. ... The act of faith is no longer to follow your lantern, but to put it down.[22]

The notion that we should, in some way, live 'in harmony with nature' is of course an ancient one, and had always carried the implications both that we should be aware how small a part of nature we really were, and that we should acknowledge the law written in our hearts and history—the laws, amongst other things, of justice, love and chastity. Wells and his New Republicans ('the scientifically trained middle class') chose instead to model their lives on 'nature', conceived as a constant struggle to 'succeed'. Everything is integral, but some things ('weak and silly and pointless things') serve only by being destroyed. The New Republicans, as above, will have no pity for such 'contemptible and silly creatures', and 'to make life convenient for the breeding of such people will seem to them not the most virtuous and amiable thing in the world. ... but an exceedingly abominable proceeding.'[23] Wells was not alone. The French philosopher Henri Lichtenberger, writing on Nietzsche:

There are unfortunates whom it is inhuman to relieve. There are degenerates whose death should not be delayed. ... Let us kill all those who are ripe for death, let us have the courage not to retain among us those who are falling, but let us push them so that they may fall even more quickly.[24]

What Darwinism and Malthusianism actually meant in living political thought and practice was that *justice did not matter*. Darwin himself had disparaged social practices that meant we were 'breeding from the worst stock',[25] and expected the inferior races to decline

---

[22] Wells, *ibid.*, p. 248

[23] *Ibid.*, p. 257f.

[24] Henri Lichtenberger *The Gospel of Superman: the philosophy of Friedrich Nietzsche*, trans. J.M. Kennedy (T.N. Foulis: Edinburgh, 1910), cited by Dan Stone, *Breeding Superman: Nietzsche, Race and Eugenics in Edwardian and Interwar Britain* (Liverpool University Press: Liverpool, 2002), p. 71. For yet more in this style see Richard Weikart, *From Darwin to Hitler: Evolutionary Ethics, Eugenics and Racism in Germany* (Palgrave Macmillan: New York, 2004).

[25] 'There is reason to believe that vaccination has preserved thousands, who from a weak constitution would formerly have succumbed to smallpox. Thus the weak members of civilized societies propagate their kind. No one who has attended to the breeding of domestic animals will doubt that this must be highly injurious to the race of man. It is surprising how soon a want of care, or care wrongly directed, leads to the degeneration of a domestic race; *but excepting in the case of man himself, hardly anyone is so ignorant as to allow his worst animals to breed*': Charles Darwin,

and die. Just this excuse was offered by the influential Biblical scholar W.A.Albright for the Israelite invasion of Palestine, that 'superior' peoples had a right to exterminate 'inferior'.[26]

Stories like this have had a bad effect, not only on those who have been killed, expropriated and humiliated by demon-led or story-led aggressors, but also on those who have been infected by them, who have thereby lost their ordinary sense of human dignity and decency, and lost any chance of making new friends among the peoples they have been led to despise. They are bad stories, very much as ordinary literary judgement would recognize similarly bad stories, ones that corrupt their readers, debasing their taste and judgement.

> The chief enemy of excellence in morality (and also in art) is personal fantasy: the tissue of self-aggrandizing and consoling wishes and dreams which prevents one from seeing what is there outside one.[27]

Stories, in short, are dangerous, and idolatry is the enemy of excellence. And for that very reason we have good reason to wish to maintain *some* sort of control on the stories people tell. Militant atheists do have a point, even if the targets of their anger and disapproval are not the only possible targets. Even more casual atheists, and liberal believers, however much they may wish 'to live and let live', may have good reason to ridicule or even prohibit certain stories, and to seek, like Plato's Guardians, to drive out their authors. We in the West may have had our fill of torture and execution, for the moment, but it would be over-optimistic to declare that we will never use such tools—especially if we also maintain that there are no objective rules of justice, nor anything 'really wrong'. If there is nothing 'really wrong', then torture and execution, even for 'thought crimes', aren't really wrong. Of course, we may be cautious about re-introducing penalties like these as long as we think it possible that *we* might be their victims: but the more that we can distance ourselves from the

---

The Descent of Man (Princeton University Press: New Jersey, 1981; a facsimile of the 1871 edition), vol. 1, p. 168 (my italics).

[26] Keith W. Whitelam, *The Invention of Ancient Israel: The Silencing of Palestinian History* (Routledge: London, 1996), pp. 79–86, citing W.A. Albright, *From the Stone Age to Christianity: Monotheism and the Historical Process* (Doubleday: New York, 1957).

[27] Iris Murdoch, *The Sovereignty of Good* (Routledge & Kegan Paul: London, 1970), p. 59; see also *ibid.*, p. 86: 'good art shows us how difficult it is to be objective by showing us how differently the world looks to an objective vision'. An 'objective' vision, remember, is not a neutral nor a patronizing one.

thoughts that are to be penalized the stronger will be our wish to drive them out. Our very fear of being accused of harbouring them may make us all the more eager to denounce them—as has happened many times in the past.

So this story is dangerous too: the story, that is, that we have power and authority to drive out demons or demonic stories. And unfortunately it does not only infect those 'in authority'. Civil and ecclesiastical authorities, indeed, may sometimes be faced by *popular* unrest, by a widespread demand to find and destroy iniquity, whether the enemies are reckoned atheists, witches, communists, paedophiles—or religious fundamentalists. They may be compelled to establish formal courts and procedures to satisfy that popular demand (and also, of course, give it authority). It is the very same problem that I described before: how to ensure that the gods of human life, Olympians, including the dreadful passion of righteous indignation, can be made to serve the peace:

> These gods are visions of the eternal attributes, or divine names, which when erected into gods, become destructive of humanity. They ought to be the servants, and not the masters of man, or of society. They ought to be made to sacrifice to Man, and not man compelled to sacrifice to them; for when separated from man or humanity, which is Jesus the Saviour, the vine of eternity, they are thieves and rebels, they are destroyers.[28]

Quite what Blake meant by 'man or humanity, which is Jesus the Saviour' requires further examination. Let it stand for the moment merely as a gesture towards the right criterion for judging, and forgiving, stories.

Truth and Imagination

Theology, or all religious discourse, may be treated, that is to say, as Narrative, and assessed by different methods than is Science (though science itself may also constitute or create new stories). It is an important insight, and one that will be useful in considering how best to read 'scriptures'. It may at least provide an opening, to help those unfamiliar with 'religious' thought and practice to work out

[28] William Blake, 'A Descriptive Catalogue' (1809), *Complete Writings*, ed. G. Keynes (Oxford University Press: London, 1966), p. 571.

what on earth their 'religious' neighbours mean by it.[29] But perhaps it isn't an insight that can be taken quite as gospel.

I introduced the notion in a preliminary bid to explain how *good* answers might be distinguished from *bad* ones in the 'religious' sphere. Whereas scientific theories are to be judged by their ability to predict precise results which other, rival, theories cannot manage, 'religious' theories, so it seems, cannot be judged 'objectively'. Either *no-one* has any authority to speak about such things, or else—by what must seem a grossly circular argument—the particular theory that is to be judged right itself identifies the proper judge (whether this be the Pope, the Bible or the local preacher). 'I believe in the Church's teaching because the Church tells me that it is correct.' Comparison with literary judgement at least opens up the possibility that we can conceive of better or worse stories, better or worse readings of a story, without recourse to arbitrary judgements of that sort. Literary—or more generally, artistic—classics are ones that survive the generations, and speak as clearly (though sometimes with a rather different implication) to one population, century or region as another. 'Great religions' are similarly catholic (that is, *kath'olou*: for the whole). Merely fashionable or parochial artistic or religious works will perish quickly. 'The Last Judgement is an Overwhelming of Bad Art & Science', according to Blake.[30] We shall see straight when we see 'with imagination', by recognizing our involvement in the creation of a *Mental* Reality.

> 'What', it will be Question'd, 'When the Sun rises, do you not see a round disk of fire somewhat like a Guinea?' O no, no, I see an Innumerable company of the Heavenly host crying 'Holy, Holy, Holy is the Lord God Almighty.' I question not my Corporeal or Vegetative Eye any more than I would question a Window concerning a Sight. I look thro' it & not with it.[31]

Blake's vision is not as peculiar as some have thought. At any rate, even or especially *materialist* observers would also insist that in seeing the sun they are seeing something far greater than 'a round disk of fire'. They are seeing a furnace vaster than the earth. And the proper response to *that* is awe.

29] See Stanley Hauerwas, *The Peaceable Kingdom: a primer in Christian Ethics* (SCM: London, 2003; 1st published 1983).

30] 'A Vision of the Last Judgement' (1810), *Complete Works*, op. cit., p. 617.

31] *Ibid.*

> High in the empty air blazed and streamed a great fire, which burnt and blinded me every time I raised my eyes to it. I have lived many years under the meteor of a fixed Apocalypse, but I have never survived the feeling of that moment. Men eat and drink, buy and sell, marry, are given in marriage, and all the time there is something in the sky at which they cannot look. They must be very brave.[32]

But very few believers will be entirely happy to suppose that their own creed is no different in kind from *Star Trek* (which has also served to represent a civil possibility, a future for us all, a dream of peace[33]), or that all they do in seeing the 'spiritual significance' of things is awaken their own imaginative powers. The materialist who sees a solar furnace would at least be a little disconcerted to discover that he was 'really' living in *The Truman Show* (1998) or its equivalent, where 'the sun' was only a spotlight, and that he was consoling himself with fantasy. Likewise the 'religious' believer. Eamon Duffy, movingly describing his own temporary but devastating loss of faith:

> I could find no way of holding on to the values of Christianity while denying the account Christianity gave of reality. It wouldn't do to say that, yes, the world *was* a bleak place subject to inexorable material forces, and yet that one might as well structure one's life by values like love and selflessness and compassion, because they were really very attractive. I didn't see how righteousness could be reduced to some sort of pleasant and useful hobby like carpentry or crocheting, something to fill in the time till the hearse came to take me away. And I couldn't make any sense of the idea of defeated virtue for its own sake. I once saw an appalling newsreel of the Russian invasion of Hungary, in which a man rushed into the streets with a national flag which he brandished defiantly in the path of an oncoming tank, till it rolled over him with a noise like crackling sweetpapers. Was goodness like that; was Jesus like that? I found that I simply couldn't see righteousness as *pathetic*, a lost cause, like defeated Jacobite squires drinking to the King over the water who would never come into his own. I didn't see how one could affirm the

---

[32] G.K. Chesterton, *Daylight and Nightmare* (Dodd, Mead & Co: New York, 1986), p. 18.

[33] See Jennifer E. Porter & Darcee L. McLaren (eds.), *Star Trek and Sacred Ground: Explorations of Star Trek, Religion and American Culture* (SUNY Press: New York, 1999). See also my 'Science Fiction and Religion' in David Seed (ed.), *Blackwell Companion to Science Fiction* (Blackwell: Oxford, 2005), pp. 95–110.

> beatitudes, and yet assert that in no circumstances whatever would the meek inherit the earth.[34]

Duffy also points out that a collapse of faith (like his) is far more likely to be caused by some sudden personal trouble than by any merely 'scientific' or 'philosophical' discovery, and that there is nothing especially 'modern' about the event. His own rediscovery of 'faith' was indeed the effect of a sort of 'choice' ('I knew I had to choose, between the bleak valueless world of [Camus'] Outsider and the world of human significance, where love and forgiveness and celebration were possibilities'), but not an invention.

> Faith is a direction, not a state of mind; states of mind change and veer about, but we can hold a direction. It is not in its essence a set of beliefs *about* anything, though it involves such beliefs. It is a loving and grateful openness to the gift *of* being. The difference between a believer and a non-believer is not that the believer has one more item in his mind, in his universe. It is that the believer is convinced that reality is to be trusted, that in spite of appearances the world is very good. When we respond to that good, we are not responding to something we have invented, or projected. Meaning is not at *our* beck and call, and neither is reality. When we try to talk *about* that reality we find ourselves talking *to* it, not in philosophy but in adoration, for it is inescapably personal, and most luminously itself in the life and death of Jesus.[35]

Other believers, of course, might dispute some of this, not sharing Duffy's own Catholicism, or even his Christianity. But the overall description may still sound right. Faith is an imaginative project, which can be chosen: a *choice* to trust reality (precisely, *despite* appearances). There is some slight confirmation that this 'works', but the project does not depend on its always being easy. Believers may be as distressed, as desperate as anyone, and yet find, somehow, that there is a light still shining in the darkness. If this were only an imaginative exercise, a story that we tell ourselves, it must soon fail.

Strangely, when not excoriating the Creator for the evils of this world, most militant unbelievers will reckon that accounts like Duffy's are far too pessimistic. Surely, they say, all *normal* people find their comfort in companionship, in art and science and scholarship, in sports and sex and serendipity. If these palliatives fail us

---

[34] Eamon Duffy, 'When Belief Fails', *New Blackfriars*, 66 (1985), pp. 208–216: p. 214.

[35] *Ibid.*, p. 215.

there are medications that may help. We're depressed, they say, because we think we *should* be happy. Accepting that the world and ourselves 'just happened' we can get what minor joys we can, and bow out gracefully. As an older variety of atheist and materialist insisted, there is a four-fold remedy for all anxiety: 'Don't fear the gods; nor death; goods are easy to obtain; evils are easy to endure'.[36]

The remedy, perhaps, is not all that convincing. Epicurus, like other ancient philosophers, advised us to restrict our desires to ones that we could satisfy, and learn to accept that there were evils we could not mend. His creed was not conducive to scientific nor to technical advance, and the slave population, at least, of the ancient world found other creeds more relevant to their condition.

But whichever creed is helpful, there is still the question: which is true? And is there any relevant *criterion* for us to judge truth by? 'Does a firm perswasion that a thing is so, make it so?'[37] Blake causes his imagined Isaiah to answer Yes, but the claim is hardly plausible (at least I am firmly persuaded that it is not). And Blake himself acknowledged that merely believing something does not make it true.

> It is an easy thing to laugh at wrathful elements,
> To hear the dog howl at the wintry door, the ox in the slaughter-house moan;
> To see a god on every wind and a blessing on every blast;
> To hear sounds of love in the thunder-storm that destroys our enemies' house;
> To rejoice in the blight that covers his field, & the sickness that cuts off his children,
> While our olive & vine sing and laugh round our door, & our children bring fruits & flowers.
> Then the groan & the dolor are quite forgotten, & the slave grinding at the mill,
> And the captive in chains, & the poor in the prison, & the soldier in the field
> When the shatter'd bone hath laid him groaning among the happier dead.
> It is an easy thing to rejoice in the tents of prosperity:
> Thus could I sing & thus rejoice: but it is not so with me.[38]

---

[36] Summarized from Diogenes Laertius, *Lives of the Philosophers*, vol. 10, on Epicurus.

[37] Blake, *Marriage of Heaven and Hell* (1790–3), pl. 12: *Complete Works*, op. cit., p. 153.

[38] Blake, *Vala*, 2nd Night, lines 408–18: *ibid.*, pp. 290–1 (Enion speaks).

Schleiermacher's evocation of a happy family Christmas, with its message of motherly love and new beginnings, celebrated in music rather than intellectual discourse, is certainly moving, and likewise influential.[39] But the original story is a grimmer and more realistic one than 'family Christmases' suggest, and Christmas is immediately followed by memories of martyrdom and slaughter. Schleiermacher may be right to say that 'all radiant, serene joy is religion',[40] but it does not follow that all religion is a radiant, serene joy. Maternal—and paternal—hormones may cast a glow on the event, but all such feelings pass. In a merely naturalistic, atheistic universe they are no more than a drug to make it easier to cope, for a while, with the knowledge that with every birth a future death is born—and that every life is littered with failures, follies, things that need repentance.

What we more easily believe will often depend on circumstances, internal and external, that are outside our control. Such transient beliefs may be equated with mere mood swings, and *faith* is better conceived, with Duffy, as a *direction*, but even such directions, it seems clear, don't guarantee their truth. 'Beloved, believe not every spirit, but try the spirits whether they are of God: because many false prophets are gone out into the world'.[41] They must be judged 'by their fruits', but what fruits are considered good criteria will vary with the faith. Which seems to leave us where we were. We cannot properly *assess* any particular creed or purpose without ourselves endorsing some particular creed or purpose: that is, we cannot *prove* our creeds in any terms that will satisfy unbelievers. Nor is it enough to respond that there are after all some basic, instinctual axioms, some things that *everyone* considers good and beautiful. Perhaps there are, but there are also many differences, and many different priorities. We may at this point simply resign ourselves to an anti-realist position: to be 'true' is only to be seriously believed by 'us'; to be 'good' is only to be seriously approved by 'us' (and who 'we' are is an arbitrary commitment). Even if there is a common 'human' reality (which is itself contentious), humanity is no more than an experiment in living, and likely to be outlived by insects. But this

---

[39] Friedrich Schleiermacher, *Christmas Eve: Dialogue on the Incarnation,* trans. Terrence N. Tice (John Knox: Richmond, 1967; 1st written 1805). The text is illuminatingly discussed by Jeremy Begbie, *Resounding Truth: Christian Wisdom in the World of Music* (SPCK: London, 2008), pp. 142–52.

[40] *Ibid.*, p. 63

[41] *1 John* 4.1.

last is indeed a surrender, a collapse of faith—and of course also deeply incoherent. If that is how things are, then there is after all a way things are, whether we like it or not. If we would be wrong to think otherwise then there is at least *that* fact of the matter.

The alternative is simply to insist that faith is possible, and even required of us, and that it is, precisely, faith in reality. A 'firm perswasion' does not make things true, but some such firm persuasions are still true, and all attempts to deny them lead down to despair.

Metaphysics

But perhaps there is a different route to clarity. Ever since Immanuel Kant's supposed destruction of traditional metaphysics, it has seemed that we must accept his word that reason must give way to faith. If all our rational endeavours are limited to the world such creatures as us perceive or conceive then 'the real world' inevitably escapes our grasp. Oddly, we have perhaps forgotten that this theme had a long pre-Kantian history. It is an axiom of post-Platonic theory, after all, that the One (which is to say, the ultimate 'explanation', ultimate 'value' and ultimate 'reality') lies 'beyond reason and existence',[42] and that nothing we can say of it is ever exactly true. The very best efforts of dialectic reason may lead us at last to appreciate the lovely forms of things, but the explanation for those forms' identity, beauty and existence is not itself a form, an entity, or anything that can be described by reason. In this context, one of the many oddities of modern atheistical argument is the claim that we don't explain complexity by invoking another complex being (we can of course explain particular examples of complexity by invoking some one complex cause). Exactly so: which is why traditional theists have sought explanations quite outside that frame. 'God' does not name a complex entity, but the irreducible unity from which all things—maybe—stem (or at any rate, if they don't, we are left with no understanding of their uniformity, nor any reason to believe in it).

I have argued elsewhere that traditional theistic arguments cannot so easily be dismissed.[43] At the very least, they are significant for any proper understanding of what it is that theists actually believe (which is not, emphatically, that there is a Bogey in the Sky: on which more below). Those arguments, like every other, depend on premises, and rules of inference, that can, in a sense, be rejected. Indeed,

[42] Plato, *The Republic*, 509b.

[43] See *God, Religion and Reality* (SPCK: London, 1998).

for some enquirers the point of 'arguments for God's existence' is not to establish that God *does* exist, but to *rebut* those premises and rules of inference. But 'reasoning' of this sort is perhaps, after all, misleading.

A passage from Northrop Frye, describing how one might feel if shipwrecked like Crusoe on a deserted island, is perhaps enlightening:

> Looking at the world as something set over against you splits your mind in two. You have an intellect that feels curious about it and wants to study it, and you have feelings or emotions that see it as beautiful or austere or terrible, You know that both these attitudes have some reality, at least for you. If the ship you were wrecked in was a Western ship, you'd probably feel that your intellect tells you more about what's really there in the outer world, and that your emotions tell you more about what's going on inside you. If your background were Oriental, you'd be more likely to reverse this and say that the beauty or terror was what was really there, and that your instinct to count and classify and measure and pull to pieces was what was inside your mind.[44]

In even momentarily accepting that division between 'Oriental' and 'Occidental' minds, Frye erred. The rationalistic, objectifying, analytic attitude is only one strand of Western history, and only recently dominant. Our predecessors would have thought that the better way of approaching reality is in awe, in trembling delight, in a fall of barriers, in letting go the merely individual, false self. Plotinus, for example, wrote as follows:

> Intellect also, then, has one power for thinking, by which it looks at the things in itself, and one by which it looks at what transcends it by a direct awareness and reception, by which also before it saw only, and by seeing acquired intellect and is one. And that first one is the contemplation of Intellect in its right mind, and the other is Intellect in love, when it goes out of its mind 'drunk with the nectar'; then it falls in love, simplified into happiness by having its fill, and it is better for it to be drunk with a drunkenness like this than to be more respectably sober.[45]

44] Northrop Frye, *The Educated Imagination* (Indiana University Press: Bloomington, 1964), p. 17.

45] *Enneads* VI. 7 [38]. 35: A.H. Armstrong, *Plotinus*, vol. 7 (Loeb Classical Library, Heinemann: London, 1988), p. 197. I attempt a more detailed analysis of this and similar Plotinian passages in 'Concluding Remarks' in Panayiota Vassilopoulou & Stephen R.L. Clark (eds.), *Late Antique Epistemology: Other Ways to Truth*

Does this seem peculiar? Drunkenness is more usually assumed to be a retreat from the 'real world'. 'Wine in large quantity produces in men much the same characteristics which we attribute to the melancholic, and as it is being drunk it fashions various characters, for instance irritable, benevolent, compassionate or reckless ones. ... We are often in a state of grieving, but could not say why, while at other times we feel cheerful without apparent reason'.[46] Most of us, most of the time, would perhaps think it better to be 'in our right minds', 'sober' and 'unemotional' (at least in the sense of *not* being overwhelmed by shifting and inappropriate moods). Rationally minded atheists may well consider that 'faith' is indeed like 'drunkenness', and that there may be genetic antecedents for believers' susceptibility. Looking back to my earlier remarks about literary and artistic imagination, it is possible to be kindly tolerant of people who are absorbed, for a time, in episodes of their favourite soaps or costume dramas (as we may also tolerate an occasional binge), while reckoning obsessive fans are foolish, no longer able to discriminate between their fantasies and what is 'really true'.[47]

But what precisely validates the atheists' 'waking world' as more than their *own* fantasy? The world as we see or hear it is private and delusional in a way that we can only escape by intellectual awakening: 'the fool on the hill sees the sun going down, and the eyes in his head'—that is, the eye of reason—'see the world spinning round'.[48] The real world has many copies, many virtual representations, but there must be, on pain of eternal scepticism, some cognitive state that meets reality directly. Those moments, as they are for us, are ones in which the Real is directly experienced, not merely argued to. And usually forgotten very quickly: as p. 27 above, 'it is as if people who slept through their life thought the things in their dreams were reliable and obvious, but, if someone woke them up, disbelieved in

(Palgrave Macmillan: Basingstoke, 2009), and 'Plotinus on Becoming Love' in Michael McGhee & Michael Chase (eds.), *Philosophy as a Way of Life* (forthcoming).

[46] Aristotle, *Problemata*, 30. On the long association of drunkenness, melancholia and intellectual interests, see R. Klibansky, E. Panofsky, F. Saxl, *Saturn and Melancholy* (Nelson: Edinburgh, 1964)

[47] Others might agree with the poet Simonides' wry judgement that his work was not well received by the Thessalians 'because they were too stupid to be deceived' (Plutarch, *De Poetis Audiendis*, 15d).

[48] Paul McCartney, 'The Fool on the Hill', *Magical Mystery Tour* (1967)

what they saw with their eyes open and went to sleep again'.[49] We live, as a rule, among phantoms. 'The things which one thinks are most real, are least real'.[50] Plotinus seems to equate that occasional recognition of reality with our recognition of *beauty*. 'These experiences must occur whenever there is contact with any sort of beautiful thing, wonder and a shock of delight and longing and passion and a happy excitement. One can have these experiences by contact with invisible beauties, and souls do have them, practically all, but particularly those who are more passionately in love with the invisible, just as with bodies all see them, but all are not stung as sharply, but some, who are called lovers, are most of all'.[51]

Properly understood, to be is to be beautiful. 'Beautifulness is reality'.[52] 'For this reason being is longed for because it is the same as beauty, and beauty is lovable because it is being'.[53] But even these realities, these beauties, only excite us when they are, as it were, illuminated. Without that, it is as if we were 'in the presence of a face which is certainly beautiful, but cannot catch the eye because it has no grace playing upon its beauty. So here below beauty is what illuminates good proportions rather than the good proportions themselves, and this is what is lovable. For why is there more light of beauty on a living face, but only a trace of it on a dead one?'[54] Something is saying to us: 'Wake Up!'

Of course this moment can be rejected. We can persuade ourselves that 'beauty' is only a projection of erotic fancy, associated with a momentary intensification of sensual awareness. 'Obviously' such lovers are mistaken.

There is a passage from a later, neglected philosopher, namely Lev Shestov, that may make the point, and perhaps suggest an answer.

> In his *Metaphysics of Sexual Love* Schopenhauer brilliantly develops the idea that love is only a fleeting illusion. The 'will' desires to realize itself once more in an individual, and so it suggests to John that Mary is a rare beauty and to Mary that John is a great hero. As soon as the goal of the 'will' is achieved, as soon as the birth of a new being is assured, the will abandons the lovers to

---

49] Plotinus, *Enneads* ,V.5.11.

50] *Ibid.*

51] *Enneads*, I.6 [1].4, 16f.

52] *Enneads*, VI.7.23f.

53] *Enneads*, V.8 [31].9, 41.

54] *Enneads*, I.6 [1].4, 23f.

> themselves and they then discover with horror that they have been the victims of a dreadful mistake. John sees the 'real' Mary—that is, a dense, stupid, and ill-natured woman; Mary, on her side, discovers the real John—a dull, banal, and cowardly fellow. And now, after the delusions of love have been dissipated, the judgements Mary and John pronounce on each other agree perfectly with the judgements of all, with what *semper ubique et ab omnibus creditum est.* For everyone always thought that Mary was ugly and stupid and John cowardly and foolish. Schopenhauer does not doubt in the least that Mary and John saw true reality precisely when they saw what everyone else saw. And not only Schopenhauer thinks so. This is again *quod semper ubique et ab omnibus creditum est.* But it is precisely because this truth appears so unquestionable that there is good reason to raise the question of the legitimacy of its pretensions. Did John and Mary really deceive themselves during the short time when, the 'will' having kindled its magic flame in them, they abandoned themselves to the mysterious passion that drew them together and they saw each other as so beautiful? May it not be that they were right precisely when they were alone in their opinion and appeared to all others as poor idiots? May it not be that at that time they were in communion with true reality and that what their social natures oblige them to believe is only error and falsehood? Who knows!'[55]

Plotinus does of course himself insist that the judgements of an assembly are likely to iron out individuals' errors,[56] and so might be expected to accept the common judgement.[57] But are we so sure that it *is* a common judgement that such lovers are mistaken? Perhaps even they will lose conviction, as Schopenhauer suggested, but is it *obvious* that they know better then? In 'ordinary' life, after all, it may be usual to think of others (human or non-human) simply as the furniture, or the tools, or obstacles, inhabiting our own supreme existence. And yet we all 'know', in our saner moments, that this is not so. Militant atheists especially—it is one good thing about them—are assured that the *real* world does not depend on us, that real things are not just tools or obstacles or stuff for our own fantasies. Yet why should we, or they, much care for this? Unless reality is

---

[55] Lev Shestov, *Potestas Clavium*, ed. and trans. Bernard Martin (Ohio University Press, 1968), Pt. 1, ch. 6: taken from http://shestov. by. ru/pc/pc1_2. html (accessed 24th April 2008).

[56] *Enneads*, VI.5 [23].10, 18f.

[57] *Enneads*, IV.4 [28].31, 30.

indeed 'attractive' why should we bother to escape the virtual realities created, we are told, as 'the fittest' (the most productive) of whatever rival forms? And why should we seek to unify our realities, in the conviction that there is one real, rationally accessible system? It would, exactly on materialist terms, be fairly rare to see and appreciate the *truth* of things: so why not take more seriously the option that it is on these rare occasions that we do, and that *faith* is to hold on to the memory and hope revealed in them? Once, I was awake. Once, Winston Smith still 'knew' that 2 plus 2 makes 4.[58]

Once again, if there are no real obligations beyond what 'we' have bothered to create as *legal* or *professional* obligations, it is difficult to see what offence can be committed by living, as far as we can, in what we think is beauty. If there are such real obligations then they may be displayed, exactly, in the recognition of real beauty. Our contact with the 'metaphysical' (that is to say, with the reality transcending ordinary experience) lies in these moments. 'And the Word became flesh and dwelt among us, and we beheld his glory, the glory as of the only begotten son of the Father, full of grace and truth'.[59]

And how do we confirm that this is real? Only by the repeated attempt to live up to that vision, and the repeated appeal for help in that endeavour. Asking for it to be proved beforehand is even sillier than it would be to expect a scientific hypothesis to be *proved* before we bother to try testing it.

Prayer

We can learn from Hindu tradition that there are three routes to freedom: *karma, jñāna, bhakti*.[60] The route of action (*karma*) is to do one's duty, as that is defined by gender, caste, age and circumstance—or by the sort of summons to a larger justice that has animated prophets and reformers. *Jñāna* is the path of metaphysical contemplation, and is not that far removed from the sort of intellectual re-ordering of our lives and minds that militant atheists advise (though they do so without joy). *Bhakti* involves a personal devotion to some god:

58] See George Orwell, *1984* (Penguin: Harmondsworth, 1954; 1st published 1949), pp. 68, 200–5, 223, 233.

59] *John* 1.14.

60] Interestingly, 'Rabbi Simon the Just said that the universe stands on three things, on Torah, on divine service, and on the practice of charity (*Mishnah*, Perkei Avot, 1.2)': Norbert M. Samuelson, 'On the symbiosis of Science and Religion: a Jewish Perspective': *Zygon*, 35 (2000), pp. 83–97: p. 95. Samuelson, plausibly, identifies Torah with the study of physical nature as well as the Hebrew texts—so the threefold pattern is repeated.

Vishnu, Shiva, Devī, Ganesha or Surya. It is this devotion, manifested in private or public prayer, with whatever personal style or churchly ritual, and directed to whatever god or guru, that is most despised by militants. Considered as a way of acquiring a particular favour, so they say, it is obviously ineffective. Considered simply as 'devotion' to an imagined deity, it is contemptible: what sort of God, they say, is pleased by servile praise and special pleading? Actually, even believers have often thought much the same. 'Those who fight bravely, not those who pray, are to come safe out of the wars',[61] as Plotinus robustly taught us. Palmerston rejected a request to establish an official fast day to ward off a cholera epidemic in 1853, saying that 'the Maker of the Universe has established certain laws of nature for the planet in which we live, and the weal or woe of mankind depends upon the observance or the neglect of those laws ... and it is the duty of man to attend those laws of nature and to exert the faculties which Providence has thus given to man for his own welfare.'[62] Clarfield goes on to say that 'Charles Kingsley, a sanitary reformer and liberal clergyman, went even further. He felt that the Lord had already responded to prayers for a stay of cholera by revealing the origins of the disease through the work of scientists; thus, new prayers would be "unappreciative of divine knowledge so revealed"'.[63]

Sophisticated believers do not pray to effect a particular result, as though God or the gods were in our power, but rather to act out, to express, their devotion and respect. Matteo Ricci, the sixteenth-century Jesuit missionary, offered a similarly 'expressive' account of Chinese rituals that involved the presentation of food or drink 'to their ancestral spirits':

> They [the Chinese] do not believe that the dead will come to eat or even need these things. They say that there is no other way to express their love and gratitude to the dead. Some told me that these rituals are set up for the living people, not the dead — that is, to teach the children and the ignorant to respect their parents that are still alive. [...] In any case, they do not think that the people who are gone are gods or spirits, thus they do not pray for any-

[61] *Enneads*, III.2 [47].32, 36f.

[62] A. Mark Clarfield, 'An old prayer for modern medicine' in *Canadian Medical Association Journal*, Dec 2002, 167, pp. 1365–67, citing S. M. Turner, *Contesting cultural authority: essays in Victorian intellectual life* (Cambridge University Press: Cambridge, 1993).

[63] *Ibid.*

> thing. It has nothing to do with idolatry. Hence it seems not to be superstition.[64]

Francis Galton's laborious demonstration that European royalty, despite being regularly prayed about, 'are literally the shortest lived of all who have the advantage of affluence'[65] depended on the assumption that believers must suppose that prayer is materially efficacious and that long life is unequivocally a good (and also on the even less plausible assumption that no-one was praying *against* the royals!). It is more likely that even those who prayed most assiduously for their sovereigns were hoping for nothing more than that strength should be available to them to meet their dreadful responsibilities (and it is not as absurd as Galton suggests to think that sovereigns—especially in the late nineteenth century—had rather more to put up with than the usual aristocracy or gentry did).[66] Prayer is not considered a magic rite, in any major religion. Nor do believers claim to know so clearly what is really *good* for those they pray for.

Galton acknowledged, though perhaps ironically, that prayer might help the one who prayed, but urged that a similar effect might be had by a non-theistic meditation:

> A confident sense of communion with God must necessarily rejoice and strengthen the heart, and divert it from petty cares; and it is equally certain that similar benefits are not excluded from those who on conscientious grounds are sceptical as to the reality of a power of communion. These can dwell on the undoubted fact, that there exists a solidarity between themselves and what surrounds them, through the endless reactions of physical laws, among which the hereditary influences are to be included. They know that they are descended from an endless past, that they have a brotherhood with all that is, and have each

[64] Matteo Ricci, *China in the Sixteenth Century: The Journal of Matteo Ricci: 1583*–1610, trans. Lous J. Gallagher (Random House: New York, 1942), p. 96. I owe this reference to Yang Xiao of Kenyon College, Ohio, and discuss it a little further in 'Discerning the Spirits: Healing and the Moral Problems of Efficacy', in Sarah Coakley (ed.), *Spiritual Healing: Science, Meaning, and Discernment* (Eerdmans, forthcoming).

[65] F. Galton, 'Statistical Inquiries into the Efficacy of Prayer', in *Fortnightly Review*, 68, 1st August 1862 (available at http://www.abelard.org/galton/galton.htm, accessed 11th January 2008). The ninety-seven in his sample lived, on average, for 64.4 years, while the 1,179 of English aristocrats, for example, managed an average of 67.31.

[66] His reference to the 'easy country life and family repose' of the clergy (who lived, on average, for five years longer) also suggests that he knew as little of the life of late Victorian clergy as he did of royalty.

> his own share of responsibility in the parentage of an endless future. The effort to familiarize the imagination with this great idea has much in common with the effort of communing with a God, and its reaction on the mind of the thinker is in many important respects the same. It may not equally rejoice the heart, but it is quite as powerful in ennobling the resolves, and it is found to give serenity during life and in the shadow of approaching death.[67]

Why it is thought more rational to believe in an 'endless past' and 'endless future' (for which we have no evidence at all) than in an eternal God, I do not know. Nor do I know what evidence beyond the personal and anecdotal Galton had for the claim that this sense of cosmic unity ennobles the resolve and gives serenity in times of trouble as certainly as more traditional belief. There might also be some doubt about the sincerity of Galton's 'brotherhood with all that is', given his involvement in Eugenics (though he would have rejected much that later passed under that name with horror). But he was right to refer to 'the effort to familiarize the imagination with this great idea': such an effort is required in any belief-system that would direct attention away from the immediate and everyday. This is one origin of ritual and ceremonial readings: merely to infuse the imagination with the truths we think we know, but constantly forget. 'Prayer purifies the mind and prepares it for the contemplation of reality.'[68] Prayer, especially public prayer, unites us in a congregation of the faithful, freed for a moment from the pull of personal affairs (though all those who engage in it can also testify that such personal affairs keep creeping into their thoughts).

That prayer may be both expressive and consoling perhaps needs little argument. If it really had no other effect than these it would still, most probably, be worth its price. But is it possible to make a larger claim? Is there any way in which the act of prayer gives reason to believe? Galton's approach would deny this: if we treat prayer as we might treat some new drug or surgical procedure, we must first engage in careful control experiments (far better controlled than Galton's statistical analysis). Such experiments have been attempted, with patients being randomly prayed for, with and without their knowledge. It is not clear that prayer, so tested, 'works' (though at least it does no harm, so long as more material treatments

---

[67] *Ibid.*

[68] Maximus Confessor, 'Four Hundred Chapters on Love', 1.79, *Maximus Confessor, Selected Writings*, trans. George C. Berthold (SPCK: London, 1985), pp. 43f.

are not abandoned). But what if prayer did 'work' on those terms, as some have thought it did? Would this give us any good reason to believe that there were gods, and that they did respond to prayer? It is more likely, if prayer like that did 'work', that some other theory would at once be devised to explain it: perhaps a theory that subverted some easy materialist certainties by proposing that our *thoughts* and *hopes* have power, or that we are really united at some level. Would this necessarily have any religious sense? It is doubtful that it would, even if the conclusion were that the world of our experience was merely virtual, and 'real causes' lay entirely outside its frame. That might serve as *allegory* of the religious view, but it could not, of itself, confirm religion. What if it turned out that sorcerous prayers to harm our enemies were also very effective?

This is as much as to say that it is pointless to test 'the efficacy of prayer'. Either it is not efficacious, as Galton supposed, or else it is, but its success need have nothing to do with religion. This is not surprising. Though we are enjoined to *test* the spirits, whether they are of God, this can't be by discovering whether they deliver the goods we wanted: Mephistopheles might do the same. Trying to make the gods serve *our* ends is axiomatically the wrong approach: piety is serving the gods' ends, and prayer is the discovery of what those ends will be. When we pray for rain (for example), at the right season, it is so that rain is experienced as an answer to our prayer, not so that it occurs on time. When we pray for healing or long life, for ourselves or others, it is to place ourselves and them at God's disposal—or rather, to realize that we are. When our prayers amount to curses, we are at another power's disposal.

What role does prayer have in the contest with which this chapter has been concerned, between religion and experimental science? Treating prayer as a technique is to miss its point entirely. But it does not follow that prayer has no epistemological effect. We find out what God or the gods 'desire' through prayer, if it is honestly undertaken (as of course it may not be). We try out 'the religious hypothesis' by prayer, and are confirmed in it (or not) by its effect in us. Personally and anecdotally, at any rate, it seems to me that prayer has just the effect it promises. It does not follow that we will always relish that effect. Be careful, as the saying goes, exactly what you pray for: you may get it.[69]

[69] See Larry Dossey, *Be Careful What You Pray For... You Just Might Get It* (HarperOne: New York, 1998), for a slightly different slant on the effects of prayers (and curses). His warning, like mine, is against the use of magic.

3

Understanding Scripture

Reading Scripture

Militant atheists are generally well-persuaded that they have read the Hebrew and Christian scriptures more attentively than have believers, and are eager to point out the contradictions, follies and appalling wickedness that they apparently contain. Till recently Islamic Scriptures perhaps had a more sympathetic hearing, and the Hindu scriptures have more usually been attacked by theists or by Buddhists than by atheists. More sympathetic readings of the scriptures, employing whatever tools of allegory and literary discrimination, are regarded as merely hypocritical. Here as in other matters there is sometimes a strange alliance between the militants and scriptural fundamentalists, persuaded that there is no other way of reading scripture than the 'literal' or 'historical'. 'Liberal' readers are heretics or hypocrites.

But militants are not, of course, the only people to have worried about the Scriptures. Chesterton gives the following words to his Father Brown, in 'The Sign of the Broken Sword':

> Sir Arthur St. Clare was a man who read his Bible. That was what was the matter with him. When will people understand that it is useless for a man to read his Bible unless he also reads everybody else's Bible? A printer reads a Bible for misprints. A Mormon reads his Bible, and finds polygamy; a Christian Scientist reads his, and finds we have no arms and legs. St. Clare was an old Anglo-Indian Protestant soldier. ... Of course, he found in the Old Testament anything that he wanted—lust, tyranny, treason. Oh, I dare say he was honest, as you call it. But what is the good of a man being honest in his worship of dishonesty?[1]

1] G.K. Chesterton, *The Innocence of Father Brown* (1911); reprinted in *The Father Brown Stories* (Cassell: London, 1929), pp. 266–7; see S. Zizek, 'Why Heidegger Made the Right Step in 1933', *International Journal of Žižek Studies* [2007 Oct 21], 1:4.

The Scriptures need to be interpreted as a whole, and within an appropriate oral tradition. 'If one may not delve into the sayings of Scripture and the Fathers with a speculative mind, the whole Bible falls apart, Old and New Testament alike.'[2] Without that context, taken *out* of context, particular passages are often peculiar, absurd or wicked. But this is not to say that nothing can be learnt from a relatively straightforward reading, nor to insist always on 'allegorical' as against 'literal' meanings. The very meaning of 'literal' and 'allegorical' is often not entirely clear. Someone who says, for example, that he was 'literally over the moon when he heard the news' does not expect to be asked how many miles over, what escape velocity he had achieved, or what fuel was used. 'Literally' here means 'emphatically' or some such, not 'non-metaphorically'. It may well be true that he was over the moon, in the sense he meant, even if pedants (and philosophers) snigger at him. Similarly, I suggest, someone who says she believes that the Bible is 'literally true' almost certainly does not mean that every sentence of the Bible has a clear 'historical' implication, but rather that the Bible is 'not mistaken', that its 'truth' is certain however difficult it may sometimes be to disentangle what truth that is. What genre any particular passage of 'the Bible' belongs to is contested, even within the mainstream Christian tradition. Certainly not every passage is offered as 'historical truth'. *The Song of Songs*, for example, is not a historical document recording the thoughts and actions of a particular woman and her man, even if—which is possible—this was the original intention of the poet who wrote it. Its significance, as part of Scripture, is for the faith community which put the texts together to determine.[3] The early chapters of *Genesis* have been understood anagogically from very early (see Philo of Alexandria), and their usefulness in the tradition is as such.

Available: http://zizekstudies. org/index. php/ijzs/article/view/64/129; and G. Fried, 'Where's the Point? Slavoj Žižek and the Broken Sword': *International Journal of Žižek Studies* [2007 Dec 31] 1:4. Available: http://zizekstudies.org/index.php/ijzs/article/view/83 /146. I am grateful to Paul Taylor (Leeds) for these references.

[2] Maximus the Confessor at his trial (in 654 AD) in response to the suggestion that we should do no more than read the 'simple words of Scripture': *Patrilogia Graeca*, 90. 149a, cited by Hans Urs von Balthasar, *Cosmic Liturgy: the universe according to Maximus the Confessor*, trans. A.M. Allchin (Ignatius Press: San Francisco, 2003), p. 53.

[3] See Nelson Pike, *Mystic Union: an essay in the phenomenology of mysticism* (Cornell University Press: New York, 1992), pp. 66ff.

> If the Manichees were willing to discuss the hidden meaning of these words [the opening chapter of *Genesis*] in a spirit of reverent inquiry rather than of captious fault-finding, then they would of course not be Manichees, but as they asked it would be given them, and as they sought they would find, as they knocked it would be opened up to them. The fact is, as you see, people who have a genuine religious interest in learning put far more questions about this text than these irreligious wretches; but the difference between them is that the former seek in order to find, while the latter are at no pains at all to do anything except not find what they are seeking.[4]

Augustine goes on to say that though there is nothing wrong in interpreting the text 'literally' and 'historically', there is also an anagogical significance, here and elsewhere.

> If there is no other way of reaching an understanding of what is written that is religious and worthy of God, except by supposing that it has all been set before us in a figurative sense and in riddles, we have the authority of the apostles for doing this, seeing that they solved so many riddles in the books of the Old Testament in this manner.[5]

The story of the Flood,[6] for another example, is a story about someone's daring to do what his neighbours think absurd, and being vindicated; a story about the survival of a remnant through catastrophe; a story about something that contains and preserves the seeds of everything; a story about being born again, after baptism; a story that offers some reason for God's allowing us to eat animal-flesh;[7] a story asserting that all humankind is closely related. Of course, it might also have a historical implication, and many commentators amused themselves in seeking to work out how to house and feed the different animals, or wondering how *global* the cataclysm was. From the eighteenth century onwards the notion of the Flood played a significant role in the interpretation of geological strata and fossil evidence of apparently drowned animals. Perhaps the most signifi-

---

[4] Augustine, *On Genesis: a refutation of the Manichees* (388/9 ad), Bk. 2, 2.3: *Augustine on Genesis,* trans. E. Hill (New City Press: New York, 2002), p. 72.

[5] *Ibid.*; see also Garry Wills, 'Radical Creativity': *MLN*, Vol. 89, No. 6, Comparative Literature. (Dec., 1974), pp. 1019–1028, citing Augustine, *City of God,* Bk. 11.

[6] *Genesis* 6–9. See Norman Cohn, *Noah's flood: the Genesis story in Western thought* (Yale University Press: New Haven, 1996).

[7] Though, properly understood, the concession does *not* permit the actual killing of animals for food: 'this bond doth give thee here no jot of blood', as Portia points out to Shylock (*The Merchant of Venice* Act IV, Scene 1, Line 302).

cant moral of the story, when that was taken as one *founded*, at least, on historical fact, was that there had been worlds, or world-ages, before our own, and that our world also could be swept aside. To that I shall return. But historical fact was not the original point, nor even the reason why the story still speaks even to those who doubt its *geological* veracity. The whole notion of a 'documentary history' in the sense that we may now expect is something that has developed, historically, and was not available to the original human authors of the corpus that was gradually composed into 'The Bible'. What the Bible is saying may still all be true, even 'literally' (that is, emphatically) true, even if the 'historical' inferences that have sometimes been drawn from its record are—sometimes—inaccurate.

Staying with the Flood for a moment, it may also be worth noting that, on present evidence, humankind has indeed passed through at least one evolutionary bottleneck,[8] and we are all very closely related as a result. That 'the Flood' was a truly global affair is unlikely, on current geological theory and information; that there was some such catastrophe, covering 'the known world', at a crucial time in our prehistory may well be true,[9] and that the Noahic survivors did also bring with them the seeds and ancestors of many non-human kinds. But the point of the story for most of its readers lies in our *personal* history, not in the natural world's.

That is probably the mainstream view amongst Christian believers at the moment: namely, that some parts of the Bible reflect historical realities, even when two or more versions of the same events are included without comment (the human authors having no way of deciding between them), but that the main point of including anything in the Bible was advisory. On the other hand, it might be worth reflecting that all histories, including the current consensus history, are artefacts, composed by human historians to fit their preconceptions. Critics who are alert to the social and cultural context of the

---

[8] This is inferred from ongoing interrogation of genetic similarities and dissimilarities, principally in our mitochondrial DNA. Our line survived, as other hominid lines did not, but not necessarily because of any particular virtue or superior genetic inheritance.

[9] This has been the dominant Anglican interpretation since it was proposed by John Pye Smith in 1839: see Cohn, *Noah's Flood*, op. cit., p. 124; see also *ibid.*, p. 43. Just possibly, it was the flooding of the Black Sea around 5,500 BC that lies behind the Sumerian story also recorded in very different forms in *Gilgamesh* and *Genesis* (see William Ryan & Walter Pitman, *Noah's Flood: the new scientific discoveries about the event that changed history* (Simon & Schuster: New York, 1998)), but there may be other candidates. Floods, after all, even catastrophic and land-changing floods, are not infrequent.

texts they study are sometimes strangely blind to their *own* social and cultural context. Suppose for a moment that the most 'literal', even mythological, interpretation of the Christian tradition is true: we are living in occupied territory, where fallen humanity and rebel angels conspire to construct some picture of the world that will divert us from the truth. In that context it might actually be true that the Bible is 'real history', and that the fables which seem to us to be inconsistent with it are, precisely, fables. Choosing to believe this, obviously, could not be a matter of a neutral assessment of 'the evidence', since by hypothesis the 'evidence' that is most feverishly pressed on us is likely to be wholly specious. Imagine yourself living in George Orwell's Oceania (in *1984*): in that context, some small group of rebels who stood by real history would be routinely mocked (and sometimes executed) by 'the authorities' who controlled what 'evidence' was available. Do we *know* that we aren't living in Oceania? Perhaps we are looking back to a genuinely global upheaval, even an intrusion upon the 'natural order', a Singularity, such that we can infer nothing about that World Before from present circumstances, but only from the stories Noah and his kindred told. *Probably*, this is false—but how exactly shall we show it?

Hermeneutical Traditions

The scriptures of any faith were composed by people, at particular times and places with particular motives and beliefs. The *Hermetic Corpus*, for example, was probably composed in the third or fourth centuries A.D., even though it claims to be a record of ancient Egyptian wisdom, from which both Plato and Moses were at one time thought to have borrowed. Its reputation was such that Marsilio Ficino was asked to turn away from translating the Platonic dialogues to translate the *Corpus* first. When Casaubon demonstrated, from internal evidence, that it was really a product of late antique Platonism, its authority amongst academic scholars and philosophers was diminished—though it has remained an inspiration in more esoteric circles. For many years it was supposed that the Egypt it imagined into being, a land of magicians and philosophers, was wholly unlike the real, historical Egypt. Actually, it appears that rather less was wrong with its picture than sceptical philosophers supposed, but it is probably still correct to read it for evidence of late antique and Renaissance Platonism rather than for insights into early Egyptian thought. We cannot easily use it as evidence that

Plato and Moses borrowed their thought from Egypt, though it is not entirely absurd to suppose that that is, partly, true.

Scholarly discussion of the *Corpus* is mostly devoted to tracing its likely origins in earlier Greek thought, and its influence on the Renaissance. But it also has an 'esoteric' life, amongst those attracted by its blend of Platonising philosophy, romantic prophecy and advice on how to live. For them its historical origins are not entirely relevant: they 'believe' in it because it speaks to them in terms they understand and love, not because they are—separately—persuaded that its author lived before Moses. Rather the reverse: if they are inclined to suspect that Casaubon was, in essence, incorrect, and that it *does* preserve an Ancient Wisdom, it is because they are moved by it. And if it were finally proved that it was composed by Alexandrian pupils of Ammonius (for example), and that the ancient Egyptians would not have understood a word, this would not matter much. Nor would they necessarily be much moved if it were proved that the prophecies it contains were *originally* no more than an exaggerated lament for Egypt as it was in the authors' day.

> A time will come when it will appear that the Egyptians paid respect to divinity with a faithful mind and painstaking reverence—to no purpose. All their holy worship will be disappointed and perish without effect, for divinity will return from earth to heaven, and Egypt will be abandoned. ... In their weariness the people of that time will find the world nothing to wonder at or to worship. This all—a good thing that never had nor has nor will have its better—will be endangered. People will find it oppressive and scorn it. They will not cherish this entire world, a work of god beyond compare. ... No one will look up to heaven. The reverent will be thought mad, the irreverent wise; the lunatic will be thought brave, and the scoundrel will be taken for a decent person. ... Whoever dedicates himself to reverence of mind will find himself facing a capital penalty. ... The fruits of the earth will rot; the soil will no more be fertile; and the very air will droop with gloomy lethargy. Such will be the old age of the world: irreverence, disorder, disregard for everything good.[10]

The application of those prophecies is determined by the way that its *readers* hear them. It is a feature of our life here-now that the gods have gone away—and will one day return.

---

[10] *Asclepius* $25–6: *Hermetica*, trans. Brian P. Copenhaver (Cambridge University Press: Cambridge, 1992), pp. 81–2. After this the Master and Father will restore the world.

The Hermetic tradition has its sacred texts, and those accumulated texts are remembered and preserved, precisely, as Hermetic. Scholars are entitled to consider them 'objectively', and seek to describe their origins and original intent. But even if it were discovered that one of those texts was first written as a joke, it might still remain a serious contribution to the tradition.[11] Its *meaning* would be what Hermeticists read in or into it, and not what its first author, perhaps, intended. Another text beloved of neo-pagan Hermeticists, Apuleius' *The Golden Ass,* culminates in his hero's restoration to humanity, and initiation into the Isis cult: it is possible that the concluding chapters, in which he is required to undergo a series of initiations, at considerable expense, merely confirm—for Apuleius—his status as an ass. But this is not how the text has been read by esotericists: if it were *only* a pornographic comedy (which, of course, in part it is) it would not have had such influence.[12]

The Bible, of course, has had still greater influence. Here too scholars may rightly devote themselves to identifying the origin and original meanings of the many texts it contains. It may be especially important to notice what those texts were first written to oppose: the 'Priestly' author(s) of *Genesis* 1.1–2.4a,[13] for example, undoubtedly knew the Babylonian stories of the Creation and the Flood. We glimpse more of their intentions in observing how different their stories are: at the very beginning the earth 'was without form and void', but there is no independent principle of chaos for the Creator to overthrow; the sun, moon and stars may govern day and night, but they do not govern us, being no more than 'signs for festivals and for seasons'.[14] But the authority of these stories does not lie with their human authors. Even more obviously than in the case of the *Hermetic Corpus* there is a community of believers which has *selected* and affirmed those texts for its own purposes. What they mean, to that community (or rather to the network of communities that together

11] The nineteenth-century Platonist Thomas Taylor wrote *A Vindication of the Rights of Brutes* in parody of Mary Wollstonecraft's *Vindication of the Rights of Women*: this does not prevent its being an influential text in the gradual expansion of human sympathies to animals.

12] See Julia Haig Gaisser, *The Fortunes of Apuleius and the Golden Ass: A Study in Transmission and Reception* (Princeton University Press: New Jersey, 2008) for a study of the novel's influence.

13] Commonly called P, to distinguish him or them from the earlier 'Yahwist' author(s) of *Genesis* 2.4b–3. 24, called J, who was working with a different set of stories.

14] *Genesis* 1.14.

form the whole Christian church, militant here in earth), is not wholly determined by what they meant (or maybe meant) to their original authors. From the earliest days of the church the Hebrew Scriptures were mined for prophetic references to Christ: many of those references are, to our eyes, strained beyond belief, and even those that make some sense were, almost certainly, not *written* originally with that reference. The Hebrew Scriptures as they are read within the Jewish tradition often don't say the same thing as when they are read within the Christian, even though the mere *words* are identical. The story of Pierre Ménard, invented by Borges, has some relevance: Ménard wanted to write *Don Quixote,* and Borges imagines that he succeeded. 'Cervantes's text and Ménard's are verbally identical, but the second is almost infinitely richer',[15] since Ménard's must be read within a different time and culture. Even within Jewish tradition, the scriptures as they are read now, after many more centuries of Rabbinic exegesis, are enormously richer than they were at first. Indeed, since Rabbinic exegesis allows different words to be read from the merely consonantal text, different sentences from an unpunctuated sequence, and different, allegorical meanings from what may at first seem 'literal', there seems to be no necessary limit to the ways that scripture can be read.[16]

Should there be limits? Secular critics have sometimes (often) supposed that the only proper interpretation of the scriptures must be compatible with what *they* take to be the truth (namely, that there are no miracles, no accurate prophecies, no providence). Whatever *really* happened must have been only the sort of thing that they suppose now happens. They could never let themselves find out that something unusual, even something unique, actually did happen, since they have ruled this out already. They could not learn from any historical record that Jesus was and is the one Son of God, since they already 'know' that nobody is unique, and have altered the records to say so. They are, of course, at liberty to follow this prescription, though it is perhaps a little odd that they are willing to accept scriptural testimony about 'natural' things, while also supposing that scriptural testimony about the 'supernatural' is wholly false. It is

---

[15] J.L. Borges, 'Pierre Ménard, Author of the Quixote', *Labyrinths*, ed. Donald A. Yates & James E. Irby (Penguin: Harmondsworth, 1970), pp. 62–71

[16] See, for example, the witty exegesis of the early chapters of *Genesis* in Shira Halevi, *The Life Story of Adam and Havah: a new Targum of Genesis* 1.26–5.5 (Jason Aronson: Northvale, New Jersey, 1997). Traditionally, 'targum' blends translation with interpretation, without troubling to cite sources or defend that interpretation as the 'correct' one.

also odd that they should deny non-secular critics a similar liberty to interpret scripture in terms of what *they* take to be the truth (namely, that Christ is risen).[17] At the very least, the 'supernaturalist' interpretation is the more familiar and influential: that is what the scriptures meant to the community that uses them. Without that attributed meaning they would never have been gathered together at all.

> The Christian Bible is the Church's book. It was assembled by the Church under the twofold conviction, first, that these particular texts tell the Church's own story, the story of God's dealings with his people for the sake of bringing to completion his purposes for creation as a whole, and, second, that it is in reading these texts that we can expect to hear the voice of God. There is no other reason for the Bible to exist.[18]

So far this is, in effect, a merely sociological or literary observation, and applicable to many other texts, both sacred and profane. If we wish to read Homer's *Iliad,* it is pointless to deconstruct it first, replacing it with a newly invented story about the Mycenaean assault on a trading city by the Hellespont. Even if *The Book of Mormon* was written by Joseph Smith (and not by the prophet Mormon), its meaning *now* is what it means to Mormons. The Hebrew and Christian scriptures have at least this much 'external' validation, in comparison with *The Iliad* and *The Book of Mormon*, that there are *other* written histories, and archaeological finds, which partly confirm their stories.[19] But perhaps we can also accept that there might be another sort of validation. If the Bible is, in some sense, 'the Word of God', it has a different sort of author than the merely human. Neither the original authors, nor the community that has selected just these texts, is what is speaking to us.

---

[17] See Alvin Plantinga, 'Two (or More) Kinds of Scripture Scholarship', *Modern Theology* 14. 2, 1998, pp. 243–77; republished in Craig Bartholomew, C. Stephen Evans, Mary Healy, & Murray Rae (eds.), *Behind the Text: History and Biblical Interpretation,* (Paternoster Press: Carlisle, 2003), pp. 19–57; see also Alvin Plantinga, *Warranted Christian Belief* (Oxford University Press: New York, 2000), and Murray A. Rae, *History and Hermeneutics* (T. & T. Clark: Edinburgh, 2005).

[18] Rae, op. cit., p. 141.

[19] There is an odd tendency amongst modern critics to suppose that where those *other* sources describe things differently, the Scriptures must be wrong: even on secular terms, they are usually as likely to be right. See Iain W. Provan 'Knowing and Believing', in Bartholomew et al., op. cit., pp. 229–66: 'it is entirely unclear what are the truly defensible grounds for such an epistemological privileging of extrabiblical texts; for these texts certainly do *not* provide us with immediate access to "the way it was" — not even to "the way it was" for the peoples who produced them, much less for the Israelites' (*ibid.*, p. 255).

Must this be ridiculous? The Scriptures, as we know, are full of seeming contradictions, both historical and moral. If they are indeed an assembly of texts from different dates and authors, this is to be expected, just as there are multiple versions in Greek literature of the story of Orestes. Even if they are to be conceived as a whole *community*'s selection, it is not all that odd that the selection, made for many particular reasons, still preserves that multiplicity. But how can a single author or, especially, a single Author, so fail to offer a coherent narrative? One response is that indeed the Bible is coherent, as long as it is properly understood: where there are seeming contradictions, the passages must be read together and the underlying unity detected. Nothing can be inferred from any scriptural passage that is truly incompatible with the primary themes: specifically, the commandments to love God and our neighbour.[20] This rule may sometimes demand, as Augustine saw, that we read a passage 'allegorically', as meaning something else than, on the surface, it seems to say.

But there is another possible response.[21] Why is it that we expect an author to be 'consistent', or 'a book' to be 'coherent'? Whether a book is a description of what has happened or a prescription for what should, it may be as various and perplexing as the world itself. It is a merit, perhaps, in detective fiction or in crossword puzzles that there be no contradictions, but why should we expect the world itself, or our duties in it, to be so easily and coherently portrayed?

> Do I contradict myself?
> Very well then I contradict myself;
> (I am large, I contain multitudes.)[22]

'The World', as we experience it, is multiple: not only do different observers see things differently, the very same observer, in different moods or moments, may have no single vision. Something even odder may be true. The speculative physicists Stephen Hawking and Thomas Hertog have recently suggested that all possible histories

---

[20] *Matthew* 22.35–40, *Luke* 10.27–8; see also *Leviticus* 19.18. One of Richard Dawkins's errors is to suppose that only fellow Israelites were to benefit from this instruction. On the contrary: 'when an alien settles with you in your land, you shall not oppress him. He shall be treated as a native born among you, and you shall love him as a man like yourself, because you were aliens in Egypt' (*Leviticus* 19.33–4).

[21] See 'Deconstructing the Laws of Logic', *Philosophy*, 82 (2008), pp. 1–29

[22] Walt Whitman, 'Song of Myself'(1855) $51, *The Portable Walt Whitman*, ed. Mark van Doren (Viking Press: New York, 1945), p. 134.

have been traversed up to the present moment, and that, correspondingly, we are ourselves responsible for determining what 'really' happened.[23] Just as there are many possible futures stemming from this moment, there have, perhaps, been many possible pasts. It would seem to follow that the more *accurate* narrative is, exactly, the one with the most superficial contradictions![24] As a matter of faith we may suppose that the *real* world contains no contradictions, that it is exactly and unambiguously *what is*, and that there is—somewhere, somehow—a coherent account available that exactly maps that unity. But we don't have that account, either of 'matters of fact' or 'matters about our duties', and it is foolish always to dismiss one well-authenticated version merely because it clashes (as far as we can see) with some other well-authenticated version. Much of the time, we must persevere with both, not only because we have no idea which one will, in the end, after whatever development, prove 'true', but because, for all we know at present, they are *both* true—or as nearly true as anything we think could be. Maybe the message of the Bible is just this: that the world is multiple, and that the unity from which it stems is not for us to see.

> There were editors, even final editors, who could have ironed out all these contradictions but who chose, importantly, not to resolve them, and in the process they bequeathed a text that foregrounds the many ways 'a people' is constructed.[25]

Which *bit* of the Bible we should concentrate upon or allow to influence us here-now will depend on what 'here-now' is intended. Sometimes the apparent contradictions will indeed point beyond themselves to a discoverable resolution. Sometimes they won't, and we shall be bound, to our cost, by both.

> Those who heard asked, 'Then who can be saved?' He answered, 'What is impossible for men is possible for God'.[26]

We may believe that there is a way through contradiction, somehow to reconcile opposing demands or different stories, but we don't always know what it is. And if we don't, how shall we dismiss one half of the purported contradiction?

---

[23] Amanda Gefter, 'Mr Hawking's Universe', *New Scientist*, 22 April 2006, pp. 28–32

[24] See also J.L. Borges, 'The Garden of Forking Paths', *Labyrinths*, op. cit., pp. 44–54.

[25] Schwartz, op. cit., p. 10.

[26] *Luke* 18.26–7.

Explanations, Therapies and Demons

Casual as well as militant atheists will often say that 'religion' used to explain the world, but 'science' has done it better. It was natural enough, they say, to imagine that storms were caused by a weather-worker in the heavens, that living things—at least in the beginning—were moulded out of clay, that there was 'a god on every wind and a blessing on every blast'.[27] But now we have better explanations, in 'impersonal' terms, whose further implications can be tested. 'Religious' explanations are either arbitrary and untestable, or else (if they are given a little content) false.

There are so many problems with this easy declaration that it is hard to know where to start. What sort of thing is 'explanation'? What is an 'impersonal' explanation, and why must it be superior? What is 'science', and what sort of 'tests' are relevant to a 'religious' claim?

Why should we believe that 'religion' offered an 'explanation'? According to the stories recorded by Snorri Sturluson (1178–1241), the world began with the appearance of a giant cow, Audhumla, the nurse of the giant Ymir: she licked away at a salt-lick amid the ice until the figure of Buri, the ancestor of the Aesir, was revealed and woke.[28] Did Snorri suppose the stories he was relying on were ever meant to *explain* anything, or that Audhumla was ever worshipped? Both Babylonians and Norsemen described how the world, our world, was made from the decaying corpse of a primeval monster: Ymir or the dragon Tiamat.[29] Did they expect to find particular traces? When the ancient Egyptians described the sun's passage across the sky, are we to suppose that they seriously suggested that there was a very large and invisible dung-beetle trundling the sun across the heavens, every day, and that this was a sufficient and helpful 'explanation' of what would otherwise be *odd*? That they did not mean this as an 'explanation' might also be suggested by the fact

[27] Blake, *Vala* 2nd Night, line 410, op. cit., pp. 290–1

[28] Snorri Sturluson, *The Prose Edda*, trans. Jean I. Young (Bowes & Bowes: Cambridge, 1954), p. 34.

[29] Tiamat lurks in the background of the Hebrew Scriptures, as Rahab or the Dragon in the Deep, but has no personality or independent being there: see Hermann Gunkel, 'Influence of Babylonian Mythology upon the Creation Story' (1895) in Bernard W. Anderson (ed.), *Creation in the Old Testament* (SPCK: London, 1984), pp. 25–52. Gunkel is very sure that *Genesis* chapter I is 'a faded myth', a transformed and less poetic version of the Babylonian story. Alternatively, it is an attempt to rediscover the original truths behind the Babylonian imagery, or the memory of those truths. I acknowledge further that there *may* be some distorted metaphysical significance even in the widespread myth of a dead monster, some echo of the Lamb that was slain before the foundation of the worlds.

that they were also ready to describe the boat of the sun in which God travelled from east to west (and back again beneath the earth), or the arch of the heavens as a goddess poised forever on toes and fingertips. These aren't even *competing* explanations, but ideographic representations or romantic stories or even, possibly, jokes. They aren't explanations, since (obviously) they don't *explain*, nor competing explanations since the Egyptians showed no concern with the contradictions.[30] Of course, we too can live with contradictions: the idea that only stupid people can gaily contradict themselves is silly. Even those anthropologists who have suggested that savages (and ancient Egyptians) had a 'primitive mentality' indifferent to logic, were eager to concede that we do too! Even physicists are stuck with competing models which cannot, imaginatively, be reconciled.[31] Eliminating contradictions from science and from our ordinary lives is, at least, a long-term project. We know much better than the Egyptians what the sun is doing daily, but still talk about 'sunrise', 'noon' and 'sunset'. We know that there is no 'sky'. Even those philosophers who are most eager to abandon 'folk psychology' (with its talk of minds, intentions, feelings, and desires) have found no other language, no other mind-set, with which to expound and advocate their creed. The creed that 'truth is one, without a flaw'[32] is itself a *creed*, a doctrine followed in faith. But when we try to find 'an explanation' of some otherwise odd event (and it takes a while to wonder whether we should also bother to explain quite ordinary events) we are indeed attempting to *unify* our world, to eliminate, exactly, an oddity.

So the idea that the Egyptians were trying to *explain* the sun requires more defence than I have seen. That the sun passes across the heavens every day is the sort of *ordinary* event that only sophisticates will question, and they only by beginning to see that it is *odd*. Describing the sun's passage as a dung-beetle's rolling a ball of

[30] See John A. Wilson, 'Egypt' in H. & H.A. Frankfurt, John A. Wilson & Thorkild Jacobsen, *Beyond Philosophy* (Penguin: Harmondsworth, 1949), pp. 39–136: pp. 53ff.

[31] 'In this respect physicists are like ordinary people. If they can't resolve a contradiction, and the contradiction is not pressing, they just disregard it and give their attention to those aspects of the theory (or theories) that are pleasantly consistent': Shimon Malin, *Nature Loves to Hide* (Oxford University Press: New York, 2001), p. 90.

[32] As the Lady Philosophy said or suggested to Boethius, *The Consolation of Philosophy* (524 a. d.), trans. V.E. Watts (Penguin: Harmondsworth, 1969) Bk. 5, ch. 4: p. 154.

dung, and also as the sun-boat's sailing, is not an explanation, since—if anything—it makes the passage *odder*, and less a single story than it was. Nor are they explanations in the sense that modern scientists prefer: ones that suggest new ways of interfering with this or another process. Can the beetle be diverted? Can the sun-boat spring a leak? Will the goddess who is the sky get cramp or suddenly decide her exercise is over? What would it be like for the sky to go away?

Such tales aren't invented to explain, but rather to incorporate what happens in an enjoyable story.[33] Maybe the Egyptians found it funny to glance up at the sun's disc and think of it as a dung-ball. Or maybe they found it inspiring to glance down at the indefatigable dung-beetle and be reminded of the sun's reliable passage. When Pharaoh went sailing they saw the sun in him, and the sun was daily present to them as a celestial sign of Pharaoh's rule. There is a certain resemblance here to 'science', as scientific theories are presented to the public. Most of us believe in dinosaurs, and even nowadays begin to believe that birds are their descendants. The story does have some explanatory content, but its chief purpose and effect is to enliven hearts. Thinking of chickens as miniature tyrannosaurs appeals to the child in all of us! Most of us are willing to believe that the cosmos began from an explosive singularity, that the echo of that event is all around us, that the heavier elements from which we're made were forged in the depths of stars and scattered through space by supernovas. We are, literally and emphatically, star-dust. All these theories may have explanatory content, but they are believed 'romantically', in much the same spirit as we dream of Middle Earth, or Star Trek.

Two questions, at least, must follow. First, were any of the Egyptians (and any other 'religionists'), after all, doing something more like 'trying to explain'? Second, is there any advantage in moulding our romantic stories to the results of 'explanation'? Both questions need to be spelt out more clearly. In both cases, what is it 'to explain'?

I have already suggested that the effect, at least, of 'explanation' is to make something less 'surprising', 'odd' or 'arbitrary'. We ask 'why', when something has happened that we don't recognize as

---

[33] For further discussion of the difference between 'explanation' (*Erklären*) and 'understanding' (*Verstehen*) see G.H. von Wright, *Explanation and Understanding* (Cornell University Press: Ithaca, 1971); Paul Ricoeur *Memory, History, Forgetting*, trans. Kathleen Blamey and David Pellauer (University of Chicago Press: Chicago, 2004).

usual. Asking the question about very *usual* things requires us to show why the usual things should really not be true. 'Why is the sky dark at night?' Ordinarily, this may elicit only a baffled reply that night-time just is when the sky is dark, or—a little more usefully—that's when the sun is down, or else when our side of the earth is turned away from the sun. The question gains strength and difficulty if we entertain the idea that the cosmos is infinite and homogenous: if that were true then every point in the sky should be occupied by a star (however unimaginably far away it is). And in that case, the whole sky should be as bright as day, as bright—indeed—as the surface of a star. It follows that the cosmos isn't infinite and homogenous,[34] and that's why the sky is dark at night. Explanation, especially of the obvious, moves from acceptance through puzzlement to eventual re-acceptance.

Whenever it is suggested that our first human ancestors were *puzzled* by the world in which they found themselves, and sought out curious 'explanations' of an animistic sort ('thunder must be like Great Uncle's temper tantrums, so there is an even greater Uncle in the sky'), we are being asked to conceive that these first people opened their eyes on a world no-one had seen before. But, as should be obvious especially to evolutionists, there were no such 'first people': the world they lived in was the usual and expected world, and 'explanations' of such ordinary things come very late in history. The 'explanations' they are supposed to have invented have actually been invented, as explanations of 'religion', only by their successors. *Real* religion, even 'primitive' religion, is a different matter entirely. Snorri and the Egyptians weren't explaining things, but playing with them.

'Why is this night different from all other nights?' That question is asked, by custom, at the Passover meal, and evokes a story about having been slaves in Egypt, and escaping.[35] Is that story voiced as an *explanation*? The Passover story could indeed be called 'an aetiological myth', and does 'explain' the various oddities of the Passover meal, but not in the same way as Olbers' Paradox is

---

34] This is a brief account of Olbers' Paradox, first noticed by Kepler. There are a few other twists to the argument, of no present importance.

35] The differences are enumerated, by the youngest child present at the *Seder*, as follows: 'On all other nights, we may eat either chometz or matzoh; on this night, only matzoh [unleavened bread]. On all other nights, we eat all kinds of vegetables; on this night, we must eat maror [bitter herbs]. On all other nights, we do not dip even once; on this night we dip twice. On all other nights, we may eat either sitting or reclining; on this night, we all recline.'

explained. The ritual is explained by being interpreted: the point is not—or at any rate not only, and not chiefly—to say what had to have been true in the past for this event to be as it is. The point is to say what it is that is being remembered and invoked. The same is true, perhaps even more strongly, in the case of other rituals. It is not really as if ingenious theorists were asked to explain some strange piece of behaviour (strange in whatever context) and devised some more or less imaginable story to say how it came about. 'Aetiological myths' aren't 'scientific' or even 'historical' hypotheses, but narrative interpretations of a ritual, or a familiar fact, often with a view to making it unfamiliar. Why do we die? Why does childbirth hurt? Why don't we all speak one language? Telling a story about how things might be different, and maybe were, is a way of attending to the everyday. The story interprets the event, and does not (in the modern sense) 'explain' a thing. Sometimes the aim is to make it marvellous. Sometimes it is only to remind us that things don't have to be like this.

Or is there something else still to be said? The Christian Gospels tell us that Jesus expelled demons, and so changed people's lives, This is not to say that the Gospel-writers were seeking to establish an hypothesis, that the conditions we may label 'mental disorders' can be cured by an authoritative command to go away, and must therefore be caused by entities which can understand and be compelled to obey plain Aramaic. Plotinus mocked those who said so:

> When they say they free themselves from diseases, if they meant they did so by temperance and orderly living, they would speak well; but in fact they assume that the diseases are evil spirits, and claim to be able to drive them out by their word; by this claim they might make themselves more impressive in the eyes of the masses, who wonder at the power of magicians, but would not persuade sensible people that diseases do not have their origin in strain or excess or deficiency or decay, and in general in changes which have their origin outside or inside. The cures of diseases make this clear too. With a vigorous motion of the bowels or the giving of a drug the illness goes through the downward passage and out, and it goes out too with bloodletting; and fasting also heals. Does the evil spirit starve, and does the drug make it waste away? ... If it came into the man without any cause of disease, why is he not always ill? But if there was a cause, what need is

> there of the spirit to produce the illness? For the cause is sufficient by itself to produce the fever.[36]

I mention Plotinus's argument chiefly to make it clear that it is simply not true that 'everyone', back then, believed in the power of exorcists and magicians. But it is not, perhaps, quite so absurd to believe in demons: militant atheists, after all, believe that 'believers' are infected by mental microbes, and apparently suppose that these can be dispelled by sermons! St. Paul did not entirely disagree.

> The Powers from which Paul would protect his Colossian correspondents are not evil spirits in the sky, but philosophy, tradition, rules and rituals, food laws and ascetic practices, the basic elements of religion, and even the good angels.[37]

Philosophy and psychotherapy alike may offer 'talking cures' almost as efficacious as surgery or drugs. Maybe the Gospel writers really did believe, maybe the Lord believed, and most probably the victims themselves believed, that there were demonic beings who could interfere with us, and be ordered away (but might sneak back again). The writers didn't intend to *prove* the story true by describing how a Jewish Hasid cured madmen. Rather they—perhaps—believed the story true already, and were ready to read the events accordingly. We, of course, know better.

But suppose for a moment at least that the story really was, and still is, true. Nowadays demons or devils are imagined simply as evil beings: the 'possessed', it is thought, are wicked beyond the norm, 'inhumanly'. There are people who are either missing something vital, who have lost 'their souls' or never had 'a soul', or else are infested by a malevolent intelligence that wholly suppresses ordinary human feeling or subtly exaggerates some one impulse into monstrous form. A belief in 'devils' may have a more humane effect than believing that there are those who have no 'soul': devils can be driven out, but who can create new souls? The fantasies have a point even if they are not explanations, and even if there are other ways to change. But it is worth recalling that the Gospel writers were not blaming *evil* on the demons, but sickness, including *mental* sickness, of a kind that divided the victims from the congregation. The point

---

36] *Enneads*, II.9 [33].14: Armstrong, op. cit., vol. 2, pp. 277–81. I have discussed the Plotinian position, and other attitudes to 'spiritual healing' in 'Discerning the Spirits: Healing and the Moral Problems of Efficacy', in *Spiritual Healing: Science, Meaning, and Discernment*, ed. Sarah Coakley (Eerdmans, forthcoming).

37] Wink, *Naming the Powers*, op. cit., p. 82.

of the healing miracles was to make the victims 'clean': that is, to bring them back from solitude, to restore them.

'Mental disorders', as they affect both victims and their carers, do seem like demons. The phenomenology of such sickness, overwhelmingly, is of an alien and contemptuous presence, denying the victim any sense that she has ever done right, or ever could. Even experienced and firmly secular therapists will identify some things that the victim does or says as the words and actions of '*the disease*', the alien thing. That thing is often very clever, and makes use even of the victim's virtues, her wish to take care of others, her eagerness to take on other burdens, her all too accurate sense that she is herself a burden. We may rely on medication to dispel some of the clouds, but this is rarely, if ever, quite enough. We may offer 'talking cures', and try to identify and rebut the core assumptions that the disease imposes. If only, we may sometimes hope, the victim could *believe,* even for a moment, that the disease could be ordered off, that someone with authority could command the devils away and the victim back to life. We act out the story, and call on any helper that we can. Consider the Navaho Blessing Way, from which this chant or prayer is taken:

In beauty may I walk.
All day long may I walk.
Through the returning seasons may I walk.
On the trail marked with pollen may I walk.
With grasshoppers about my feet may I walk.
With dew about my feet may I walk.
With beauty may I walk.
With beauty before me, may I walk.
With beauty behind me, may I walk.
With beauty above me, may I walk.
With beauty below me, may I walk.
With beauty all around me, may I walk.
In old age wandering on a trail of beauty, lively, may I walk.
In old age wandering on a trail of beauty, living again, may I walk.
It is finished in beauty.
It is finished in beauty.[38]

This is the root idea of exorcism, after all, and not so different, in its essence, from the techniques with which a loving parent may dis-

[38] I have taken this particular version from http://my.opera. com/Nyingje/blog/show.dml/192715; see Charlotte J. Frisbie & David P. McAllester (eds.), *Navajo Blessingway Singer: The Autobiography of Frank Mitchell, 1881–1967* (University of New Mexico Press, 2003) for an account of what it is like to be a singer.

tract or comfort or encourage a weeping child. Sometimes, somehow, the effort works: the accusing presence is silenced, and the victim is reminded that she is, after all, alive, and that her sins are forgiven. But it is what happens afterwards that matters more: maybe the demon is silenced, even driven away, but it will return unless some constant watch is kept.[39]

Phenomenologically, some disorders feel like possessions. Phenomenologically, they may sometimes be dispelled. Little more than this is needed to make sense of the Gospel stories. But given that this *is* how it feels, to victims, carers and professionals, perhaps we can also ask if this is how it is? Perhaps, after all, there are demons which are something more than common delusions, something more than common fears that have no being outside the human mind. In saying there aren't, after all, we moderns aren't simply disputing a few first-century writers, but the common sense of all humanity across the world.

> The refusal of modern 'enlightenment' to treat 'possession' as an hypothesis to be spoken of as even possible, in spite of the massive human tradition based on concrete experience in its favor, has always seemed to me a curious example of the power of fashion in things scientific. That the demon-theory will again have its innings is to my mind absolutely certain. One has to be 'scientific' indeed, to be blind and ignorant enough to suspect no such possibility.[40]

Uncovering Evil

Amongst the many signs that militant atheists are really devotees of a particular 'religion' is their eye for evil, their refusal to countenance wrong-doing merely on the ground that it is 'traditional', or that it embodies an inspiring story. Richard Dawkins' response, following Nicholas Humphrey's, to a television documentary in which Inca sacrifice of children was given sympathetic treatment by an overtly nationalist presenter is a good example. This, he says, is outrageous: 'How dare they invite us... to feel uplifted by contemplating an act

---

39] *Matthew* 12.43–45; see Dossey, *Be Careful what you pray for,* op. cit, p. 205.

40] William James, *William James on Psychical Research,* ed. Gardner Murphy & Robert O. Ballou (Chatto & Windus: London, 1962, p. 207: cited by Dossey, op. cit., pp. 203–4.

of ritual murder: the murder of an ignorant child by a bunch of stupid, puffed up, superstitious, ignorant old men?'[41]

Dawkins' expressed belief that it wouldn't have happened if the child, and those ignorant old men, had only realized that the sun (in whose name, perhaps, the sacrifice occurred) is 'really a ball of hydrogen' is, of course, staggeringly naïve. By all the available standards of their day those stupid old men were experts.[42] And why should being 'a ball of hydrogen' be incompatible with being—or more probably, standing for—a god (or devil)? Is it only 'religious believers' who indoctrinate and kill their children? Is there nothing dangerous, for example, in the conviction that our children are merely bearers of 'our' genes, experiments in living, having no 'rights' beyond the ones accorded them by convention? There are, unfortunately, 'secular' philosophers who see little wrong in infanticide, and thoroughly 'secular' regimes that leave orphan children to rot. It is also at least a little difficult not to wonder whether abortion differs all that much from infanticide. But let us agree that Dawkins (and Humphreys) were right to be enraged. That is, there really is something wrong. But are they *entitled* to be enraged? They may be right in what they believe, but themselves lack any real reason to believe it.

> If it be true (as it certainly is) that a man can feel exquisite happiness in skinning a cat, then the religious philosopher can only draw one of two deductions. He must either deny the existence of God, as all atheists do; or he must deny the present union between God and man, as all Christians do.[43]

'God's not existing', in this context, means that there is no transcendent Right, and that is therefore nothing 'wrong' in taking such delight in skinning cats, or sacrificing children—except that *some* of us don't like to do it, nor like its being done. We may, of course, be moved to obliterate the civilization that approves such things (as invading Europeans, and invading Israelites before them, have been

---

[41] Richard Dawkins, *The God Delusion* (Bantam: London, 2006), cited by Cornwell, op. cit., pp. 105f. I recall the programme myself, and had a similar reaction.

[42] See Edwin Black, *War against the Weak: Eugenics and America's Campaign to Create a Master Race* (Four Walls Eight Windows: New York, 2003) for a detailed account of other 'experts', who imprisoned, sterilized and castrated people they deemed 'unfit', in defiance of law, the American Constitution and ordinary decency. No doubt they were fools, but they were neither ignorant nor stupid by the standards of their time.

[43] Chesterton, *Orthodoxy*, op. cit., p. 6.

moved to forbid child sacrifice, cut down sacred trees or deface statues). Conversely, our growing distaste for such invasions—and their tendency to end up killing children—may give us cause to be more tolerant: 'live and let live' is at least a more peaceful solution than cultural (and often literal) genocide. If there is no Real Right, no eternal righteousness, but only 'our' various attempts to 'get along', then moral rage of the kind that Dawkins actually favours seems obtuse. Is he *enraged* by ichneumon wasps, or cannibalistic chimpanzees? Is it really impossible to understand, and so to accept, even such social orders as he would not like himself (being himself the product of a different order, owing its moral sense to a particular history and civilization)? Perhaps it should be.

When did 'we' start to reject child sacrifice? As far as European history goes the answer is twofold. In the first place, Israel rejected it, and also the gods (or devils) who demanded it. The principal moral of the story of Abraham and Isaac[44] is that Abraham's people were forbidden to kill children not because they impiously denied the gods their due, but because any God worth worshipping forbids such murders. Abraham, in the story, was being tested—but so was God. There was a conflict, obviously, in Abraham, between his natural parental love, his hopes for the future, and his obedience to the voice which had pulled him away from the land and religion of his fathers (and incidentally promised him a son). It was *not* a conflict between the voice and the established ethics of his day, and neither would his immediate neighbours have thought him either insane or wicked—any more than the Incas thought child-sacrifice obscene. Abraham, *pace* Kierkegaard's analysis, was not 'transcending morality', but establishing its limits, discovering the nature of the God he served. In the second place, it was Rome which opposed Carthage—not just as a trading rival, but as the locus of the Phoenician cult of Molech, who required that living children be thrown into his fire.[45]

44] *Genesis* 22.1–19; see also *Leviticus* 18. 2: 'you shall not surrender any of your children to Molech and thus profane the name of your God'.

45] See J.B. Rives, *Religion and authority in Roman Carthage from Augustus to Constantine* (Clarendon Press: Oxford, 1995) for an up-to-date account of Carthaginian religion, which did indeed involve child sacrifice. Whether 'Molech' is the name of a distinct imagined deity (as is most likely: see John Day, *Molech: A God of Human Sacrifice in the Old Testament* (Cambridge University Press: Cambridge, 1990)), a title (meaning 'King') of Baal Ammon, or a misinterpretation of '*lmlk*', meaning 'as a sacrifice', makes no difference to the reality of small, burned bodies.

It is important, of course, to understand these rituals and the societies that relied on them. People don't do such things for no reason, and the reasons they have reveal a lot about their cultural and economic needs. They may even be displaying *virtue* of a sort. In judging the sins of our ancestors, the things they did which we now think deplorable, it is also as well to remember that our descendants may think the same of us. How many children, after all, do *we* sacrifice each year, predictable victims of our worship of convenience and speed?[46] But by the same token it is well to remember that all those judgements may be right, and that our reforming ancestors may have had good reason for their rage.

> The consuls of Rome and the prophets of Israel ... were at one in what they hated. It is very easy in both cases to represent that hatred as something merely hateful. It is easy enough to make a merely harsh and inhuman figure either of Elijah raving above the slaughter of Carmel or Cato thundering against the amnesty of Africa. These men had their limitations and their local passions; but this criticism of them is unimaginative and therefore unreal. It leaves out something, something immense and intermediate, facing east and west and calling up this passion in its eastern and western enemies.[47]

Canaanites and Carthaginians—along with many other tribes across the world—imagined that there was Someone who wanted children dead. The Hebrew Scriptures (and the Roman Laws) denied that God or the gods desired it—but maybe there was indeed *something* that did.

> It was Moloch [sic] upon the mountain of the Latins, looking with his appalling face across the plain; it was Baal who trampled the vineyards with his feet of stone; it was the voice of Tanit the invis-

[46] According to the UK Department for Transport's figures (http://www.dft.gov.uk/pgr/statistics/datatablespublications/accidents/casualtiesgbar/roadcasualtiesgreatbritain2005) '141 children were killed on the roads in 2005, 25 less than in 2004, a fall of 15 per cent. The total number of children killed or seriously injured fell by 11 per cent to 3,472'. By 2006, the number killed or seriously injured (3,294) was less than half the average for the years 1994–8 (6,860) (statistics taken from http://www.dft.gov.uk/ 162259/162469/ 221412/221549/227755/rcgb 2006v1.pdf). This is still many more than the Incas (probably) killed. Of course, they knew which ones they had it in mind to kill: does this make us better?

[47] G.K. Chesterton, *The Everlasting Man* (Hodder & Stoughton: London, 1925), p. 142.

> ible, behind her trailing veils, whispering of the love that is more horrible than hate.[48]

In other words, the codes which required such sacrifice are not to be considered simply another primate possibility, one that 'we' would rather not indulge but must allow, but as something radically wrong, something to be rejected root and branch, with just as much vehemence as our ancestors rejected other demons (but perhaps with more humility). For it is just such righteous rage that may also lead to murder, and the Inquisition. The rumour of child murder was made an excuse, not all that long ago, for murdering Jews. The Inquisition was established to root out views that were seen as dangerous (and the Spanish Inquisition, in particular, was active in a newly liberated nation). As Chesterton said, 'to understand the Spanish Inquisition it would be necessary to discover two things that we have never dreamed of bothering about; what Spain was and what an Inquisition was.'[49] Our ancestors had reasons—and so do contemporary would-be Inquisitors. Those who now suggest that torture should be used in 'the war against terror' would do well to remember that Innocent IV (1243–54) licensed torture in 1252 for what seemed to him good reasons—and thereby gave the opponents of his church a reason to hate it that has still not entirely run its course.

Is this relevant to Dawkins' rage? For at least two reasons, yes. In the first place, it is just this righteous rage which is, paradoxically, almost our best evidence for Righteousness. It is easy enough to play with sceptical ideas, but the pain of a stubbed toe will usually convince us (I do not say correctly) that there *is* a material world. It is easy enough to preach that there is no such thing as Righteousness (on which, more below), but the sight of a small, burnt body must persuade us that there is a *moral* world. 'There are certain deeds that cry out to heaven. ... The imperative to save a child from murder, even at the cost of killing the putative murderer, appears to be curiously immune to relativizing analysis'.[50]

And in the second place, it is just this righteous rage that is itself an easy tool for demons. The more that militant atheists react against

---

[48] *Ibid.*, p. 171. It is likely that Chesterton drew his picture of Carthage largely from Gustave Flaubert's *Salammbo* (1862), and Flaubert (1821–80), in turn, from Roman and Rabbinic sources. But the picture was not wholly false.

[49] G.K. Chesterton, *St Francis of Assisi* (Hodder & Stoughton: London, 1923), p. 13.

[50] Peter Berger, *A Rumour of Angels: Modern Society and the Rediscovery of the Supernatural* (Penguin: Harmondsworth, 1970), pp. 85–6.

the evils of religion, the more they seem to display just such a religious fury. It is a matter of record that the great atheistical empires of the twentieth century, like earlier empires, humiliated, persecuted and killed 'religious' people. Their motives for doing so, no doubt, were mixed, but may well have included just such righteous *and religious* rage against 'the unbeliever'—those who did not believe, that is, in the imperial creed. Religion is indeed very dangerous—because it is often a vehicle for demons or—equivalently—an excuse for murderous contempt and rage, all the more murderous for being self-righteous. Militant atheism, in important respects, amounts to a religion—despite the astonishingly ignorant response made by many such atheists that 'religion' is essentially a belief in supernatural entities, and 'atheism' the simple rejection of that belief.[51]

The sacred scriptures of all the great religions may be used for evil, especially by those who have forgotten what they're for. Understandably, it is chiefly the Jewish and Christian scriptures that most modern militant atheists address: understandably, since militant atheism is itself a sort of Christian heresy. The Christian Churches have themselves sometimes caricatured the Hebrew Scriptures, seizing on the revisionist remarks of Jesus Christ and his apostles to suggest that pre-Christian Israel was dominated by a legalistic and small-minded spirit. The Sabbath was made for Man, and not Man for the Sabbath.[52] Human needs take precedence over ritual demands.[53] An executed felon, condemned by popular vote and ecclesiastical and imperial authority, strips those powers bare and leads them 'captives in his triumphal procession'.[54] 'We', his followers, will judge angels.[55] In the coming world there will be no temple,[56] for all that is most worshipful will be found in the body of Christ, his people. Orthodox Christians, of course, don't endorse the Marcionite heresy, that 'the God of the Old Testament' is no more

[51] The claim is ignorant in imagining an essentialist account of 'religion', in speaking of 'the supernatural' without any attempt to analyze what is meant, and especially in simply ignoring the point that is being made by mentioning those features of militant atheism that most resemble the worst aspects of theistical religions.

[52] *Mark* 2.27.

[53] *Matthew* 5.23–4; 23.23.

[54] *Colossians* 2. 15: see Wink *Naming the Powers*, op. cit. pp. 55–60.

[55] *1 Corinthians* 6.3.

[56] *Revelation* 21.22.

than Nobodaddy,[57] but 'Christian Humanism', so to call it, at least prefers the divinized Christ, the form of humanity taken up into the Godhead (rather as Socrates has been embedded in Philosophy). And where is that Christ except in his faltering, sinful, ever-hopeful Church? 'God' is not in the heavens, and 'only Acts & Is, in existing beings or Men'.[58]

> Only when a person sees humanity as a living community of individuals, cultivates humanity as a community, bears its spirit and consciousness in his life, and within that community both loses his isolated existence and finds it again in a new way—only then does that person have the higher life and peace of God within himself. ... Everyone in whom this genuine self-consciousness of humanity arises enters within the bounds of the church.[59]

This is also the hopeful vision of much modern science fiction, imagining terrestrial humanity's advance into the skies, where cruel and stodgy empires fall—in imagination—before the courage and kindliness of ordinary people. 'God', as the term very often is understood, can only stand for inhuman laws and senile civilizations: MegaBig Incorporated, Galactic Engineers. The truly worshipful God is With Us.

Militant atheism is a very natural outgrowth of this strand, which is plainly not the whole of Christendom. In its nature it is alarmingly open to infection by another mental microbe, one that has sometimes seemed endemic in the Christian Churches: namely, anti-Semitism. As Cornwell has pointed out, it is worrying that Dawkins cites an anti-Semitic diatribe in his case against the humane effects of the Christian gospel, apparently without realizing the source, or troubling to check the theory.[60] Worrying, but not entirely surprising.

---

[57] See William Blake, 'Poems from the Notebook 1793' (op. cit., p. 185): 'Old Nobodaddy aloft farted & belch'd & cough'd , /And said, "I love hanging & drawing & quartering /Every bit as well as war & slaughtering"'.

[58] Blake, *The Marriage of Heaven and Hell* (1790–3) Plate 16: op. cit., p. 155

[59] Schleiermacher, *Christmas Eve*, op. cit., p. 83.

[60] Cornwell, op. cit., pp. 77–84, commenting on Dawkins' uncritical use of the work of John Hartung ('Love Thy Neighbor: The Evolution of In-Group Morality': *Skeptic*, 3 (1995), accessible http://www. lrainc. com/swtaboo/taboos/ltn01. html) in his argument that both Israel and Jesus intended to require only a love of *Jews*. There is doubtless *some* truth in Hartung's argument (and Kevin McDonald's: see especially *The Culture of Critique: An Evolutionary Analysis of Jewish Involvement in Twentieth-Century Intellectual and Political Movements* (Praeger: Westport, CT, 1998)) that the Jewish nation has, in effect, been breeding itself for high intelligence, and that other nations and lineages have

The Christian Churches have themselves often fallen for this folly, but we should perhaps have learnt a little better. The Hebrew Scriptures, we are probably now readier to realize than in some ages past, are themselves 'humane', and God as He appears in them is very far from the over-powerful and greedy infant that Marcion and Dawkins have imagined. Correspondingly, 'the New Testament' does not reject the Old, not even when Paul deconstructs the demands of the ritual law. In neither Old nor New Testament is everything exactly as it should be: how could it be, when 'all human life is there'?[61] And so is the God who is understood as the great liberator, who brought Israel out of the land of Egypt, and Jesus Christ from the dead. Nobodaddy is nowhere.

'I will even own', says Crito in Berkeley's *Alciphron*, 'that the Gospel and the Christian religion have often been the pretexts for [feuds, factions, massacres and wars]; but it will not thence follow they were the cause. On the contrary, it is plain they could not be the real proper cause of these evils; because a rebellious, proud, revengeful, quarrelsome spirit is directly opposite to the whole tenor and most express precepts of Christianity. ... And secondly, because all those evils... were as frequent, nay, much more frequent, before the Christian religion was known in the world'.[62]

---

sometimes felt threatened by Jewish success in this. This is no excuse for misrepresenting what Jews, including Jesus, have actually taught and practised, nor for claiming (as both Hartung and McDonald do) that David Irving is a serious historian.

[61] 'The power of the Bible is largely that it gives an unvarnished picture of human nature and of the dynamics of history, and also of religion and the things that people do in its name': John D. Collins, 'The Zeal of Phinehas: the Bible and the Legitimation of Violence', in *Journal of Biblical Literature* 122 (2003), pp. 3–21: p. 20.

[62] Berkeley, *Alciphron*, op. cit., p. 190. Consider for example the unspeakable cruelties of which the Assyrian king Ashurnasirpal II (883–59 BC) boasted in the inscriptions at Nimrud: he had 'rebels' flayed, impaled, maimed and burnt alive, not in honour of any god at all except his own conceit.

4

The Abolition of Man

The Paradox of Objective Value

It is fashionable to suppose that evaluative judgements cannot be ordinarily, 'factually', true, even if they are ones that any sensible or decent judge would make. 'Facts', it is supposed, are one thing, and 'values' quite another. It follows that there can be no 'objective values': to be valuable is only to be valued by sensible or half-way decent people (that is, by people much like us). Some philosophers conclude that 'moralizing' judgements rest upon an error, consequent on the mistaken belief that there are indeed such values; others that 'moralizing' never amounted to anything more than sensible evaluation, that no-one ever really intended to suggest that there were 'objective values'.[2] These fashionable opinions can be made to seem banal. If 'facts' are only those truths that would or could be admitted by anyone, whatever her moral character or purposes, then they obviously carry no evaluative implications. A fact that no-one could acknowledge without admitting, logically, that there was something they should do, or that they were themselves in need of moral reformation, would not be counted as a fact. Facts, so defined, imply no Values (if A is compatible with both B and not-B, A does not imply B). Again: 'objectivity' is merely being ready to put aside all evaluative attitudes, and 'objective values' are therefore self-contradiction, the kind of values that can be recognized as such without

[1] An earlier version of this chapter appeared as 'Objective Values, Final Causes': *Electronic Journal of Analytical Philosophy*, 3 (1995), pp. 65–78 (http://ejap.louisiana. edu/EJAP/1995. spring/clark.abss.html: accessed 3 January 2008). See also 'Orwell and the Anti-Realists': *Philosophy*, 67 (1992), pp. 141–54, and 'Objectivism and the Alternatives' in E. Morscher, O. Neumaier, P. Simons (eds.), *Applied Ethics in a Troubled World* (Kluwer: Dordrecht-Boston-London, 1998), pp. 285–94.

[2] See 'Mackie and the Moral Order', *Philosophical Quarterly*, 39 (1989), pp. 98–144, a review of Ted Honderich ed., *Morality and Objectivity: Essays in Memory of John Mackie* (Blackwell: Oxford, 1987).

supposing they are valuable at all. Again: values, if they existed, would be utterly unlike whatever existent things weren't values (they would, in John Mackie's phrase, be queer[3]): they could not be absorbed into a larger mathematical synthesis, as other properties and things can be. What could it even mean to suggest that there could be natural laws connecting 'being morally wrong' with 'being more alkaline than acid' or 'being heavier than lead'? Could 'moral rightness' be a natural force alongside gravity and electro-magnetism? And even if such surds existed after all, how could they affect us? We'd believe and feel exactly the same things even if there were no 'objective values'. So our believing or feeling that there are can never be accounted knowledge: we only really *know* that p if the fact that p plays a serious part in making us believe in it.

All this is fallacy. The thesis that there are no real objective values, which I addressed in part in an earlier chapter, is both more substantial and less certain. The reason that so many moderns think it trivially true is that they have forgotten what objective values are, and why they have been forgotten. They have also ignored the real implications of their supposed non-existence. The truth is that, if there were no values, there would be no facts, nothing that all reasonable people *should* believe. If values don't exist, then nothing does, and no-one. Such nihilism has at least two forms: the radical, and the conventional. To reject them both is to adopt an older realism (once called Platonism). Of course there are truths that specify what we should do. Of course there are real standards to which things should aspire. Of course some things at least exist because they should. Of course we *should* seek to see them 'without prejudice'. And not everything that exists can be absorbed into a single mathematical system (our own subjectivity, for example, cannot be).

To understand why we have forgotten all this, we need to see why, for a while, we needed to forget, and so to understand what is good about 'objectivity'.

The Anthropocentric Synthesis

According to the Stoics the world (or everything that is the case) is a *cosmos* (that is, an ordered whole). Nothing exists or happens without a reason, and that reason is the maintenance of rational order, as it can be known by members of the rational community of gods and humans. To understand the shape and behaviour of things-in-the-world we need to see what good they do. On the one

[3] J.L. Mackie, *Ethics: Inventing Right and Wrong* (Penguin: Harmondsworth, 1977).

hand, every single thing exists as an example of its type, and its deficiencies or disabilities or disastrous accidents are mapped against its 'nature'. To find out what you should do you must first identify the various things you are (human, citizen of the world, child, parent, town councillor): 'each of these titles, rationally considered, always suggests the actions appropriate to it',[4] and those inappropriate. On the other hand, even apparent errors are just as much a part of 'nature overall'. Worm-eaten acorns are in one way damaged. In another they are just what the cosmos needs. Deranged or greedy people are in one way 'against nature' (namely, human nature). In another they too must serve a larger purpose (like boils, scabs and fevers).

The cosmos, the Stoics said, exists to reveal the ordered system flowing from the Divine Mind, and to sustain that ordered system in the Human Mind. It follows—they imagined—that everything is ours, and non-rational beings achieve their goal in serving us. Pigs are no more than locomotive meals, with souls instead of salt to keep them fresh. Wetlands exist to be drained, and forests to be cut down. Were it not that exercise is good for us, the cosmos would have provided drainage ditches and cut planks to order. Not using the material for worthy ends is simply laziness, and what one tribe of people lazily ignore (or employ in some different fashion) another may virtuously seize. 'Land in Asia, Africa and the Americas was there for European exploitation, because Europe understood the value of land in a way impossible for the natives'.[5]

---

[4] Epictetus, *Discourses*, 2.10: A.A. Long and D. Sedley, *The Hellenistic Philosophers* (Cambridge University Press: Cambridge, 1987), vol. 1, p. 364.

[5] Edward W. Said, 'Zionism from the Standpoint of Its Victims' in *Social Text*, 1 (1979), pp. 7–58: p. 27. Cf. Friedrich Engels, *Neue Rheinische Zeitung*, 15th February 1849: 'Will Bakunin accuse the Americans of a "war of conquest", which, although it deals with a severe blow to his theory based on "justice and humanity", was nevertheless waged wholly and solely in the interest of civilization? Or is it perhaps unfortunate that splendid California has been taken away from the lazy Mexicans, who could not do anything with it? That the energetic Yankees by rapid exploitation of the California gold mines will increase the means of circulation, in a few years will concentrate a dense population and extensive trade at the most suitable places on the coast of the Pacific Ocean, create large cities, open up communications by steamship, construct a railway from New York to San Francisco, for the first time really open the Pacific Ocean to civilization, and for the third time in history give the world trade a new direction? The "independence" of a few Spanish Californians and Texans may suffer because of it, in some places "justice" and other moral principles may be violated; but what does that matter to such facts of world-historic significance?' Yes, it matters.

Stoic moralists, of course, would not have thought that people should cut down forests, torment pigs or pollute the streams to satisfy a cruel or luxurious taste. Those tastes would be 'unnatural', and those who indulged them would be unvirtuous, foolish, mad: no true companions for the gods. Really, only the wise owned everything—and their wisdom, paradoxically, would be shown in regretting and condemning nothing, not even the apparently 'unnatural', which is really just as much a part of divine order as the apparently virtuous. But the main message of Stoic moralism is still that every mortal thing exists to make people possible, and people exist to serve the whole by knowing it. Nothing we can positively do in the world can make that world a better place, but it is, perhaps, completed by our knowledge of it. People (or wise people) are the world become self-conscious.

It should be clear how slippery these arguments can be. By some Stoic or Stoicising accounts a wilderness is nothing valuable. Only when it has been drained, farmed, built upon will it be worth preserving. Other (perhaps more realistic) accounts suggest that wilderness may be a necessary side-effect of processes that are themselves essential for the rational good. Others again may wonder if such wilderness may be 'redeemed' simply in being known as part of the one cosmos. But that last story may begin to tip the balance away from strictly anthropocentric theories. If the wilderness is redeemed by being known it can only be because it is worth knowing (and would be worth existing even if we didn't know it). More often it is assumed that nothing that is non-rational can rightly be valued 'as an end'. Everything but rational community itself is valuable only as a means, and the reason such things exist is because the cosmos is in love with us.

The Stoic cosmos is an ordered whole. In that it is like many an archaic cosmos, as it also is in its hierarchical implications. Everything should keep its place. In one way, everything is equal, equally required by the one order that defines the only (and therefore the best possible) world. In another there are natural rulers, natural subjects, natural predators and natural prey. The notion of 'the food chain' as it is understood in popular fiction identifies the topmost predator with the most noble: consider that reactionary fiction, Disney's *Lion King*. Order, fertility and peace can only be restored when the rightful predator is acknowledged lord. True wilderness emerges when 'the balance' is disrupted, when 'natural law' is ignored, when the noblest predator eats too low down the chain, when outsiders take up residence. The idea that 'Nature always knows best' (and may even allow a brief disastrous step to make the point for us) defines an order in which our duties are mostly obvious: if we are prey, to be eaten.

De-Moralizing Nature

So the cosmos exists to do us good, and every thing in it is 'healthy' (or as good as it can be) if it visibly serves the needs of people, or of superior people. The ideal was not invented by the Stoics. Everything that people can find useful people have always reckoned must be meant for them. Everything that can be judged diseased, disabled or just 'out of place' bears witness to our recognition of real norms in nature, and those norms must 'fit together' in a larger purpose (surely, ours). To live rightly must be to live in accordance with nature's plan, as that is manifested in the world around us. Predation, dominance, and territorial control are facts of life. We ought to make a proper, careful use of things because they wouldn't be there at all if we weren't meant to use them. Those who, in their turn, use us should be honoured for it. Those who rebel should be reckoned mad, and hunted down.

The ambiguity in Stoic doctrine that I have already mentioned can issue in very different creeds. On the one hand, we should hunt down rebels, and all other creatures that can be judged 'unnatural'. Maybe they are creatures of the Evil One, an enemy whose purposes do not include our good. On the other, even such rebel creatures (and maybe the Evil One) can only serve God's purposes even in their own despite. 'Bed-bugs are useful for waking us, and mice encourage us not to be untidy'.[6] In practice it hardly matters. It is axiomatic that things would not be as they are if they did not do some good, and that good typically, or so we usually suppose, is ours. Ordinarily sensual humanity may think it good to eat and drink and be merry; those with longer views may think the real good is to live in rational community, to follow duty, to understand Necessity. All of us interpret our good (that is, what we want) as what the cosmos wants, what makes the cosmos good.

But all of this, we must conclude, is also fallacy. 'In seeking to show that Nature does nothing in vain—that is, nothing that is not to man's advantage—they seem to have shown only this, that Nature

[6] Chrysippus, according to Plutarch, *On Stoic Self-contradictions*, 1044d (Long and Sedley, op. cit., vol. 1, p. 328).

and the gods are as crazy as mankind'.[7] The fact that we can make use of things does not prove that they were made for us. And this is especially true if there are many things we cannot really use at all, or that run counter to any ordinary purposes of ours.

> Who gave the wild donkey his freedom, and untied the rope from his proud neck? I have given him the desert as a home, the salt plains his own habitat. ... Is the wild ox willing to serve you or spend a night beside your manger?[8]

Even if we stopped trying to interpret everything as 'made for us', and thought instead of all the things that seem to be good for others, we might reasonably suspect that the others were also making use of what, by chance, existed. Maybe nothing at all exists 'in order to do good', though many things that exist can, more or less, be used. Maybe if we really found things lying around that perfectly provided for our purposes we might reasonably suspect a larger purpose: if, for example, we had only to close our eyes and wish, to find, at once, the tool or machine or house we needed. Maybe such magic would be bad for us (as failing to preserve our moral tone), and what we find is really better (the material for tools, machines or houses). But even the things best suited to our use have other properties that are disabling: pigs can't only be locomotive meals. And some things, seemingly, are of no 'use' at all, to us or anyone (at any rate, we can't imagine a use for them).

The scientific revolution began with the denial of final causes.[9] Instead of supposing that things existed 'to do good', or that we understand them best when we see what good they do, we chose instead to see simply how things happened: how, not why. Because we were no longer concerned (in scientific mode) with the good things did or might do, we could no longer judge them more or less successful, more or less obedient. Instead of supposing that 'Nature does nothing in vain', let us instead suggest that everything that 'Na-

[7] Benedict Spinoza, *The Ethics and Selected Letters*, ed. S. Feldman, trans. S. Shirley (Hackett: Indianapolis, 1982), p. 58. Spinoza was himself a Stoic, and as dismissive of the interests of 'animals' as was Chrysippus (also of 'womanish sentiment'): see 'The Description and Evaluation of Animal Emotion' in C. Blakemore & S. Greenwood (eds.), *Mindwaves* (Blackwells, 1987), pp. 139–49.

[8] *Job* 39.5–6.

[9] Another way of looking at the event is to see it as the outcome of the Reformation and Counter-Reformation rejection of Renaissance paganism: it became desperately important to empty reality of any imaginative, passion-exciting significance. See Ioan P. Couliano, *Eros and Magic in the Renaissance,* trans. Margaret Cook (University of Chicago Press: Chicago, 1987).

ture does' is pointless. 'For nothing has been engendered in our body in order that we might be able to use it. It is the fact of its being engendered that creates its use'.[10]

On this account there are no inbuilt norms. Without us, without our projected purposes, there could be no optical illusions, no zodiacal signs, no war-horses, no weeds. Less obviously, there are not even entities of the kind we usually think 'natural' (oaks, cattle, people). To be an oak tree, after all, is to be something that grows according to a preset plan, against which deviation, accident or disease can be plotted. On the Stoic account even diseased oaks are as the cosmos truly requires them to be, but it is possible to identify them, locally, as trees that have not quite grown as they should, or as trees usually do. How do we identify a tree if there is no way, even locally, that they should grow? How do trees differ from convenient rock-formations or crystal growths? We can describe the latter, of course: that is, we can say that the rocky substance 'over there' reminds us of a pillar, or a bee-hive, or a human figure. But no one seriously thinks that those identifications are anything but subjective. That the rock looks like a bee-hive played no part in its growing where it did: it might as easily have looked like Aunt Agatha (perhaps it does). An acorn that is not even locally 'designed' to grow into an oak, and is much more likely to end up as some squirrel's supper, is not, objectively, an acorn, any more than it is, objectively, a present, a missile, a symbol or a philosophical example. Calling a piece of stuff, or an aggregate of elementary bits, by one name or another says nothing about what 'it' is. The constellation, say, of Cassiopeia, exists only in our imagination: is there any singular thing that exists outside it? All we can truly say is that some elementary bits stay stuck together longer than some others. Epicurean thought is very close to Buddhist thought in this. In the *Questions of King Milinda* (which is Menander, ruling in the second century BC. in north-west India) the Buddhist philosopher Nagasena explains to Menander that no complex entity is anything but a collection of parts: better still, such words as seem to name that complex entity are only convenient designations for what has no substantial being. 'Nagasena' itself is 'but a way of counting, term, appellation, convenient designation mere name for the hair of the head, hair of the body. ... brain of the head, form, sensation, perception, the predispositions and consciousness. But in the absolute sense there is no ego

[10] Lucretius, *On the Nature of Things*, 4. 830ff: Long and Sedley, op. cit., vol. 1, p. 58

to be found'.[11] The more interesting form of Epicurean doctrine may lead naturally to a sort of Buddhist enlightenment: once disruptive desires have been abandoned, what is left, *Nirvana*, is the end of suffering, not in complete unconsciousness but in a sort of openness to anything that happens. But this is probably not what most Epicureans nowadays acknowledge.

Whereas Stoic moralists supposed that every creature aimed, or was aimed, at preserving its own being, Epicurean moralists identified pleasure (and the absence of pain) as what appetitive creatures (such as us) desired, or what the desires that compose us were. Stoics reckoned that we felt pleasure ('normally') in activities we needed to perform to live. A fetishistic preference for pleasure even when it harmed us was, locally, irrational, even if the cosmos as a whole (apparently) required that some of us should make this 'error'. Epicureans, on the other hand, thought life could be worth living only if it brought us pleasure (principally, to avoid misunderstanding, pleasures of friendship, beauty, peace, that have no consequential pains attached). Whereas Stoic moralists reckoned that what things (really) were determined what use was to be made of them, an Epicurean moralist might think that any use was equally 'appropriate' (and therefore none was appropriate in the Stoic sense). Mice do not exist to keep us from being untidy, nor to encourage us (as they did Diogenes the Cynic) to travel light, nor even to produce more mice. They have no real point at all, and there is therefore no particular proper way to use them: they might as well be dinner, or art-objects, or grain-thieves. How many uses can you think of for a pebble, or for half-a-mouse?

Unregulated hedonism, of a sort that Epicureans would despise, easily concludes, for example, that any pleasurable contact of two skins is 'as good' as any other. Whereas the older (post-Stoic) moralism reckoned that the proper use of sexual organs was made clear by 'nature', more recent, radical 'amoralism' judges that anything can be the object and occasion of a 'sexual' desire. Sexuality, indeed, is nothing special. Masturbation, bestiality, sodomy, cunnilingus, fellatio, pederasty, necrophiliac practices, sado-masochism and fertile coition are all and only ways that some of us (does 'we' identify a real

---

[11] S. Radhakrishnan & C. Moore (eds.), *Sourcebook of Indian Philosophy* (Princeton University Press: New Jersey, 1957), pp. 281–4. See Thomas McEvilley, *The Shape of Ancient Thought* (Allworth Press: New York, 2002) for a detailed and convincing argument that the Mediterranean and Indian milieux were closely connected, and that philosophical ideas and arguments flowed easily between them.

class?) get pleasure. None are more 'natural' than another, even if some are 'dangerous' in the eyes of those who still believe that there are real entities involved, and most of them aren't procreative. Any judgement between them can only be conventional, not natural. The same, presumably, applies in questions about diet: apples, grubs, mice, dogs and human babies are only conventionally distinguished. All are edible, and the different labels that 'we' make for them are only like the different labels that food-faddists give to different cuts of cow. 'No-one who is anyone would serve rump-steak in place of tournedos or long-pig in place of turkey for Thanksgiving Dinner.'

It would be wrong to assume that all 'Stoics' would defend the common-sense morality of Western Europe, or that all 'Epicureans' would despise it. On the contrary, it is a matter of record that those who believe in objective values, natural norms discoverable by reason but independent of our wishes and beliefs, may decide that common sense morality is wrong: incest, cannibalism and regicide may not be 'really' wrong precisely because some things—most notably, complaining—really are. One reason, oddly, why some moralists have denied that values could be objective is that they cannot let themselves believe that they themselves might get things wrong.[12] To avoid the possibility of any real challenge to their own moral convictions they prefer to found those convictions simply on their own determination to abide by them. *Their* 'firm perswasion that a thing is so' apparently *does* 'make it so', as far as this sort of moralist is concerned. The price of never being wrong, of course, is never being right. Conversely, those who disbelieve in objective values upon some other pretext may, for that very reason, adopt an unremarkable conventionalism: having no other standards to appeal to, and without any obligation to respect truth or consistency, they fall back upon contemporary custom. No-one who is anyone takes stands. Once we have been persuaded that our 'values' are historically and psychologically contingent, that we might have been as eager to promote a different set, how can we resist our enemies' persuasions?

Some modern Epicureans even reinvent a kind of 'realism': if there are no real obligations, then the old distinction between facts that we were all bound to admit and fictions that could only bind a few (that is, between 'hard facts' and 'values') is inane. All truths (that is, all claims we *should* admit) are only conventionally binding, and therefore equally real. Stoics and others could distinguish

12] See T.D. Perry, *Moral Reasoning and Truth* (Clarendon Press: Oxford, 1976).

'truths by nature' and 'truths by convention', what a man was 'really' worth and what he was worth 'in society'. All Epicureans can distinguish is what they value and what others do: why make a fuss?

But 'quasi-realists' are not my concern. The more interesting sort of radical objectivist has lost all faith in her own being. Being a person, or the same person as before, is being someone who can take responsibility for what one does, or who is held responsible. In the absence of real values, real responsibilities, there are no real persons, nor real identities. Whereas our realist predecessors could object to punishing a traitor's family for crimes that they did not commit, post-moderns have no warrant for the distinction. Such 'punishments' would probably be effective, and we might as well insist upon the moral identity of a family or gene-line as of 'a single being'.

No-one founds societies to protect atoms against atom-smashers (or not, at any rate, for that reason): why trouble to defend 'matter in that state known as living'?[13] Even pleasure and pain, which have retained a slight importance, must diminish once identities are gone, once we no longer trouble ourselves about what damage 'we' (who is that?) may suffer. Everything is mutable material, and as such immortal. 'We are the rocks dancing'—and will be even when we have reduced the rocks and every other living thing to sludge.

Plato and the Book of Genesis

Stoics believed that everything was for a purpose, and that purpose was to provide for rational community. Epicureans denied that anything had a purpose, but claimed that a certain kind of human friendship could make life 'worth living' in the midst of chaos.[14] In historical fact, both schools insisted that 'we' had no obligations toward non-human animals. Whether they were 'meant' for us or not, we were 'entitled' to treat them as if they were. Older injunctions to respect the good in horses, trees or streams could only, at best, be allegorical. It does not seem to have occurred to any philosopher of the time that we could ever damage Earth Herself, or that desertification, erosion or pollution could ever have been 'our fault'. No doubt the Stoics would have explained such 'natural catastrophes' as good for us, and Epicureans would have reckoned to make local use of them. The one major school of philosophers that

---

[13] So Arthur Keith (1866–1955) inquired, in defence of vivisection: 'Stephen Paget Memorial Lecture', *British Medical Journal* (1932), pp. 1184ff.

[14] Epicureans turned Buddhist in the way that I have suggested might have another view, but this development would take too long to examine clearly here.

defended animals, and might have noticed natural catastrophes as, occasionally, symptoms of moral decay, were Platonists.

By Platonic standards, what there actually is need not be what there ought to be. But what there actually is retains such being as it has by being *like* what ought to be, by Platonic standards. To be at all is to be, or almost to be, something: that is, to be becoming beautiful. It was just because, unlike Stoics and Epicureans alike, the Platonists insisted there were other things than the material, that they could judge the world, and human action, to be less than perfect, while still insisting that perfection had an influence. Philo of Alexandria, expounding the Hebrew Scriptures with the aid of Plato, laid the foundations for later Jewish, Christian and Islamic developments. So far from being anthropocentric the post-Platonic synthesis was theocentric — and that God was a circle whose centre was everywhere, and whose circumference nowhere. God could not be contained in human life, even if human beings were summoned to share the divine life. Nor could God's purposes be exactly known, let alone the means He chose to realize them. As even Descartes was to observe: 'Just as the same craftsman could make two clocks which tell the time equally well and look completely alike from the outside but have completely different assemblies of wheels inside, so the supreme craftsman of the real world could have produced all that we see in several different ways'.[15]

The God celebrated in the Hebrew and post-Hebraic scriptures did not *need* secondary causes, even if He chose to create them. It follows that, if He did create them, He wished them to exist for their own sake, because He thought them 'good'. That, despite appearances, He also wished to do them good, was a further article of faith. 'He hates nothing that He has made: why else would He have made it?'[16] The God celebrated in post-Platonic philosophy poured out the world, in all its multifarious kinds, because no smaller universe would do to represent His Beauty. The world perpetually sustained by God, Hebrew and Platonic, always contained the possibility of failure. The creatures made to embody Beauty, in its different kinds, might come to regard themselves as 'independent' beings, whose welfare must depend on grabbing what they could from others. Because they came to forget that they were all rays from a single

---

15] René Descartes, *The Philosophical Writings of Descartes* (Cambridge University Press: Cambridge, 1985), trans. John Cottingham, Robert Stoothoff, Dugald Murdoch, vol. 1, p. 289.

16] *Wisdom of Solomon* 11.25

Brightness, fragments of a grand mosaic, they grew to hate and fear each other. The moment of return is when we look at others, real others, and know that they are not ourselves, not ours, not even very like us, and thereby reacquaint ourselves with the life, the beauty, that fills everything in so many, very different ways.

Analytical philosophy, perhaps, is not very likely to awaken us to beauty. The title, after all, has often been associated with the fallacies with which I began this chapter. But Platonists can 'analyze' as well as any. Even if their efforts do not wake us up, they may still help to persuade us that we are awake when we experience Otherness, and when we see things in the light of Day. In the madman's universe everything is targeted at him or her. 'What has history to do with me? Mine is the first and only world! I want to report how I found the world!'[17] To this there can, in a way, be no reply except to hope that 'the hammer of a higher God could smash [this] small cosmos, scattering the stars like spangles, and leave [him] in the open, free like other men to look up as well as down'.[18] But de-moralizing nature may be a necessary *askesis*. When Wittgenstein urges us to 'remember that the spirit of the snake, of the lion, is [our] spirit',[19] he can only seriously be speaking of the spirits of moralized snakes or lions, heraldic beasts. In order to avoid interpreting snake or lion behaviour in that inappropriate way, and to recall the projected spirits, we may reasonably insist, for a while, that we will only speak of their 'objective movements', motions that have no moral weight (beyond the mere, remaining implication that we should face the facts).

Objectivists of the modern kind pretend that there are 'facts' accessible to everyone that have no moral weight at all. Because those are the only facts they will admit, they have to exclude pretended facts about King Oberon,[20] the lives of plants, the inner space

---

[17] Ludwig von Wittgenstein, *Notebooks 1914–16* (Blackwell: Oxford, 1961), 82e

[18] Chesterton, *Orthodoxy*, op. cit., p. 10

[19] Wittgenstein, op. cit., 26 October 1916.

[20] See Thomas Sprat, *History of the Royal Society* (Chapman: Oxford, 1722:, 3rd ed.: http:// books.google.com/books?id=YTYJAAAAQAAJ; 1st published 1667), p. 340f: 'The poets of old ... to make all things look more venerable than they were, devised a thousand false *Chimaeras:* on every *Field, River, Grove* and *Cave,* they imposed a *Fantasm* of their own making. ... All which abuses if those acute Philosophers [the Schoolmen] did not promote, yet they were never able to overcome; nay, not even so much as King Oberon and his invisible army. But from the time in which the *Real Philosophy* appeared there is scarcely any mention of these Horrors. For this we are beholden to *Experiments,* which though they have not yet completed the discovery of the true world, yet they have already

of beasts. Quasi-realists, acknowledging that the objectivizing project cannot be completed, pretend to restore the world we found at first. Neither route is satisfactory. On the one hand, facts to be facts at all have moral weight (and those concerning the inner lives of our fellow beings especially). On the other, they have that weight precisely because they're real. It cannot be true that 'pigs feel pain' means only that 'pigs should be included in our moral universe',[21] since one important reason why they should be is that they do. The discovery that they do, and should be, is a revelation of an Otherness beyond the lies we spin. The demand that we be objective is, exactly, a moral demand.

> We must see things objectively, as we do a tree; and understand that they exist whether we like them or not. We must not try and turn them into something different by the mere exercise of our minds, as if we were witches.[22]

Platonists insist that 'he that will find Truth must seek it with a free judgement and a sanctified minde'.[23] Part of the requirement is that we do not grab things for ourselves, nor project our fancies on the waiting world: 'as those Philosophers that Tully complains of in his times... which made their knowledge only matter of ostentation, to venditate and set off themselves, but never caring to square and govern their lives by it. Such as these doe but Spider-like take a great deal of pains to spin a worthless web out of their own bowels, which will not keep them warm'.[24]

If, for a while, we have allowed ourselves to think 'objectively' it was to purge nature (nature, that is, as we experience it) of our own conceits. Just so, Chesterton suggested, Christians of the early middle ages had to turn aside from nature for a while. Gardens, woods and the stars themselves were polluted (that is, the world of nature

---

vanquished those wild inhabitants of the false worlds that used to astonish the minds of men'. The theological, ideological origin of the 'experimental philosophy' could hardly be more clearly stated.

21] Richard Rorty, *Philosophy and the Mirror of Nature.* (Princeton University Press, 1979), p. 190.

22] G.K. Chesterton, *Illustrated London News* 22nd Nov 1913, in *Complete Works*, vol. 29 (Ignatius Press: San Francisco, 1988), p. 589, cited by A. De Silva in *Brave New Family*, ed. A.D. Silva (Ignatius Press: San Francisco, 1990), p. 15. For a further defence of realism see G.K. Chesterton, *Heretics* (John Lane: New York, 1905), pp. 304f.

23] John Smith, 1644: C.A. Patrides (ed.), *The Cambridge Platonists* (Cambridge University Press: Cambridge, 1969), p. 137.

24] John Smith, *The Cambridge Platonists*, op. cit., p. 133

as it features in our imaginative experience was polluted) by the perversions of late paganism.[25] Only when four centuries of ascetic practice had purified the imagination could St.Francis rededicate the natural world. 'Man has stripped from his soul the last rag of nature-worship, and can return to nature'.[26] When we can face the world as Other than ourselves, we can at last interpret it. Neither 'objectivists' nor 'quasi-realists' do either. Stoics and Epicureans made the attempt, but lost their way. It is precisely because things-in-themselves are worth knowing, because they embody real values, that we ought to rise above immediate prejudice, personal affections and dislikes, projected spirits. If there were no real values independent of our will there could be no real reason to transcend our prejudice.

> Insight is the moment in time when the mind's eye glimpses immutable Truth; it is Time touching Eternity, a foretaste of eternal blessedness, an experience of God.[27]

The Choice before 'Environmentalists'

The very term, 'environmentalist', is a misnomer. The world and our fellow creatures have a larger brief than simply to 'environ' us. Many an anthropocentric Stoic, or sub-Stoic, could entertain the shallower forms of ecological concern. Only very stupid creatures foul their nests, poison their land and kill the golden goose. Stoics and Epicureans alike could also find some fault with our priorities: maybe we 'need' to use the world we find, but 'need' is not the verb that applies to hamburgers, cosmetics or large cars. Every moral and religious tradition in the world till now has objected to *pleonexia*, the greed for more, and also to usury, despoliation, sacrilege. No-one till recently imagined we could ever 'own' the land. Our problem is that, having begun to disenchant, de-moralize, the world (for good and sufficient reasons) we forgot to pause. Some (most of us) cheated all along. We only disenchanted part of the world, the parts 'we'

---

[25] G.K. Chesterton, *St. Francis of Assisi* (Sheed & Ward: London, 1923), pp. 29ff.

[26] Chesterton, *St Francis*, op. cit., p. 39

[27] Philip Cary, *Augustine's Invention of the Inner Self: the legacy of a Christian Platonist* (Oxford University Press: New York, 2000), p. 72, summarizing Augustine's view. Cary notes (*ibid.*, pp. 69–71) that the Roman Church has ruled against 'ontologism' ('the notion that we see all things in God') on the grounds that the universal laws and structures we discover are *created* things, not uncreated Forms in the mind of God. But though, as created things, they could indeed have been different, and though *our* conception of them is not God's, they are still *founded* on the uncreated Word, and we don't understand them aright without acknowledging this.

wished to use, but went on giving worship to our human friends (which is not, of course, all humankind). A few of us have begun to empty even humankind, and even 'ourselves', of worship: there is only stuff, to be made the occasion of whatever pleasures still remain unwithered. The only real answer is to remember why we began the objectivizing programme. 'God never intended that a creature should rest satisfied with its own candle-light, but that it should run to the fountain of light, and sunne it self in the presence of its God'.[28] Sometimes, to hear what others say, we simply must shut up. It does not follow that we should never speak thereafter, nor ever actually listen to what they say in answer.

The visions which I have labeled 'Stoic' and 'Epicurean' have much the same effect. On Stoic terms the creatures with which we surround ourselves exist to serve our purposes. Cereals, cattle, horses, dogs and human slaves are judged good or bad according to their usefulness. All of them, in historical fact, have been bred and tamed so as to have some chance of being useful. Epicureans (reasonably) doubt the claim that any of these creatures came into existence for our sake. But for that very reason, that they exist for no-one's sake, they can be used remorselessly for any purposes we have. Disenchanting nature is only a device for making it available for purposes that were not countenanced within the earlier, 'Stoic' synthesis. What I have called 'Platonism' is a better route. The creatures who share the world with us exist (as the Stoics saw, in part) to embody and preserve real values. To be at all is to be something, and the thing in question is identified as worth existing by the very effort with which whatever is persists in being. As Spinoza saw, following the Stoics, 'the effort with which each thing endeavours to persist in its own being is nothing but the essence of the thing itself'.[29] To understand it is to see why it exists, and to see that it can never be merely a means to some other creature's good.[30] Spinoza himself fell back, like the Stoics, into the anthropocentric error of supposing that the good of other, non-human creatures might justly be neglected[31] because their goods are of less importance, to us, than ours.

The message of the deeper sort of 'environmentalist' is that there is a world 'out there', embodying more beauties than our own imagi-

---

28] Nathanael Culverwell, 1652: Patrides, op. cit., p. 11.

29] Spinoza, op. cit., p. 109

30] Spinoza, op. cit., p. 168

31] Spinoza, op. cit., pp. 175, 193

nations can create. Platonists, unlike some other ancients, can accommodate the truth that things change and vanish from the world. Nothing in the world will last forever. Maybe even the world itself will not. While it lasts, in all its changeful and variegated beauty, it merits our respect and love. Certainly those who neither respect nor love it because, they say, they are superior deserve no credit. 'He who boasts of the dignity of his nature and the advantages of his station, exhibits his folly as well as his malice.'[32]

One of the many errors that have been made by modern critics—and also by some believers—rests on a misreading of the account in *Genesis*. When Man (Humanity) is made 'in the image of God' and instructed to 'rule' fish, birds and 'every living thing that moves upon the face of the earth',[33] the easy assumption is that we are to rule for our own benefit. But the sort of rule that is intended is not what 'kings' imagine, or the sort of kings that people too often get.[34] Reading that humanity is 'made in God's image', we should ask what the likeness is meant to be. What is it that *Genesis* has shown God doing? What is it that we are assigned to imitate?

> A jealous dispute broke out [among the disciples]: who among them should rank highest? But [Jesus] said, 'In the world, kings lord it over their subjects; and those in authority are called their country's "Benefactors". Not so with you: on the contrary, the highest among you must bear himself like the youngest, the chief of you like a servant'.[35]

So also John Paul II,

> In his desire to have and to enjoy rather than to be and to grow, man consumes the resources of the earth and his own life in an excessive and disordered way. At the root of the senseless destruction of the natural environment lies an anthropological error, which unfortunately is widespread in our day. Man, who discovers his capacity to transform and in a certain sense create

---

[32] Humphrey Primatt, *The Duty of Humanity to Inferior Creatures,* ed. A. Broome (London, 1831; 1st edn. 1776), p. 22. The original, complete edition has been republished in *Animal rights and souls in the eighteenth century,* ed. Aaron Garrett (Thoemmes Press: Bristol, 2000), vol. 3. Some texts read 'the disadvantages of his station'.

[33] *Genesis* 1.26–8

[34] See *I Samuel* 8.6–19, where the people of Israel want to have a king, as other nations do, in place of their obedience to the covenant, and Samuel warns them, in the Lord's name, of the kind of king they'll be getting.

[35] *Luke* 22.24–6.

> the world through his own work, forgets that this is always based on God's prior and original gift of the things that are. Man thinks that he can make arbitrary use of the earth, subjecting it without restraint to his will, as though it did not have its own requisites and a prior God-given purpose, which man can indeed develop but must not betray. Instead of carrying out his role as a co-operator with God in the work of creation, man sets himself up in place of God and thus ends up provoking a rebellion on the part of nature, which is more tyrannized than governed by him.[36]

We are not to be 'kings', as the world understands that term. In co-creating we must recall that we are working *within* an existing, blessed creation. In governing we must act—as Plato also advised[37]—for the good of those we govern.

Stripping Away Significance

The title of this chapter is drawn from C.S. Lewis's finest philosophical work, in which he pointed out that moral values were being casually described, without argument, in works purporting to be about English literature, as merely subjective responses. The infection has spread even further since his day (as he would not have been surprised to note). Academics are now regularly asked to conduct 'ethical reviews' of any research they may propose. Medical ethicists and experimental scientists (especially) may speak of 'ethical constraints' against certain forms of invasive experimentation. Some—including many atheistical philosophers—are as firm as any in their moral judgements. But it is noticeable that animal experimentalists (especially), when challenged to explain what 'ethical constraints' might be, will almost always declare that they are no more than *social* obstacles. Right and Wrong, they suppose, are only social constructions. By the same account the difference between 'humans' and 'non-humans', 'male' and 'female', 'native' and 'foreign' are also 'social constructions', and ages and societies that draw the lines a little differently aren't 'wrong' (though 'we' dislike them). Nothing 'out there in the world' can serve as a standard against which to test our 'ethical constructions' at least in the way that 'scientific theories' are tried out against something 'out there in the world'.

36] *Centesimus Annus* (1 May 1991) $37: taken from http://www.vatican.va/holy_father/john_paul_ii/encyclicals/documents/hf_jp-ii_enc_01051991_centesimus-annus_en. html (accessed 4 April 2008): my thanks to a member of christianveg@yahoogroups. com for this reference.

37] See Plato, *The Republic*, 1.342e.

An associated theme (or mental microbe) is disparagement of the 'yuk factor'. It may be acknowledged that there is widespread dismay at one or another proposal (say, for genetic engineering or experimental intervention—grafting a human ear onto a mouse's back, or keeping a monkey's head—but not its body—'alive', or breeding headless chickens), but all that is needed is for 'the public' to be educated into understanding what advantages may be won by this or any other immediately 'distasteful' act. The *advantages* are somehow beyond analysis or dispute: the 'yum' factor, oddly, is considered 'rational' whereas the 'yuk' is not. Enthusiasts will almost always add that 'the public' used to find other things disgusting too, and has already learnt that it is *wrong* to do so!

As so often Chesterton imagined an appropriate response.

> Don't you see that that dreadful dry light shed on things must at last wither up the moral mysteries as illusions, respect for age, respect for property, and that the sanctity of life will be a superstition? The men in the street are only organisms, with their organs more or less displayed.[38]

Let us suppose for a moment that the 'moral mysteries' are indeed created only by our human involvement in the universe, by our reflection on our own and others' preferences and feelings. In the absence of any creatures with a point of view or preferences, all states of matter, we may say, were neutral. Once there are living creatures this is not so, but there may still be no single, unitary valuation possible: prey and predator have different *local* interests. Even then they may not have different *global* interests: it is not in the predator's interests that none of the prey survive, nor in the prey's that predation wholly halt. Even before there were self-reflective creatures (such as us) the same processes that have engineered animal organs and behaviour patterns engineered inhibitions, compassionate feelings, and even 'a sense of fairness'. Why should we abandon these constructions merely because, in a way, we can? What possible *obligation* could we have to do so if there are no obligations? And if there are no obligations, and we should (?) teach our children so, how shall we expect them to behave?

> There must ... of necessity, in every State, be a certain system of salutary notions, a prevailing set of opinions, acquired either by private reason and reflection or taught and instilled by the gen-

[38] G.K. Chesterton, *The Poet and the Lunatics* (Darwen Finlayson: London, 1962; 1st published 1929), p. 70

> eral reason of the public, that is, by the law of the land. … Nor will it be any objection to say that these are prejudices; inasmuch as they are therefore neither less useful nor less true, although their proofs may not be understood by all men. … The mind of a young creature cannot remain empty; if you do not put into it that which is good, it will be sure to receive that which is bad. Do what you can, there will still be a bias from education; and if so, is it not better this bias should lie towards things laudable and useful to society? … If you strip men of these their notions, or, if you will, prejudices, with regard to modesty, decency, justice, charity, and the like, you will soon find them so many monsters, utterly unfit for human society.[39]

The mainstream view of late has been that 'nature' is a war for survival. It may seem that creatures can cooperate, but 'all that is happening' is the effort of 'the selfish gene' to replicate itself within whatever sphere it works.[40] Whatever of parental or filial or more open love or loyalty is seen it's 'really' only a device to secure more samples of some gene or other in a future mix. So our children, in being taught this, are being taught not to be deceived. Weirdly, we teach them not to respect their elders, not to acknowledge any moral force in love or loyalty, not to believe in higher unities. And when parents object to seeing their children reared to despise such ethical endeavours (and implicitly to despise even the scientist's own would-be rational creeds), they can be dismissed as failed manipulators, or as unconscious agents of a mental microbe. As David Stove observed, the claim that 'nothing but expediency will restrain anyone from brutalizing, from maiming, from murdering—his brother, his mate, his parents or his child'[41] is a direct incitement to crime.[42] Some of those who preach such nihilism are themselves honourable:

---

[39] George Berkeley, 'Discourse to Magistrates': *Works*, ed. T.E. Jessop & A.A. Luce, vol. 6 (Thomas Nelson: Edinburgh, 1953), pp. 203f

[40] I leave aside for the moment any criticisms of the very notion of 'a gene', and the simple-minded notion that it is such 'genes' that are 'selected' in the course of evolution.

[41] M.H. Ghiselin, *The Economy of Nature and the Evolution of Sex* (University of California Press: San Francisco, 1978), p. 247.

[42] David Stove, *Darwinian Fairytales* (Avebury: Aldershott, 1995), p. 74. The claim was addressed by Plato in the story of Gyges' Ring (*The Republic* Bk. 2). See J. Budziszewksi, 'Accept No Imitations: the rivalry of naturalism and natural law' in William K. Dembski, ed., *Uncommon Dissent: Intellectuals who find Darwinism Unconvincing* (ISI Books: Wilmington, Delaware, 2004), pp. 99–114 on the unsuccessful attempt somehow to derive a simulacrum of traditional morality ('natural law') from Darwinian Theory.

precisely because they are honourable, they seem unable to understand how accidental their own honour is. Like other, political, radicals convinced that 'the established order' deserves no respect they believe that everyone would be as kindly as they are themselves if that order vanished. Less kindly people (like myself) are far too well aware of what lies on the far side of the civil peace.[43] Strangely, the very same people as insist that there are no *real* values are surprised and hurt when anyone infers that their word cannot be trusted. If someone tells you that it is not wrong to lie, why do you believe that he is not lying?

It may take a while for the full effects of radical scepticism to be observed, but they can be imagined.

> The morals of a people are in this like their fortunes; when they feel a national shock, the worst doth not shew itself immediately. Things make a shift for a time on the credit of old notions and dying opinions. But the youth born and brought up in wicked times, without any bias to good from early principle or instilled opinion, when they grow ripe must be monsters indeed. And it is to be feared, that age of monsters is not far off.[44]

We can hope that what children are taught in schools will have less influence than their 'natural' respect and love for parents and each other. But of course such inbred inhibitions cannot, for us, be the only answer. One of Darwin's sillier remarks was that if bees were rational creatures they would consider it their 'sacred duty to kill their brothers, and mothers would strive to kill their fertile daughters, and no-one would think of interfering'.[45] It was a silly remark because, once rational, they would plainly be able to question their own innate impulses—as readily as we can question even those impulses whose *evolutionary* logic we can understand (to kill step-children and foreigners, for example, as well as to care for our own young). Sometimes this questioning may be only a comparison, even a conflict, between equally natural impulses (neither step-children nor foreigners are so different from our own children and immediate kin as to be quite easily despised). But it may also rest on

---

[43] See 'Anarchists against the Revolution' in M. Warner & R. Crisp (eds.), *Terrorism and Power* (Edward Elgar: London, 1990), pp. 123–37; republished in *The Political Animal* (Routledge: London, 1999), pp. 75–91.

[44] G. Berkeley, 'Discourse to Magistrates', *Works*, vol. 6, op. cit., p. 221; see also *Alciphron*: *Works*, vol. 3, op. cit., pp. 130f (Crito speaks).

[45] Charles Darwin, *The Descent of Man* (Princeton University Press: New Jersey, 1981: a facsimile of the 1871 edition), vol. 1, p. 73.

exactly the same intuition as 'science': namely, that there is a larger world than *ours*, that we *ought* to remember that we are not, individually, the only or the most important entities there are. We *ought* to remember that others are as real as we, that the one world on which we have such different perspectives, sustains and will outlast us all. We cannot, must not, wholly abandon innate inhibitions or traditional advice, but we also cannot wholly rely on either.

The Golden Rule, expressed in very many ages and societies, is to treat others as we would ourselves be treated—not only with a view to *encouraging* such gentle treatment (sometimes it doesn't) but to follow the rule that a caring intelligence *would* give. The morally right thing to do is what we would be asked to do by someone with the interests of each at heart, and reliable knowledge of the effect of what we do. We *ought*, that is, to do what God requires, or what God *would* require if there were indeed a God. Unfortunately, of course, we are not ourselves so altruistic, or intelligent, or knowledgeable as always to know what this would be: that is what is wrong with 'playing God', that it requires more knowledge, more compassion, more intelligence than we can muster.[46] It is also often to claim an authority that is not ours—not *God's* authority, that is, but our fellow creatures'. One of the risks that even virtuous people face is that, having good intentions and even good information, they forget that they may have no legal or moral *right* to act on those intentions. Better to attend to such small things as come our way than entertain large dreams of world-creation! Better to love our neighbour than humanity at large (because our neighbour can at once protest that we have misunderstood her needs). Better contest present iniquity than plan utopia. 'Loving humanity' is sometimes an easy fantasy, a cloak for our own egotism.

This compromise has long been known,
This scheme of partial pardons,
In ethical societies
And small suburban gardens—
The villas and the chapels where
I learned with little labour

46] See Gordon Graham, *Genes: a philosophical inquiry* (Routledge: London, 2002), pp. 145ff. Graham points out that the *wrongness* of playing God does not depend, as some have supposed, on there being a God whose authority we would be usurping. Quite otherwise, it is even rasher to play God if there isn't! *God* may forgive us our temerity: it is not obvious that *Nature* will.

The way to love my fellow-man
And hate my next-door neighbour.[47]

Good scientists and scholars acknowledge the moral force of *truth,* and even if they have no option but to believe in their own best image of that truth, it is still the truth itself, and not their image of it, that demands devotion. 'I had promised to show you, if you recall, that there is something higher than our mind and reason. There you have it—truth itself! Embrace it if you can and enjoy it!'[48] The error of the bad scientist that Chesterton's poet exclaims against is, simultaneously, that he mistakes his personal passion for the truth, and that he fails to perceive the moral *force* of truth, the demand made on us by real things.

But surely, not everything that is true is worth discovering, nor everything real worth worship? That was the Stoic error that I described before. What we need to see is beauty, not as a projection of subjective thrills, but as the norm at work within even the meanest creature.[49]

Everything that exists is the present record of past struggles to embody beauty, pressed into shape by internal and external factors. On the one hand, Dawkins is—in a way—correct to find the actual organism (say, a fig) of more compelling interest and beauty than even the wildest stories told about such figs by people less well acquainted with the 'real', ongoing world.[50] On the other, he would be wrong to deny the experienced, humane significance of figs (and every other creature). All things come to us with an aura, a mist of social and subjective meanings—and this is not wrong unless that mist obscures for us the real thing, the independently real creature. Stripping significance away from the world we inhabit may some-

---

[47] G.K. Chesterton, 'The World State' in *Collected Poems* (Methuen: London, 1933), p. 16.

[48] Augustine, *De Libero Arbitrio,* 2.13.35: *The Teacher, The Free Choice of the Will & Grace and Free Will,* trans. R.P. Russell (Catholic University of America Press: Washington, 1968), p. 144. It is said that the citizens of Lampsacus, on the death of Anaxagoras in 428 BC, 'erected an altar to *nous kai aletheia,* mind and truth, because they had gathered that these were his gods (or that this was his god)': G.E.M. Anscombe, 'Paganism, Superstition and Philosophy' (1985): *Faith in a Hard Ground,* op. cit., pp. 49–60: p. 56 (after Diogenes Laertius, *Lives of the Philosophers,* 2.3.10).

[49] See Aristotle, *De Partibus Animalium,* 1.645a15f.

[50] See Richard Dawkins, *Climbing Mount Improbable* (Penguin: London, 1997), cited by Cornwell, op. cit., p. 34.

times be a necessary exercise, a purification,[51] but only so that the world can be re-clothed.

51] I have examined some of the history and significance of this powerful metaphor in 'Going Naked into the Shrine: Herbert, Plotinus and the Constructive Metaphor' in D. Hedley & S. Hutton (eds.), *Platonism at the Origins of Modernity* (Springer: Dordrecht, 2008), pp. 45–61

5

Can Animals be our Friends?

Pythagoras and the Eternal Self

One of the stories told about Pythagoras is that he rebuked a man who was beating a dog, with the words 'That's a friend of mine—I knew him by his voice.' The story is told to illustrate, maybe to mock, Pythagorean belief in metempsychosis, in the thought that souls migrate into new bodies when their present body dies. It is a belief found all across the world, though not every believer thinks that their soul might end up in a non-human body. I don't myself think that doctrine is absurd. Standard philosophical arguments against its mere possibility, whether these are Aristotelian or modern materialist, seem to me to beg every question going. That there are *theological* arguments against its truth, at any rate within the Abrahamic traditions, is a lot more plausible. If we here-now are to hope for the Resurrection, and if God holds *persons* to be supremely valuable, it does seem that we are destined to be the soul-body composites that we currently are forever.[2] My immortal self, so the Christian Councils at any rate have decided, is Stephen, and not the Soul that now animates this person and has animated and will animate however many entities with different names and sensibilities. This may not be the only possible Abrahamic, or even the only possible Christian position: if it's right, it still isn't right 'of necessity', but only what the

---

[1] An earlier version of this chapter was presented to a colloquium at the University of Chester in September 2007, and published, in brief, as 'Can Animals be our Friends?' in *Philosophy Now*, 67 (May/June 2008), pp. 13–16. See also 'How Alien are Animals?' in Pierfrancesco Basile & Leemon B. McHenry (eds.), *Consciousness, Reality and Value: essays in honour of T.L.S. Sprigge* (Ontos Verlag: Heusenstamm, 2007), pp. 245–58.

[2] See Paul Williams, *The Unexpected Way: on converting from Buddhism to Catholicism* (T & T Clark; London & New York, 2002), pp. 80–83

Creator has in fact determined. But let this pass: the *truth* of metempsychosis, though a serious issue, isn't my concern.

I shall also not address the converse, Neo-Cartesian arguments against the possibility of animal consciousness, beliefs, desires and affections. Those arguments depend on the mere assertion that thought and feeling is impossible without a certain sort of language, a doctrine that makes the *acquisition* of language, by a human infant or the human species, a mere miracle. Oddly, those who deploy the argument in philosophical circles don't usually acknowledge the theological implications. My experience is that the arguments, and associated specious appeals to Ockam's Razor, the custom and practice of humankind, and—in appropriate circles—the Bible, seem plausible only to those with a real stake in the conclusion. I shall take it for granted that no likely reader seriously disputes the thesis that vertebrates at any rate have a point of view, are conscious, that there is 'something it is like to be' a bat, a cat or crocodile.[3] It is probably also common sense to suppose that there is something it is like to be a worm, a wasp or a common octopus.[4] But of course it doesn't immediately follow that their points of view are ours, or that they inhabit anything like the same 'moral universe' as we do. After all, plenty of human beings don't seem to do that either!

Pythagoras recognized a friend. Let's leave it at that, for now. Pythagoras' heart went out to the dog when he heard his yelps: in that moment, he became a friend. It is not the only possible reaction to an animal's complaint. A story is told of the Rabbi Judah that when he heard a calf complaining on the way to slaughter, he rebuked him, saying that it was for this that the calf had been created. For this insensitivity he had toothache for thirteen years until one day he saved a weasel's life, and was pardoned.[5] At least Judah gave the calf an answer. The commonest reaction of all, of course, is simply to ignore the noise, which cannot really be a *complaint*, nor an appeal for justice, nor even a cry for help. Animals, after all, are merely animal. And even those late antique philosophers who lived

---

[3] The expression was first coined by T.L.S. Sprigge, in 'Final Causes', *Aristotelian Society Supplementary Volume*, 45 (1971), pp. 149–70, and used in the context of an interesting argument for panpsychism by Thomas Nagel in 'What is it like to be a bat?' *Philosophical Review*, 83 (1974), pp. 435–50, reprinted in *Mortal Questions* (Cambridge University Press: Cambridge, 1979).

[4] See my 'Impersonal Minds' in Anthony O'Hear (ed.), *Minds and Persons* (Cambridge University Press: Cambridge, 2003), pp. 185–209.

[5] Richard H. Schwartz, *Judaism and Vegetarianism* (Lantern Books: New York, 2001), p. 29, citing *Baba Metzia* 85a, *Midrash Genesis Rabbah* 33.3.

out a Neo-Pythagorean or Neo-Platonic tradition mostly made just the same distinction, in order to defend their very un-Pythagorean resort to blood sacrifice. But maybe they were wrong.

Common Sense about Friends and Animals

The context of my present argument is current, Western, common sense. On this view, non-human animals are neither vehicles for just the same sort of soul as human animals, nor are they merely insentient mechanisms. They are animate, sentient creatures, but they are not 'human'—and neither are they all the same. The sociologist Sherry Turkle can speak of sitting silently, watching children pulling the wings off butterflies, because she supposes that butterflies are 'far enough from being alive in the way that a person is alive to make its mutilation and killing almost acceptable'.[6] I am not sure that a British sociologist could have been quite so indifferent, or so easily persuaded that the children 'are not simply being thoughtless or cruel', but merely and commendably playing with their ideas and feelings about life and death. No doubt the children don't really know what they are doing: it is up to the adults in their life to correct them (and certainly not to refrain because it would be 'judgemental' to make any comment). But it is still true that we do commonly make distinctions: I doubt if even Turkle would have been quite so laid back if the children were dismembering vertebrates (and of course the vertebrates would have objected violently, and there would have been more mess). Amongst invertebrates only the common octopus (and not even its closest relatives) is given the same protection as vertebrates by the Animal Procedures Act of 1986. Philosophers working within the mainstream Western tradition often make a simple distinction between human and non-human animals, as though chimpanzees were more like worms than they are like people, but common sense does not agree. We make both objective and subjective distinctions: that is, we divide animals both by their own innate properties and by our own attitudes to them. We treat vertebrates and insects differently because, we suppose, they are innately different. We treat dogs and pigs differently because they mean different things to us, though we recognize that their intelligence and sensitivity are much the same. Friendship, to preempt discussion, involves objective and subjective elements: my friends, perhaps,

[6] Sherry Turkle, *The Second Self: computers and the human spirit* (Simon & Schuster: New York, 1984), pp. 31f: see http://name.umdl.umich.edu/heb01158.0001.001 (consulted 22 April 2006).

share some objective properties, but not all who have those properties are therefore my friends, even if I happen to know them. So my question, can animals be our friends, should really be replaced by a different and much lengthier pair of questions: which animals, if any, can be our friends, and what is friendship?

Some animals clearly like our company, and like to be petted—even, so my daughter tells me, giant tortoises. Tradition tells us that even certain insects—namely, bees—cooperate more eagerly with certain humans than with others. Conversely, some humans get on more easily than others with animals of one sort or another. Liking one another's company and even some physical contact is at least an element in friendship, but probably not the only one. Traditionally, amongst our household pets, dogs may be counted friends, but cats, it is supposed, just like the warmth, the scent, the touch of humans (and of course the food they offer). That this is entirely accurate, I doubt: the distinction is one of human culture rather than objective judgement, and its value is largely that it draws attention to the things we expect of 'friends'. Feline affection, for example, is not expected to be either faithful, obedient or protective, whereas we take it for granted that dogs will guard and obey us until death. Once again, I am not sure that this distinction is objectively correct: canine fidelity can also be interpreted as the sort of pack loyalty that is easily transformed to rivalry, and cats too sometimes seem both faithful and concerned. But the cats of our 'imaginary' are their own masters in ways that dogs are not, and so cannot, we think, be 'friends'.

By Aristotle's account of friendship, on the other hand, masters and slaves cannot be really friends, since the master does not take any of the slave's goals as his own: the slave, indeed, has no acknowledged goals, beyond the satisfaction of immediate desires and the release from fear. *Natural slaves*, in Aristotle's political ontology, have no conception of doing what is right, nor any chance of a 'life well-lived'. Still less have any non-humans any share in moral action or in a life well-lived. In actual practice, of course, there may be shared affections, loyalties, and reciprocal obligations even between slave and master, even between man and dog. Since many or most *actual* slaves are slaves unjustly (not being 'natural slaves') the relationship may ascend a step, to the sort of 'unequal friendships' in which the merit of the friends so differs that their relationship is feudal rather than egalitarian. Rather than sharing the same advantages of friendship unequal friends get different gains, offer different honour to each other. This may not look like *friendship* as such at all; Aristotle, after all, was discussing *philia*, the vital bond of Greek societies that marks off what is 'one's own', a relationship much more 'political' than 'romantic'. But perhaps this is still a useful model, and one we can extend to the non-human. Relationships can be either reciprocal or complementary—a distinction drawn by animal behaviourists who haven't, probably, read Aristotle.[7] It is important to commonsensical tradition that our 'animal companions' be inferior in those respects that matter most to us, and acknowledge their subservience—which is another reason why we are uncertain that cats are ever friends. Dogs that too obviously control their households are in need, we suppose, of therapy. Dog-owners who mourn their pets too openly embarrass themselves and others.[8] Those who feel more sorrow at their pets' death than at any human relatives' decease experience the grief that dare not say its name. Does not their sorrow prove that they had given their hearts to something less than human, preferring mindless affection to the real challenges of *human* intercourse?[9] Their dogs were, in a way, *philoi*, but the *philia* was of the unequal kind, and the feudal superior ought not to lose his dignity in grief.

Aristotle's analysis has further advantages. Even among more equal 'friendships' there are distinctions. The commonest sort is 'for pleasure': *philoi* who take pleasure together in games, or drink, or even more intellectual pursuits. A second kind of *philia* is the business partnership, for profit. Only the third kind is counted, by Aristotle, as *true philia*: the case where *philoi* recognize each other as good, as just what they themselves would wish and hope to be, as 'other selves' for whom it would be proper and even easy to die. Such *philoi* share a conception of the life well-lived, and value their own virtues expressed more openly in the other. They love each other as themselves. Aristotle held it would be slavish to live 'for another', taking the others' ideals and interests as one's own, except in just these cases, where *philoi* take their pleasure, and their profit, in a single noble enterprise. Only human beings can be such *philoi*, and only what we call *ethical* human beings, those who do all and only what they conceive is *right*—which excludes most of us, especially in this

---

[7] R.A. Hinde, 'Interactions, relationships and social structures', in *Man,* 11 (1976), pp. 1–17: p. 7: cited by Barbara B. Smuts, *Sex and Friendship in Baboons* (Aldine de Gruyter: New York, 1985), p. 61.

[8] See Avery D. Weisman, 'Bereavement and Companion Animals' in *Omega: Journal of Death and Dying,* 22 (1990–1), pp. 242–8

[9] See Kennan Ferguson, 'I ♥ my dog' in *Political Theory,* 32 (2004), p. 373f.

hedonistic age. But the other forms of *philia* have this much in common with the best, that *philoi* do things together, that they are partners in some enterprise. Inferior partners follow their superiors' plans. Equal partners are jointly committed to the same endeavour.

So what about non-human animals, especially of the sort that human beings domesticate and rule? Of course, by Aristotelian and commonsensical standards, such animals don't share our plans, except at the level of pleasure, or maybe profit. Human and cat may both have pleasure in the other, even if not the same pleasure. Human and dog may profitably join in hunting or herding, each with their own goals and alert to each other's profit. But can such partners ever share a conception of what it is right to do, or of a life well-lived? Aristotle's answer was that they could not—because the notion of 'what is right, noble, beautiful' is something only visible to the eye of intellect. Other Platonists—for Aristotle himself was a kind of Platonist—were prepared to suppose that any animate being had some connection with that intellect, even if its eye was, for the moment, blind. They could therefore imagine that non-human animals were sometimes moved by 'moral beauty', even if they could not articulate that emotion or that vision. But that possibility is another item that I shall not address—largely because I don't know how we could settle the question. Instead, it is worth asking whether our contemporary common sense, not being Platonist, has any grounds for saying that animals can't manage what we manage. If ethics, so to speak is *not* objective in the way that Platonists believe, what other option have we than to think 'the good' is simply what we approve of, what we like and recommend to others whom we like? And non-human animals can have just such sentiments.

> Different as they are from language-using human beings, they are able to form relationships not only with members of their own species, but also with human beings, while giving expression to their own intentions and purposes. So that the relationships are far more clearly analogous to human relationships than some of the philosophical theorizing that I have discussed would allow. Some human beings indeed and some nonhuman animals pursue their respective goods in company with and in coopera-

> tion with each other. And what we mean by 'goods' in saying this is precisely the same, whether we are speaking of human or dolphin or gorilla.[10]

Whether or not there is an objective element in ethics, even Platonists can agree that *sentiment*, and not mathematical reason, is our ground of moral judgement. Our ethics are the ethics of a certain sort of social mammal, programmed to care for our offspring and our immediate kin. In some species that care seems carefully confined: chimpanzees seem wholly indifferent to more distant relatives, feeling no impulse to care for them,[11] and even willingly killing members of any rival group (as people also do, but usually needing some rationalized excuse for murder). But this need not be a universal feature. Experiments suggest that other primates will forego advantages rather than cause others pain—and rather more strongly that some scientists won't. In other species it is even possible for affectionate care to reach out *beyond* the species—to human observers' surprise. Recent cases noted in the media include the snake that lives contentedly with the hamster intended for its lunch, or the lioness that persisted in adopting oryxes.[12] Young chimpanzees can play with young baboons: maybe some day a pair will maintain that connection into adulthood, uncorrupted by their company. Sociobiologists may believe that this is or would be in some sense 'an error', a bit of inheritable behaviour that cannot be really 'fit', and so must always be rare. My own guess is that 'fitness', in this ethically neutral sense, is not so easy to calculate (on which more below). At the very least, it is obvious that the *human* capacity for caring for more distant kin, and even for the non-human, has not restricted our reproduction. On the contrary, it is the humans incapable of caring that are rare: we call them psychopaths. There may, sometimes, be small psychopathic populations, but more generous attitudes are as likely to be common.

---

[10] Alastair Macintyre, *Dependent Rational Animals* (Open Court: Chicago, 1999), p. 61. See further Marc Bekoff, 'Wild justice and fair play: cooperation, forgiveness, and morality in animals', *Biology and Philosophy,* 19 (2004), pp. 489–520.

[11] Joan B. Silk, Sarah F. Brosnan, Jennifer Vonk, Joseph Henrich, Daniel J. Povinelli, Amanda S., Susan P. Lambeth, Jenny Mascaro & Steven J. Schapiro, 'Chimpanzees are indifferent to the welfare of unrelated group members' *Nature,* 437 (2005), pp. 1357–9 (http://userwww.service.emory.edu/~sbrosna/Manuscripts/Silk%20et%20al%20Nature%202005.pdf: accessed 18 April 2006).

[12] http://news.bbc.co.uk/2/hi/asia-pacific/4627950.stm; http://news.bbc.co.uk/2/hi/africa/ 1905363. stm

So mutually caring companionships are already more than pleasurable associations (the first and commonest form of *philia*) and more than quid-pro-quo partnerships (the second). They depend on a kind of mutual liking, a recognition of common sentiments and attitudes, that is the sentimental origin of ethics. Primatologists are not entirely wrong to use 'spatial proximity and grooming as measures of affinity between individuals', even if they are too quick to include 'the probability of future copulations' in their account of what they call friendship.[13] It is perhaps notable that adult male baboons are connected most easily to female baboons, of roughly their own age: they don't have many or any independent same-sex 'friendships'.

> Female baboons, in general, are wary of males. This is understandable: males sometimes use their larger size and formidable canines to intimidate and bully smaller troop members, Females, however, were apparently drawn to their male Friends, and they seemed surprisingly relaxed around these hulking companions, The males, too, seemed to undergo a subtle transformation when interacting with female Friends. They appeared less tense, more affectionate and more sensitive to the behavior of their partners.[14]

This sort of friendship offers an escape from the normally agonistic and antagonistic nature of baboon—and other primate—society. We aren't always rivals, or need not be. And generosity goes along with justice: it is possible to feel aggrieved that our associates and almost-friends aren't 'playing fair', and there is evidence that non-humans feel the same.[15] On the one hand we are eager to find associates to care for who will also care for us. On the other we are sensitive to betrayals, and united in a desire to see fair play.

None of this need be reckoned the result of any rational good will, any deliberate intent to comfort or console or take revenge. I am willing to assume that their behaviour is indeed the product of unreasoned sentiment, and even that these sentiments have been 'selected' as being 'fit'. But it doesn't follow that just because non-humans cannot *deliberately* prefer their friends' welfare to their own that they are therefore to be reckoned merely selfish. Nor does this follow from any post-Darwinian extravagance about the metaphorical selfishness of

---

13] Smuts, op. cit., p. 38.

14] Smuts, op. cit., p. 61.

15] Sarah F. Brosnan & Franz de Waal, 'Monkeys reject unequal pay', *Nature* 425. 2003, pp. 297–9 (http://www.emory.edu/LIVING_LINKS/capuchins/Brosnan Nature/Manuscripts/BrosnanUnequalPay.pdf accessed 18 April 2006)

genes. If they cannot distinguish the real good of others from their own comfort in companionship (as we can do) they lie 'before' that distinction. What they feel is something that, in us, can sometimes be separated: one of Owen Barfield's 'ancient unities'.[16]

Words and the Wordless

I described this as an 'hedonistic age', in which it is hard to persuade anyone that much matters more than pleasure or relief from pain. But it is also a strikingly *verbal* one: it is widely assumed that those who cannot talk can't really amount to much, even if only a few neo-Cartesians (with whom, you remember, I don't intend to argue) can bring themselves to believe, and even they half-heartedly, that those who cannot talk don't think or feel. Traditionalists who wish to defend the rights of the unborn, the infantile, the imbecile or senile, have to insist, in an ancient language, that because they are human, the imbecile and infant *must* have souls and be deserving of the same respect as rational adults. John Paul II, in *Evangelium Vitae*, makes the point, in rebuking

> the mentality which tends to equate personal dignity with the capacity for verbal and explicit, or at least perceptible, communication. It is clear that on the basis of these presuppositions there is no place in the world for anyone who, like the unborn or the dying, is a weak element in the social structure, or for anyone who appears completely at the mercy of others and radically dependent on them, and can only communicate through the silent language of a profound sharing of affection.[17]

But why, even within the older tradition, are the non-human not allowed this silent language? Where did we get the idea that only those in *human* form have the sort of souls that allow it? Why does even such a civilized theologian as Nicholas Lash unthinkingly contrast 'human beings' and 'things', as though these classes exhausted the terrestrial universe, saying that 'there is a difference between listening to a waterfall and listening to another person, and in the natural scientist's world there are only waterfalls'?[18] Even Augustine, who absorbed too much of the Stoic attitude to animals, and was

[16] Owen Barfield, *Poetic Diction: a study in meaning* (Faber: London, 1952, 2nd edn.), pp. 86ff.

[17] *Evangelium Vitae* 25th March 1995 at http://www.vatican.va/holy_father/john_paul_ii/encyclicals/documents/hf_jp-ii_enc_25031995_evangelium-vitae_en.html, §19.

[18] Lash, op. cit., p. 85.

eager to distance himself from his youthful Manichaeanism, acknowledged that many people will understand their *dog* better than they understand or appreciate a foreigner.[19] Our initial experience is often of a household where creatures of several species more or less get along: it is the outsider, the foreigner, even if of our own species, that is suspect.

The answer to my historical question is not the one that too many writers still suppose: it was not Biblical Christianity that imposed a radical disjunction between human and non-human, though there are now self-styled 'Bible Christians', especially in the States, who seem to think it part of their creed that no-one should care for animals, probably in reaction against what they suppose—not wrongly—to be the implications of evolutionary theory. Nor was it 'Greek Thought' that left us in the West this heritage, though—as I have just suggested—there were elements in that tradition that helped create the division. Nor is it reasonable to suggest that we should change things for the better by adopting 'Non-Western', Oriental or Amerindian thought patterns (which are as diverse as our own, and often even less animal-friendly).[20]

Stoics and Epicureans both rested much of moral law on some form of social contract theory,[21] and explicitly excluded those who could make no verbal contracts. Stoics also reckoned that it was only amongst human beings that there could be 'friends of God' and co-proprietors of everything, since only humans shared God's intellectual capacities (it didn't follow that *all* human beings could be friends of God, nor that they all deserved respect).[22] Platonists, who founded moral law on our intuition of the Good, and its embodiment in the 'dance of immortal love', might be expected to have a more animal-friendly outlook, whether or not they believed in metempsychosis. Platonists, including Aristotle, were also open to the recognition that there were no stable or definite boundary lines in nature, and that our formal taxonomies were only a way of thinking. Despite this, we somehow inherited the notion that boundaries

19] Augustine, *City of God*, Bk. 19, ch. 7.

20] See Rod Preece, *Animals and Nature: Cultural Myths, Cultural Realities* (University of British Columbia Press: Vancouver, 1999)

21] Though why such contracts should generate *moral* obligations remains, to me, obscure: brigands may make bargains, of a sort, with others of their gang, but ought they to abide by them?

22] This may be one unfortunate origin of the idea that everything done 'for the sake of science' is permitted (which is as much as to say that *scientists* own everything). At any rate, I can find no other excuse for this delusion!

are definite and stable, despite all the obvious counterexamples. Hybridization is either impossible or somehow rather deplorable (I shall address some of the problems this creates for transgenic engineering in a later chapter).

Language creates distinctions, and above all the distinction between those who have it and those who don't. We are then easily persuaded that verbal distinctions correspond to natural kinds—and that we must defend those boundaries.

One of Darwin's most dangerous ideas—not only his, but one that he did much to popularize—is that species are not natural kinds, but only varieties grown just a bit more different, just sufficiently different in fact as to prevent most interbreeding. A species is a reproductively isolated set of interbreeding populations, isolated either by geography or temperament or physiology. Within such isolated super-populations, genetic drift, formal convergence, and even natural selection work their magic, but there need be no species-nature universal among and peculiar to all members of a particular species. This is why 'speciesism' does indeed have the same form as 'racism', even though species are better defined than races. If we could see the whole collection of individuals belonging over time to the species in which we have an interest, we should see very few, if any, wide disjunctions.

Speciation may still be a Good Thing, whereas 'pseudo-speciation', whether based on race, class or creed, is not. 'Without isolation [that is, without speciation] all organic beings would have been nearly uniform, and all would have belonged to a single type, which would be the one best fitted to getting food and for propagating its race: a half-animal, half-vegetable, and a ruthless cannibal.'[23] Speciation allows many more creatures to share the world, by diversifying their talents and tastes, and cooperating in the construction of a living world more diversely beautiful, and more stable, than the uniform world imagined by Hutton.[24] The price is that everyone has a commitment towards, and sentiment in favour of their own particular species-life and their very own conspecifics. But those commitments and sentiments are not the

---

[23] F.W. Hutton, *Darwinism and Lamarkism* (Duckworth: London, 1899), p. 105

[24] One of the most striking examples of this is to be found in the cichlid fishes of the African Great Lakes, whose rapid speciation, and concomitant specialization, allows many more organisms a life, each in its own ecological and behavioural niche: see Denis Alexander *Creation or Evolution: do we have to choose?* (Monarch Books: Oxford, 2008), pp. 98–9.

only ones, nor even necessarily the most powerful. Conspecifics, after all, are also our chief rivals and competitors! It may actually be easier to value one's dog than a stranger: the dog, after all, is a valuable member of one's household, and whether or not he is a friend he is certainly *philos*. And for those who like to play sociobiological games, there is no reason why our *genes* should care which gene-pool they populate. They have as strong an interest, in Dawkins-speak, in their survival outside our species as within. It is true that variants, at least among eukaryotes, mostly spread within a species, but it is not so long since our ancestors *were* one species: our separation is the relatively recent thing.[25] And it has been suggested that it may also be a temporary thing: if technophiliac humanity embraces the full potential of genetic engineering, then the species-barriers are coming down. We shall all recover the prokaryotic mode of life—for bacterial populations are not isolated species-communities even now.[26]

> Now, after some three billion years, the Darwinian era is over. The epoch of species competition came to an end about 10 thousand years ago when a single species, Homo sapiens, began to dominate and reorganize the biosphere. Since that time, cultural evolution has replaced biological evolution as the driving force of change. Cultural evolution is not Darwinian. Cultures spread by horizontal transfer of ideas more than by genetic inheritance. Cultural evolution is running a thousand times faster than Darwinian evolution, taking us into a new era of cultural interdependence that we call globalization. And now, in the last 30 years, Homo sapiens has revived the ancient pre-Darwinian practice of horizontal gene transfer, moving genes easily from microbes to plants and animals, blurring the boundaries between species. We are moving rapidly into the post-Darwinian era, when species will no longer exist, and the evolution of life will again be communal.[27]

---

[25] And it is clear that our isolation, even now, is not complete: viral infection spreads genes across species boundaries: Alexander, op. cit., p. 118 describes the viral population as 'a giant gene production factory, generating a constant stream of new information, some of which is taken up and adapted for use by other genomes'.

[26] Some of this material is also addressed in 'Elves, Hobbits, Trolls and Talking Beasts', in Celia Deane-Drummond & David Clough (eds.), *Creaturely Theology* (SCM Press: London, forthcoming).

[27] Freeman Dyson, 'The Darwinian Interlude' in *Technology Review* March 2005, at http:// www.technologyreview.com/read_article.aspx?id=14236&ch=biotech, after Carl Woese, 'A New Biology for a New Century' in *Microbiology and Molecular Biology Reviews*, June 2004. In another sense, it is worth noting, it is only

Dyson does not draw any particular morals for our present situation, though he sketches a future in which home biotech packs are readily available: 'There will be do-it-yourself kits for gardeners who will use genetic engineering to breed new varieties of roses and orchids. Also kits for lovers of pigeons and parrots and lizards and snakes, to breed new varieties of pets. Breeders of dogs and cats will have their kits too.'[28]

Modern thought has drifted far from the metaphysical and biological theories that, once upon a time, validated the conviction that non-human creatures were all so different from 'us' that we could not possibly be 'friends'. Each of us, human or non-human, is the product of a set of genes almost all of which are widely shared between species: there are probably no specifically human genes, no genes that belong only and entirely within 'the human genome', and no specifically human patterns of behaviour. There is a risk that we shall slide into a future where individual self-hood is forgotten, where the world-hive generates whatever mobile units, with whatever functions, that it temporarily desires. One thing that may preserve us from this future is the memory of friendship, the memory, that is, that individual creatures *matter*, that a soul is worth the saving. Chesterton could think, or at any rate conjecture, that it was only *human* souls worth this, and that any attempt to equate human and non-human led only to the inhuman. But he also suggested, 'for those who like such biological fancies, ... that we stand as chiefs and champions of a whole section of nature, princes of the house whose cognisance is the backbone, standing for the milk of the individual mother and the courage of the wandering cub, representing the pathetic chivalry of the dog, the humour and perversity of cats, the affection of the tranquil horse, the loneliness of the lion.'[29]

Those who suppose that animals cannot be our friends do so because they doubt that animals are ever real individuals, whose

---

the vast and rapidly breeding bacterial and viral population that evolves at a molecular level by the strictly Darwinian means of random variation, and differential reproduction of those variations. In multicellular and especially bisexual organisms things get much more complicated very quickly.

[28] Freeman Dyson, 'The Future of Evolution', 'originally a talk for fiftieth anniversary of the death of Teilhard de Chardin at Marist College, Poughkeepsie, 14 May, 2005', published by Metanexus Institute 13 October 2005 http://www.metanexus.net/metanexus_ online /show_article2.asp?id=9361 (accessed 26 April 2006). This paper incorporates material from the one in Technology Review.

[29] Chesterton, *What's Wrong* op. cit., p. 263f.

soul is worth the saving. Animals are to be valued, if at all, entirely for the good they do us. On this account, it is not unreasonable, though it may well be utterly impractical, to require cloned copies of dead pets. Those who more truly loved their non-human companions would no more desire this outcome than a lover would be pleased by the substitution of his beloved's twin, or a well-designed replica. In friendship we encounter an individual, not a type, and don't transfer our loyalties so quickly.

This study involves a triangular affair. In one corner are the traditionalists, maintaining with whatever excuse or metaphysical conviction, that non-human and human animals are 'ships that pass in the night', whose interests and ideas are entirely opaque to each other. 'A turkey [for example] is more occult and awful than all the angels and archangels.'[30] Any friendship that may seem to exist between such different entities can only be superficial, a mere liking for the other's physical presence. And though Chesterton insisted that we should *respect* these other, inscrutable creatures, the practical effect of the doctrine is to endorse most of our existing, exploitative, destructive practices. In the second corner are the modernists, for whom species boundaries are temporary and easily subvertible, and whose metaphysics hardly allow the real existence of individuals at all (though they may retain some superstitions on the subject). The practical effect is very much what Chesterton feared: the transformation of persons as well as animals into tools. And in the third corner are those, like myself, who acknowledge that species makes little difference, but wish to insist on the reality of those we love or might love. *Homo sapiens* is a species: *Humanity* is an ideal.

Stratford Caldecott has summarized the thought of Hans Urs von Balthasar as follows.[31]

> As a natural faculty, even before it is 'supernaturalized' by the indwelling of God's Holy Spirit at baptism, the spiritual intellect or *apex mentis* is the organ of metaphysics. It is recognized in all religious traditions, and the knowledge of universals which it gives (however distorted and confused after the Fall) is part of the common heritage of humanity. This is the faculty which perceives all things as symbolic in their very nature; that is, as expressing the attributes of God. Thus Hans Urs von Balthasar writes: 'The whole world of images that surrounds us is a single

---

[30] G.K. Chesterton, *All Things Considered* (Methuen & Co: London, 1908), p. 220

[31] Stratford Caldecott, 'Liturgy and Trinity: Towards an Anthropology of the Liturgy': http: //www.tcrnews2.com/caldecott.html (accessed 4/4/2006)

field of significations. Every flower we see is an expression, every landscape has its significance, every human or animal face speaks its wordless language. It would be utterly futile to attempt a transposition of this language into concepts.... This expressive language is addressed primarily, not to conceptual thought, but to the kind of intelligence that perceptively reads the *gestalt* of things.'

Whatever name we give it ('intellect', 'imagination' or 'heart'), what Balthasar has in mind here is a faculty that transcends yet at the same time unifies feeling and thought, body and soul, sensation and rationality. It is the kind of intelligence that sees the meaning in things, that reads them as symbols—symbols, not of something else, but of *themselves as they stand in God*. Thus in the spiritual intelligence of man, being is unveiled in its true nature as a gift bearing within it the love of the Giver. Ultimately things—just as truly as persons—can be truly known only through love. In other words, a thing can be known only when it draws us out of ourselves, when we grasp it in its otherness from ourselves, in the meaning which it possesses as beauty, uniting truth and goodness. This kind of knowledge is justly called *sobria ebrietas* ('drunken' sobriety) because it is ecstatic, rapturous, although at the same time measured, ordered, dignified. It is an encounter with the Other which takes the heart out of itself and places it in another centre, which is ultimately the very centre of being, where all things are received from God.

We know things truly only through love, and love is a recognition of something Other, something single. Animals become our friends, we become their friends, when they look back at us, and we are confronted by the mystery of the Other which is at the root also of our own being. Suddenly, we realize that they are *alive*.[32] They are not to be respected merely because they are rather *like* us, but because in many respects they aren't. Non-humans aren't, in human terms, as clever as we are, but neither are we, in their terms, as clever as *they* are. Language is not all important, and the boundaries it creates are there to be transcended. We can 'communicate through the silent language of a profound sharing of affection'. Pythagoras heard his friend, and knew him by his voice.

---

[32] I do not deny that this realization may sometimes horrify us: that horror is one reason why atheism is sometimes attractive. But it is open to us, along with Plotinus, to *welcome* the reality: 'beautifulness is reality' (*Ennead*, I.6 [1].6, 21), and the proper response is awe.

6

What's Wrong with Darwinian Evolution?

Social Darwinism

Any examination of the nature of faith must touch on the theory that is widely supposed to have supplanted it. There is a kind of conspiracy between militant atheists and 'fundamentalists' to insist that 'real' religion is anti-Darwinian. One response is nearly universal amongst educated believers: namely, that God may as easily create the world by evolutionary stages as by discrete, creative actions. This is certainly true, but it is perhaps not the end of the story. Any serious attempt to question the theory is likely to be misrepresented, when it is not simply ignored. I have myself found that Darwinists often seem incapable of believing that any question could possibly be intended seriously: they suppose that the critic simply *must* be ill-informed, or stupid, or with some personal, concealed, agenda that depends on denying obvious truth. This is a very strange attitude for people who think themselves scientists, or at any rate 'scientific'. Physicists are allowed to question Einstein, or quantum mechanics, or superstring theory, or even the Big Bang. They are even allowed to mention God.[2] Mainstream biologists display, at

---

1] Some of this material has also been used in my *G.K. Chesterton: Thinking Backward, Looking Forward* (Templeton Foundation Press: West Conshohocken, 2006). I also spoke on the topic at the conference in honour of John Hedley Brooke, on *Science and Religion*, held at Lancaster University in July 2007.

2] Though Frank J. Tipler notes that, in the USA at least, any physical theory implying or even seeming to imply that God exists is considered scandalous, and a reason for rejecting the theory out of hand: see Frank J. Tipler, 'Refereed Journals: do they insure quality or enforce orthodoxy?' in Dembski *Uncommon Dissent*, op. cit., pp. 115–30.

times, a quite intolerable conceit, and its concomitant deafness to all enquiry.

It is important always to distinguish different elements in evolutionary theory. It is one thing to say that biological history reaches back for many million years, and that the fossil record suggests very strongly that there were many creatures alive in the past of other kinds than any we can see here-now. It is another to agree that the present similarities, both phenotypical and genotypical, of existing creatures suggest that those creatures are genealogically related, and may indeed all stem from some one primordial ancestor. It is yet a third thing to suggest that undirected variation and natural selection are together enough to explain the past and present diversity of living creatures, and that the Enlightenment decision to abandon 'final causes' in our account of nature (of which I spoke before) has now been vindicated. The first two theses are ones that, personally, I find attractive. The third seems to me to be unproven, perhaps unprovable, and clearly very dangerous.

It is dangerous especially in the form that we now identify as 'Social Darwinism' (though whether that differs from *Darwinism* in any significant detail is obscure). G.K. Chesterton debated publicly, in 1931, with Clarence Darrow, the lawyer on the side of 'science' in 'the Monkey Trials',[3] and remarked afterwards that 'he felt as if Darrow had been arguing all afternoon with a fundamentalist aunt, and simply kept sparring with a dummy of his own making'.[4] His own opposition to Darwinian—not yet *neo-Darwinian* – theory did not rest on any 'fundamentalist' or literalist interpretation of Biblical texts or Christian doctrine, nor was it obscurantist or 'anti-scientific'. His approach guides mine.

The Darwinism that he opposed—and Bryan opposed—was an ethical and metaphysical doctrine that denied the ancient standards of justice, love and chastity. In the words of H.G.Wells, writing in

[3] See also G.K. Chesterton, *Fancies versus Fads* (Methuen: London, 1923), pp. 179ff; see Edward J. Larson, *Summer for the Gods: The Scopes Trial and America's Continuing Debate over Science and Religion* (Harvard University Press: Boston, 1998) for an account of the political and economic context of the trial; Stephen Jay Gould, *Rocks of Ages: Science and Religion in the Fullness of Life* (London: Jonathan Cape, 1999) gives a good understanding of William Jennings Bryan's humanitarian motives (Bryan being Darrow's adversary in the Scopes Trial). It must be noted that the Broadway play (1955) broadly based on this episode, *Inherit the Wind,* and the later film (directed by Stanley Kramer, 1960) are thoroughly misleading.

[4] Maisie Ward, *Gilbert Keith Chesterton* (Sheed & Ward: London, 1944), p. 497

1904, 'if the universe is non-ethical by our present standards, we must reconsider those standards and reconstruct our ethics.'[5] Wells drew the conclusion that we should cooperate with the Darwinian process, and thence that we should kill off all inferior or inconvenient forms.[6] Everything is 'integral', but some things ('weak and silly and pointless things') serve only by being destroyed. The New Republicans of Wells's imagination, remember, will have no pity for such 'contemptible and silly creatures', and 'to make life convenient for the breeding of such people will seem to them not the most virtuous and amiable thing in the world ... but an exceedingly abominable proceeding. ... The procreation of children who by the circumstances of their parentage, *must* be diseased bodily or mentally ... is absolutely the most loathsome of all conceivable sins.'[7]

There were social Darwinists and eugenicists who did not go quite so far—at least in public. But Chesterton was right that a similar creed could be found in hidden places. Consider Father Brown's rebuke to a gaggle of dons at dinner: 'It is Capitalism you take for granted; or rather the vices of Capitalism disguised as a dead Darwinism. Do you recall what you were all saying in the Common Room, about life being only a scramble, and nature demanding the survival of the fittest, and how it doesn't matter whether the poor are paid justly or not? Why *that* is the heresy you have grown accustomed to.'[8] On the global stage the matter could be even worse:

> The colonial ideal of such men as Cecil Rhodes did not arise out of any fresh creative idea of the Western genius, it was a fad, and like most fads an imitation. For what was wrong with Rhodes was not that, like Cromwell or Hildebrand, he made huge mistakes, nor even that he committed great crimes. It was that he committed these crimes and errors in order to spread certain ideas. And when one asked for the ideas they could not be found. Cromwell stood for Calvinism, Hildebrand for Catholicism: but Rhodes had no principles whatever to give to the world. He had only a hasty but elaborate machinery for spreading the principles that he hadn't got. What he called his ideals were the dregs of a Darwinism which had already grown not only stagnant, but poi-

---

5] Wells, *Anticipations* (1902) ch. 9: in *Anticipations and Other Works* (Fisher Unwin: London, 1924), p. 248

6] *Ibid.*, pp. 253f

7] *Anticipations* pp. 257f

8] The Crime of the Communist' in the *Scandal of Father Brown* (Cassell: London, 1935), p. 178f

> sonous. That the fittest must survive, and that any one like himself must be the fittest; that the weakest must go to the wall, and that any one he could not understand must be the weakest; that was the philosophy which he lumberingly believed through life, like many another agnostic old bachelor of the Victorian era. All his views on religion ... were simply the stalest ideas of his time. It was not his fault, poor fellow, that he called a high hill somewhere in South Africa 'his church'. It was not his fault, I mean, that he could not see that a church all to oneself is not a church at all. It is a madman's cell. It was not his fault that he 'figured out that God meant as much of the planet to be Anglo-Saxon as possible'. Many evolutionists much wiser had 'figured out' things even more babyish. He was an honest and humble recipient of the plodding popular science of his time; he spread no ideas that any cockney clerk in Streatham could not have spread for him. But it was exactly because he had no ideas to spread that he invoked slaughter, violated justice, and ruined republics to spread them.[9]

It is against this background that we need to consider Chesterton's lifelong aversion to Darwinian Theory,[10] and also the present widespread antagonism towards Darwinian Theory, especially in America. What Darwinism and Malthusianism actually meant in living political thought and practice, as I remarked in an earlier chapter, was that *justice did not matter.* Perhaps this was not the proper, 'scientific' meaning of his theory (on which more later), but it was the social meaning.

In fact, there was a further implication. Wells and others thought that evolution happened with disarming speed. "We can realize now, as no one in the past was ever able to realise it, that man is a creature changing very rapidly from the life of a rare and solitary ape

---

[9] 'The Sultan', from *A Miscellany of Men* (HIS press: Norfolk, 2004; 1st published 1912), p. 128f.

[10] It is worth adding that he named Darwin himself as one of those of whom the English should be far more proud than they were of the arts of conquest: 'It would not be in the least extraordinary if a claim of eating up provinces and pulling down princes were the chief boast of a Zulu. The extraordinary thing is, that it is the chief boast of a people who have Shakespeare, Newton, Burke, and Darwin to boast of. ' ('In Defence of Patriotism', in *The Defendant* (1901) http://www.gutenberg.net/dirs/1/2/2/4/12245/12245-h/12245-h.htm. He offered cogent criticisms especially of Burke and Darwin, but this was compatible with a profound admiration for their intellectual powers, and a recognition of their global significance.

to the life of a social and economic animal."[11] He accepted Arthur Keith's estimate that there had been changes in the face and skull within the last five thousand years.[12]

Human beings—as long as we did not wantonly preserve the silly and contemptible, nor helped them procreate—would swiftly evolve still further, into all appropriate forms. It is hardly surprising that Chesterton saw that on these terms, "[T]he employer need not mind sending a Kaffir underground; he will soon become an underground animal, like a mole. ... Men need not trouble to alter conditions; conditions will so soon alter men. The head can be beaten small enough to fit the hat. Do not knock the fetters off the slave; knock the slave until he forgets the fetters."[13] It is by these techniques after all that we have bred domestic beasts to servitude, because we have been bold enough to kill or castrate "poor stock." And what *counts* as poor stock will depend on the uses that we have for them.

> The sub-conscious popular instinct against Darwinism was ... that when once one begins to think of man as a shifting and alterable thing, it is always easy for the strong and crafty to twist him into new shapes for all kinds of unnatural purposes. The popular instinct sees in such developments the possibility of backs bowed and hunch-backed for their burden, or limbs twisted for their task. It has a very well-grounded guess that whatever is done swiftly and systematically will mostly be done by a successful class and almost solely in their interests. It has therefore a vision of unhuman hybrids and half-human experiments much in the style of Mr. Wells's Island of Dr Moreau ... The rich man may come to be breeding a tribe of dwarfs to be his jockeys, and a tribe of giants to be his hall-porters.[14]

Wells's contempt at 'the spectacle of a mean-spirited, under-sized, diseased little man, quite incapable of earning a decent living even

[11] H.G. Wells, *Mr Belloc Objects*, op. cit., p. 53. Wells's claim is simply mistaken: our ancestors, even if they were more like modern apes than we are, were certainly not solitary. See Wiktor Stoczkowski. *Explaining Human Origins: Myth, Imagination and Conjecture,* trans. Mary Turton (Cambridge University Press: Cambridge, 2002) for an excellent account of the mythological origins of much popular and even 'scientific' speculation about prehistory.

[12] Wells, op. cit., pp. 30f, after Arthur Keith at the Royal Society of Medicine Nov 16th 1925. Something like this may perhaps turn out to be true: see recent work by Henry Harpending described at http://www. physorg. com/news116529402. html (accessed 20 December 2007). Harpending does not suggest that this gives any support to proposals to deny some populations equal rights.

[13] *What's Wrong,* p. 22

[14] *What's Wrong,* p. 259

for himself, married to a some underfed, ignorant, ill-shaped, plain and diseased little woman, and guilty of the lives of ten or twelve ugly ailing children'[15] could be conjoined with happy admiration of some other human animals, adapted to their station. What he looks forward to, it seems, is an imitation of the form of life achieved by the social insects or the denizens of his Moon.[16] In fairness to Wells, it should be noted that only a few years later he denounced the attitude that says 'when the convict tramps past us—"There goes another sort of animal that is differentiating from my species and which I would gladly see exterminated"'.[17] Maybe Chesterton had influenced him for the better (or maybe he admired the convict precisely for being *criminal*: that is, for not subscribing to outworn, superstitious norms of decency and justice).

Darwinists typically supposed that there were inferior (often mistakenly called 'less-evolved') races, both human and nonhuman. They also thought that individual specimens might be inferior, and that it was important that social arrangements should reveal this inferiority.

> Among the innumerable muddles, which mere materialistic fashion made out of the famous theory, there was in many quarters a queer idea that the Struggle for Existence was of necessity an actual struggle between the candidates for survival; literally a cut-throat competition. There was a vague idea that the strongest creature violently crushed the others. And the notion that this was the one method of improvement came everywhere as good news to bad men; to bad rulers, to bad employers, to swindlers and sweaters and the rest. The brisk owner of a bucket-shop compared himself modestly to a mammoth, trampling down other mammoths in the primeval jungle. The business man destroyed other business men, under the extraordinary delusion that the eohippic horse had devoured other eohippic horses. The rich man suddenly discovered that it was not only convenient but cosmic to starve or pillage the poor, because pterodactyls may have used their little hands to tear each other's eyes. Science, that nameless being, declared that the weakest must go to the wall; especially in Wall Street. There was a rapid decline and degradation in the sense of responsibility in the rich, from the merely rationalistic eighteenth century to the purely scientific nine-

[15] *Anticipations*, p. 264

[16] See *The First Men in the Moon* (1901); see *What's Wrong*, p. 263 on the 'soul of the hive' as described by Maeterlink.

[17] *The Problem of the Birth Supply: Anticipations and other works*, p. 322

> teenth. The great Jefferson, when he reluctantly legalised slavery, said he trembled for his country, knowing that God is just. The profiteer of later times, when he legalised usury or financial trickery, was satisfied with himself; knowing that Nature is unjust.[18]

It was also a doctrine that the ruling classes chose to impose upon the public. 'In the lower classes the schoolmaster does not work for the parent but against the parent. Modern education means handing down the customs of the minority, and rooting out the customs of the majority.'[19] Specifically, it meant instructing children to despise everything their parents thought and felt,[20] including any residual respect for justice. The issue was only marginally about a scientific theory—the theory, that is, of gradual change through differential reproduction. It was about the implications of that theory as it was expounded by men ignorant of the actual theory. The same is probably true of William Jennings Bryan, who led the prosecution team in Tennessee, and had been influential in banning the teaching of 'evolution' (that is, racist and imperialist theories masquerading as science).[21]

The problem was made worse because Darwinians, even Darwin himself, did not have a clear notion of *inheritance*, nor of 'genes'. Children inherit many things from their parents, not all of them by way

[18] 'The Return to Religion' in *The Well and the Shallows* (Sheed & Ward: London, 1935).

[19] *What's Wrong*, p. 248

[20] See also M. Canovan, *G.K. Chesterton: Radical Populist* (New York and London: Harcourt Brace Jovanovitch, 1977), p. 56.

[21] The book that was the occasion for the Scopes Trial was George William Hunter's *A Civic Biology: presented in problems* (American Book Co: New York, 1914), which contains such passages as this: 'Parasitism and its Cost to Society. —Hundreds of families such as those described above exist today, spreading disease, immorality, and crime to all parts of this country. The cost to society of such families is very severe. Just as certain animals or plants become parasitic on other plants or animals, these families have become parasitic on society. They not only do harm to others by corrupting, stealing, or spreading disease, but they are actually protected and cared for by the state out of public money. Largely for them the poorhouse and the asylum exist. They take from society, but they give nothing in return. They are true parasites. The Remedy.—If such people were lower animals, we would probably kill them off to prevent them from spreading. Humanity will not allow this, but we do have the remedy of separating the sexes in asylums or other places and in various ways preventing intermarriage and the possibilities of perpetuating such a low and degenerate race. Remedies of this sort have been tried successfully in Europe and are now meeting with some success in this country' (taken from http://en. wikipedia.org/wiki/Civic_Biology, accessed 18 June 2007). This was not an isolated or eccentric suggestion.

of DNA, and the features which were usually identified as disabilities or diseases were, to our eyes, socially rather than biologically engendered.

> In a popular magazine there is one of the usual articles about criminology; about whether wicked men could be made good if their heads were taken to pieces. As by far the wickedest men I know of are much too rich and powerful ever to submit to the process, the speculation leaves me cold. I always notice with pain, however, a curious absence of the portraits of living millionaires from such galleries of awful examples; most of the portraits in which we are called upon to remark the line of the nose or the curve of the forehead appear to be the portraits of ordinary sad men, who stole because they were hungry or killed because they were in a rage. The physical peculiarity seems to vary infinitely; sometimes it is the remarkable square head, sometimes it is the unmistakable round head; sometimes the learned draw attention to the abnormal development, sometimes to the striking deficiency of the back of the head. I have tried to discover what is the invariable factor, the one permanent mark of the scientific criminal type; after exhaustive classification I have to come to the conclusion that it consists in being poor.[22]

Two inferences were open to Darwinians of this stamp. The first and simplest was to conclude, with Wells, that

> It has become apparent that whole masses of the human population are as a whole inferior in their claim upon the future to other masses, that they cannot be given opportunities or trusted with power as the superior peoples are trusted, that their characteristic weaknesses are contagious and detrimental in the civilizing fabric, and their range of incapacity tempts and demoralizes the strong. To give them equality is to sink to their level, to protect and cherish them is to be swamped in their fecundity.[23]

So his New Republicans will sterilize and kill all those considered surplus to requirements. They may control them by "scientific" torture,[24] but will usually find it easier to kill offenders. 'They will contrive a land legislation that will keep the black or yellow or mean-

---

[22] "A Criminal Head" in *Alarms and Discursions*, http://www.gutenberg.net/dirs/etext06/aldsc10. txt.

[23] *Anticipations*, p. 250.

[24] *Anticipations*, p. 259

white squatter on the move' to prevent their procreating.[25] It was Wells's expectation (and incidentally, Darwin's) that 'the inferior races', including 'mean-white' trash, would be extinguished unless they could prove useful. Consider also Ernst Haeckel and his Monist League: 'The "redemption from evil" [for the ill, deformed and criminal] should be accomplished by a dose of some painless and rapid poison.'[26] Consider the members and supporters of the Eugenics Society, with their sub-Nietzschean dreams of breeding 'supermen', and disposing of 'the unfit' by whatever easy means. No doubt some of them 'didn't really mean it', but 'there is something disquieting [to put it very mildly] about the "respectable" members of the society, most of whom would have been horrified by the slightest whiff of Bolshevist barbarism, sitting in their comfortable lounges discussing the need to eliminate the unfit, without seriously considering the terrible implications of realizing such vague visions.'[27] And some of them really did mean it.

An alternative inference, founded in a suspicion that perhaps not all inherited characteristics are inherited 'through the seed', was to remove children from their parents and their peers, to rear them under proper 'scientific' guidance, or at least—as above—to break down parental influence. As Chesterton said, '[N]obody could pretend that the affectionate mother of a rather backward child *deserves* to be punished by having all the happiness taken out of her life. But anyone can pretend that the act is needed for the happiness of the community'[28]—or the imagined 'health' of the race. The practice

---

[25] *Anticipations*, p. 263.

[26] *Wonders of Life* (Harper: New York, 1904), pp. 118f, cited by D. Gasman, *The Scientific Origins of National Socialism* (Macdonald: London 1971), p. 95. Militant atheists—and perhaps especially Amazon reviewers—are enraged by the suggestion that Darwinism had anything to do with the Holocaust. They retort at once that anti-semitism was endemic in Christian Europe, and needed no assistance from biologists. What they choose to forget is that it was not only Jews that suffered: the Nazis followed the 'best intellectual advice' (as above) in killing imbeciles and lunatics before they advanced on homosexuals, Jews and Gypsies, all conceived as 'degenerate' and deserving no respect. Edwin Black in *War against the Weak,* op. cit., has shown, with extensive documentation, that the programme of genetic cleansing was initially devised in America, with the active support of philanthropists and doctors. It is not surprising that Chesterton had a low opinion of such 'philanthropy'.

[27] Stone, op. cit., p. 85. Bolshevist barbarism, of course, might actually have threatened *them*: their own schemes, they could imagine, were threats only to the poor, the 'feeble-minded' and the alien immigrant.

[28] Chesterton, *Fancies versus Fads*, p. 91.

continued, at the expense of the poor, and the native populations of conquered countries, for many decades. Only very recently have governments even begun to apologize.

I should add that eugenicists of either sort drew entirely the wrong inferences from evolutionary theory, even if all we minded or should mind about is having some descendants. It is the more *diverse* lineage that is likeliest to have the resources to continue in a changing world: if only those who seem *at present* to be the 'fittest' are allowed to breed, according to whatever fashionable and usually unreasoned account of 'fitness',[29] our future possibilities are restricted. In the end, if this were permitted, the human population would be as monotonous, as vulnerable and probably as damaged as any fashionable breed of domestic creature. Only in the clearest and most certainly destructive cases is it reasonable to try and eliminate 'a gene': who knows what other characters we would lose in the attempt, and what other possibilities in changed times?

Some Problems with Scientific Darwinism

Chesterton also voiced some merely scientific objections to the original theory, ones that had been raised almost from the beginning (for, contrary to scientific myth, the opposition to Darwin's theory in the early years was led by scientists, not clerics). First, that the theory required that each new stage must be both viable and profitable long before the final version appeared. 'If a thing can fly it may survive, and if it has a wing it may fly; but if it cannot fly with half a wing, why should it survive with half a wing?'[30] One immediate response is that the genealogical route to having a wing does not pass through a stage of having half a wing, but rather (say) through having feathers and gliding flaps: organs that perhaps work less well than a developed wing, but well enough to give an advantage to the owner. There *must* have been a pathway from the wingless to the winged condition, each stage *must* have given a Darwinian advantage, and

[29] Black, op. cit., records the efforts of America's eugenicists to have all imaginably hereditary 'weaknesses' eliminated, including myopia, migraine, illiteracy—and not being 'Nordic' enough. What else they would have eliminated alongside these 'weaknesses', by whatever oppressive and unconstitutional means (sterilization, castration and imprisonment) they apparently never paused to consider.

[30] Chesterton, *Fancies versus Fads*, op. cit. p. 187; see also *G.B. Shaw* (Bodley Head: London 1935, 2nd edn.), p. 284, where he comments on the 'coincidence that animals should grow organs which are useful at the moment, while at the same moment they grow organs that will be useful centuries hence'.

none emerged more rapidly than they would 'at random'. But these remain articles of faith, not empirical observations. The more recent form of this objection has to do with the notion of 'irreducible complexity': cases, that is, where the whole system has to be working together to be viable, and does not seem to be composable from earlier systems or subsystems unless some sort of forward-looking intelligence is at work (the example most often cited—and also often disputed—is the bacterial flagellum, a bidirectional propeller, but actually almost all organic systems have a similar character). Committed Darwinists are of course unanimous in insisting that such complexities must after all have developed from earlier, simpler systems by undirected variation and natural selection, but it is not entirely clear that they have established even that this *could* have happened, let alone that it did. Their argument seems to be that there *must* have been such indirect Darwinian pathways simply because Darwinian Theory rules.[31] This is not satisfactory. It is one thing, as it were, to show that the butler *could* have committed the crime (perhaps by some technique of which we can give no detailed or refutable account), and quite another to prove he did.[32] Special creationists are rarely allowed to get away with 'explaining' features of the natural world by saying that God did it, somehow or other, for some unknown reason. It is odd that Darwinists so often appeal to an exactly parallel maxim: that the form of a living creature is certainly the outcome of unknown 'natural' processes selected by some circumstance we cannot now identify, merely because, perhaps, it could have been.[33]

A second objection turns on the actual absence in the record of the many intervening stages that each lineage must have had, if Darwin were correct. Darwin himself acknowledged the difficulty. Their absence has easy explanations: the whole record is so patchy that we

[31] See William A. Dembski, *The Design Revolution; answering the toughest questions about intelligent design* (Intervarsity Press: Leicester, 2004), pp. 110ff.

[32] As Alvin Plantinga points out in a review of *The God Delusion*, the form of Richard Dawkins' argument in *The Blind Watchmaker* is that 'We know of no irrefutable objections to its being possible that p; Therefore p is true': 'The Dawkins Confusion: naturalism ad absurdum', *Christianity Today/Books and Culture*, March/April 2007. 13, pp. 21ff: http://www.christianitytoday.com/bc/2007/002/1.21.html, accessed 19th April 2008.

[33] 'Cladists' are generally content to discover, through the analysis of hereditable characteristics, that particular creatures belong in some particular line of descent, a clade, without troubling to invent any fables about how the variations happened: see Henry Gee, *Deep Time: cladistics, the revolution in evolution* (Fourth Estate: London, 2000). This seems a commendable restraint.

are lucky to have as much as we do. But though their absence does not disprove the theory, it can hardly—as Chesterton observed—establish it. If a horned devil had walked along the beach at Brighton we could conceive any number of reasons why its footprints can't be found—but no-one would sensibly suggest that their absence proved the story![34] More seriously (and to anticipate a later issue), talk of 'missing links' tends to suggest that certain creatures—and in the end *all* creatures—are no more than a passing phase, rather than creatures 'in their own right'.[35] Those who thought that there were once 'partially human' people were all too likely to think that there are still such 'partial humans', 'less evolved' creatures destined to extinction:[36] those, like Chesterton, who believed that all human beings were *people*, were inclined to believe that humanity—and maybe other creaturely kinds—appeared abruptly.[37]

The third—and until the 1930s the most serious—objection is that only asexual organisms, reproducing parthenogenetically, can guarantee to pass their advantageous features on. Suppose it is true that one particular creature has some feature that enables it to beget or bear more offspring than its rivals. It does not follow at all that its offspring will have that feature. Until the rediscovery—and better understanding—of Mendelian genetics the dominant opinion was that inheritance was *blended*: the children of a tall man and a shorter woman might be taller than their mother, but not as tall as their

---

[34] Chesterton, *Fancies versus Fads*, op. cit. p. 192. Genomic analysis, unavailable in Darwin's day, does something to fill in the gaps—or at least gives us some reason to agree that there really are identifiable 'clades'. Whether variation has always been gradual or has, occasionally, been abrupt is not easily decidable from either the fossil evidence or from genomic analysis.

[35] Cf. F. Nietzsche, *Thus Spake Zarathustra* 'The Salutation' (Dent & Sons: London, 1933), p. 249: 'You are mere bridges: may men higher than you stride over you. You signify steps: therefore do not be angry with him who climbs over you to his height'.

[36] See James A. Herrick, *Scientific Mythologies: How Science and Science Fiction forge New Religious Beliefs* (Intervarsity Press: Downers Grove, Illinois, 2008) for an account of the pervasive influence of these ideas in science fiction and pseudo-science.

[37] See Chesterton, *The Everlasting Man*, p. 47: 'I shall waste no further space on these speculations on the nature of man before he became man. His body may have been evolved from the brutes; but we know nothing of any such transition that throws the smallest light upon his soul as it has shown itself in history.' We do now know rather more about the psychological characters we share with other creatures, but there is still some reason to doubt that past transitions were merely *gradual* ones.

father. The tendency would always be to revert to the average height within that population (a notion that was itself employed by Eugenicists as an 'argument' against 'miscegenation'[38]). Occasional freaks might have more immediate offspring, but not necessarily more descendants. Only the discovery that inheritance might sometimes be particulate offered a solution. So until that discovery Darwin's theory, however elegant, could not be made to work. It was a metaphor, not a mechanism, and Chesterton was right to say that it was moribund.[39]

Fourthly, Chesterton was right to suspect the very idea of 'Fitness':

> We breed cows for milk; and not for a moral balance of particular virtues in the cow. We breed pigs to turn them into pork and not to exhibit their portraits as pictures of perfect and harmonious beauty. In other words, we can breed cows and pigs precisely because we cannot really criticize cows and pigs. We cannot judge them from the point of view of the Cow Concept or the Pig Ideal.[40]

Particular features may explain why certain organisms have more offspring, in a particular context. But whether their combination adds up to a harmonious whole is something that we cannot predict—as Wells too had said. Even physical beauty 'is neither a simple nor a constant thing; it is attainable through a variety of combinations.'[41] Chesterton amplified the point:

> Mr. Wells' point was this. That we cannot be certain about the inheritance of health, because health is not a quality. It is not a thing like darkness in the hair or length in the limbs. It is a relation, a balance. You have a tall, strong man; but his very strength depends on his not being too tall for his strength. You catch a healthy, full-blooded fellow; but his very health depends on his being not too full of blood. A heart that is strong for a dwarf will

38] See Black, op. cit., p. 274, citing Adolf Hitler's borrowings from American Eugenicism: 'any crossing of two beings not at exactly the same level produces a medium between the level of the two parents'.

39] In fact, the situation, arguably, hasn't much changed: it is easy enough to *say* that some phenotypical variation can be created by random variation at the molecular level, to be preserved and refined through later generations (that is, simultaneously retained and altered), but all stages of this process remain obscure.

40] Chesterton, *Avowals and Denials* (Methuen: London, 1934), p. 59; *Brave New Family* p. 204.

41] *Anticipations and Other Works*, p. 313;

> be weak for a giant; a nervous system that would kill a man with a trace of a certain illness will sustain him to ninety if he has no trace of that illness. Nay, the same nervous system might kill him if he had an excess of some other comparatively healthy thing. Seeing, therefore, that there are apparently healthy people of all types, it is obvious that if you mate two of them, you may even then produce a discord out of two inconsistent harmonies. It is obvious that you can no more be certain of a good offspring than you can be certain of a good tune if you play two fine airs at once on the same piano. You can be even less certain of it in the more delicate case of beauty, of which the Eugenists talk a great deal. Marry two handsome people whose noses tend to the aquiline, and their baby (for all you know) may be a goblin with a nose like an enormous parrot's. Indeed, I actually know a case of this kind. The Eugenist has to settle, not the result of fixing one steady thing to a second steady thing; but what will happen when one toppling and dizzy equilibrium crashes into another.[42]

If that is a problem for Eugenists, it is also so for 'Nature'. If natural selection works on particular attributes, then it will—almost certainly—fail to preserve even the most immediately 'fit' beyond a few generations. Commercially bred turkeys may provide the flesh the breeders' customers require: they would not last long in the wild. If, on the other hand, it is the whole organism that is or is not 'fit', the particular contributions of hereditable properties will be incalculable, nor can we have much reason to suppose that variations in those properties will be preserved. The presently popular idea that it is single 'genes', genotypic variations linked to specific phenotypic characters, that compete to reproduce themselves is at best a gross simplification (and an unhelpful criterion for picking out 'a gene' in any case).[43]

---

[42] See Chesterton, *Eugenics* (1922), ch. 6: (taken from http://www.dur.ac.uk/martin.ward/ gkc/books/Eugenics.html).

[43] It used to be that 'a gene' was a set of codons, not necessarily contiguous, that together instruct the relevant cell, if it 'chooses' to obey, to construct some particular protein (itself made up of many amino-acids), though there is no one-for-one correspondence of gene and protein (since there are many more proteins than there are genes to ask for them). Other codons or sets of codons act to turn 'genes' on or off. Yet others, so far, may only be backups, or even parasites. Recent studies suggest that inheritance is even more complicated than we thought, and the notion of 'a gene' even more contestable. See Helen Pearson 'What is a gene?,' *Nature*, 441, 398–401 (25 May 2006). By popular extension, a gene is whatever feature of the genome that appears to be present in an organism displaying one particular feature, and not in organisms that don't (or by yet

Chesterton's fifth problem with Darwinism, and probably the one that exercised him most, was that Darwinists, unlike earlier evolutionary theorists, denied that there were distinct 'natural kinds', and so conceded, as p. 136 above, that there were and might be 'partial humans'.

> If evolution simply means that a positive thing called an ape turned very slowly into a positive thing called a man, then it is stingless for the most orthodox; for a personal God might just as well do things slowly as quickly, especially if, like the Christian God, he were outside time. But if it means anything more, it means that there is no such thing as an ape to change, and no such thing as a man for him to change into.[44]

Darwinists suppose that populations change gradually, and also (which is different) that there can never have been a first *human* couple, radically different in nature from their immediate parents. Indeed, as I have pointed out before, conspecifics do not, on Darwinian terms, need to share any particular nature (though they may of course be alike in many respects—and also like creatures not of 'their own species'). Even modern scientists have not always seen the implications of this doctrine, notably that there can be no distinctively *human* rights, as there is nothing distinctively and uniquely human.[45] Maybe so, but there is more to be debated here.

---

further extension, whatever feature appears quite often in such an organism, and less often in those that don't: the 'gay gene', for example, belongs, at best, in this last camp, and has little predictive—or any other—value). See also Denis Noble, *The Music of Life* (Oxford University Press: Oxford, 2006) for an up-to-date, readable discussion of genome, proteome and whole organism.

[44] Chesterton, *Orthodoxy*, op. cit., p. 22. In *The Everlasting Man* (op. cit., p. 26) Chesterton drew on H.G. Wells's *The Time Machine* (1895) to show that whether something happened 'slowly' or 'quickly' was entirely subjective: 'in that sublime nightmare the hero saw trees shoot up like green rockets, and vegetation spread visibly like a green conflagration, or the sun shoot across the sky from east to west with the swiftness of a meteor'. Talking of an organism's changing, of course, is very misleading: what we are really speaking about is a change in the population to which particular organisms belong. Even if a *population* of prehominids changes only slowly into a population of hominids, it might still be true that the *hominids* in that population differ from *prehominids* not 'by degrees', but 'in kind'.

[45] See Richard Dawkins, 'Gaps in the Mind' in P. Singer & P. Cavalieri (eds.), *The Great Ape Project: Equality beyond humanity* (Fourth Estate: London, 1993), pp. 80–7, and also my own 'Is Humanity a Natural Kind?' in T. Ingold (ed.), *What is an Animal?* (Unwin Hyman, 1988), pp. 17–34 (reprinted in *The Political Animal* (Routledge: London, 1999), pp. 40–58.

The Gradual and the Catastrophic

A personal God can do things 'slowly' as well as 'quickly'. One reason that Darwinian evolutionary theory was attractive to so many, despite its scientific difficulties, was precisely that it made change *gradual*. The other ideological reasons for its popularity, that it seemed to provide a rationale for racist, imperialist and oppressively capitalist notions, were, perhaps, not entirely Darwin's fault. His own loss of faith, after all, was triggered by his daughter's death and expressed in horror at the abuse of power. If 'the world of nature', perceived as thoroughly unjust, is not the sort of world that a decent creator-god could make, then human injustice cannot be right either. Even the profiteer that Chesterton pilloried, as being 'satisfied with himself, knowing that Nature is unjust', should have known better. Those who condemn a creator-god's indifference or cruelty should not themselves be cruel or indifferent. In rejecting the work of 'our master, the selfish gene' (as both T.H. Huxley and Richard Dawkins have sought to do), we are acknowledging that there is indeed a higher source of value (that is, that there is a God).

Geological discoveries were an earlier challenge to Biblical history. Some influential persons feared that if the Mosaic history turned out not be entirely accurate an amoral atheism would prevail, and the worst features of the French Revolution be the inevitable result.[46] Others proposed that Mosaic history could be essentially true, even though the world was older than it might at first have appeared. There were earlier ages, marked by the fossils of unfamiliar creatures, which seemed to have perished suddenly. The European imagination was very ready to see signs of the Flood, or perhaps of *many* such floods. Those worlds were swept away, by processes that might or might not sometimes be visible nowadays, and new biospheres created in their stead. Imaginative historians were divided on this matter. Some supposed that God had intervened 'directly' on such occasions; others that He had merely ordained that comets should do the work for Him, or that the way the continents were put together led, expectably, to their occasional collapse. In either case, the present state of things was not the only way things could be. In either case, they might suddenly be changed. Maybe the new worlds were entirely new. Or maybe they were

[46] See Cohn, *Noah's Flood,* op. cit, pp. 102–7, pp. 121–9.

developed from some seed, some remnant, from the older world they displaced.[47]

Darwinian Theory offered an alternative to Cuvier's catastrophism:[48] there were no *sudden* changes, no discontinuities. It was enough that the world changed, that the character of populations changed, continuously (even though we could not always, or ever, find any records of these continuous changes). Each generation was just a little different from the previous one, and we could, in principle, conceive that all the generations of living things were a single, subtly varying population. Our hope for the future would be that subtle variations would continue. Some lineages might end abruptly, but all those that survived at all would suffer no sudden transformation. They would simply be getting 'better'—or so people usually inferred (and even Darwin was not immune to the suggestion). Strictly speaking, Darwinian selection does not *improve* the lineage in any sense that we would ordinarily accept: there is no guarantee that the recognizably *virtuous* (whatever sort of virtue they possess) will have more descendants than those without such virtues. There is no guarantee even that the ordinarily *successful* will have more descendants—though Darwin's own exposition of the theory sometimes suggested this. It is simply false to say that we admire or seek to emulate only those characteristics (physical or moral or economic) that are likely to produce (or have in the past produced) more descendants than their rivals. It is slightly more plausible that sexual desire is usually directed towards potential mates who offer some evidence that they can provide descendants. But for that very reason there is little evolutionary need to be especially discriminating in our choices: almost any reasonably healthy specimen of the opposite sex will serve! And as a matter of—very welcome—fact we *don't* all desire the same persons, nor even the same body-types. If we did, and there were an agreed list of more and less desirable mates, no-one but the pair at the top of the two lists (the male and female) would get what they preferred. Everyone else would be stuck with a partner that they considered less desirable, and almost all of us with someone who barely achieved a rank! Fashion may encourage us to dream about particular body-shapes and

---

47] This is now a very common theme in science fiction, whether the catastrophe is past or future: either humanity escapes from our doomed earth in a new Ark, or else some equivalent Ark is identified as the origin of our present world. What exactly these stories mean for their readers is uncertain.

48] See Cohn, *Noah's Flood,* op. cit., pp. 111ff on Georges Cuvier (1769–1832).

complexions, and even to emulate them, but it does not follow that later generations will reflect those dreams. Present-day Western fashion, notoriously, favours very youthful looks, especially in females: these may not be the characteristics that encourage successful breeding. A later age may indeed be puzzled that we males seem to prefer the pleasures of sex to the pleasures of actual procreation,[49] in lusting after those characteristics that are least likely to be linked to, or to survive, child-bearing.

The profile of a given population may vary from one generation to another, but we usually don't know in what direction, nor whether it will continue to vary in the same direction (why should it?), or for how long. Even now, when different local populations are increasingly in contact with a wider world, there are different pressures upon different regions and in different times, and the populations may still develop into different varieties. The easy belief that 'modern medical care' has called a halt to evolution[50] is confused: on the contrary, by preserving more variations than would otherwise, 'in the wild', survive, we may be accelerating it (just as evolution is accelerated after a mass extinction, when competition is not so intense). At the least we are merely altering, a little, and in various ways, which lineages have more descendants. Both allopatric and sympatric speciation remain serious possibilities for the human stock, even without an interplanetary diaspora, or a catastrophe. *Probably*, the human population (which might once have evolved into distinct biological species) will merge into a single whole, *largely* composed of dark-haired, black-eyed, smooth-skinned mesomorphs rather less than six-feet tall (with frequent throwbacks to earlier types as recessive genes—for example, those for red hair, fair skin and freckles—are matched in the breeding pairs). But that out-

---

[49] In passing: the idea that marriage is ordained 'first, for the procreation of children... second, for a remedy against sin, and to avoid fornication... and thirdly, for the mutual society, help, and comfort that the one ought to have of the other' (*Book of Common Prayer*) may sound strange to sensualists everywhere (that is, to all of us, sometimes), as may the doctrine that all 'acts of love' should be open to the possibility of procreation (implying, perhaps illicitly, that contraception is against the natural law). Of course I share those feelings—but it is both merely realistic and also properly respectful to remember that procreation is not merely an accidental and inconvenient effect of sex. If sex were *really* detached from procreation (as it is not yet, at any rate for heterosexuals) it would be something different, and not necessarily something greater.

[50] As Alexander, op. cit., p. 233 supposes, possibly with a view to persuading himself that our descendants will remain Christ's conspecifics: I think this is theologically confused, as well as scientifically rash.

come is not certain: maybe quite other characters, ones that we haven't even noticed, will have, statistically and over the very long run, many more descendants than the ones we notice. Current theory suggests that most Europeans are descended from one or another of seven women, living in different ages of the world,[51] but no-one has offered any reason at all to suppose that those seven women were in any real sense any 'fitter' than their contemporaries (nor that we have inherited anything very special from them, save their mitochondria).

Darwinian Theory, in its popular form at least, suggests that our descendants will, in some respects, be 'better' than we are (though probably not in any sense that we would be *bound* to consider an improvement). It also suggests that we would *recognize* our descendants (with perhaps some effort): they will not be of a *radically* different sort, at least until after many ages. They in their turn won't have much reason to think us utterly alien. The contrasting, catastrophic, theory suggests both that there may be some sudden change to call a halt to our endeavours, and that the world to come, even if we have descendants there, may find our world incomprehensible.

> As were the days of Noah, so will be the coming of the Son of man. For as in those days before the flood they were eating and drinking, marrying and giving in marriage, until the day when Noah entered the ark, and they did not know until the flood came and swept them all away, so will be the coming of the Son of man.[52]

And again:

> By the word of God the world that then existed was deluged with water and perished. But by the same word the heavens and earth that now exist have been stored up for fire, being kept until the day of judgement and the destruction of ungodly men.[53]

This is not a comfortable thought, though it is one that has had more resonance in the past century than it did in the late nineteenth. We too dream of apocalypse: a sudden change in our circumstances, brought on in consequence (why not, in judgement?) of human

---

51] Brian Sykes, *The Seven Daughters of Eve* (Bantam Press: London, 2001).

52] *Matthew* 24.37–9.

53] *II Peter* 3.5–7

behaviour, whether this be a nuclear winter or global warming.[54] But we still prefer to believe that changes will be 'gradual', that there will be no sudden shift, and that all such changes will be ones that 'we' can adapt to (while acknowledging that many of us will not). Unfortunately, there does seem reason to suspect that some changes are *not* gradual, but both sudden and radically transformative. On the far side of the Change, all things are different, whether that Change was something that has happened before, in accordance with some discernible 'natural law', or else something unprecedented, 'miraculous', an invasion from Elsewhere (and are we sure that we could always tell the difference?).

If we are to carry on living we must somehow persuade ourselves that life is indeed worth living, even if under judgement. Perhaps that is only possible if we can somehow also believe that the Change can be survived, somehow, or that the World-to-Come will not be wholly alien, not be entirely 'hell'. Unfortunately, perhaps, some varieties chiefly of American Protestantism have interpreted this to mean that we needn't be concerned about what we do: either the Lord will guarantee us (that is, prosperous Westerners) our continuing enjoyment of natural goods and glories (and ensure that this has no global consequence), or else He will at least ensure that there will be a Remnant taken up and saved (coincidentally, of prosperous Westerners). Neither conviction can be easily supported from Christian, Jewish or Islamic tradition. On the contrary, Rabbinic exegesis of the days before the Flood, as I remarked before, is of a prosperous and gleefully immoral world which bears a strong resemblance to the prosperous West! Maybe indeed a Remnant will be saved, but it is more probable that they will be the presently downtrodden, the ones already familiar with a hand-to-mouth existence, and without any confidence in any earthly powers.

Modern Neo-Darwinian Theory usually acknowledges that catastrophes have occurred, and evolutionary flowerings follow them, as the survivors move out into the changed environment, swept clean of most old species. In that sense, the modern theory, in this as in

---

[54] Even those politicians who have at last and grudgingly admitted that the world is warming up, and that this is an effect of human policies, imagine that the world, once warmer, will somehow settle down, that there will be some happy limit to its warming. Unfortunately, we have no *scientific* evidence of this outcome: as far as the evidence goes, the world may carry on warming until everything but thermophile bacteria are dead. See James Lovelock, *The Revenge of Gaia: Why the Earth Is Fighting Back – and How We Can Still Save Humanity* (Allen Lane: London, 2006).

other matters, is no longer quite Darwinian. 'Natural selection', in most 'normal' times, acts mainly to preserve existing adaptations, pruning away less profitable deviations. Only in the context of relatively sudden change is there scope for any new variation to survive, perhaps in temporarily isolated enclaves. Where those variations come from, and whether their appearance is truly random, with respect to any 'benefit' they bring, we still have very little idea.[55] It helps us believe that there will be a future, even in changed conditions, without requiring us to anticipate a fully radical change in who and what we are. The theory still identified as Darwin's, in other words, remains a metaphor, not a mechanism, and one that is widely accepted, still, for largely 'romantic' reasons, having to do with how we feel. Those who reject the theory, as they understand it, may also be doing so for largely romantic reasons. There is one more reason to reject it that is not 'romantic', but—precisely—rational.

Darwin's Doubt

The final problem for Chesterton was Darwin's Doubt (as described on an earlier page): 'With me the horrid doubt always arises whether the convictions of man's mind, which have been developed from the mind of the lower animals, are of any value or are at all trustworthy. Would anyone trust in the convictions of a monkey's mind, if there are any convictions in such a mind?'[56] It is no answer at all to say that *good* logic has been selected to survive, that it has passed the test of

---

[55] Michael J. Behe, in *The Edge of Evolution: the search for the limits of Darwinism* (Simon & Schuster: New York, 2007), has argued that whereas very simple changes, of the sort that makes the malaria parasite immune to chloroquine, are plausible, given enough time and a large population, more complex accumulated changes, leading seamlessly—in the sense that each small change is beneficial—from one sort of creature to another, could not reasonably be expected even in geological time unless they are *not* random. He may be mistaken, but his critics do not seem to me to prove this merely by asserting that there *must* have been, 'by chance', such intermediate, beneficial steps amid a host of damaging variations. The drunkard *must* have been merely lucky in his trek across a busy highway, since he has arrived. It makes more sense to wonder *how* he did. Tipler, op. cit., pp. 126–30 (though I agree—as I shall argue in the next section—with his insistence that Darwinian Theory amounts to 'an abdication of human intelligence' (after John Paul II)), has mistaken the sense of 'random': the claim is not that the variations are 'uncaused', but that they have no principled relation to any benefit that might be needed by the lineage in which they occur. But Tipler may still be right to suppose that Darwinian theorists misunderstand causality.

[56] Charles Darwin in F. Darwin (ed.), *The Life and Letters of Charles Darwin* (Murray: London ,1887), vol. 1, pp. 315–6). See Alvin Plantinga, *Warrant and Proper Function* (Oxford University Press: New York, 1993

nature, that *human* convictions work or have worked. In the first place, *bad* logic has survived as well (or we would need no logic classes!), and misplaced conviction. In the second, it has survived (it is said) not because it is *true,* but because it proved 'useful'. In the third, its past survival offers no guarantees for any future success. In the fourth, once we have begun to doubt ourselves, and reason, reason can give no answer that is not already doubtful. The alternative conviction, that reason is, as it were, a god's eye-view of truth, is one that has had great influence on the growth of science. Somehow, we can hope to see things not as they merely seem to creatures of our kind but 'as they are'. Without that conviction science dissolves into a merely pragmatic instrument, or set of instruments, for managing our lives. Aliens might have no such strategy. That is the true nightmare of Darwinian science:

> It is an act of faith to assert that our thoughts have any relation to reality at all. If you are merely a sceptic, you must sooner or later ask yourself the question, 'Why should anything go right; even observation and deduction? Why should good logic not be as misleading as bad logic? They are both movements in the brain of a bewildered ape'.[57]

Something like the ancient doctrine still seems necessary, that we must have *faith* in reason, and reject all systems that sap that faith. 'No truth which I find can deny that I am seeking the truth. My mind cannot find anything which denies my mind.'[58]

At the very least, Darwinian or Neo-Darwinian Theory cannot be the last word about our condition: for if it were, it would indeed be the very last word of all, the idea that eats up all others, and itself.[59] Chesterton knew better.

One very strange response to this argument is simply to insist that 'science *does* work', that this needs no explanation, and that atheists can be scientists as easily as (more easily perhaps than) theists. This is a strange response since it so plainly misses the point. If there is a wet umbrella in the porch, that is *evidence* at least that someone has been out in the rain, simply because if someone had gone out, the

---

[57] Chesterton, *Orthodoxy*, op. cit., p. 20f.

[58] 'The Long Bow', *Alarms and Discursions* (Methuen: London, 1910), written after reading one of Wells's novels, probably *The Island of Dr Moreau* (1910).

[59] Strangely, Darwinists like Daniel C. Dennett actually acknowledge (in *Darwin's Dangerous Idea: Evolutions and the Meaning of Life* (Allen Lane: London, 1995)) that Darwinism is, as it were, a 'universal acid', without admitting that it also, inevitably, undermines their own theories.

umbrella would probably be wet, and if no-one had it probably would not be. Of course, there might be other explanations for the umbrella's wetness, but if we are only to compare the two hypotheses ('someone went out with it'; and 'no-one did') the former is far more likely. It would be no reply to the argument to say, 'The umbrella *is* wet, and there's an end of it'. Similarly, it would be far more likely that we had some way of seeing truth if something like theism were correct, than if it weren't. In so far as we are persuaded that we *can* see truth, we have some reason to believe that theism is correct, just as we have some reason to believe that someone went out in the rain.

Conversely, if we insist that nobody went out, that no-one could possibly have gone out, that there was no possible exit, we must begin to doubt that the umbrella is really wet: perhaps it is merely glossy. It may be difficult to doubt our immediate sensory judgements (though not impossible), but we have no such *sensory* assurance that we have a route to cosmic truth, even if we have managed to tell good stories to ourselves. If naturalistic atheism and neo-Darwinian Theory are correct, we have—if anything—some reason to suspect that we have no such route. All our attempts to find out the truth are no more than extrapolations from the limited sphere in which our guesses are pragmatically confirmed (at least to the point of not *preventing* procreation). Science was born, as a matter of more or less ascertainable fact, in a monotheistic culture (both Islamic and Christian): the Chinese, despite being at least as intelligent as Europeans, had no particular reason to believe that there was a unified and rationally discernible system of reality, and were therefore content with *local* successes, particular technical triumphs.[60] On modern atheistical terms they were quite correct. Immanuel Kant's legacy was the pessimistic claim that we can't expect to know or even conceive anything outside the framework of our very finite minds. Darwin's legacy was an even more pessimistic one: our minds are

60] See Joseph Needham, *The Great Titration* (Allen & Unwin: London, 1969). There are probably many other available explanations for the different histories of Chinese and European science, including the fact that China had a unified bureaucratic system unfriendly to innovation. This too may have a moral for our future.

only the tools that a social primate needed, once, to procreate. 'The Universe is not only queerer than we suppose, but queerer than we *can* suppose'.[61]

And this, as Chesterton said, is bad theology![62]

Intelligence and Natural Norms

That there is Intelligence at work in the world, as Plotinus said, is generally admitted easily. Things don't happen quite 'at random', but follow discoverable patterns, laws or regularities of a sort that sustain all things in being, not necessarily forever but for long enough for there to be, exactly, *things*. We might imagine for ourselves a world where this wasn't so, but the more effort we put into the imagination the less we can call the result 'a world' at all. In the first stages of the imagination we might suppose that acorns could hatch chickens or a swarm of bees as easily as oaks, that objects fall at whatever speed they wish and in any preferred direction, that water might burst into flame or the sun occasionally suck warmth from its surroundings. But of course if this were happening all the time, there would be no acorns, chickens, bees or water. No characters could be expected to endure even for an instant, and so there would be no characters at all—only a sort of 'blooming, buzzing confusion' (to borrow William James's phrase[63]). It is not by chance that we don't live in that world, for in that world there could be nothing anything like us. Where everything is possible, and just as likely as anything else, then nothing actually occurs at all.

In this first sense of 'intelligence', that is, it is indeed an obvious and universal truth that there is indeed a world, and axiomatically a world filled with intelligence. Not everything happens quite 'at random'. Another early speculation, associated now with a Greek philosopher and mystic called Empedocles and with the Epicurean school, was that this condition might perhaps be merely what has survived from a primordial 'chaos'. Once upon a time, things really were 'like that': no particular forms were stable, and there were no

---

[61] J.B.S. Haldane, *Possible Worlds and Other Essays* (Heinemann: London, 1927), p. 286. Richard Dawkins has taken to quoting this, apparently without seeing that it is the death of reason.

[62] G.K. Chesterton, 'The Blue Cross' in *The Innocence of Father Brown: FBS*, op. cit., pp. 21, 27.

[63] William James, *The Principles of Psychology* (Harvard University Press: Cambridge, MA., 1890), vol. 1., p. 488, speaking of a baby's initial impression of the world. Actually, it is likely that the baby's world has a structure from the start, precisely because the world itself has a structure.

general truths about what might follow what. Empedocles and the Epicureans then proposed that, quite by chance, particular forms emerged that managed to sustain themselves in being or to reproduce themselves by infecting their surroundings with some similar forms. Gradually order emerged from chaos (and it is no surprise that *we* inhabit an ordered part or period of the totality).[64] The particular imagery employed in this speculation now seems weird, but the basic idea remains: present order is only what survives from chaos; 'in the beginning' everything imaginable occurs with equal probability, but only a few such happenings can sustain a world like ours. The idea is invoked to 'explain' the curious fact that the universe of our experience is 'fine-tuned', almost uniquely fit for the emergence of stars, planets, living things. Obviously all the other 'universes' that are less well suited to the existence of things like us are unobserved, from within, by anything like us: we are bound to be living in a world that suits us. The fact that we are is evidence, of a sort, that there are indefinitely many other worlds or universes or primordial somewhats where we aren't.

'Evidence of a sort': actually, the story is as far from an *explanation* as can easily be imagined, and wholly unscientific, by the standard that is usually invoked against 'religious' explanations, that no empirical discovery could conceivably count against it. If we choose to 'explain' an odd event merely by saying that all imaginable events must happen somewhere, we are disclaiming any need to *explain* this one at all. If all imaginable events occur somewhere we are still living in chaos, and there is no limit at all on what may happen next instant or next door. If we correct the story, and say instead that all 'physically possible' worlds exist somewhere (all worlds consistent with primordial law, with varying adjustments for what seem to be 'contingent'—that is, unnecessary, random—facts about the relative strengths of gravity, electromagnetism, the weak and the strong nuclear forces (and so on), we are simply stating that the primordial state is *not,* after all, chaotic. Some law rules, even if that law allows many variant instantiations. Each version of the 'Big Bang' determines a particular sort of universe, and events within those universes are coordinated, somehow, by the presence of a particular set of laws and 'chance' (if they were) beginnings. Even if there were many such variants (and we have no *empirical* reason to believe there are) it must still be worth noticing that *this* world is astonishingly

---

64] John Brunner, *Traveller in Black* (Methuen: London, 1978) offers a fantasy version of this notion.

well-suited for the existence of living things like us (and we have no *empirical* reason to believe that any other sort is possible). The Order of Things appears to include the probability of life: at the very least it is 'pre-adapted' for biology.[65]

The Many Worlds hypothesis, in its various forms, is endearingly metaphysical. This does not, of itself, make it unthinkable, but it does raise one obvious question: if atheists are allowed to posit indefinitely (infinitely?) many Other Worlds in order to make it seem a little less improbable that this world here should be 'fine-tuned', why may I not posit *One* Other World, indefinitely (or infinitely?) 'large' (that is, the Divine)? That there is *One* infinite and eternal at least has some advantages over the suggestion that there are infinitely Many: it actually explains the unity of reality in a way that the Many Worlds hypothesis doesn't, and it is also quite likely to be checkable. I shall return to that.

The 'Intelligence' at work consists, so far, only in the overruling presence of an intelligible order. The world of our experience (and obviously we experience no other world) is orderly: however wide and long it stretches there is something that is 'the same' in all of it. Wherever we look we find the same laws, the same relationships. Wherever we look we find that *mathematics* rules: it is, as Eugen Wigner pointed out, 'unreasonably effective', at least if we suppose that we have made it up! The conclusion must surely be that we haven't. One way of gesturing toward the universal law is to speak of the Principle of Least Action: it is as if every moving particle (including photons) 'choose' the pathway between their beginning and their end by selecting that which requires the least action (in the simplest case, the least time). When this principle was first identified, in the eighteenth century, its quasi-theological nature was acknowledged: modern physicists are a little shyer![66]

It is easier, at first sight, to think of the *biological* world in Neo-Empedoclean terms, at any rate if we pay no attention to its ori-

---

[65] See Michael J. Denton, *Nature's Destiny: how the laws of nature reveal purpose in the universe* (Simon & Schuster: New York, 1998) p. 387: 'whether one accepts or rejects the design hypothesis, whether one thinks of the designer as the Greek world soul or the Hebrew God, there is no avoiding the conclusion that the world *looks* as if it has been uniquely tailored for life: *it appears to have been designed.*'

[66] See A. Zee, *Fearful Symmetry: the search for beauty in modern physics* (Princeton University Press: New Jersey, 1999; 2nd edn.), pp. 103–9.

gins.[67] Perhaps the orderliness of procreation and the elegant complexity of biological form is simply an effect of 'random variation' and 'natural selection'. The forms that have survived are the ones, exactly, that have survived: they continue to vary 'randomly', but only within an ordered context. Simple mutations in the procreative process may make offspring just a little different from their parents, but not entirely different. The process, we are told, is 'blind', in that the variations are not created with a view to any success: even if longer beaks or a darker skin would be clearly advantageous in a particular setting, there is no mechanism to produce *those* variations any more often than a shorter beak and lighter skin. Is this compatible with 'Intelligence' in any stronger sense, of a kind that depends on 'forethought' or 'design'? The Darwinian answer is that it is not: Intelligence of a sort is at work in all things, but not a forward-looking intelligence. Progress (so to call it) depends at least as much on the *failure* of order as on its force.

But of course this judgement depends on a particular concept of Intelligence and of Intelligent Design. Oddly, while mainstream biologists insist that a forward-looking Designer would do things differently, actual engineers and creative artists in the human world increasingly employ, exactly, the techniques of 'random variation' and 'selection' that they have copied from Darwinian Theory. But in that case an Intelligent Designer, even one with all available knowledge of how things work (because it *is* that knowledge), might more easily operate by just this 'trial and error'. Even a divine creator

---

67] Since evolution through random variation and natural selection depends on the existence of a mechanism for procreation, there is a serious difficulty about supposing that this mechanism can itself be produced by random variation and natural selection. The more complicated and ingenious the mechanism turns out to be the harder it is to solve what seems to be a *logical* not merely an empirical impasse. There are of course some theories that purport to solve the problem, but none with any real authority. Simply saying that there just *must* have been a much simpler copying system once upon a time is not an argument. One might as well say that there just *must* have been fairies once upon a time.

might prefer to let His creation roll and try out all available variations, rather than preempt a real discovery of what works best.[68]

Actually, we do not know that literally *all* available variations are produced, 'at random'.[69]. There are lots of variations, it is true, that—to our eyes—do nothing for the offspring or its lineage (and are, most often, eliminated by the premature death or lowered fertility of the creature in question). But the problem precisely is that a genetic variation may have many different phenotypical results, and these will survive and breed, or not, depending on the circumstances and the 'choices' that they make. What doesn't 'work' at one time, may well work at another. So Intelligence may be working with more forethought (as it were) than we suppose, but even if it isn't there is no easy distinction in this matter between Intelligence and Chance. In a divinely ordered world what 'works' is what God lets work.

Finally, even if we concede that there is a difference, and that blind Darwinian Evolution (defined by the dogma that 'the process has no direction, and no foresight'[70]) *could* generate our present world, it must surely still be far more likely that it has been generated by 'design'. Our world, after all, would be far more probable if Design were King than if it weren't. Only if Design were itself vastly improbable would this argument fail, and Darwinians have only four arguments to suggest that this is so.

First, that the world we live in is full of misery, and has been so for many million years. This is no more than the familiar 'argument from evil', and invalid on many counts.[71] George Berkeley's mock-

[68] Further exploration of what the traditional divine property of 'omniscience' requires would take me too far afield: briefly, its scope is not as obvious as atheistic critics seem to think. Some theists would happily insist that there *are* things that even omniscience doesn't (yet) know, but even the more orthodox could reasonably observe that even if God *does* know what the outcome will be (or rather, eternally is) He does not determine it: the outcome is the product of innumerable choices and 'chance' events which He observes.

[69] There seems to be some evidence that bacterial populations at any rate adapt more rapidly to harsh conditions (the presence of antibiotics, for example) than steady, random mutation would predict: see Hunter, op. cit., p. 77.

[70] Noble, op. cit., p. 110. Note that this is not a *discovery*, but an axiom.

[71] See John Hick, *Evil and the God of Love* (Macmillan: London, 1966) for a scholarly account of the history of this trope, and the usual answers, both 'Irenaean' and 'Augustinian'. The currently more popular answer, endorsed for example by Alexander, op. cit. is the 'Irenaean': for there to be persons of our kind we need to have *developed* in the context of a law-governed but dangerous and uncertain world. I do not myself consider this an adequate response, and prefer some form of

ery is perhaps the only answer: 'he who undertakes to measure without knowing either [the measure or the thing to be measured] can be no more exact than he is modest, … who having neither an abstract idea of moral fitness nor an adequate idea of the divine economy shall yet pretend to measure the one by the other'.[72] It is especially odd that atheists should ever rely upon this argument, since it turns on the flat declaration that there are some things, some *absolute evils*, which can neither be justifiably permitted nor redeemed. Theism, or at any rate mainstream theism, is the faith that there are no such evils: that there are more ordinary evils, desperately in need of redemption, may be true, but this does not refute (rather, it affirms) the possibility of redemption.

The second argument is that we are *badly* designed, if we are designed at all: no sensible engineer, we are told, would so often use existing organs for some novel purpose when it would be more 'efficient' to rearrange the whole or simply start again.[73] This is a strange claim, even if it were really true that the examples of such 'bad design' were real, since it rests on a culturally mandated preference for radical reconstruction rather than organic growth. Presumably any 'sensible' town designer would demolish all existing buildings, roads and landmarks in order to install his currently preferred utopia (and the next designer along would do the same). This is not a good idea, and a genuinely sensible designer would be more inclined to work always with what is already 'given'. Noble asserts, mistaking Paley's argument from watch to watchmaker, that 'now we can see that life is full of design faults, false trails, and imperfect compromises. We can still wonder at the intricate beauty of life on earth, but we no longer think that its logic is the best there could be'.[74] But who said it was? It is, on the contrary, a familiar theme in orthodox religion that this is *not* the best world there could be, and that whatever pattern is intended for it by its Creator is constantly evaded or inadequately expressed. And it is also a familiar theme

---

the Augustinian: see my 'Progress and the Argument from Evil' *Religious Studies*, 40 (2004), pp. 181–92. But this is another story.

72] *Alciphron* (Crito speaks): *Works*, op. cit., vol. 3, pp. 251f.

73] Stephen Jay Gould, *The Panda's Thumb: more reflections in natural history* (Norton: New York, 1980). Oddly, it is also sometimes supposed to be an argument against 'Design' that there have apparently been occasions in earth's history when exactly that occurred: an existing biosphere was swept away, and lesser entities given a chance to grow ('as in the days of Noah').

74] Noble, op. cit., p. 111.

that a world *entirely* controlled by any single pattern would not be what our hearts, or the Lord, require.

The third argument advanced against invoking Design is that any such Designer must be as complex as the world it made, and is therefore no real 'ultimate' explanation for complexity. This is a complex of confusions, to which there are at least three responses. The first is to observe that not all Design arguments have to do with 'ultimate' explanations: if an archaeologist determines that a particular pile of rocks is the relic not of 'natural forces', nor even termites, but of an architect, a team of builders, a whole nation of people who desired such buildings, she may be explaining what is relatively *less* complex by reference to what is *more*. It may still be the best available explanation. The second response, if we are concerned with *ultimate* explanations, would be that insofar as it is true that 'God' names something complex, this would be as much as to say that such 'complexity' is a primordial datum, and our world is itself a simpler, cruder, copy of that reality (as Platonists have always held). But the third response is perhaps the most cogent: 'God' is a label for something wholly simple (in the sense that it is not composed of any prior things).

> Only the infinite and all-powerful substance which created all things is simple, of one form, unqualified, peaceful and undisturbed. Every creature, on the other hand, is a composite of substance and accident and in constant need of divine Providence since it is not free from mutability.[75]

The Design that springs from It is single, uniform, coherent, omnipresent precisely because its Origin is One.[76] The atheistical argument has simply borrowed a theological or metaphysical claim (that the ultimate explanation must, in a sense, be simple, unitary, incomposite, and so on, because to explain just is, in a way, to simplify) and sought to suggest that this requirement is met by material atoms. But atoms do not themselves constitute a 'simple' explanation: there are too many of them, at too many times and places. There just *is* an eternal rain or swarm of infinitely many atoms, as the Epicureans suggested, without any reason for their existence or their infinitely diverse properties: which is not an *explanation* at all. If

[75] Maximus Confessor, 'Four Hundred Chapters on Love', 4.9: op. cit., p. 76.

[76] All these points have been made, clearly and repeatedly, by Alvin Plantinga: see, for example, 'The Dawkins Confusion: naturalism ad absurdum', *Christianity Today*, March/April 2007, Vol. 13, No. 2, p. 21 (http://www.christianity today.com/bc/2007/ 002/1.21.html, accessed 28th August 2008).

there is to be an explanation of the material world it lies first of all 'aloft', in the Intelligence that rules all things. That Intelligence, as Plotinus pointed out, is itself, in a way, a complex thing, constituting all the forms of being there are in a systematic unity. For him, the further explanation of its being at all lies in the One's simplicity. What is it, in Hawking's phrase, that 'breathes fire into the equations'?[77] *How* things are is determined by what has been called the *Logos*. *That* they are is determined by the single Will.

The fourth argument is that if there were a Designer, there would be more variety: why should a Designer place all the planets in a single plane rather than giving each its own unique location or direction; why should terrestrial life display the nested hierarchies that evolutionists interpret as signals of shared ancestry?[78] It's a strange argument: any designer—even the most Divine—is likely to create variations on some favourite themes! And like all the others, it rests upon unvoiced and unexamined assumptions about what God would do.

The final reason, so it seems, for atheistic evolutionary theorists to reject all this is not an *argument* at all, but a blinding prejudice: they simply do not want to allow even the barest possibility that the God of Abraham is real. Amazon reviewers especially may sometimes have some valuable and valid criticisms to make of the various books that criticize popular evolutionary theory or defend 'Intelligent Design', but rapidly revert to rants about the failings of that imagined deity and the wickedness of anyone with whom they disagree. They believe in 'blind evolution' because they cannot bear the supposed alternative. This is not necessarily an epistemological error: theists; after all, may *disbelieve* in eugenics because they have a similarly fierce attachment to the Word of God.[79] But it is at least a little odd that anyone should refuse to believe there is a God merely

[77] Hawking, *A Brief History*, op. cit

[78] See Hunter, *Science's Blind Spot*, op. cit., pp. 57–8, 71–2.

[79] And the only *argument* I have ever seen against Philip Gosse's suggestion, in *Omphalos* (Routledge: London, 2003; 1st published 1858), that God could have made the world complete with organisms and materials that would seem to indicate a long prehistory is that 'God would not deceive us' (so Alexander, op. cit., pp. 139–41, 213). How we know this I at least *don't* know. Alexander believes that the Bible assures us that God does not deceive: it was for exactly that reason, because of what the Bible told him, that Gosse himself supposed that God had started the world, like any novelist, as it were *in medias res*, and carefully enlightened His people on the subject, if we cared to believe His words. Metaphysical, and even supposedly scientific, argument is often covertly theological!

because they don't like His imagined character: are we suddenly to suppose that Reality must bend to suit our wishes? Why may I not refuse to believe in geological ages because I don't like *their* imagined character?

There is still some reason to try to achieve a coherent vision of the whole, putting aside presuppositions. It may even be that biologists are working, without due thought, with a long-outmoded concept of causality. Physicists are likelier to insist that the *later* stages of a world-line are as significant as the earlier, that temporal priority is not *explanatory* priority. The fact that we are here (maybe, most strongly, the fact that the peoples of the final end-time are, in their perspective, 'here'[80]) may be what determines what past variations have occurred and been selected. Particles take the path of least action: so may the universe as a whole, as a spatio-temporal expression of the Single Formula which governs all things.

If Darwin's Doubt must lead us to conclude that science itself depends on Intelligence's being at work in everything (since otherwise there would be no good reason to expect that our 'intelligence' was more than a set of more-or-less useful algorithms which could not be relied upon beyond their original setting), then we must also conclude that there are real norms, or forms. Once this is agreed we must also admit that there is no good reason to exclude the action of such norms or forms or even 'final causes': deciding not to mention them was a philosophical or theological decision, designed to wean us away from unduly anthropocentric images. It wasn't an absurd decision, but it must not be taken so seriously as to prevent any chance of understanding.

Biological species are not natural kinds, but it does not follow that there are no natural kinds, nor that there are no norms or forms on which the process of evolutionary change converges. Convergent evolution is indeed an obvious fact. Whereas we might reasonably expect, in a truly Darwinian or neo-Darwinian universe, that every fresh evolutionary beginning (whether after a cataclysm, or in some newly isolated region) would generate utterly different types (very much as Stephen Jay Gould supposed), the truth is that although living creatures are indeed diverse, they are not *wildly* and bizarrely diverse. Marsupial wolves don't look or behave very differently

---

[80] As Hawking himself has suggested, remember, without incurring Dawkins' public wrath: see Gefter, 'Mr Hawking's Universe', op. cit.

from placental wolves. Sharks, mackerel, dolphins, sea-lions and the rest, with different immediate ancestries, will nonetheless be very similar. Eusociality has been devised by bees, ants, termites, naked mole-rats—and with appropriate divergences, by hominids. That different lineages can generate very similar forms may perhaps be evidence that they all carry the genetic wherewithal for appropriate adaptations—as the master-gene for *eyes* is carried in many different kinds, some of them being eyeless.[81] 'Junk DNA'—DNA that cannot now code for any proteins, and *seems* to have no present function in the genome—may actually be a library of usable ideas. Or else the natural laws that govern all things themselves direct appropriate variations. We don't *know* that this is false, and the mere claim that there are no such directing forces and no stored pre-adaptations, has very little weight against the overriding argument that there *must* be norms—or else our own intelligence has no authority, to be either accurate or demanding. We have good reason to insist that *intelligence* rules all (or else there are no reasons).

That we have evolved, and that we are cousins of all living creatures here on the third planet of the Sun, are both very likely true (unless this is a virtual reality very unlike the real truth). This 'common descent with variation' is what people often mean by 'evolution',[82] but neo-Darwinians trade too easily on the plausibility of 'evolution' so understood and the post-Darwinian Theory that 'random variation' and 'natural selection' must be responsible, by themselves, for all the lives we see. Perhaps they are. This last claim remains what it always was: a strange hypothesis that is indeed a 'universal acid', destroying all sense of justice, and intelligence. Living in that bare world is a more difficult task than anyone, perhaps, but Nietzsche saw. Why should we attempt it?

---

[81] G. Halder et al. (1995). Induction of ectopic eyes by targeted expression of the eyeless gene in Drosophila. *Science*, 267 (24th March 1995):1788. This is not a wholly uncontroversial theory, and some theorists would still suggest that camera-eyes evolved separately, amongst jellyfish (cubozoans), marine worms, three sorts of gastropod, cephalopods, ogre spiders and vertebrates, making use of pre-existent material, and converging on very similar results (see Simon Conway Morris, *Life's Solution: inevitable humans in a lonely universe* (Cambridge University Press: Cambridge, 2003), pp. 151–8). Convergence—the presence of similar structures in very distantly related species, and perhaps with very different developmental processes—also suggests that evolutionary transformations are 'guided'.

[82] And that, as Michael J. Behe says, 'is *very* well supported': op. cit., p. 12.

7

Waking Up

Morals in the Dream of Life

I have on several occasions mentioned dreams. Sometimes, following Chesterton, I have suggested that it is an axiom of sanity that we are not dreaming. Sometimes I have half-endorsed Marx's judgement that religion is a *dream*—a dream of a better future. Sometimes I have followed Marcus Aurelius in pointing out that our ordinary lives are, after all, like dreams, and even referred with sympathy to the notion that we are living a merely *virtual* reality created in a slightly later age, or even in the cosmic end-times when almost all the creatures there have ever been are living. None of these remarks are exactly in contradiction, but it must be important to allow them all a merely appropriate power. We certainly need to remind ourselves that what we do does count, that—in that sense at any rate—we are not dreaming. But maybe we also need to wonder if—in a way—we are, and may wake up.[1]

How, either way, we should behave is perhaps the easiest question. 'Whether it's reality or a dream, doing what's right is what matters. If it's reality, then for the sake of reality; if it's a dream, then for the purpose of winning friends for when we awaken.'[2] It might seem at first that in a *waking* world we have more reason to think of the long-term effects and social implications of our actions, whereas in a *dream,* we can do what now comes naturally. That, after all, is what we do in dreams as these are ordinarily understood. If we *knew* we were dreaming, we could enjoy ourselves much more.

Or maybe not. It is only *our* judgement, after all, that dreams don't count: other ages and other nations have supposed the contrary, that

[1] I addressed this metaphor for the afterlife in 'Waking-up: a neglected model for the After-life': *Inquiry*, 26 (1983), pp. 209ff.

[2] Pedro Calderón de la Barca, *Life's A Dream.* (University Press of Colorado: Boulder, 2004; 1st published as *La vida es sueño* in 1635), p 137f (Sigismund speaks).

they matter very much. And even on our terms, they may. If we are dreaming now, we may wake up, and be ashamed. If we are dreaming, maybe there are others who can share our dreams. Maybe our dreams are tests, to see how we might behave—as Calderon's king tests Sigismund in the strange play that I quoted. Even if many of the creatures we encounter in this dream are props, such that there is no other real dreamer following the story from that point of view, we don't know that. Whatever we do to others in the dream we might find ourselves enduring in another venture. Better to treat others (even if they are figments) as we'd wish ourselves to be treated—since that is how we *will* be treated when we log in again.

> There is no accident in a man's becoming a slave, nor is he taken prisoner in war by chance, nor is outrage done on his body without due cause, but he was once the doer of that which he now suffers; and a man who made away with his mother will be made away with by a son when he has become a woman, and one who has raped a woman will be a woman in order to be raped.[3]

I acknowledge that one catch with this, and many other accounts of karmic retribution, is that the victims of oppression may then seem to deserve it,[4] but this would be an error. Even if some do, it does not pay us to exact that vengeance.

Another moral is more plausible. Dream goodies turn to ashes in the morning, much like fairy gold. Spending our dream energies on accumulating 'stuff' is silly. Better to lay up treasures for ourselves 'in heaven', in the real waking world, if we can do it.[5]

The hope of heaven (and a corresponding fear of hell) is often supposed to be the principal difference between believers and unbelievers. Some recent militants, indeed, imagine that any 'belief in God' is sold entirely with the promise of unending life. There may be some truth in this, but it is hard to prove that *every* religion offers such a hope. Many may tell stories of particular heroes who were taken up to heaven or to the Elysian Islands, but most of us aren't heroes, and expect no more than *genealogical* survival. Even those religions that teach us not to fear death may do so only by reminding us that we are still alive, or that glory counts for more than a prolonged old age! Popular Greek religion in the days of Plato, for example, had no spe-

---

[3] Plotinus, *Ennead*, III.2 [47].13, 11ff

[4] See 'Indian Ethics' in John Skorupski (ed.), *Routledge Companion to Ethics* (Routledge: London, forthcoming).

[5] *Matthew* 6.19–21; see also 19.21.

cial hopes of survival. Many pious Jews did not concern themselves with 'life after death'. A belief in reincarnation is not a belief that this person here, this Stephen, will be eternal: quite otherwise, what is eternal is something that this person here can hardly recognize. God or the gods or Atman may be immortal, but in knowing that, we know that we are not.

And yet there is also some sense in the remark of an old man in conversation with Unamuno: 'if there is no life after death, what's the point of God?'[6] Or of Paul the Apostle: 'if in this life only we have hope in Christ, we are of all men most miserable'.[7] Whatever hopes we have, of course, it is difficult to deny that there are also fears. As Plato knew:

> Cebes laughed. 'Suppose that we are afraid, Socrates', he said, 'and try to convince us. Or rather don't suppose that it is we that are afraid. Probably even in us there is a little boy who has these childish terrors. Try to persuade him not to be afraid of death as though it were a bogey.' 'What you should do', said Socrates, 'is to say a magic spell over him every day until you have charmed his fears away'.[8]

The magic spell that Socrates has in mind is *argument*, and especially an argument for the real existence of eternal truths that we remember and can make central to our being. I shall propose in a later section that there are forms of this proposal still influential even or especially amongst the atheistical. But first let us confront the bogey.

Why do we find the prospect of death so fearful? This may seem like the sort of foolish question that only philosophers ask. Why is there anything? Where do past times go? How do words have meaning? How can we justify inductive argument? Why do parents love their children? Why is the sky dark at night? Of course we fear death as the greatest evil, the destroyer of delights and separator of companions. The very elderly or very ill may at last be reconciled to it, but even they would generally accept the offer of a fresh, new life! The Epicurean response that we have no reason to fear being dead (since we never will *be* dead) is generally thought to miss the obvious point: that it is—exactly—not-being that we fear (as well, of course,

---

[6] Miguel di Unamuno, *The Tragic Sense of Life*, trans. J.E. Crawford Hutch (Macmillan: New York, 1921), p. 5.

[7] *1 Corinthians* 15.19.

[8] Plato, *Phaedo*, 77e–78a.

as the messy, painful and embarrassing process of 'becoming dead'). Courage is the capacity to carry on living in the face of death (for the alternative is dying—that is, not-living—before we're dead). The familiar paradox of courage is that unless we are willing to risk death we cannot achieve anything that we wish by living. Those who seek to secure themselves against the possibility of death will fail: they will die in any case, and not have lived beforehand.

Perhaps this is why politicians so frequently declare that suicide-bombers are cowardly. On the face of it, it is a strange remark: they have spent their lives, after all, to achieve the ends they serve. Their action may be murderous or stupid, but it would seem they can't be exactly *cowards*. But the goal of courage is to live in beauty, in the service of a greater life. The goal of suicide-bombers, so it seems, is death.

> They have but two objects, to destroy first humanity and then themselves. That is why they throw bombs instead of firing pistols. The innocent rank and file are disappointed because the bomb has not killed the king; but the high priesthood are happy because it has killed somebody.[9]

After the Madrid bombings in 2004 an al-Qaeda tape (released on March 14) stated: 'You love life and we love death', and similar sentiments have been recorded from other Jihadist sources, giving strength to the notion that there is an Islamic Death Cult. It is understandable, at least, that non-believers find themselves a little nervous of believers, especially of those who believe there is a world to come, a life after death. Atheists suppose that such believers are either hypocritical (since they take steps to live) or dangerous lunatics (as crazy as the followers of Jim Jones in Johnstown in 1978). But there is a third possibility (at least): that those who truly believe in immortal life believe also in *this* life.

> If a man say, I love God, and hateth his brother, he is a liar: for he that loveth not his brother whom he hath seen, how can he love God whom he has not seen?[10]

Or as Plotinus put it in response to the menacing Gnostics of his day:

> It does no good at all to say 'Look to God', unless one also teaches how one is to look. ... In reality it is virtue which goes before us to

---

[9] G.K. Chesterton, *The Man who was Thursday* (Arrowsmith: Bristol, 1908), p. 48; see also p. 65f.

[10] *1 John* 4.20

> the goal and, when it comes to exist in the soul along with wisdom, shows God; but God, if you talk about him without true virtue, is only a name. Again, despising the universe and the gods in it and the other noble things is certainly not becoming good. … For anyone who feels affection for anything at all shows kindness to all that is akin to the object of his affection, and to the children of the father that he loves. But every soul is a child of That Father.[11]

Death Cults, despising this world here and all who are involved in it, are at the very least bad manners. It is one thing to agree that we need to awaken, to see things in their proper ranks and places, and quite another to suppose that we must therefore wreck the dream. On the contrary, *waking up* is waking to the real existence of our neighbours, rejecting fantasy, making the best of things. 'Loving God' does not demand that we love creatures *less.*

Thinking of General St. Clare's fornication, deceit and cruelty, Father Brown allowed him some theological good faith (as it were): '"certainly he would have said with steady eyes that he did it to the glory of the Lord."'. He adds '"My own theology is sufficiently expressed by asking which Lord?"'[12]

> Therefore choose life, that both thou and thy seed may live.[13]

Waking from the Dream

The metaphor of 'waking up from life' has been neglected by philosophers, though not by poets or evangelists. Most recent secular philosophers have sought to show that 'surviving our own deaths' is a contradiction. Some more religiously-inclined philosophers have borrowed themes from science fiction to suggest that we could after all be 'resurrected' or 'uploaded', and so survive as indistinguishable duplicates of the persons that we were. The stories never quite convince. If I can be resurrected once, after all, it can happen many times. All that our normal theories could agree is that in this case there will be many duplicated Stephens, none of whom are Me. If I can be uploaded, what is this but to say that a computer network can recall my works and words and even extrapolate (perhaps) to what I *would* say if I lived? We can of course *pretend* that this is what we

---

[11] Plotinus, *Ennead,* II.9 [33].15, 33–16.10.

[12] Cited by G. Fried, op. cit., from 'The Sign of the Broken Sword'. The same question, obviously, arises with respect to those who rape and murder in alleged obedience to the Koran.

[13] *Deuteronomy* 30.19.

wanted, but it plainly isn't. Whatever it is that makes me Me will not be captured by these methods. The one advantage of such stories is to show that we can't flatly say what *God* could do, if we can't even be sure what *we* could do. If it is possible for us to think that someone or something made some centuries hence will be all of Me that matters (and some writers seem to think that's true), it must also be possible for God to retain or resurrect Me, if He wishes.[14]

But the metaphor of awakening has a wider reach. One of the commonest of sentimental epitaphs is Shelley's verse on the death of Keats:

> Peace, peace! He is not dead, he doth not sleep—
> He hath awakened from the dream of life ...
> He lives, he wakes—'tis Death is dead, not he.[15]

What Shelley meant, who knows? His poem continues by suggesting that Keats 'is made one with Nature. ... He is a portion of the loveliness which once he made more lovely', and later still he urges that 'the One remains, the many change and pass; Heaven's light forever shines, Earth's shadows fly; Life, like a many-coloured glass, stains the white radiance of Eternity, until Death tramples it to fragments.' What remains eternally, we might conclude, is abstract, universal, not the particular, maddening and delightful poet. What matters in us, as Plato might have said, is indeed immortal, since what matters is that immortal part. Socrates still lives, in a way, because he is identified with true philosophy: in his brief mortal life he made himself an icon. The parts of him that *aren't* immortal don't much matter: they are no more than mortal flummery.[16]

'Waking from the dream of life' is also a slogan much employed by occultists of many kinds, whether Western Vedantin, Buddhist or fans of the movie *The Matrix* (1999). It is often associated with the fear or fantasy or shrewd observation that we are being deceived by

---

[14] See John Hick, *Death and Eternal Life* (Collins: London, 1976) for some examples of these gambits.

[15] P.B. Shelley, 'Adonais' (1821): *Poetical Works*, ed. Thomas Hutchinson & G.M. Matthews (Oxford University Press: London, 1970), p. 440.

[16] See Plato, *The Symposium*, 211e: 'what if a man had eyes to see the true beauty—the divine beauty, I mean, pure and clear and unalloyed, not infected with the pollutions of the flesh and all the colours and vanities of mortal life—thither looking, and holding converse with the true beauty simple and divine?'

Powers (as Plato also suggested[17]), and a complacent belief that the writer is himself awake. Better perhaps to dream.

But it may still be worth exploring the idea that on our deaths we wake. In the merely science fictional story, of course, we wake to a natural universe of one sort or another. Maybe that real waking world will be much like this one: we are dreaming only a costume drama from our relatively recent past, that fascinating century on the cusp of the Singularity. Or maybe it will be that stranger world, feasting on the Hawking radiation of black holes, at the very end of the cosmos: we have dreamt ourselves into a distant past—or even a weird fiction—to explore the strangenesses of individualized and mortal-seeming life. In the former case, our waking selves will probably be as mortal as our dream-selves think we are (though maybe longer lived). In the latter case, our waking selves will be stranger than we can think, but will still, we can suspect, be as ignorant of the Why and Wherefore of the world as we. To them there will be little difference between terrestrial 21st century humans, Neanderthals from fifty millennia before, and engineered post-humans in the photosphere of Sirius. Probably there will be little difference between humans, crows and butterflies.

Those fantasies are at once impossible to imagine in any detail or with any force of truth, and also impossible to refute. But any of these waking selves, it seems, will be in exactly the same position as we are: namely, that they won't *know* that they're waking. They too must have the suspicion, even more than we do, that their lives are only dreaming. Once the suspicion has been raised, it seems, we can only live by faith—and what shall that faith be?

> Since, then, there exists soul which reasons about what is right and good, and discursive reasoning which enquires about the rightness (*dikaion*) and goodness (*kalon*) of this or that particular thing, there must be some further permanent rightness from which arises the discursive reasoning in the realm of soul. Or how else would it manage to reason? And if soul sometimes reasons about the right and good and sometimes does not, there must be in us Intellect which does not reason discursively but always possesses the right, and there must be also the principle and cause and God of Intellect. He is not divided, but abides, and as he does not abide in place he is contemplated in many beings, in each and every one of those capable of receiving him as

[17] In that best known of philosophical allegories, The Cave, the shadow play is cast on the cave wall by hidden puppeteers: Plato, *The Republic*, Bk. 7.514aff.

> another self, just as the centre of a circle exists by itself, but every one of the radii has its point in the centre and the lines bring their individuality to it. For it is with something of this sort in ourselves that we are in contact with god and are with him and depend upon him, and those of us who converge towards him are firmly established in him.[18]

Plotinus's argument is that reasoning has a starting point in principles we simply 'know' already, and that this 'knowing self' cannot be divided from the things it knows. 'If [Intellect and the intelligible] are not the same, there will be no truth',[19] for even intellect would only experience some *image* of reality, and never be able (obviously) to compare that image with the real.[20] The real, waking world, the one from which we need to fear no further waking, is something that, in a way, we remember.

The implication for our 'immortality' is simply this: that our real selves, the beauties that eternally we are, are eternally known in God. We are occasionally conscious of this, perhaps, and then slip drowsily backward to enjoy the dream. 'Often I have woken up out of the body to my self', Plotinus says, 'and have entered into myself, going out from all other things. ... Then after that rest in the divine, when I have come down from Intellect to discursive reasoning (*eis logismon ek nou*), I am puzzled how I ever came down, and how my soul has come to be in the body.'[21]

Scientific Enlightenment

> I told myself that when one is asleep one believes all sorts of things and finds oneself in all sorts of situations; one believes in them absolutely, without the slightest doubt. When one wakes up, one realizes the inconsistency and inanity of the phantasms of the imagination. In the same way, one might ask oneself about the reality of beliefs one has acquired through one's senses or by reason. Could one not imagine oneself in a state which compares to being awake, just as wakefulness compares to being asleep? Being awake would be like the dreams of that state, which in turn would show that the illusion (of the certainty) of rational knowledge is nothing but vain imagination. Such a state might be the

---

[18] Plotinus, *Ennead*, V.1.11; see 'A Plotinian Account of Intellect': *American Catholic Philosophical Quarterly*, 71 (1997), pp. 421–32.

[19] Plotinus, *Ennead*, V.3.5, 23–4

[20] See my later chapter on the implications of this argument for the right idea of God.

[21] Plotinus, *Ennead*, IV.8.1.1–3

> one that the mystics (Sāfis) claim, for they assert that, when they become totally absorbed in themselves and completely abstract from their senses, they find themselves in a state of mind which does not agree with what is given by reason. Perhaps this state is none other than death? Did not Allah's messenger, peace be upon him, say: "Men are asleep; in dying they awaken." Life here below may be a stream, compared with life beyond. After death, things would appear in a different light, and, as the *Qur'an* says, "We have lifted your veil, and today your sight is penetrating." Then these thoughts came to my mind and gnawed at me I tried to find some way of treating my unhealthy condition, but this was in vain. They could be dispelled only by reasoning, which is impossible without recourse to the first principles of knowledge. If these are not admissible, no construction of a proof is possible.[22]

Does this seem very strange? Perhaps it is. But the shift from here-and-now to a sort of higher insight, a waking-up to realize where and what we are, is not reserved to 'believers'. Nor is it only 'believers' who might begin to worry about 'the illusion of certainty'. Quite otherwise: it is traditional believers who more readily find a place at least for Here.

What is the real world, according to modern materialists, and what are we? It is, by ordinary human standards, Very Big and Very Old. We have been told, repeatedly, that the Medieval Church enforced belief in Aristotelian physics and Ptolemaic astronomy, and that the cosmos they described was 'cosy' and 'anthropocentric'. It is part of the self-understanding of all modern science that Copernicus, Galileo, Bruno, Lyell and Darwin have helped us break out from the cosy crystal spheres of the medieval cosmos. Nowadays we

---

[22] Abu Hamid Muhammad Ibn Muhammad Ibn Ahmad al-Tusi al-Ghazali (1058–1111*), Deliverance from Error and Mystical Union with the Almighty* (1106/7)*: a Translation of* al-Munqidh min *al*-Dalal by Muhammad Abulaylah, ed. George F. McLean (Council for Research in Values & Philosophy: Washington, DC 2002), p. 66 (accessible at http:// www.ghazali.org/books/md/IIA-02main.htm). There is some dispute about the origin of Muhammed's supposed saying (*ibid.*, p. 115n32). The Koranic verse is (*Qaf*) 50. 22. Al-Ghazali's escape from sceptical despair, unlike Descartes', was by a direct experience of God's light: 'My disease grew worse and lasted almost two months, during which I fell prey to skepticism (*safaa*), though neither in theory nor in outward expression. At last, God the Almighty cured me of that disease and I recovered my health and mental equilibrium. The self-evident principles of reason again seemed acceptable; I trusted them and in them felt safe and certain. I reached this point not by well-ordered or methodical argument, but by means of a light God the Almighty cast into my breast, which light is the key to most knowledge' (*ibid.*, p. 67).

'know' that the earth is orbiting a minor star in one spiral arm of an ordinary galaxy, that the cosmos is billions of years old, and that terrestrial life has evolved over many millions of years without a guiding goal. We 'know' that we only see a small segment of the electro-magnetic spectrum, smell a limited range of chemicals and hear hardly any sounds. We 'know' that there are no cosmic standards of beauty, righteousness or even simple kindness. We 'know' that we only 'fall in love' because our genes command it. We 'know' that we may be all wiped out by a pandemic, a change in solar radiation, a passing comet, volcanic action, or a nearby supernova, and that no-one at all will notice that we are gone.[23] We 'know' that there are no privileged times, places, scales or species. We 'know', in short, that almost everything we feel and think is false—and yet we hardly notice this at all. The one significant new literary genre born in the twentieth century is science fiction, which at least attempts to make these changes real to us—and all respectable critics think it's stuff for kids. It only becomes half-way respectable if it can be understood merely to allegorize our present situation and emotions, and certainly not if it attempts to describe the cosmos we all 'know' exists.

What is it really like to live in the convictions taught us by modern scientism? Clearly, it requires us to *wake up,* to stick our heads out from the cosy world, to leave the cave behind—as Plato taught us long ago. The problem is not only Darwin's Doubt, that we can see no reason to suppose that creatures such as us would have the wherewithal to understand the cosmos, nor any reason to try. Nor is it only that the attempt to live as if in the wider world would leave us blind and stammering in the old (as Plato also warned us). The main problem is that it seems that we must abandon all old ways of feeling and believing and, somehow, make up the new. We must somehow decide how 'human' we wish to be,[24] or what 'humanity' demands of us when we look back at ourselves, as it were, from Nowhere.

No doubt this can appeal. Modernism itself is, in some moods, the conviction that the 'old ways' are no more than superstition. And what we know of human history may tend to confirm that judgement. 'History is a nightmare from which I am trying to awake', so

---

[23] As Nietzsche pointed out: *On Truth and Lies in an Extra-Moral Sense,* op. cit (see p. 13 above).

[24] E.O. Wilson, *On Human Nature* (Harvard University Press: Cambridge, MA., 1978), p. 208; I have discussed this further in 'Posthumanism: engineering in the place of ethics': Barry Smith & Berit Brogaard (eds), *Rationality and Irrationality: Proceedings of the 23rd International Wittgenstein Symposium* (ÖbvetHpt: Vienna, 2001), pp. 62–76.

James Joyce caused his Stephen Daedalus to say in response to a jolly anti-Semite.[25]

> Human nature is a hodgepodge of special genetic adaptations to an environment largely vanished, the world of the Ice-Age hunter-gatherer. ... We are forced to choose among the elements of human nature by reference to value systems which these same elements created in an evolutionary age now long vanished. *Fortunately, this circularity of the human predicament is not so tight that it cannot be broken through an exercise of will.*[26]

We ought to abandon all those ancient ties and theories, and begin again. But why? Some have imagined that we can find a new goal simply in reproduction, scattering our genes across the sidereal universe, in whatever mutated form will, maybe, work. What other criterion than this can we imagine? 'Human behavior — like the deepest capacities for emotional response which drive and guide it — is the circuitous technique by which human genetic material has been and will be kept intact. Morality has no other demonstrable function'[27] — that is, or so Wilson declares, there is nothing else that it consistently does, and that explains the particular shape it takes. Our aim *must* be to facilitate the survival of 'human genes'. 'The individual is an evanescent combination of genes drawn from [the human gene-pool], one whose hereditary material will soon be dissolved back into it.'[28] But what justifies or compels our thinking *that* goal unalterable? When C.S. Lewis described the planetary angel Malacandra's conversation with the corrupt scientist Weston, he can hardly have imagined that anyone would so readily admit the charge:

> You do not love any one of your race ... You do not love the mind of your race, nor the body. Any kind of creature will please you if only it is begotten by your kind as they are now. It seems to me ... that what you really love is no completed creature but the very seed itself; for that is all that is left.

---

[25] James Joyce, *Ulysses*, Episode 2: 'Nestor' (Oxford University Press: Oxford, 1993; 1st published 1922), p. 34. My thanks to the many members of the e-list philos-l who supplied me with this reference.

[26] E.O. Wilson, op. cit., p. 196 (my italics); though cf. *ibid.*, p. 88: 'It would be premature to assume that modern civilizations have been built entirely on genetic capital accumulated during the long haul of the Ice Age' — there has been time to diversify and alter.

[27] *Ibid.*, p. 167

[28] *Ibid.*, p. 197

Weston retorts by appealing to 'a man's [fundamental] loyalty to humanity', and the angel continues:

> I see now how the lord of the silent world has bent you. There are laws that all *hnau* know, of pity and straight dealing and shame and the like, and one of these is the love of kindred. He has taught you to break all of them except this one, which is not one of the greatest laws; this one he has bent till it becomes folly and has set it up, thus bent, to be a little, blind Oyarsa in your brain. And now you can do nothing but obey it, though if we ask you why it is a law you can give no other reason for it than for all the other and greater laws which it drives you to disobey.[29]

Others regard this scattering of our seed as about as silly an aim as dispersing plastic ducks across the ocean (probably somewhat sillier: at least the latter may tell us something about ocean currents, and there is a certain excitement when we happen to find such a duck, and can conceive of its travels[30]). A grander scheme, perhaps, is to accumulate all knowledge, until in the last days of the universe the system is complete, whatever the long-ago ancestry of those end-time creatures and creators. It is 'grander', but no less futile, no less absurd.

Waking up from parochial, sectarian, nationalistic or professional pre-occupations itself casts doubt on all our dreaming days, and so on all the plans and motives that once sustained us. Creating any new motives for ourselves, especially in the light of galaxies and cosmic ages, seems quite hopeless. Our ancestors might imagine, with some plausibility, that they could build some monument '*aere perennius*', longer-lived than bronze, whether this was a human lineage, a work of art, a religion, or a theory. They might also, without much self-deception, think it made a difference, that it mattered. But *we* know—or suppose we know—that all ages die, and that our tiny world is an accident. Anything 'of value' we might make or think is 'of value' only to us here-now, and will not last. Any 'new beginnings', of science or art or politics, are unimportant to anyone but ourselves—and we are insignificant already. It is not surprising that

---

[29] C.S. Lewis, *Out of the Silent Planet* (Pan Books: London, 1952; 1st published 1938), p. 163. '*Hnau*' means 'rational animal'; '*Oyarsa*' is the title of a planetary ruler in Lewis's mythology. See also my *Civil Peace and Sacred Order* (Clarendon Press: Oxford, 1989), p. 145.

[30] In fact, the ducks' travels were begun by accident (see *Times Online*, 28th June 2007: http://www.timesonline.co.uk/tol/news/uk/article1996553.ece, accessed 24th March 2008), but we can easily imagine some similar, more deliberate, project!

we mostly fall asleep again, to whatever parochial, sectarian, nationalistic or professional pre-occupations have the greatest strength for us.

For some, this problem is specious. The absence of real values and the vastness of time and space that sensibly diminish our importance will not affect our passions. It is still possible to enjoy meals, and sex, and sunsets, even though we know these are of no cosmic interest or significance. This may be because they have never had any *sacramental* sense of meals, or sex, or sunsets, or think it easily enjoyed by occasional self-deception. But waking to the 'real world' is still, as Socrates said, to practice *dying*,[31] to think much less of all these local lusts and fancies, to look down on ourselves as from a height, to be 'alienated', to be 'alien'.

One way of conceiving this possibility is indeed through science fiction, by imagining how 'machine intelligences' or utter aliens think, rather as our ancestors could imagine how 'angels' think, being discorporate, non-local, thoroughly non-sensual minds. For them, as for waking scientists, there no privileged times, places, scales, spectra or points of view. Whereas our biology picks out just those features of the 'real world' that we 'need to notice' if we are to reproduce our kind, machine intelligences and angels move around the scales, times, places as they will. For them nothing is foregrounded as of more essential significance than anything else, and the fall of a maple-leaf is as momentous as the fall of Rome. There are no long times or short times.[32] We like to feel that *our* time-rate, like our size, is central, just as our ancestors imagined that the Earth was central (though they did not suppose it was therefore very important[33]).

---

[31] Plato, *Phaedo,* 62c ff.

[32] See Chesterton *The Everlasting Man*, op. cit., p. 26.

[33] On the contrary, for medieval Christendom the Earth was very nearly at the *bottom* of the world, pretty close to 'the pits', even the fixed stars were so far off that the Earth was a mathematical point in comparison (Boethius *Consolation of Philosophy* (524 a.d.) Bk. 2, ch. 7: op. cit., p. 73). Macrobius's *Commentary on the Dream of Scipio*, trans. William Harris Stahl (Columbia University Press: New York, 1952) preserved Cicero's 'Dream of Scipio' (originally the concluding section of his *Republic*, lost till the 19th century) through the Middle Ages: both Cicero (106–43 BC) and Macrobius (fl. 400 AD) speak of the Earth as, relatively, a point, and emphasise how huge, how distant and how beautiful the stars are in comparison. The whole cosmos in its turn could be imagined as 'a little thing, the size of a hazel-nut ... which exists now and forever because God loves it' (Julian of Norwich *Revelations of Divine Love* trans. Clifton Wolters (Penguin:

Scientific wakefulness also requires us to conceive that 'time' as we ordinarily experience it is an illusion: there is no single 'present' everywhere, and the sense we have that 'the past' is what is no longer, 'the future' what is not yet determinate, is utterly misleading. All times, as well as all places, scales, rates of change and points of view, are as real as this here-now (which differs, of course, for me and you as I write and you read this). Having 'the Mind of God' in the Stoic or scientific sense requires an *impersonal* attitude, one in which no motions are more significant than others. Chesterton, remember, voiced the problem through one of his poet-heroes, speaking of a 'dry light shed on things'.[34] That dry light, he also agreed, might sometimes do good, 'though in one sense it's the very reverse of knowledge, it's actually suppression of what we know. It's treating a friend as a stranger, and pretending that something familiar is really remote and mysterious'.[35] We need to know things from the inside as well as the outside, as Plotinus also knew:

> If one likens [reality] to a living richly varied sphere, or imagines it as a thing all faces, shining with living faces, or as all the pure souls running together into the same place, with no deficiencies but having all that is their own, and universal Intellect seated on their summits so that the region is illuminated by intellectual light—if one imagined it like this one would be seeing it somehow as one sees another from outside; but one must become that, and make oneself the contemplation.[36]

How this is to come about may be another story.

Harmondsworth, 1966), ch. 5, p. 68. In no case are this earth or humankind itself supremely significant.

[34] *The Poet and the Lunatics*, op. cit., p. 70

[35] 'The Secret of Father Brown' (1927): *Father Brown Stories*, op. cit., p. 817.

[36] *Ennead*, VI.7 [38].15, 25–16, 3. Armstrong, op. cit., vol. 7, p. 136.

8

What is God?

Understanding Words and Pictures

I have already touched on the problems of reading scripture 'blind', as though 'the real meaning' of the texts could be discerned without attention to the community that collected and endorsed them. A similar problem arises for those who consider the 'arguments for God' abstracted from the common practice of believers. Those arguments have, it is true, been helpful to philosophers, in allowing them to reason about the difference between predicative and existential propositions, about the nature of time, and truth, and power. All sorts of paradoxes can be devised to while away the time, and some of them result in greater clarity about what we say and do. Can an omnipotent God make a stone too heavy for Him to lift? Does an omniscient and timeless God ever know that a war is over? Can an invulnerable God ever understand what *pain* is? More serious questions can be raised about the existence of 'evils' of a kind that a benevolent God would surely wish should not exist, and an omnipotent God ensure did not. But it is not clear that anyone who concentrates on these questions is really talking about *God* in the sense believers mean. Militant atheists especially are inclined to suppose that it is easy to say what 'believing in God' amounts to: surely it must just be to suppose that there is an entity with certain well-known properties (omniscient, omnipotent, benevolent; bodiless, timeless, and inscrutable) whose actions can be identified in the here and now, even though they can't be understood. It must be just like thinking there are visiting extra-terrestrials, or fairies, or the Loch Ness Monster, and thinking this so firmly that everything is evidence for the belief, and all counter-evidence easily dismissed.

Even in the abstract, in the realm of philosophical theology, this is entirely wrong. Whatever is meant by 'God' must exist, if at all, in every possible world, and there can therefore never be any possible scenario incompatible with His existence. He cannot be a contingent being, dependent on internal parts or external circumstances for His being (as extra-terrestrials, fairies and the Loch Ness Monster would be). He has no 'properties' at all, in the sense that He might lose them or have had different ones; nor is He a member of any class of things, and everything we say of Him is subtly or not-so-subtly false. At the same time, God is *essentially* worshipful: not just any powerful being, even one that cannot be resisted.[1] This is not merely the talk of speculative philosophers: it is embedded in the creeds of every great religion, both Abrahamic and (with appropriate translations) Buddhist. There are, at the same time, *stories* which are offered as a way of thinking ourselves into 'the right frame of mind', but those stories are, expressly, not to be taken as straightforward truths. 'We know that "God" is not a proper name, and that the Holy One is not a thing, a being of some particular kind'.[2]

Consider how the Annunciation, for example, is represented in Orthodox icons or Western pictures (that is, the occasion when Mary was informed that she would or could be the mother of the coming Christ[3]). On the one side Mary sits, perhaps in a blue gown, and with a lily beside her, in a vase. On the other, a winged figure, clothed perhaps in gold. Windows open behind the pair, looking out over a green landscape. The lily, historically, is there because painters felt a need to give the vase a purpose, and also stands for purity. The vase is there because, in the *Protoevangelium* or *Book of James* (an early apocryphal Gospel, not accepted into the canon), Mary was getting water from a well. She is wearing blue to signify that she is or will be Queen of Heaven. The angel has wings because they fly so far and fast. The picture, in short, is in part a cryptogram, a message to be interpreted, not a replica of some past actual scene as it might have been observed by some other human witness. This is not, even now, an unfamiliar pattern: pictures of long-dead dinosaurs don't strictly represent what would have been seen (by whom?), but simply summarize some current theories about how such creatures worked. We don't know even what *we* would have seen if we were wished back there and then. We certainly don't know what was *actually* seen, by whatever non-human witnesses. Models, pictures, and even narra-

---

[1] Consider one of A.E. Van Vogt's inventions, the marsh gas turned into a 'galactic spirit' (*The Voyage of the Space Beagle* (Grayson & Grayson: London, 1951): this is a being capable of mass destruction, who feeds on death, present at every point of its galaxy. It may, in some sense, have 'god-like powers', but no serious believer would suppose that it was *God*.

[2] Lash, op. cit., p. 59.

[3] *Luke* 1.26–38.

tives, are only ways of conveying (we hope) some truths: they aren't ever exactly 'literal'. *The Acts of the Apostles* records that the risen Christ 'was taken up, and a cloud received him out of [the apostles'] sight'.[4] It does not follow that this is what we would have seen, even if the story is, in a way, quite accurate (that is to say, it conveys what was intended).

Both popular stories and philosophical abstractions somehow convey a message, but it isn't one that will be understood without attention to the larger realm of 'religious belief and practice'. The point is not that we must believe before we can understand (though that may also, sometimes, be true), but that all these stories and abstractions need a context, every bit as much as remarks about DNA, or quarks, or singularities. Expecting to understand them all by a simple, unguided reading or inspection is absurd (unless it is a claim to personal inspiration). Even Protestants convinced that the Scriptures are made clear to every earnest enquirer must still acknowledge (as Augustine said[5]) that they learnt their *alphabet* at least from other humans, and that they come to the Scriptures primed to understand them, exactly, as the Word of God.

The same issues arise in thinking about Nirvana or the Buddha-nature, and readers who come to the founding texts of Buddhism with the conviction that a 'fresh look' will show them what was really, originally, meant, are likely to make as many grotesque errors. Those founding texts, after all (like the Hebrew, Christian and Islamic scriptures), were collected and composed by believers for believers. But my concern at the moment is with Abrahamic theism, and especially the Christian tradition. The question remains: what is God?

What, in the proper religious context, is it for God to be omnipotent, omniscient and the rest? Actually, it might be better to use less Latinate expressions: God is conceived as all-powerful and all-knowing. The first claim is that 'there is nothing in death or life, in the realm of spirits or superhuman powers, in the world as it is or the world as it shall be, in the forces of the universe, in heights or depths—nothing in all creation that can separate us from the love of God in Christ Jesus our Lord':[6] worries about whether God can sin, or sneeze, or make a mistake in calculating Pi, or make a stone He

---

[4] *Acts* 1.9

[5] See Augustine, *De Doctrina Christiana*, Preface (http://ccat.sas.upenn.edu/jod/augustine/ddc1.html)

[6] *Romans* 8.38

cannot lift (and all the rest) are quite irrelevant.[7] The second claim, of omniscience or of omnipresence, is that nothing is hidden from God:

> If I ascend up into heaven, thou art there! If I make my bed in Sheol, behold, thou art there! If I take the wings of the morning and dwell in the uttermost parts of the sea, even there shall thy hand lead me, and thy right hand shall hold me. If I say, 'Surely the darkness shall cover me'; even the night shall be light about me. Yea, the darkness hideth not from thee; but the night shineth as the day: the darkness and the light are both alike to thee.[8]

God is that than which none greater can be conceived, but not in the sense that He is, as it were, 'the largest number'. Mathematically, there is no such number (as any imagined instance can be surpassed merely by adding 1). Physically, there might be a largest actual set, such that there is no class of things that is in fact more numerous, or else a largest single entity, such that there is nothing larger, but this would—in both cases—be 'as it happens' and not of necessity. We might always be able to imagine some additional perfection, as we can imagine an additional extension, and therefore deny that there either is or could be anything with no imaginable lack. But in imagining such perfections, we do implicitly acknowledge a *direction*, a criterion according to which the addition is '*more* perfect', 'greater'. 'God' stands for that direction, and not any instance: not something to be exhausted, but forever surpassing anything we conceive. Without that criterion, that direction, there is only difference and change, and nothing to say that any change or difference is for the better.

Gods and the Wow Factor

It is already evident that the presence of 'a god' is known *emotionally*, and that we may invoke it by familiar rituals. 'A festival', so one of Schleiermacher's characters insists, 'is founded only to commemorate that through the representation of which a certain mood and disposition can be aroused within men.'[9] Even in polytheistic cultures a god is not just a very long-lived and powerful being, whom

[7] For the record: the description 'a stone that cannot be lifted by someone who can lift every stone' makes no sense, and it is no diminution of God's power to agree that He can't make such a stone (any more than a round square), since there is no such thing. Alternatively, if we hesitate to impose even the laws of logic on Omnipotence, then He can live with the contradiction of being both able and unable to lift such a stone if He so chooses (that is, if He makes the stone).

[8] *Psalms* 138[139].8–12

[9] Schleiermacher, *Christmas Eve*, op. cit., p. 77. Christmas, he adds, is meant 'to incite joy'. For a further examination of the point, putting more emphasis on the

sensible human beings placate or seek to avoid, any more than a 'fairy', in such cultures as believe in fairies, is a pretty winged person about the size of a butterfly whose biology we might hope to disentangle.[10] Gods, fairies, demons cast a 'glamour' round them: indeed, they *are* that glamour. They are the Wow Factor in experience. As I said in an earlier chapter, Sex, War, Curiosity, Artistic Creativity and Trickiness (to give them their abstract titles) are powers we have to deal with. We appreciate their presence not by simple sight, but by the *manner* of our experience. 'Man is a shadow's dream (*skias onar anthropos*), but when god sheds a brightness then shining light is on earth and life is sweet as honey':[11] the god that Pindar had in mind on that occasion was Success.

In a purely polytheistic culture (though it may be that there are few of these: our own age may be one of very few candidates) there is no reason to rank one god above another. All have their devotees, and may resent devotions given elsewhere, but with no single, overmastering power to regularize their relations. Pagan Greeks, as I have already suggested, had some hopes that the bright sky, who is Zeus,[12] could enforce at least the duties of hospitality and oaths once taken. Living beneath that sky—living particularly under the *Greek* sky, perhaps—it is difficult to think that secrets can be kept, or consequences avoided. Once upon a time, perhaps, Titanic impulses ruled all the world, and suffered no pangs of guilt.[13] Once upon a time, perhaps, that age of Cronos was an age of innocence (or else an age

---

feeling of absolute dependence, see Jeffrey VanderWilt 'Why worship?: Schleiermacher speaks to the question': *Scottish Journal of Theology*, 56 (2003), pp. 286–307.

[10] See 'How to Believe in Fairies' in *Inquiry*, 30 (1988), pp. 337–55

[11] Pindar, *Pythian*, 8.95ff

[12] A.B. Cook, *Zeus: a study in ancient religion* (Cambridge University Press: Cambridge, 1914) mustered etymological, literary and cultic evidence for the identification of Zeus with the sky (see especially vol. 1, pp. 1–62). His account is marred by the then-fashionable conviction that this must have been a 'primitive' idea, surpassed by anthropomorphic representations of Zeus as, he suggests, a weather-working magician. This would be a more interesting notion if it were William Blake's: 'God appears and God is light to those poor souls who dwell in night, but does a human form display to those who dwell in realms of day' (Blake *Auguries of Innocence* (1803) lines 129–32: *Complete Works* op. cit., p. 434). Ken Dowden's *Zeus* (Routledge: London, 2006) is a short and helpful survey of ancient and modern concepts of the god.

[13] Interestingly, rabbinic exegesis of the Flood narratives suggested that the ante-diluvian world was immensely prosperous and easy (Cohn, *Noah's Flood*, op. cit., pp. 32f), and that its inhabitants were utterly immoral: that age, just like the age of Cronos, might be considered good or bad depending on one's attitude.

for animals). Since that age's overthrow it is the God of Justice we must hope is ruling,[14] but the other gods must also be acknowledged. Prohibiting or trying to prohibit sex, or drunkenness, or violent sport, or curiosity, may well turn out to be disastrous, but any of those gods or moods or passions can also be, as Blake said, 'thieves and rebels'.[15]

Our own unconscious metaphysics may prevent our seeing this straight. We suppose, in something like a post-Aristotelian way, that real entities are distinct and countable, localized, corporeal substances, with particular histories. Hearing that the Greeks (and others) believe in 'gods', we imagine that these must be just such entities, though irritatingly divorced from our conditions. But it is possible that the Greeks (and others) were rather pre-Platonic: real entities are ones with real intrinsic natures, which appear and reappear in many different moments and under different names. It is what we call 'universals' that are the real things, and 'we' are only their playground or arena.

> Eternity is passion, girl or boy
> Cry at the onset of their sexual joy
> 'For ever and for ever'; then awake
> Ignorant what Dramatis Personae spake.[16]

We can admit that there is, to our eyes, something odd in this. Aristotelian common sense is confident that, for example, *people* smile and yawn. Both smiles and yawns are infectious: are we to wonder whether it is the *same* smile, the *same* yawn that flits across a company? If two or more people are thinking or feeling *the same thing*, in what sense is there a single thing they think or feel? Does it exist without them? Platonists may sometimes answer 'Yes'. At any

---

[14] See Hugh Lloyd-Jones, *The Justice of Zeus* (University of California Press: San Francisco, 1971).

[15] William Blake, 'A Descriptive Catalogue' (1809): *Complete Works*, op. cit., p. 571 (see p. 44 above). This remarks reflects an older story, mentioned in the Koran: 'We created you and then formed you and then We said to the Angels, "Prostrate before Adam" and they prostrated except for Iblis. He was not among those who prostrated. God said, "What prevented you from prostrating when I commanded you?" He (Iblis) replied, "I am better than him. You created me from fire and You created him from clay". God said, "Descend from heaven. It is not for you to be arrogant in it. So get out! You are one of the abased. " (*Koran* Surah 7 (al-A`raf), 11–13). See also *Life of Adam and Eve* aka *Apocalypse of Moses*, chs. 13–14.

[16] W.B. Yeats, 'Supernatural Songs 8: Whence had they come?', *Collected Poems* (Macmillan: London, 1950), p. 332.

rate this reply may be heuristically convenient.[17] We can *examine* the thing that is shared, and learn from it. Gods, angels, demons, fairies, are part of the human universe—and also, probably, of the pre-human too. We live among enchantments, and also dream of freedom. Religion, on the one hand, provides a set of symbols, rituals and readings to give gods a place. On the other hand, at least some forms of religion also offer a release. In Greek antiquity Dionysus subverts all gender roles and urban decency to allow his worshippers a taste of being gods. Abraham is called away from Haran and the gods of his forefathers. The people of Israel are led out of Egypt. Gautama abandons both caste responsibilities and the ascetic life to discover an escape from *dukkha*, from the Wheel turned round by anger, greed and ignorance.[18] Hindus distinguish the path of the gods, *deva-yana*, which leads to liberation, from the path of the ancestors, *pitri-yana*, that leads only round the Wheel.[19] And atheists also dream of an escape. There is—all these traditions tell us—something greater than all usual gods and phantoms. *Magna est veritas, et praevalet*.[20]

So if gods are, in our terms, *states* or *energies*, what state or energy is God? Aristotle's reply is that God *is theoria*, and in living thus 'theo-

---

[17] Especially since the Aristotelian belief in *substances* like people, distinct from other categories (qualities, quantities, relations and the rest), is usually now dismissed as an artefact of language: I do not say that it should be. But if moderns are willing to abandon that common sense distinction they may as well admit the reality of yawns and smiles and gods.

[18] Interestingly, a similar threesome can be found in Epicurean thought: anger, fear and indolence are mingled with soul-particles in the composite living being (Lucretius, *On the Nature of Things*, 3.268ff: 'So heat and air and the invisible power of breath, mixed up, create one nature, together with that mobile force which causes them to move and so give sensitive movement to the whole body'). There is at least a resemblance between the Epicurean and early Buddhist ways: on the possibility of mutual influence between the Mediterranean and Indian milieux see Thomas McEvilley op. cit.

[19] Charles Upton, *Folk Metaphysics: Mystical Meanings in Traditional Folk-Songs and Spirituals* (Sophia Perennis: San Rafael, CA, 2008), p. 23. The source is *Rig-Veda* X. 88. 16, a hymn to Agni, 'who hath spread abroad the radiant Mornings, and, coming with his light, unveils the darkness'. See also *Bhagavad-Gita* 8. 26: 'These two paths of the world, the bright and the dark, are considered to be eternal; proceeding by one of them, one reaches the supreme state from which there is no return. Proceeding by the other, one returns to the mortal world and becomes subject to birth and death once more.'

[20] 'The truth is great, and prevails': *I Esdras*, 4.41 (Vulgate version). Note that the opposite of Truth, in this context, is Unrighteousness. In Greek, the opposite of Truth (*aletheia*) is Forgetting (*lethe*): see *God's World and the Great Awakening* (Clarendon Press: Oxford, 1991), pp. 48ff.

retically' we live by what is most divine in us, and at the same time what is most really human.[21] Quite what *theoria*, contemplation, is may be as difficult a question as what God is: in fact, it is nearly the same question. Consider also the writer known as John: 'God is love; and he that dwelleth in love dwelleth in God, and God in him'.[22] And what 'Love' is may be as difficult a question. And finally consider the late third century Platonist, Plotinus, as he struggles to explain what he means by 'the One': it is 'the productive power of all things',[23] the power of everything to live, to act, to generate. The One is everywhere—but not because it fills a pre-existent space. Rather every place and every entity exists in love. The One *is* Love (though whether he means exactly the same by this as John is another matter).[24].

In all these cases God is a state, an energy, a power. And in all three cases, reflection led to the conclusion that He was, in effect, a trinity.[25] Contemplation requires an object, but this cannot be one separate from the spectator. Love requires a beloved. Becoming a god in this new sense is joining in the dance, the feast, the life of the Blessed Trinity.

> It is like a choral dance: in the order of its singing the choir keeps round its conductor but may sometimes turn away so that he is out of their sight, but when it turns back to him it sings beautifully and is truly with him; so we are always around him—and if we were not, we should be totally dissolved and no longer exist—but not always turned towards him; but when we do look to him, then we are at our goal and at rest and do not sing out of tune as we truly dance our god-inspired dance around him.[26]

To be even momentarily 'elevated' is to be in the presence of a god. It does not follow that *not* being elevated implies its absence. Con-

---

[21] 'We must not follow those who advise us, being men, to think of human things, and, being mortal, of mortal things, but must, so far as we can, make ourselves immortal, and strain every nerve to live in accordance with the best thing in us; for even if it be small in bulk, much more does it in power and worth surpass everything': Aristotle, *Nicomachean Ethics* ,10.1177b30ff.

[22] *I John* 4.16

[23] *Ennead*, III.8.10; see Eric D. Perl, 'The Power of All Things': *ACPQ*, 71 (1997), 301–13.

[24] *Ennead*, VI.8.15

[25] Saying 'He' is not to impute a gender, but to resist the easy conclusion that the One is 'impersonal' just because He is also not a person.

[26] *Ennead*, VI.9 [9].8, 38ff

sider the notion of a 'hidden god', known not in strength but in weakness. Plato was prepared to conceive of a genuinely *just,* or *righteous,* person, who was universally abused, tortured and condemned to a felon's death. By common standards (not only ancient Greek standards) he would be thought a wretch, a failure, 'one hated by the gods'. Plato, and later philosophers also, believed that he might still be 'happy' (as we misleadingly translate the term '*eudaimon*', which is to say: being on good terms with his god), that there would be something quite untouched by failure and disgrace. A merely subjective interpretation of this paradox (that the righteous man is happy even in the Bull of Phalaris—a notorious instrument of death by torture) might be that the 'righteous man' would still know that he was doing the right thing, would be content with the consequences of his defiance. But maybe the catastrophe, realistically, could go still further:

> Barbed wire enclosed an arbitrary spot
> Where bored officials lounged (one cracked a joke)
> And sentries sweated for the day was hot:
> A crowd of ordinary decent folk
> Watched from without and neither moved nor spoke
> As three pale figures were led forth and bound
> To three posts driven upright in the ground.
> The mass and majesty of this world, all
> That carries weight and always weighs the same
> Lay in the hands of others; they were small
> And could not hope for help and no help came:
> What their foes liked to do was done, their shame
> Was all the worst could wish; they lost their pride
> And died as men before their bodies died.[27]

Even righteous pride may perish, and yet somehow there still be something untouched, impervious, a god. Plotinus supposed that the higher soul to which we should awaken is already 'There' (in the alongside, Real World), and exists in its felicity whatever happens here.[28] Even in the bull of Phalaris, even in the utmost agony, 'there is another which, even while it is compelled to accompany that which

---

[27] W.H. Auden, 'The Shield of Achilles': *Collected Shorter Poems 1927–57* (Faber: London, 1966), p. 295.

[28] Plotinus, *Ennead,* IV.8 [6].8

suffers pain, remains in its own company and will not fall short of the vision of the universal good'.[29]

One of the oddest claims of Christian theologians is that 'the Greeks' could not have accepted the idea that any god could endure crucifixion. To this there are two replies. The first, who then accepted it? The second, that they plainly could, and did. *Success* might well have been the standard criterion of worth, but both philosophy and traditional story had words of praise for *failure*. Heracles, who was the other (and now less familiar) 'Son of God' admired and followed in the early centuries AD, was the rightful king of his people, forced into servitude, performed astonishing feats, was betrayed by a close companion, died a death by torture—and was called up to the heavens. The Heraclean and Christian stories aren't identical, and neither are the morals drawn from them, but the Heraclean story shows that even pagans knew that gods have different standards of success.[30]

So, once again: what's God? The villains of Auden's poem, and of real life, condemn their enemies to a disgraceful death as a way of destroying even their reputation and the cause they serve. But it happens often enough that their attempt backfires: it is *they* who are judged wanting, and their victim rules unconquerable from the tree. Sometimes it may indeed be the victim's visible calm bravery that effects the result: Diogenes Laertius's *Lives of the Philosophers* accumulates examples of such philosophical defiance to perturb us academics. Even today there have been real life cases. But the victim need not be visibly brave to achieve the greater result: we are moved by innocence, by abject pain, by utter disgrace inflicted on the helpless, irrespective of the *bravery* they display. In brief, we see a god—even in the moment when the victim no longer does.

The easy way (for moderns) into this way of seeing is still via Story. But as Duffy points out, it is difficult to sustain ourselves

---

[29] Plotinus, *Ennead*, I.4 [46].13, 6ff. Charles Williams attempted to represent this simultaneous identity and difference in *All Hallows Eve* (Faber: London, 1945).

[30] To avoid misunderstanding: the popular claim that early Christianity (merely another Jewish sect) was infected, probably by that much-maligned figure Paul of Tarsus, with all sorts of pagan stories (conception by divine action, virgin birth, resurrection, atoning sacrifice) is wholly without merit. Christian missionaries were not unlike Cynics (followers of Diogenes of Sinope who adopted Heracles as an iconic figure: see F. Gerald Downing, *Christ and the Cynics: Jesus and other radical preachers in first-century tradition* (JSOT Press: Sheffield, 1988)), but they could not have borrowed the Salvation narrative from pagans (whether Cynics, Mithraists or Isis-worshippers), since no such narrative existed. In later centuries some other sects copied some of the Christian themes, but there really is no resemblance in detail or in significance even then.

within the story if we simultaneously deny its *truth*. We may, from a distance, be able to insist that it is the *tyrants* who are judged wanting, their victims who are vindicated in the very fact of their destruction. But if this is a lie, it is the tyrants who laugh last. If there is no God, then the victims are not vindicated.

> Suppose that Socrates was wrong, that we have *not* once seen the Truth, and so will not, intuitively, recognize it when we see it again. This means that when the secret police come, when the torturers violate the innocent, there is nothing to be said to them of the form 'There is something within you which you are betraying. Though you embody the practices of a totalitarian society which will endure forever, there is something beyond those practices which condemns you'.[31]

Or as an older writer put it, 'if there is no God, then anything is permitted', in that the powerful can get away with anything, however vile (especially when they can easily—and falsely—be persuaded that Darwinian Theory rules out genuine altruism).[32]

Suppose on the contrary that Socrates was right. The Truth is not forgotten. It prevails. Holding to that conviction, of course, requires us to have a conception of that truth which makes it possible—logically and psychologically—to believe it true.

The God of Atheists

Rorty's claim of course is not, in modern terms, absurd. It is easy enough to devise a naturalistic explanation for the awed excitement that we may feel at the sight of beauty, or authority, or virtue. Such excitements, we can convince ourselves quite easily, must have given some slight advantage in fertility: creatures who felt like that had more descendants than those who did not feel like that at all, or had the feelings for quite different objects. Whether we can really tell a plausible story to explain how this was so is another matter. Con-

---

[31] R. Rorty, *Consequences of Pragmatism* (University of Minnesota Press: Minneapolis, 1982), p. xlii. See also J. Stout, *Ethics since Babel* (James Clarke & Co: Cambridge, 1990), p. 257. Stout goes on to say, contra Rorty, that he and 'the example of every remaining virtuous person, as well as whatever exemplary lives we can keep alive in memory' can still condemn the torturer (*ibid.*, p. 259). But this will be a mere act of will, and susceptible to the usual erosion of our own fidelity and memory.

[32] F.M. Dostoyevsky, *The Brothers Karamazov*, part 1, book 1, chapter 6 (Ivan speaks): see Cornwell, op. cit., pp. 70ff for a clear explanation of the meaning of this remark. As Cornwell points out, Dostoyevsky had ample, personal reason to think the suggestion plausible.

vinced Darwinians usually think it enough to say that it *must* have happened like that, even though there are other creatures in the world (it seems) who don't feel awed excitement, but only such transient desires as keep them living, feeding, breeding. Awed excitement, we can plausibly contend, may also lead to personal disaster, and an end to procreation. But perhaps, statistically, the claim is true: in our particular lineage it has, for unknown reasons, 'paid' in evolutionary terms to be *awestruck*. The objects of our awe aren't 'awful' in themselves, and any 'awesomeness' that we perceive in them has played no independent causal role in natural or human history. Mothers are convulsed with love for their newborn children (mostly), but not because those neonates are lovely: it is a hormonal surge that is needed to induce the attentive care the newborns need, and cuckoos would and do evoke the same response. Lovers find everything about their beloveds marvellous, but not because they are: without this helpful passion how could they endure each other's loathly habits? We are all affected by trumpets, waving banners and rich jewels, but not because these things have any real worth of a sort that any rational being would recognize: we are affected because the ones who weren't are dead. When the Martians arrive (as it were) they will be quite unmoved by flummery like this: 'intellects vast and cool and unsympathetic',[33] though with their own strange drives and passing fancies.

Awed excitement may be pleasant even when we no longer believe that anything is awesome, and no longer have any good reason to think that Martians—and post-human creatures who think just like them[34]—are psychopaths. Actually, the Martians do still have some undefended motives, directed toward the survival of 'their kind' and kindred. It is not clear why motives of this sort should survive the Darwinian acid any more than others. At the moment I may be moved by the thought of a struggling human lineage (or the still larger lineage that is Life on Earth). Humankind or Lifekind is a sort of god. But if all 'gods' and 'godliness' are mere projections, so also are these Kinds. Pleasure and pain—that is the pleasure and pain that is realized here-now, by me—may still retain their power, but even they have less significance than once they did.

---

[33] H.G. Wells, *The War of the Worlds* (Penguin: Harmondsworth, 1946; 1st published 1897), p. 9

[34] A less well-known tale of H.G. Wells imagines that the Martians (perhaps) have invaded more successfully, by infecting us with the mindset Wells preferred: see *Star Begotten* (Chatto & Windus: London, 1937).

'Pain' is no longer what we feel at the destruction of some real good, and neither is 'pleasure' a sign of the god's presence. They are only curious sensations, to be obtained in whatever easy way—if they really can be pleasant in the absence of a god.[35]

Militant atheists, in fact, are rarely as atheistical as they suppose. Their rage stems from real devotion and from awed excitement. It is because they suppose that 'religionists' have different and more alien gods that they despise them. In condemning 'religionists', and also in seeking to condemn the putative Creator or the literary character they find in religious writings, they bear witness to a god beyond both world and religious writings. Defiance 'is really an unconscious homage to something in or behind that cosmos which [the atheist] recognizes as infinitely valuable and authoritative: for if mercy and justice were really only private whims of his own with no objective and impersonal roots, and if he realized this, he could not go on being indignant.'[36]

The dangerous delusion that Chesterton described (see pp. 104, 171 above), whereby nothing in the world has any importance compared to the fanatic's own purposes is not quite the same as 'atheism'. On the contrary, militants might reasonably point out, the delusion may be found *especially* among those who imagine that they have God on their side and, in effect, name their own egos 'God' rather than feeling the presence of a *demanding* God quite other than their own will and fancy. Militants believe that we should open our eyes and hearts to Honest Truth—and so also do theists, more honest at least in this, that they openly acknowledge that Truth as *God* (that is, precisely as something we ought to serve, and that lies at the heart of our own being). 'I had promised to show you, if you recall, that there is something higher than our mind and reason. There you have it—truth itself! Embrace it if you can and enjoy it!'[37]

---

[35] Even masturbation, after all, needs something more than friction to be successful: it needs at least the *imagined* presence of a sexual partner, whose appearance glows more brightly by the act. And no-one, as Plotinus said, would really prefer the *appearance* of the beloved to the real thing (*Enneads,* VI.7 [38].26, 21f). Or rather, that preference for a comfortable unreality is one route to damnation: Charles Williams, *Descent into Hell* (Faber: London 1937)!

[36] C.S. Lewis, 'De Futilitate' (1924): *Essay Collection*, ed. Lesley Walmsley (Harper Collins: London, 2000), p. 680, cited by Michael Ward, *Planet Narnia: the Seven Heavens in the Imagination of C.S. Lewis* (Oxford University Press: New York, 2008), p. 211.

[37] Augustine, *De Libero Arbitrio,* 2.13.35, op. cit., p. 144.

I shall address the *metaphysics* of truth in a moment. The point here is to recognize that truth is suffused with value, for honest atheists as well as theists. Contemplatives of any honest school are freed from enchantment not because they see all things as indifferent or ugly,[38] but because every real thing is beautiful, and such as so awaken joy in those who really see it. 'They exist and appear to us and he who sees them cannot possibly say anything else except that they are what really exists. What does "really exist" mean? That they exist as beauties'.[39] 'Or rather, beautifulness is reality'.[40]

And as Samuelson points out, that the God of Israel is infinite and eternal 'means that whatever truth is known, that truth is never final and complete'.[41] What we know, even what we know as beautiful, points always beyond itself. Or as Plotinus put it, the One holds beauty as a golden veil or barrier before itself.[42]

Militant atheists don't really want to explain away their awe, even if that awe is directed simply at the elegance and splendour of the natural world (and their own intelligence in seeing it). Their impulse is rather that of monotheists everywhere: *their* God is a jealous God, willing to abide no rival. We must not make any idols for ourselves, nor trust any other feelings that we have except the one that elevates their God. More casual atheists find this as puzzling as the dogmas of more ordinary believers: they have no other criterion themselves than what at any particular moment seems most natural to believe or wish. Like many other postmodernists they are, in effect, as polytheistic as our pagan forebears—more so, since those pagans were mostly persuaded that there was one God overall, even if He stayed in—or was—the background to the easier drama of the little gods. Militant atheists, like orthodox Abrahamists, insist that there is one Truth only, that its ways are not like ours, and that all lesser 'gods' are phantoms. 'The faith and trust of the heart makes both God and

[38] That is how *fairies*, in the Celtic tradition, see things, being cynically immune to their own glamour: see 'How to Believe in Fairies' in *Inquiry*, 30 (1988), pp. 337–55.

[39] Plotinus, *Ennead*, I.6 [1].5, 18f

[40] *Ennead*, I.6 [1].6, 21; 'For this reason being is longed for because it is the same as beauty, and beauty is lovable because it is being' (V.8 [31].9, 41)

[41] Samuelson, 'On the Symbiosis of Science and Religion', op. cit., p. 94.

[42] Plotinus, *Enneads*, I.6 [1].9.

idol', and only Reality is worth our trust.[43] To this austere conviction some will respond that 'they cannot worship what they hate, or serve a god they dare not know', and prefer to make gods out 'of friendly clay and kindly stone, to warm them from the cold of Space'.[44]

One further issue: some self-styled atheists will acknowledge both that there is Intelligence at work in all the world, and that the world, so ordered, excites their admiration, even their love. They are content, in effect, to leave this unexamined, and to maintain only that they don't accept a 'personal' or an 'anthropomorphic' God. This may mean only that they don't suppose that there is an 'Old Man in the Sky', and their objection to the Abrahamic faiths (or any other theistic tradition) rests on a grotesque error, a refusal actually to listen to what theists tell them about their belief in God. Nobodaddy is explicitly rejected in all the great religions. Whatever it is we mean by 'God' it is not *that*. God is, expressly, *not* 'a person', not something dependent on an abiding lawful cosmos, with a biography, parts and passions. Human beings, according to the Abrahamic tradition, are *in some sense* 'in His image', but we are not to suppose that He is *like* anything in the earth or in the heavens. Our focus must be on something utterly beyond all images. Even Christians, who suppose that the human form has been taken up into the Godhead, that God has been truly Man and suffered along with us, are careful in how they say this.

'Pantheistic' or 'Spinozistic' atheists, content to admire a cosmic beauty but determined not to acknowledge 'the God of Abraham', are mistaken in their notion of what traditional believers think. But there may still be serious questions to address. What, after all, does it *mean* to be 'impersonal' or 'personal'? One relevant distinction lies between those who think that the Order of Things is absolutely fixed, and those who believe it is more flexible, more fluid, that it is open to possibilities. A merely Stoic or Spinozistic attitude in this has no recourse but submission: things are exactly and entirely as they *must* be, and it is foolish to complain, however often we are impelled to do so. Atheistical or misotheistical rebellion is a waste of breath. The Hebrew tradition, by contrast, *praises* those who argue with the

---

[43] The epigram is Luther's *Werke* (1833ff), 30, 1:133, 1–8), cited by Wolfhart Pannenberg, *The Apostle's Creed in the Light of Today's Questions*, trans. Margaret Kohl (SCM Press: London, 1972), p. 4.

[44] After John Buchan, 'Stocks and Stones' (1911), in *The Moon Endureth* (Thomas Nelson: Edinburgh, 1923), p. 162.

Lord, who complain, who demand that the Judge of all the earth do right. Things *don't* have to be 'like this', and there is some point appealing. It is the *impatience* of Job that gets him an answer. That God, in some strange way, is 'personal', after all, even if He is not 'a person', is as much as to say that the Order of Things is fluid, and that complaints are heard. God has subjected Himself to judgement, even the judgement of His people.

Let us suppose, for a moment, that the militant atheist's judgement is, in a way, correct. Let it be the case that the One Original 'maker of gods and men' is well represented in 'natural history', viewed as an unending struggle for survival. Let is suppose that It is indeed indifferent to the pains and tribulations of Its creation, that It cares only for Its own magnificence, and that there is no power, in heaven or earth, that can withstand Its 'anger'. What exactly is our alternative to 'worship'? It is easy enough to *say* that we can 'defy' the laws It makes, that we can rage against it, 'disdaining the coward terrors of the slave of Fate'.[45] But by hypothesis, we cannot actually prevail against It, and even our rage is something It has made. In the absence of any 'message from outside', any secret assistance from an independent power, we have no sensible recourse but Stoic resignation. And the image of Nobodaddy that militant atheists purport to draw from the Hebrew Scriptures seems to be exactly what they believe the World as a whole to be. Why then do they rage against the God they (mistakenly) detect in the Scriptures—unless they really do retain some memory, some sense, that this is not what should be, nor yet what will in the end prevail? Their anger rests on the conviction that the world *must* not be, *cannot* be, in the unyielding grip of an indifferent and unconquerable Satan.

Orthodox Argument

As I said earlier, a belief in God rarely depends on abstract metaphysics. The original faith of Israel, or so Gerhard von Rad convincingly maintained, was in the God of Israel's redemptive history, the one who gave the Law. He is acknowledged as the Maker and Redeemer of the human or the Hebrew world before He is recognized as Creator of the entire world.[46] That it was *God* who made heaven and earth is not a tautology (that whoever it was that made them made them), but a declaration. *This* is the power that stands

---

[45] Russell, 'Free Man's Worship', op. cit..

[46] Gerhard von Rad, 'The Theological Problem of the Old Testament Doctrine of Creation' (1936) in Anderson *Creation*, op. cit., pp. 53–64.

behind and within all things that are—but even if it weren't, we should acknowledge Him as the power that created Israel (the people and tradition, not the modern state). God is what we are moved and commanded by, not what we vaguely postulate, and it is often far more important to 'have faith', in the senses I described before, than to have a detailed intellectual understanding of the creeds.

> May not Christians ... be allowed to believe the divinity of our Saviour, or that in Him God and man make one Person, and be verily persuaded thereof, so far as for such faith or belief to become a real principle of life and conduct? inasmuch as, by virtue of such persuasion, they submit to His government, believe His doctrine, and practise His precepts, although they form no abstract idea of the union between the divine and human nature; nor may be able to clear up the notion of *person* to the contentment of a minute philosopher.[47]

The British especially have good reason to prefer an *inarticulate* devotion: heresy-hunting (which is a practice often associated with attempts to get things clear) has a sadly bloody history in these islands. But there are such things as 'heresies',[48] and some of them are dangerous: that, after all, is what all militant atheists, and even more casual and liberal atheists, also believe. We ought to put some effort into getting our beliefs in order, and so must practice metaphysics. Even atheistical argument is actually theological; even materialist argument is metaphysical. Judged as theology such works as Richard Dawkins' *The Blind Watchmaker* or *The God Delusion* are really very bad, not because they draw atheistical conclusions, but because they show no metaphysical or historical understanding of the doctrines they oppose, nor of the proper techniques of metaphysical argument. It is as if creationists were to criticise Darwinian Theory (as some do) without ever bothering to find out what the modern theory is, or whether there are answers to the stereotyped

---

[47] George Berkeley, *Alciphron* (Euphranor speaks): *Works*¸ed. T.E. Jessop & A.A. Luce, vol. 3 (Thomas Nelson: Edinburgh, 1950), p. 298. See my 'Berkeley's Philosophy of Religion' in Kenneth Winkler ed., *Cambridge Companion to Berkeley* (Cambridge University Press: New York, 2005), pp. 369–404. See also Lash, op. cit., p. 89: 'the primary function of Christian doctrine is regulative rather than descriptive'.

[48] Originally, a 'heresy' (*hairesis*) is a sectarian belief, a chosen set of axioms which others do not share (as it might be Stoic or Epicurean axioms and hypotheses). It later came to mean a conscious rejection of the axioms endorsed by an assembly of the faithful to which, perhaps, the 'heretic' owed loyalty. Where there are several such dissenting congregations the charge of 'heresy' means little more than that 'we' disagree with 'you', and that you, on the principles you share with us, should change your mind. As perhaps you should.

conundrums. If we are to examine and rebut what people have actually believed and practised, we need—exactly—to examine and understand what they have believed and practised. As Al-Ghazali remarked: 'To attempt to refute a system without understanding it or knowing it through and through is to do so blindfold'.[49]

Unfortunately, this may give the critics of religion—or of particular religions—an opportunity to sneer at what seem to them to be unnecessary or even ridiculous complications. That there is an intelligent and very powerful creator is at least an intelligible theory, although there is no need, they suppose, to believe it. That 'the First Cause' is something that no-one can understand, having no properties, or none in common with any finite thing, is not a theory at all, they think, and amounts to hardly more than saying that the ultimate cause of everything is altogether unknown, that *anything* is possible, that nothing could refute it. Atheists may firmly deny the first account, but do not need to deny the second. So David Hume, through his character Cleanthes, appositely enquires 'How ... mystics, who maintain the absolute incomprehensibility of the Deity, differ from Sceptics or Atheists, who assert, that the first cause of all is unknown and unintelligible?'[50] *Christian* theists who take the final step of consciously requiring us to suppose that there is One God in Three Persons, each incomprehensible and simultaneously identical and different, can only be talking nonsense. Some theists, of course, agree, and seek to affirm that God is a simple unity, and simply comprehensible. It is an easier thesis to maintain, but possibly also a false one.

One answer to Cleanthes' question about 'mystics' and 'atheists or sceptics' is that their *attitudes* differ. This isn't altogether odd. After all, we might also reckon that other creatures are, in a way, inscrutable. 'A turkey is more occult and awful than all the angels and archangels',[51] but there is a difference in *attitude* between one who supposes that the turkey is no more than meat and one who thinks it 'awful' in the ancient sense. Even our human neighbours may be inscrutable, and even our human lovers. Lovers don't need to *under-*

---

[49] Al-Ghazali, op. cit., p. 73 (chapter 2, part 2).

[50] David Hume, *Dialogues Concerning Natural Religion* (1779) pt. 4: *Hume on Religion*, ed. R. Wollheim (Fontana: London, 1963), p. 131.

[51] G.K. Chesterton, *All Things Considered* (Methuen: London, 1908), p. 220.

stand each other, but to love. 'And it is better for us to be drunk with a drunkenness like this than to be more respectably sober'.[52]

Another approach to the problem lies in *jñāna,* the path of knowledge. True scientists and scholars give their devotion to the truth, and not their own best image of that truth, even though they have no recourse but to serve truth through that image. They must admit, that is, the possibility that they are *wrong,* although they don't believe they are. But this is as much as to say that the truth lies beyond *their* reason at least, beyond any account they give of Being. This was also Descartes' insight: that in the very act of imagining ourselves mistaken we recognize that there really is a truth beyond our sense and intellect, a truth we do not know. We must believe at the same time that there is an identity between our own best image of the truth and the truth entire (if we thought otherwise then it would not be our own best image). Our own science and scholarship reveals a Trinitarian analogy: the truth entire, our image of that truth, and the conviction which unites the two as one. Any theory that divides those three makes intellectual life impossible (and this is one good reason why mainstream Christianity has outlawed such heresies as divide the Trinity or demote the Second or Third Persons[53]).

That intellectual route to Trinitarian doctrine is perhaps less appealing than the route of *bhakti*. If the intellect were the only route to God, then only the intelligent and well-informed could follow it. Some pagan philosophers would have agreed, but for that very reason—amongst others—their particular creeds were never popular! Nor should they have been, on those terms: the Lord, if He lives at all, must like the simple. *Intelligence* is a great gift, and a great responsibility, but sanctity is better. If we are to understand God through and in devotion, then this devotion itself is deity. 'God is Love', we are told in the tradition—and therefore God is Trinity. 'He, that same self, is lovable and love and love of himself' (*erasmion kai eros ho autos kai hautou eros*).[54] If there were nothing analogous, at least, to the community of love in God, then God could not, in Himself, be Love. Either there would be some good that wasn't 'there' in God (namely,

---

[52] After *Enneads*, VI.7 [38].35, quoted earlier.

[53] A failure to believe the strange dogmas of the Athanasian Creed will lead us, so it says, to be 'damned eternally': this is not a *punishment*. The Creed is intended as a road-map to lead us out of harm's way: taking the wrong turn, institutional experience shows, is not a good idea. But that is another and much longer story.

[54] Plotinus, VI.8.15: Armstrong, op. cit.,vol. 7, p. 277.

love) or else love isn't a real good at all. In so far as God is taken to be the focus of all desire, He must be Trinitarian.

In brief, the strange record of mainstream Christian theological debate was not an historical accident, a weirdly arbitrary conglomeration of disparate doctrines. It was a serious attempt to unfold, as other thinkers had also sought to unfold, the real implications of religious and philosophical devotion. Again: we do not aim to *understand* God, as if He were the effect of an intelligible law of nature or Supernature. Rather He is the focus of a certain sort of life from which all other lives and substances derive, and is known in love, and as love.

The metaphysical and theological arguments attached to these doctrines are important ones. But what matters more, in this context, is the *effect* of doctrine. What difference does it make to our lives to have a Trinitarian faith, as against a Unitarian one? Not believing in God at all amounts to not believing that there is a right way of living in which all can share, and not believing that justice will be done (which is not to say, remember, that atheists aren't 'nice' people). What can be wrong with thinking that there is one right way of living, and that the judge is single? Consider Chesterton's response:

> There is nothing in the least liberal or akin to reform in the substitution of pure monótheism for the Trinity. The complex God of the Athanasian Creed may be an enigma for the intellect; but He is far less likely to gather the mystery and cruelty of a Sultan than the lonely god of Omar or Mahomet. The god who is mere awful unity is not only a king but an Eastern king. The heart of humanity, especially of European humanity, is certainly much more satisfied by the strange hints and symbols that gather round the Trinitarian idea, the image of a council at which mercy pleads as well as justice, the conception of a sort of liberty and variety existing even in the inmost chamber of the world.[55]

As so often, one of the many charges against Christian theism, that it elevates a Celestial Monarch over all creation (and so gives credence to the claims of earthly monarchs), has been anticipated in theistic tradition. God is not 'the Boss' of folk-religion, to be conceived 'monarchically', or not entirely so: He is conceived as a community, and one which we may join. The notion is not only Christian. According to Kant, Tibetan lamas told Francisco Orazio della Penna (an eighteenth century Capuchin friar who settled in Lhasa), that

[55] Chesterton, *Orthodoxy*, op. cit., p. 99.

'God is the community of all the holy ones'.[56] What they meant, or he meant, I don't know. But we have a European, pre-Christian, witness too. Plotinus also hoped to 'join the dance of immortal love'.[57] The final sentence of his *Enneads* has often been mistranslated, as urging on us 'the flight of the alone to the Alone'—a flight doomed, obviously, to failure (as neither would then be actually alone).[58] Our 'flight', so to speak, is possible because the One exists in Many, because it exists as love.

> Plotinus's divine mind [which is also the totality of intelligible being] is not just a mind knowing a lot of eternal objects. It is an organic living community of interpenetrating beings which are at once Forms and intelligences, all 'awake and alive', in which every part thinks and therefore is the whole; so that all are one mind and yet each retains its distinct individuality without which the whole would be impoverished.[59]

Chesterton was probably wrong to think that purely monotheistic creeds always ignore the value of community, or make God in the image of a Sultan. More playful attitudes arise in them as in any other. But he was probably right to think that the *implication* of a straightforwardly monotheistic vision is that we are always 'over against' God, always slaves or property, not friends. The extraordinary claim that is made by Trinitarians is that we can join the dance—even that we *have* already joined the dance. Whether this is true or not we can only find out by trying. That it *matters* hardly needs finding out.

There is another theme of orthodox Christian faith that should appeal to atheists, whether or not it is true. The image of an impossibly distant God, creator and destroyer, who has condemned us all to life (and death), plainly excites more than derision. The more militant the atheist the more he rages against the God he doesn't believe in (and thereby testifies, remember, to a desire for justice that makes

[56] I. Kant, *Kant's Political Writings*, ed. H. Reiss (Cambridge University Press: Cambridge, 1970), p. 107.

[57] '*khoron sterixan erotos athanatou*': Porphyry *Life of Plotinus* 23. 36f, after 22. 54ff. The words are from Delphi's reported judgement on Plotinus.

[58] Plotinus, *Ennead*, VI.9.11, 51: *phuge monou pros monon*. Armstrong (op. cit., vol. 7, p. 345) translates the phrase as 'escape in solitude to the solitary', but immediately warns against taking the phrase in isolation from the rest of Plotinian thought. *Monos* here really means 'pure', or even 'Holy', not 'solitary': free of all distractions, and not self-absorbed.

[59] A.H. Armstrong & R.A. Markus, *Christian Faith and Greek Philosophy* (Darton, Longman & Todd: London, 1960), p. 27.

no sense if there is no such thing, as well as at least an *ambivalent* attitude to the truth of things). This may be intellectually odd, but it preserves a truth—a truth also preserved in Christian doctrine. 'Theism', as this is now usually understood, is actually as heretical as atheism.[60] Liberal-minded believers often attempt to edit out the more revolutionary claims about the god-man Jesus. As Chesterton points out, they err:

> The thing may be true or not; that I shall deal with before I end. But if the story is true it is certainly terribly revolutionary. That a good man may have his back to the wall is no more than we knew already; but that God could have His back to the wall is a boast for all insurgents for ever. Christianity is the only religion on earth that has felt that omnipotence made God incomplete. Christianity alone has felt that God, to be wholly God, must have been a rebel as well as a king. Alone of all creeds, Christianity has added courage to the virtues of the Creator. For the only courage worth calling courage must necessarily mean that the soul passes a breaking point—and does not break. ... Let the revolutionists choose a creed from all the creeds and a god from all the gods of the world, carefully weighing all the gods of inevitable recurrence and of unalterable power. They will not find another god who has himself been in revolt. Nay (the matter grows too difficult for human speech), but let the atheists themselves choose a god. They will find only one divinity who ever uttered their isolation; only one religion in which God seemed for an instant to be an atheist.[61]

The claim that this is *true*, that God Himself has suffered along with us, is not as alien even to pagan Greeks as some suppose, nor is it as metaphysically preposterous as simple monotheists have thought. The fact that we are ready to conceive that it *ought* to be true is evidence that it can be, even though it is difficult to construct a language or a theory to accommodate the truth, and not surprising that the result—in Christian creeds—reads very oddly to outsiders of whatever other creed. But if it isn't true we have reason to doubt that God is either omniscient or properly benevolent. He cannot be omni-

---

[60] See Walter Kasper, *The God of Jesus Christ* (SCM Press: London, 1984).

[61] Chesterton, *Orthodoxy*, op. cit., p. 102. The concluding reference is to the penultimate cry from the cross: *Matthew* 27. 46; cf. *Psalm* 22. 1. See also Charles Williams, 'The Cross' (1943), reprinted in *The Image of the City*, ed. Anne Ridler (Oxford University Press: London, 1958) and in *Charles Williams: Selected Writings*, ed. Anne Ridler (Oxford University Press: London, 1961), pp. 94–105: 'at least, alone among the gods, He deigned to endure the justice He decreed'.

scient since He can't know 'from within' what desolation is, nor even—as I observed before with reference to angels—what *time* is. He cannot be benevolent, and wish us well, since He can't know what we need to be rescued from. His justice, if He is just, is an abstraction. His power has not been tried.

So something like the Christian claim is a more satisfactory story. This does not prove it true: that, as before, is something to be discovered by trying out the life it recommends, and not by referring back to Gospel miracles. Those miracles are believed because we already believe the story.[62] We don't believe the story because we suppose strange things once happened around Jerusalem for which we seek explanations. On the one hand, there are *resemblances* (not identities) between the Gospel stories and earlier stories about saints and heroes (as I said before). Maybe they are only versions of that common stock of tales. On the other hand, if the Gospel stories are, in essence, true, we could expect there to be exactly such echoes, intimations, parodies. If the story is true, all human and cosmic history begins from there. If we think of all that history as something imagined into being by the Creator, the Gospel was, as it were, the very first chapter that He wrote.[63] And in revealing 'the Mind—the Meaning—of God' in the life of a Jewish Hasid He gave us a rather different role-model than the one that folk-religion usually imagines.

> Let *this* mind be in you which was also in Christ Jesus, who being in the form of God, did not think to snatch at equality with God, but took upon him the form of a servant, and was made in the likeness of man.[64]

---

[62] See G.E.M. Anscombe, 'Prophecy and Miracles' (1957) for a lucid account of how someone already persuaded of the general truth of theism might, from reading the Scriptures, slowly come to wonder whether indeed the Lord was active in those histories, and so at least accept that 'miracles' were probable: *Faith in a Hard Ground* op. cit. , pp. 21–39.

[63] See Martin Hengel, *The Cross of the Son of God*, trans. John Bowden (SCM: London, 1986), pp. 45ff; See also Mircea Eliade, *Cosmos and* History, trans. W.R. Trask (Harper & Row: New York, 1959), p. 16: in Rabbinic tradition, God began His creation with Zion.

[64] *Philippians* 2.5–7. See James P. Mackey *Jesus of Nazareth: The Life, the Faith and the Future of the Prophet. A Brief History* (Columba Press: Blackrock, Ireland, 2008): Mackey perhaps neglects rather too many of the texts that expect *judgement* in his exposition, but the contrast he draws between the God of Jesus and the God of too much folk religion is still to the point.

9

World Orders, World Religions

World Order and the Secularist Illusion

There are good reasons for being suspicious of the very concept of 'a religion', let alone a 'world religion'.[1] It may be useful for a hospital administrator to know a patient's 'religion'—as Protestant or Church of England or Catholic or Buddhist—but such labels do little more than identify a suitable chaplain, and connote groupings in the vast and confusing region of 'religious thought and practice' that are of very different ranks. By any rational, genealogical taxonomy of the sort that is now preferred amongst biologists 'Protestant', 'Anglican', 'Catholic' connote species, genera or families within Christianity, which is in turn a taxon within the multivariant tradition that traces its line to Abraham. 'Buddhism' includes as many variants as 'Abrahamism'. Most Abrahamists, traditionally, have been theists, but it is difficult not to suspect that Marxism and even non-Marxist militant atheism are atypical variants of the same tradition. Most Buddhists, conversely, have preferred to think of themselves as atheists, but there are Buddhist sects for which the Buddha-nature has much the same function as God. Stories, rites and doctrines flow back and forth between the traditions: one example is the story of St. Josaphat (that is, Gautama Buddha), transformed by Georgians from an Islamic source and exerting an effect on Tolstoy, and so, through Henry Salt, on Gandhi.[2] 'Religions', unlike biological spe-

---

[1] Some of the material in this section was tried out in 'World Religions and World Orders' in *Religious Studies* 26. 1990, pp. 43–57, reprinted in Charles Taliaferro & Paul. J. Griffiths (eds.), *Philosophy of Religion*, (Blackwell: Oxford, 2003), pp. 21–30.

[2] See Wilfred Cantwell Smith, *Towards a World Theology: faith and the comparative history of religion* (Macmillan: London 1981), pp. 8ff. See also Sarah Iles Johnson ed., *Religions of the Ancient World: a Guide* (Harvard University Press: Cambridge,

cies, are rarely isolated, even if particular sects do sometimes wish they were. Indeed the whole notion of 'a religion', as one species within a larger genus of 'religions' is probably a seventeenth century invention.[3]

Are we to suppose that this diversity will some day, or should some day, converge upon a single, unified 'religion'? That was certainly Immanuel Kant's hope: 'there can only be one religion which is valid for all men and at all times. Thus the different confessions can scarcely be more than the vehicles of religion.'[4] Unfortunately, every actual attempt to specify and proclaim this One Religion has merely added another vehicle (Islam, Baha'i, Vedanta, Unitarian Christianity): every such proclamation is intended to be universal, and none of them have ever converted everyone. If there is only to be one ship for the 'sea of faith' there are at least three ways of engineering it, and none—so far—have worked. The first attempt is Kantian in spirit: to identify the central, essential truths proclaimed in all religions, stripping away historical, parochial baggage. The second is syncretistic, patching a more commodious vehicle together from the flotsam of past endeavours, but without any sense that contradictions must be weeded out, or that there is a single intelligible, axiomatic system underlying the structure. The third is openly exclusivist: there will in the end be one ship only that comes safe to harbour, since the others will have sunk. The first and third endeavours, unfortunately, are not always easy to distinguish: rationalists may *believe* that they have identified the true, the central, the only rational belief, but their opponents often find them just as 'bigoted' as those who dismiss all scriptures but their own. The second endeavour has often been the main recourse of empires: what does it matter what particular gods we serve, as long as we can all struggle along together, without trying to reform or exclude anyone? So King Belshazzar gathered sacred vessels from the conquered nations, 'drank wine and praised the gods of gold and silver, of bronze and iron, and of wood and stone'[5] (rather as moderns praise the artistry of medieval cathedrals, icons, and ancient statuary). Even syncretists, of course, have limits—and the more those limits are

---

MA., 2004), on the ease with which the ancients identified their own gods with those of their neighbours and copied their rituals.

[3] See Lash, op. cit., p. 10.

[4] I. Kant, 'Perpetual Peace', *Kant's Political Writings*, ed. H. Reiss (Cambridge University Press: Cambridge, 1970), p. 114.

[5] *Daniel* 5.4.

challenged the more the syncretic cults begin to find some unifying principle by which to exclude their enemies.

Darwin's insight (or one way of seeing it) was that the undoubted similarities between different clans and species might depend on *ancestry*, not archetypes. We are all variations on a theme established millions of years ago—or so he suggested—rather than partial reflections of eternal forms. So also, perhaps, are 'religions' (that is, roughly demarcated traditions of rituals, stories, clerisies and ethical demands). The temptation to enquire whether such and such a cult is 'really Christian' may be resisted more easily when we see that there need be no 'real essence' of Christianity, but only a common ancestor. Christianity was once, as it were, a species, but has long since become a genus, family or order, and some members of the clade resemble cults of quite a different ancestry more than they do their more immediate cousins. Unlike biological species (or unlike eucaryotic species) religious cults can infect each other, or merge and separate.[6] But just as there are convergent patterns in biological evolution (so that salmon, ichthyosaurs and dolphins are alike, despite having ancestors that weren't), so also are there patterns in religious history. It is worth considering what different ways have been devised, what different orders, and so picking out those patterns. It is especially worth considering this when we can no longer isolate ourselves from other religious worlds, and must make some attempt to devise a single peace. Precisely because 'we do not want a world state', as W.E. Hocking realized, 'we do require a world morale', which is to say the beginnings of a world religion.[7] If we don't want the peace, or an imitation of peace, to be enforced with bayonets and guns, we must hope that it can be maintained by a

[6] Actually, there may be reason to think that at least *some* species (and maybe most) are the products of alliances between different organisms, especially at a microbial level. Lichens aren't *plants*, but symbiotic partnerships of algae and fungus. There are even animals, like the green underwater slug *Elysia viridis*, that have incorporated algae, and don't need to eat in all their adult lives: see Lynn Margulis & Dorion Sagan, *Acquiring Genomes: a theory of the origins of species* (Basic Books: New York, 2002), pp. 13ff. And all of us, very probably, are composed of cells originally formed by an alliance between eubacteria and archaebacteria (which belong to distinct bacterial kingdoms), later joined by oxygen-respiring mitochondria (*ibid.*, p. 7). So there is a closer analogy between 'religions' and 'species' than one might initially suppose! Religious traditions can be formed by incorporating, making friends with, once alien traditions.

[7] W.E. Hocking, *Living Religions and a World Faith* (Allen & Unwin: London, 1940), p. 264. 'Morale' means much the same as 'religion', but is perhaps a label more acceptable to atheists who imagine—falsely—that they have no personal ideology.

common moral sense (though this will probably not entirely remove the need for bayonets and guns). Even if there were a single secular authority with power over all the globe, we should still need that common sense:

> For how can there be an international law or order or working league or federation of states until there is an accepted level of moral understanding among men to give vitality to its legal code?[8]

And what sort of moral understanding might this be? As I hinted earlier, the easiest form is syncretic. This may begin in a simple wish to live and let live, to protect the liberties of everyone to follow their own faith and fancy. It may then become a slightly different goal: precisely to preserve variety, including past varieties, as our best image of the Unknown. 'Religion' in the broadest sense amounts to Art or Poetry or mere Tradition, and any such traditions may have a part to play in the global order, so long as they give their little pinch of incense to the earthly powers (and never hint that those powers will be under judgement 'when the great and terrible day of the Lord'[9] is come). Unfortunately, just this comfortable pluralism or casual polytheism may be what some sectarians most despise. When the Taliban destroyed the Buddhist statues of Bamyan they might have done so not only because they rejected *Buddhism* (so after all did almost all their critics), nor even from ethnic hatred of Bamyan civilization,[10] but because they despised—so to call it—liberal aestheticism.[11] At least it was a comprehensible excuse.

But what style of global order, global religion, *might* we adopt if only we could avoid dissension? Rationalists, syncretists and faithful believers are not entirely discrete groups: any of us may acknowledge the attractions of any of these positions. And whichever stance we favour much the same questions must arise about world order.

---

[8] *Ibid.*, p. 19.

[9] *Malachi* 4.5; see also *Revelation* 6.9–17.

[10] See http://www.hazara.net/hazara/geography/Buddha/buddha.html (accessed 1st February 2008).

[11] *The New York Times* reported on 19th March 2001 that the Taliban envoy to the US had said 'that the Islamic government made its decision in a rage after a foreign delegation offered money to preserve the ancient works while a million Afghans faced starvation. "When your children are dying in front of you, then you don't care about a piece of art. ": http://www.nytimes.com/2001/03/19/world/19TALI.html?ex=1202014800&en=10bba2601a2c3ec4&ei=5070 (accessed 1st February 2008). This was not, of course, exactly rational: destroying the statues did not feed the children.

Some projected world religions accept a division between spiritual authority and political power, and some do not. On the one side: Hindus draw an absolute distinction between Brahmin and Kshatriya; Gautama chose to be a Buddha not a Cakravartin, to guide the world through force of example rather than by force of arms; Christians, Jews and Sunni Muslims all find their authorities elsewhere than in Princes;[12] Kantians expressly distinguish sound republican governments as ones where the laws are framed by those who don't themselves enforce them. On the other side, the half-forgotten but still deeply influential experiments of Egyptian Pharaonism, Constantinian theocracy, the Imamate, Tibetan Buddhism and sundry apocalyptic cults all postulate a God-King present in the flesh.

Again: some religions presuppose a diffused authority, others a more central one. For some, any believer may speak with God's voice; for others only accredited officials may. Shall we wait for Minos (as it were), the sovereign, to bring the laws from Zeus,[13] or else trust in the collective judgement of an ordinary assembly?[14]

Another distinction, implicit in some earlier remarks, is between those who acknowledge that they live 'by faith' and those who suppose their creeds are uniquely *rational.* Buddhists and some Muslims regularly comment unfavourably on a supposedly Christian appeal to 'blind faith' and 'dependence', and insist that we should rely upon ourselves and on our own reasoning powers. The distinction makes little sense, since all reasoning (as in an earlier chapter) depends on unproven and unprovable axioms, and we cannot ourselves check everything that might be doubted by a sufficiently paranoid enquirer. Believing in oneself, as Chesterton observed, is as foolish a superstition as believing in Joanna Southcott.[15] For a Buddhist it should be more like believing in the prophecies of Merlin (who does not exist), since there is no real Self apart from the streams of consciousness. But though the distinction makes little or no sense as theory, it makes a difference in practice. Some would-be global religions—including the pseudo-religion of the Brights—will think that they can spread by the mere exposition of their doctrine, and that those who are unpersuaded must be simple-minded. Others

[12] Even the Anglican Church, though acknowledging the Sovereign as, in a sense, its 'head', does not suppose that the monarch can legislate *belief.*

[13] Plotinus, *Enneads*, VI.9 [9].7, after Plato (or ps-Plato) *Minos.*

[14] Plotinus, *Ennead*, VI.5.10

[15] Chesterton, *Orthodoxy*, op. cit., p. 5.

will also invoke ritual, art, poetry and look to kindle a vision of enlightenment that no words can teach.

What other possible world religions, or 'world-morales', might there be? One option, and one of the most powerful, must be the sort of post-Christian humanism that is embodied in our scientific-industrial civilization. It is implicit in that system that there is no moral order in nature, that everything is readily at hand as tools or material for human purposes. Nothing is sacred, save the wills of those who are accounted 'human' (which class does not necessarily include infants, imbeciles or even 'primitives'), and the superstitions of less enlightened peoples cannot long be taken seriously. Scientific industrialism, though its spokesmen regularly denounce old-fashioned dualisms of 'matter' and 'spirit', actually embodies a powerful dualism of its own, between wild nature and the technosphere. Sometimes its fantasies are of a space-travelling civilization that need never again adapt itself to a non-human environment (precisely by placing itself in that most alien and deadly space beyond the living Earth). Back in 1985 even the humane and intelligent author C.J. Cherryh wrote that 'planets are a commodity of value at two stages of a humanoid species' existence: either as cradle or as retirement home. Otherwise taken, their value is negligible, and the preponderance of them—taken with moons, moonlets, asteroids, rings and such—might well be classified as navigational hazards rather than prizes of great value.'[16] Teilhard de Chardin's fantasies of the Overmind are to be realised through computer networks, genetic engineering, bionic enhancement of sense and muscle.[17] One strand of this strange creed, perhaps less popular, is a wish to be free not only of *other* material beings (bacteria, wild animals, and primitives), but of human flesh itself, 'the meat'. Respected figures, even if mostly in California, seriously imagine that they will themselves achieve an immortal life as uploaded computer programs in a soon-to-be-cosmic web.[18] In order to hurry on this would-be apotheosis they may demand that 'scientists' must be free to do whatever

[16] C.J. Cherryh, 'Goodbye Star Wars, Hello Alley-Oop', in Sharon Jarvis (ed.), *Inside outer space: science fiction professionals look at their craft* (New York: F. Ungar Pub. Co., 1985), pp. 17–26. She has changed her mind since then, recognizing that if we ever did make a life Out There we should have to take the whole world with us—the world, that is, of bacteria, plants, wild animals and symbiotes. Surviving without them would be surviving without internal organs too!

[17] See Lash, op. cit., pp. 262f for reasons *not* to respect Chardin's opinions.

[18] See Ed Regis, *Great Mambo Chicken and the Post-Human Condition* (Penguin: Harmondsworth, 1992, 2nd ed.).

research they choose (and of course be paid to do it from the public purse). The Christian hope, they believe, is to be realized through naturalistic science, and 'Humanity', in some strange form, will one day rule the cosmos (as long as we don't falter in this crucial age).[19] 'The created universe waits with eager expectation for God's sons to be revealed'.[20]

But modern naturalism does have other faces, maybe significant enough to be identified as yet other would-be global religions (or morales). While some believers seek to detach themselves from Earth (and Flesh), others seek the closest identification with our living world. Nature Worship is as powerful a force as Human Worship, and has many half-formed sects. More usually such naturism involves an appeal to felt presences of stream and hill and forest, to the uncomplicated (or supposedly uncomplicated) emotions of non-human animals, to supposedly 'feminine' capacities of love or intuition rather than 'masculine' and rule-governed intellect. Sometimes naturists, unconsciously, draw very close to the religion of blood and soil that challenged Christendom over sixty years ago.[21]

These opposing views, of Gaia and the Technosphere, identify another real distinction amongst world-religions: some are humanist in their orientation, and others non-humanist or even anti-humanist. Is the divine (the worshipful and/or the ultimately victorious) to be found unambiguously within human life, or does it loom outside or over against it? Recent liberal theology in the developed West, as well as liberal philosophy, has been overwhelmingly humanist, to the point where true believers plainly find it difficult to understand how anyone could seriously doubt their creed. *Obviously*, the hope of human welfare (which usually means health and a longish life) is sufficient excuse for whatever use we make of anything 'non-human'. *Obviously* people have a right to be 'better off' (that is, to have the chance to enjoy whatever goods they choose). Only very gradually has the thought emerged that the costs — to the world, to non-human creatures, to the human poor — may be, even in the chosen terms, too high. Naturists, whatever strange exaggerations they may fall into, are at least attempting to construct a differ-

---

[19] See Frank J. Tipler, *The Physics of Immortality: Modern Cosmology, God and the Resurrection of the Dead* (Doubleday: New York, 1994).

[20] *Romans* 8.19: I doubt if Paul would accept the industrialists' gloss!

[21] The point has been made by, amongst others, Robert A. Pois, *National Socialism and the Religion of Nature* (Palgrave Macmillan: New York, 1986). See also my *How to Think about the Earth* (Mowbrays: London, 1993).

ent form of life that may perhaps be a little more 'world-friendly', just by not insisting that the world is made—or to be made—for us.

So global religions may be parapolitical or political, centralized or decentralized, faith-holding or intellectual, humanist or non-humanist. Some have a linear view of time, others a cyclical one. Some are Platonic, others anti-Platonic, in that they do or do not recognize the presence of something over and above the stream of particular events and atoms in which we seem to live. Some are deeply Platonic in another sense, and others not, in that some assert that the Divine is rationally incomprehensible and must be approached through poetry, love and ritual, while others are confident that human reason, somehow, can discover all things. Most are egalitarian in principle, but this is not inevitable: of all the great religions only Hinduism maintains an open hierarchy, ranking different castes according to their 'purity', and must measure itself against Jewish and Buddhist condemnation of caste structures before it should be global.[22] Some would-be global religions are tied to precise historical associations in ways that others are not: all 'religions' must be embodied in a continuing community with its particular customs and happy anecdotes (this is also true of 'the scientific community'), but Buddhist sects could probably survive the discovery that Gautama was a trickster, and every named hero, arhat, lama, bodhisattva was fictional or a fraud. Conversion to the Buddhist creed does not really require one to shave one's head, learn Pali, take another name or believe even one of the myriad stories about Gautama, his past lives, and the lives of past and future Buddhas. Conversion to an *Abrahamic* religion may demand a greater degree of historical involvement: if the real history of Israel, the early Church and the companions of Mohammed were quite other than the stories say it might be difficult to sustain the creeds. Conversion to Judaism, especially, is more like being adopted or married into a large, united family (united mainly in the style of their disagreements, maybe), but all Abrahamic faiths have something like that structure. Converts are expected to take on the style and custom of their new families, as well as the abstract doctrines. Sometimes missionaries demand too much of converts, mistaking their own personal customs or the customs of their nation for the customs of the

[22] Unfortunately, it is also possible—as Oswald Spengler expected (see *The Decline of the West: Form and Actuality*, trans. C.F. Atkinson (Allen & Unwin: London, 1926)—that the world-beast, the global state, will be caste-ridden, and all the worst features of Hinduism be re-embodied there. But let us hope it's not.

Church or the companions of Mohammed. If Papuan tribesmen, say, must be 'Westernized' (that is, given sugar, steel knives, trousers, money) before they can be 'Christianized', does that not amount to cultural genocide (maybe real genocide)? If they can 'enter the stream' (as Buddhists say), or even bow before that One who spoke through all the prophets (but Mohammed last and best of all) without ceasing to be Papuans is that not a gain? Can Christendom be exported or expanded?

The very claim on which that Christendom is based, of course, is that the Jewish Hasid is that same light that lights us all, the *Logos*.[23] There must already be something in each human tradition which can now be seen as Him—or else He isn't what the Church has said He is. No doubt those seeds or signs have been distorted—as they have also been in Europe—and the effort to distinguish truth from harmful fantasy will always, till the Day, be doubtful.

The Clash of Civilizations

According to Samuel Huntington, our current problem or opportunity is a clash or confrontation of 'civilizations', each with their own cultural, and religious, baggage.[24] Some such civilizations, in a list that is very similar to Arnold Toynbee's, have no global ambitions, and others, even if they do, are unlikely, in the foreseeable future, to realize them. But 'the West', Islam, and 'Asian' (or 'Confucian') civilization all have considerable power, which may result in confrontations as acrimonious and potentially lethal as ever 'the Cold War' between 'the West' and the USSR. This is not to deny that there may also be confrontations even *within* a civilization: our most obvious and immediate enemies, now as ever, may be our nearest neighbours. It is also all too easy to imagine that 'the Other Civilization' is unified in a way that we know 'Ours' isn't, and therefore be surprised that there are serious ideological and religious issues between, for example, Sunni and Shia, that may preclude a unified response to civilizational challenge from outside. Nor is it easy to identify 'distinct civilizations': Huntington distinguishes, for example, both 'Orthodox Christendom' (with Russia as its core state) and 'Latin American Civilization' (without any secure core state) from 'the West', while acknowledging that all three have Christian roots, but does not choose to distinguish Shi'ite Civilization (centred on

[23] *John* 1.8f

[24] Samuel R. Huntington, *The Clash of Civilizations and the Remaking of World Order* (Simon & Schuster: London, 1996).

Iran) from Sunni Civilization (in which Saudi Arabia and Pakistan both have a claim that may eventually be trumped by a post-secular Turkey[25]). But Huntington's basic thesis seems secure: people from different civilizations make different assumptions, and the merely parochial belief that 'our' assumptions are simply rational and factual ones is itself a barrier to understanding, and to any hope of peace.

The State system itself, with its self-denying rules against interference across State boundaries, is partly a pragmatic rejection of imperial invasions of a kind that might destabilize the world, but it rests on a *Late Western* assumption, that the natural political unit is a State, a body of people in a particular region with their own legal, religious and military systems, such that the citizen's first loyalty must be to that State (and Government). Such States emerged from *Western* history (quite late) and were imposed on the rest of the world by *Western* power. Elsewhere in the world (and also in earlier Western history) first loyalty is given to the Church or to the *ummah,* on the one hand, or else to families, clans or tribes, on the other. Even within a Western state, of course, there are people with other loyalties, tolerated as harmless, or feared as potential threats: Papists, Protestants, Jews, Gypsies. As long as their *public* loyalty is to the State, they can be forgiven their quirks. Loyalty to what may be the wider community is close to treason, and may be avenged as brutally.

It is possible that Christendom was more accommodating to the emergence of such territorial States than other civilizations might have been, that it is not just an historical accident that they developed in the West. The old Hellenic idea that different nations had different presiding spirits, gods or angels (to which Symmachus referred: see p. 9 above[26]) was not wholly repudiated by the Chris-

---

[25] *Ibid.*, p. 178

[26] And also Julian, *contra Galileos* 115de: 'The creator is the common father and king of all, but the various nations have been divided by him among nation-ruling gods, ethnarchs, and city-protecting gods, each one of whom controls his allotment in accordance with his own nature' (cited by D. Rokeah, *Jews, Pagans and Christians in Conflict* (Brill: Leiden, 1982), p. 157). See also Sacks, *Dignity of Difference,* op. cit., p. 54, who, oddly, blames Plato for infecting his successors with the idea that there should be a single political authority over all the world: on the contrary, Platonists believe as firmly in diversity as Sacks (see, for example, Themistius (317–87) *Oration*, 5. 70a: 'God wants Syrians to be people of one type, Greeks to be people of a different sort, and Egyptians a third variety. Even the Syrians [probably, Christians] he does not want to be alike, but he has actually broken them down into small units'). Even the Anglican *Articles of Religion* (1562) also observe that 'it is not necessary that Traditions and Ceremonies be in all

tian Churches. It was also generally agreed (as p. 199 above) that there was a difference between *political* and *ecclesiastical* power: the Sovereign, as judge and general, was not to concern himself with his subjects' *spiritual* welfare (though he was himself, in the early years of Christendom, subject to ecclesiastical censure).

> This explains why two guides have been appointed for man to lead him to his twofold goal: there is the Supreme Pontiff who is to lead mankind to eternal life in accordance with revelation; and there is the Emperor who, in accordance with philosophical teaching, is to lead mankind to temporal happiness.[27]

Those dissenting voices, in Calvin's Switzerland or the Puritans' New England, who sought to enforce a very particular belief as the condition for membership of civil society, rather persuaded the rest of us that this was not a good idea. So the natural form of civil partnership has come to be defined by the accidents of birth and territorial history: anyone born in the United Kingdom is British (since 1981, only if at least one parent is a British citizen or permanent resident) and expected, other things being equal, to serve the British Crown, the spirit imagined (probably) into being by generations of such service. Anyone may, of course (at least in a liberal state), migrate and take up citizenship, eventually, in some *other* state, but we do not concede that they may instead, while living here, affirm a different overriding loyalty, to Church, or *ummah*, or international Party, or transnational Company, and act accordingly (though liberal commentators are strangely reluctant actually to avow this allegiance: witness the hostility with which recently they greeted the suggestion that school children take an oath of allegiance, as they do in other States). The *older* laws of Christendom, and the present laws of Islam, do not concede that any putative State laws which contradict the larger laws are valid. It may still be necessary to submit to them, but not necessarily to obey them.[28]

To outsiders, the West now seems licentious: dominated by a desire for individual success, to be proved in riotous expenditure,

---

places one, and utterly like; for at all times they have been divers, and may be changed according to the diversities of countries, times, and men's manners, so that nothing be ordained against God's Word' (*Article 34*).

[27] Dante Alighieri, *Monarchy and Three Political Letters*, ed. D. Nicholl & C. Hardie (Weidenfeld & Nicolson: London, 1954), p. 93

[28] The distinction was drawn by George Berkeley in 'Passive Obedience' (1713), in *Works*, ed. T.E. Jessop & A.A. Luce, vol. 6 (Thomas Nelson: Edinburgh, 1953), pp. 15–46.

and without any restraining sense of something sacred. In other civilizations—and in the Western past—virtue is displayed in loyalty to family, to lords, to long traditions, to the very land we live in. Everyone is born into a particular station (some larger or more flexible than others), and is required to serve some wider good. Individuals do not *own* even their own bodies, and must not pollute them by drink, drugs or sensuality. Modern Westerners, as they are understood by others, all seek to ape the habits of the Very Rich, believing that there is a price for everything, and that the only purpose in life is their enjoyment. Sometimes, of course, the Very Rich can be brought up with care, to believe that they are only trustees of their wealth, responsible for carefully maintaining land, and laws, and full employment. There are also residual inhibitions, especially with regard to children. But their temptation has always been to think they owned whatever they could buy, that 'enjoyment' was purely personal. And our temptation (who are not actually quite so rich) is to assume that any virtues they display are really hypocritical. In imitating the Very Rich this is what we copy—and depend on there being people whose services we can buy.

This is a somewhat distorted picture, and Westerners may reasonably retort that 'capitalism', 'liberal individualism', 'secularism', with all their faults, have provided a healthier, wider, freer, safer life for almost everyone than any historical alternative. The West has even provided safe havens for people (peoples) who live their lives by older rules. Most educated Muslims would agree that the United Kingdom, for example, enables them to live as Muslims, in greater safety and with more liberty, than most existing States that purport to be Islamic: Shia and Sunni do not usually kill each other here, and women are guaranteed the liberties that Mohammed himself decreed. The particular difficulties created for any Western State by the presence of substantial communities with a larger loyalty and values at odds with the public values of the State will concern me later. What is at issue here is the problem posed for *international* order.

War, in any viable civilization, is for the sake of peace—though this would once have been more contentious, and may not be quite right. It is not only States and Empires that go to war. In Papua New Guinea neighbouring villages were at war, or feud, forever, and it was a mark of manhood to have killed some easy prey[29]. In many ages of the world the main virtue is the warrior's, and for a man to die in bed is a disgrace. Even Christ's wry comment that those who live by the sword shall die by it[30] was interpreted as a *promise*. Aztecs went to war to acquire new victims for their sacrifice (and the loathing this inspired in all their neighbours helped to bring them down). But this is probably not our principal problem. Those civilizations, at any rate, with global ambitions and a global reach desire a just peace, not a constant state of war (though their rulers may also get some benefit from maintaining a war-footing, a readiness for war in their various populations). The problem is that there are differing criteria for what counts as a 'just peace', and no reason for one Court to trust another. In the 'world at war', *dar al-harb*, winner takes all and will not be dislodged by anything but violence. Within *dar al-Islam* it is *Shari'a*, the body of law built up from the Koran and the Hadith by generations of scholar-judges that determines justice (and even this is not unambiguous: different versions of *Shari'a* dictate different rules). The West is engaged in constructing 'International Law' though a complex of particular treaties and the founding statements of the United Nations, but those latter statements are usually either ignored or so construed as to have no real bearing.[31] To outsiders, Western cant about international law and a just peace is simply rhetoric, having no ethical basis or any real effect. What *reason* have modern Westerners, after all, to keep their word or acknowledge any rights of property, let alone any sense of the sacred? It's difficult enough for any political unit to keep a treaty when it isn't to its taste or in what it takes to be its interests: in days gone by we might have done so for fear of the god who held our oath, but if there is no such god, or none with any *political* existence, our only reason for faithfulness is our own temporal self-interest (whatever that may be). Outsiders, knowing this, would be fools to take our word! And we

---

[29] See Robert Gardner & Karl G. Heider, *Gardens of War: Life and Death in the New Guinea Stone Age* (Random House: New York, 1968). See also Paula Brown 'Conflict in the New Guinea Highlands', *Journal of Conflict Resolution*, 26. 1982, pp. 525–46.

[30] *Matthew* 26.52

[31] The rules declare that States must intervene to prevent genocide, for example, but it is always possible to declare that even mass murder in the name of 'ethnic cleansing' isn't really *genocide* (and notice also that masterly excuse for perpetual inaction, that we should not intervene *anywhere* if we can't intervene *everywhere*). See 'Genocide, War and Consistency', in *Human Rights and Military Intervention*, ed. Richard Norman & Alex Moseley (Ashgate: Aldershot, 2002), pp. 113–31.

would be fools, correspondingly, to take theirs either, since they cannot mean it sincerely.

In the absence of a 'world-morale', as Hocking said, and especially in the absence of any common sense that oaths once given are sacred, our only recourse for peace, so it may be supposed, is a world-state, an authority powerful enough in *fact* (not law) to 'punish' (though its acts will not be *punishment* in the proper sense) or restrain. It must have a *literal* power of life and death, by its control both of the means of living and the certainty of dying: something like the 'water monopoly empires' that Karl Wittfogel suggested were the basis for 'oriental despotism'.[32]

But this too is a forlorn hope. The World-State's problem will be partly that it will be hated, and itself a cause of war. The deeper problem is that it is far too easy to suppose that it can deter revolt or disobedience: that is to suppose that everyone is really agreed on what *counts* as a deterrent. Will their individual lives matter to all potential rebels? Will any temporal condition matter? The World State's methods, as I have outlined them, rest in effect on unexamined assumptions about identity and interest—assumptions that are questioned even within the modern West. J.S. Findlay, describing the Wittgensteinian revolution, declared that there was 'no sense of "same" which corresponds more closely with the "nature of things" than any other'—that is that there are no substantial forms—and that this was—by implication—a welcome 'charter of freedom'.[33] There are no boundaries in Nature, and so no *entities* in a familiar sense at all. There may be complex, causal continuities, but my own 'identity' with the seven-year old called Stephen is no more 'real' than my putative 'identity' with, let us say, my maternal grandfather. We no longer believe in 'the angels of the nations', and can therefore acknowledge that the identity of 'ancient Gaul' and 'modern France' is only a function of what some Frenchmen may now say.[34] If we don't believe in souls (that is, unextended and indivisible identities), the same applies to 'individuals'. So why should the death or destruction of 'this' animal organism at a particular

---

[32] Karl A. Wittfogel, *Oriental Despotism* (Yale University Press: New Haven, 1957): the theory may apply more exactly to *future* empires than it actually did to the past.

[33] J.N. Findlay, *Language, Mind and Value* (London: Allen & Unwin, 1963), p. 30; see pp. 21ff above, on Dennett's deconstruction of the self.

[34] Wink, *Unmasking the Powers*, op. cit., pp. 87–107 does something to make the idea of 'national angels', as the inner aspect of the material and social unities we know as nations more plausible.

moment of time be of any special interest? We can—the rebels can—as easily identify themselves as disposable cells of a longer-lasting unit. This matches Richard Rorty's conclusion. 'Truth', or the *only truth that we could mind about*, is 'what it is better for us to believe, rather than the accurate representation of reality'[35]—though how that 'better belief' is to be identified in the absence of any real value beyond what 'we' (who? what?) now desire remains obscure. This is to reduce all argument to power politics, and truth to 'the majority vote of that nation that could lick all others'.[36]

The World-State cannot expect to control all its subjects merely by bribery and threats, since there is no bribe, no threat that will really affect them all. We may imagine that it will seek to escalate its threats: rebels will not just be killed, but they and their families will be crucified in public places (or treated as experimental animals, more privately), their cities destroyed and the land sown with salt (there are plenty of precedents for just this sort of thing). It may also escalate its bribes: loyal supporters will have full medical service, including transplantable organs from less important subjects, and access to whatever luxuries they wish. But these very escalations will create further disaffections: the more the State commands entirely by lawless violence, the less *moral* authority it wields—unless, perhaps, it teaches very successfully that there is one organism only, the World-State, that all of us are only its elements, and that 'truth' is what it says. Which is what Orwell's O'Brien would have us all believe.[37]

The World Beast and Apocalypse

Whether this is what will happen, I have no idea. But if it does, it is unlikely to be any more secure against dissension and revolt. No doubt it could be made to *seem* secure. The World State will have greater powers of surveillance and control than any past or present empire. Those powers are already being developed, and sold to the people they will control on the plea that this will increase security. In the past even the most efficient surveillance system would have its

[35] R.M. Rorty, *Philosophy and the Mirror of Nature* (Oxford: Blackwell, 1980), p. 10.

[36] Oliver Wendell Holmes Jr., 'Natural Law', *The Mind and Faith of Justice Holmes*, ed. Max Lerner (Halcyon House: Garden City, NY, 1943), p. 395, cited by Black, *War against the Weak*, op. cit., p. 119. It was Holmes, as a member of the Massachusetts Supreme Court, who in 1927 gave legal sanction to the forceable sterilization of the supposedly 'feeble-minded'.

[37] See my 'Orwell and the Anti-Realists': *Philosophy*, 67 (1992), pp. 141–54

bottlenecks: there is a limit to how much any single agent of the State can know, and agents at every level of the system have their own reasons to conceal or distort even what they *do* know. In the past even the most careful and intelligent educationalists have been unable to predict what their pupils will decide and do: each new generation offers its own descant on any theme. But the World State, we can confidently predict, will have computerized access everywhere. It will also have drugs targeted for every sort of 'illness' (including 'mental illnesses' such as dissent and heretical belief), and a precise understanding of every citizen's genes. We won't have been *forced* to allow these powers: they will be made to seem advantages that we'd be foolish to prevent. Nor will most of us even feel oppressed: the World State will not need, in its extremity, to *oppress* at all. We—or our descendants—will be drunk with love, idolatrously devoted to the Beast.

Accidents, no doubt, will happen. The bacterial population that sustains the world will itself evolve, create new plagues and new disorders. There will be earthquakes, tidal waves, volcanic eruptions, meteors. Electrical power will suddenly fail, the Worldwide Web or its descendant crash. Even the best educated and best disciplined civil servant will, for no good reason, lose significant data. But since all these things are predictable, in general though not in detail, the World State will find ways to accommodate such errors. If the natural world is, as materialists suppose, a closed system, then there seems no reason why anything should ever change (until the Sun expands into its Red Giant phase and engulfs us all). Or must we hope that something 'from outside' will break into the vision, and 'the hammer of a higher God … smash [this] small cosmos, scattering the stars like spangles, and leave [us] in the open'?[38] In history, that hammer has often been invasion, or the 'decay' of the ruling caste. If the World State's power is global, there will be no human invasion. If its psychological and genetic power is near complete there will be no ruling, military or intellectual, caste that can 'decay' (unless Plato was right in his suspicion that the breeding programme will be gradually corrupted). But we might still imagine invasion 'from outside', and the collapse of the ruling paradigm, confronted by some power that owes it nothing. The strangest and in many ways most disagreeable book of the Bible is the *Revelation of John the*

[38] Chesterton, *Orthodoxy*, op. cit., p. 10.

Divine, in which the rule of the World Beast and its overthrow are imagined. Babylon the Great, we are assured, will fall.[39]

In science fiction—the one twentieth century genre that has sought to expand our horizons and not been content with the illusions either of an unchanging or a certainly progressive order—such invasions, of course, have been extraterrestrial, whether inimical, indifferent or well-meaning. Once the barrier is breached the World State can't survive, nor would any interstellar power have similar capacities of surveillance and control. Science fiction, here as elsewhere, is the only way, it seems, that we can imagine what an earlier generation would have understood by apocalypse.[40] On the one hand, we owe our vision of the World State to such writers; on the other, we owe to them our vision of its overthrow in the realization that the World is not our own, that there will always be the chance of an irruption. Hobbits, pursued through their familiar woods by alien enemies, complain that they can't walk through their own Shire without disturbance, and are reminded that it is *not* their Shire, that others lived there before hobbits were, and will again when hobbits are no more.[41]

If the World as a whole is *not* a closed system, but 'Nature' as a merely 'virtual reality' is subject to 'Supernature', then the case is even clearer. Whatever level of control we think we have, and even if our descendants manage a more than terrestrial empire, there will be incursions from the real, waking world. Recalling that, even in the guise provided by our fantasists rather than by our visionaries, is a way of exorcising the World Beast even before it happens. The moral is that we must not hope to control all things, and should accept diversity, and challenge, and personal responsibility.

And there, perhaps, is another hope of peace: the great religions, despite their differences, are all opposed to the World Beast, to the dream of absolute control. In acknowledging how dreadful that solution to our problems would be (and, in the end, how pointless) we may all come to see that there is a peaceable future (or at least the dream of it), when 'the wolf shall live with the sheep, and the leopard lie down with the kid; the calf and the young lion shall grow up

---

[39] *Revelation* 18.2

[40] See 'Science Fiction and Religion': *Blackwell Companion to Science Fiction*, ed. David Seed (Blackwell: Oxford, 2005), pp. 95–110

[41] J.R.R. Tolkien, *The Lord of the Rings*, vol. 1 (Allen & Unwin: London, 1966, 2nd edn.), p. 93.

together, and a little child shall lead them.'[42] We have all learnt to put aside the dream of War as the proper state of humanity. But there are still worse things than War to fear, and one of them is an enforced uniformity.

> In an emerging world of ethnic conflict and civilizational clash, Western belief in the universality of Western culture suffers three problems: it is false; it is immoral; and it is dangerous. That it is false ... [is] a thesis well summed up by Michael Howard: the 'common Western assumption that cultural diversity is a historical curiosity being rapidly eroded by the growth of a common, western-oriented, Anglophone world-culture, shaping our basic values ... is simply not true.'[43]

It is immoral and dangerous, Huntington goes on, because the attempt to make it so would lead (is perhaps already leading) to open war. It is immoral and dangerous even in the form beloved of militant atheists and would-be secular commentators, according to which all merely 'religious' ideas should simply be ignored in the public space. There is no clear notion of what they would mean by 'religious', nor any clear, neutrally discernible, distinction between the ideas that they themselves think obvious and those they wish to exclude. That sort of 'secularism' amounts to ideological tyranny, most obviously when, for example, the sacred places of Aboriginal religion are treated merely as property, owned by the richer classes of a State imposed on the locale by force.

One reply might be that Huntington's analysis, rather oddly, wholly ignores two features of the West: namely, that it is in the West that 'science', in the last two centuries, has grown to dominate our thought, and that it is the West that has developed a militant atheism. Militant atheists will usually insist that their own creed is 'scientific', or even that 'science' itself depends on atheistic practice. Their expectation is that the spread of scientific method, on the back of technological success, will gradually or violently erode 'Belief', and so create a peace when no-one any longer lives for 'Religion'. If Huntington is right to suppose that the current contest is between civilizations, each founded on a distinctive and usually 'religious' mind-set, then the contest will be over when all such religions fail. Militant atheism must therefore be opposed to every civilization

[42] *Isaiah* 12.6

[43] Huntington, op. cit., p. 310, citing Michael Howard *America and the World* (Washington University: St. Louis, Annual Lewin Lecture 5th April 1984), p. 6.

except the most modern West (for even 'Confucian' civility depends on reverence for ancestors and for Heaven), and every civilization except that modern West (especially but not only Muslim civilization) must resent such atheism as yet another example of Western decadence. Rejecting God—so all outsiders think—is simply rejecting any limit to desire, and any fear of judgement.

Science doesn't in fact depend on atheism, and neither is atheism an effect of science. The origins of both science and atheism can be traced to elements especially of Christian belief and practice, and these in turn to elements of a more widely-shared sensibility. 'Methodological atheism' (that is, a decision not to worry about final causes, and the purposes of the Creator) is an occasionally useful askesis. *Genuine* atheism is utterly incompatible with the practice and hope of science, since it denies—along with Nietzsche—that our thoughts can ever expect to mirror the infinite. Genuine science is permitting the purposes and images of God to be unfolded in our hearts and minds, without expecting a premature uniformity. The sooner we acknowledge this the better our chances of global reconciliation.

As Huntington acknowledges, what counts as 'one civilization' depends on what the most active and immediate 'Other' is. In days gone by Protestant Europe could reasonably think itself a different civilization from Catholic Europe, just as Huntington now suggests that Orthodox Eastern Christendom and Latin America constitute significant 'Others' to the West. But in a larger sense Christendom contains them all—and is itself a segment of a still larger unit, the civilization born of Abraham. Islam, Christendom, Jewry—and a host of lesser sects—all share the sense that there are individual persons, summoned to share in Heaven. We may also find a common sensibility with Buddhists and Confucians, all acknowledging a Golden Rule, and all suspecting that this world here is at once a dream and a responsibility. Something *like* the 'Noahic Covenant' may perhaps be recognizable as a common heritage, compatible with many diverse nations, sects and cultures.[44] The nightmare vision of the World Beast that I sketched before is itself a plainly *false* religion: everything that the decent atheist despises. World Peace (though it

---

[44] As interpreted by Jewish tradition, that covenant prohibits 'idolatry and blasphemy, murder, theft, sexual transgression and wanton cruelty to animals' and positively requires us to establish a system of justice: see Sacks, *Dignity of Difference*, op. cit., p. 20. But of course there may be considerable ambiguity even in the prohibitions.

is unlikely to be untroubled even then) will arise more readily from realizing that peace is a *blessing*. As long as militant atheists denounce *all* gods as demons, they are—inevitably—seen as enemies, and as representatives of everything that the non-Western world despises. Wars of Religion, along with civil wars, are the worst of all: better to locate the undercurrent of agreement in religion, and the blessing of diversity.

> Whatever the degree to which they divided humankind, the world's major religions—Western Christianity, Orthodoxy, Hinduism, Buddhism Islam, Confucianism, Taoism, Judaism—also share key values in common. If humans are ever to develop a universal civilization, it will emerge gradually through the exploration and expansion of these commonalities.[45]

Enmity, Liberty and Solidarity within the State

I briefly proposed, in speaking of the Flood in an earlier chapter, that we *might* be wholly misled about our history: if we were living in Orwell's Oceania, as it were, only a few strange rebels would recall the truth. Those rebels would probably themselves be flawed: it takes a particular kind of counter-suggestible, irascible personality to maintain a solitary conviction even that 2+2 makes 4 if everyone around is saying that it makes 7. Nowadays, it seems, it is easier than once it was to find support for even the strangest deviations from the consensus world, and correspondingly easier to insist that the supposed destruction of the twin towers was a CIA or Jewish plot, that no-one ever landed on the Moon, that the Queen of England is a Lord of the Instrumentality, and that extra-terrestrial lizards established us as a social experiment no more than a thousand years ago. Most of us don't mind—there are loopy theories in plenty, and even lunatics sometimes discover truths. Isaac Newton spent most of his intellectual energies in search of the Philosopher's Stone, or in interpreting the *Revelation of John the Divine*. Ferdinand de Saussure, the father of modern semantics, saw anagrams everywhere, from Cicero to the Nibelungenlied.[46] Kurt Gödel, one of the greatest mathematicians of

---

[45] Huntington, op. cit., p. 320. I would myself dispute his claim that Western Christianity and Orthodoxy constitute 'different religions', a claim which I take to be an invalid inference from the gap between 'the West' and Russia. He is also certainly mistaken in supposing that 'in Orthodoxy God is Caesar's junior partner' (*ibid.*, p. 70).

[46] See J.J. Lecercle, *Philosophy through the Looking Glass* (Hutchinson: London, 1985), pp. 3–5: he proved his sanity by abandoning the notion as a research project when

the last century (and most others), believed that his enemies were seeking to poison him, and so starved himself to death.[47]

Great minds can be distrustful when they should really be trusting, and embarrassingly gullible when they should have qualms. So can the rest of us. Many of those who doubt the Darwinian Theory of evolution suspect that establishment scientists are liars. Some of those doubters are themselves embarrassingly persuaded that they have the Word of God Himself about the real nature of things. Many of those persuaded of Darwinian Theory, on the other hand, are similarly paranoid, convinced that anyone who doubts *their* word is ignorant or mad or stupid (and even, though they'd rather not believe it, wicked).[48] Each side imagines itself besieged by malice, and each side 'knows' the truth.

No doubt there are many other such polarities: in the United Kingdom Labour and Tory faithful in particular can seemingly believe no good of their opponents, and must ceaselessly invent vile motives even for half-way sensible proposals. In the United States, the population appears evenly divided between two groups with utterly different cultures and ethical presuppositions, each persuaded that the other is not merely wrong but wicked. Perhaps they are sometimes right. But any such division within a Nation, a State, an Empire is in the end disastrous. I must be able to think reasonably well even of those who don't agree with me, or at any rate I must be able to accept their right to contribute to that Nation, State or Empire. Otherwise, they are, in effect, a part of *dar al-harb*, and we can make no covenant with them. Our natural relationship is war.

Possibly this is so. But before we are so easily reconciled to a future of unending, pointless conflict, we should perhaps consider whether we might learn to love our enemies—who are, as Chesterton

---

there turned out to be no other evidence for this literary conceit, but he probably went on seeing them.

[47] see P. Yourgrau, *A World without Time: the Forgotten Legacy of Gödel and Einstein* (Allen Lane: London, 2005), p. 9.

[48] So Richard Dawkins in 'Put Your Money on Evolution' in *New York Times*, April 9th 1989, cited by Alvin Plantinga 'When Faith and Reason Clash: Evolution and the Bible' in *Christian Scholar's Review* XXI:1 (September, 1991): pp. 8–33 (http://www. asa3.org/aSA/dialogues/Faith-reason/CRS9-91Plantinga1.html, accessed 19th April 2008): 'It is absolutely safe to say that if you meet someone who claims not to believe in evolution, that person is ignorant, stupid or insane (or wicked, but I'd rather not consider that).'

remarked, also likely to be our neighbours.[49] Ordinary believers have indeed often been guilty of demonizing their opponents, and most especially those who were more likely to agree on many matters. Militant or even more casual atheists in the present day are often so concerned with the evils that they see in 'religious faith' that they will constantly exaggerate their neighbours' involvement in those evils. Muslims, American Protestants and the Catholic Church have been the principal target in recent years, while 'Anglicans' have been granted the doubtful credit of really being English (and therefore obviously opponents of all enthusiasm), unless they are so tactless as to suggest that they do after all believe. To judge from the more heated remarks of atheists, no 'religious believer' of any sort should ever hold high office, nor be responsible for their children's education, and neither should any believer dare to proselytize for any cause (on pain of being told that she is trying to enforce her own view on the many—a charge that is somehow silent when the would-be 'secularist' speaks). This strategy is, at the least, impractical: all policies embody some sort of ethic and metaphysic which will strike those who don't share it as unreasonable or false. Are we *all* to be silent, or only those that the secularist despises? At worst, the strategy is likely to be disastrous. If believers cannot express their honest views in public, and must see the State they live in turn in directions they deplore, they will be further alienated from that State. Why exactly should we obey the dictates of a government that dismisses all our concerns as frivolous? It seems that secularists implicitly rely on a conception of the State, the Government, as 'ordained of God', the sole judge of what is to be done and thought, while openly deriding the idea that anything can be ordained of God. Secularism, which purports to reject all 'religious' sanctions, 'has simply insured that, in the absence of any divine constraints whatever, nations are free to behave as if they had complete autonomy, as if the nation were indeed absolute: as if it itself were God, deciding the fate of nations'.[50]

---

[49] G.K. Chesterton, 'The Irishman', cited by A.S. Dale, *Outline of Sanity: Life of G.K. Chesterton* (Grand Rapids: Eerdmans, 1983), p. 224.

[50] Wink, *Unmasking the Powers* op. cit., p. 100. Wink goes on to observe (p. 102) that whereas 'a godly people would react to the threat of God's judgement [the sort that Jefferson feared, 'knowing God is just': see p. 131, above] with fear, awe, consternation', many Americans, and especially self-styled 'believers', now regard all such critiques as subversive. That is, it is 'America'—or whatever other State is being considered—that claims the place of God. Neo-Darwinian theorists

Secularists must of course dismiss the notion that the nation is a god. But in that case the State is obeyed only from fear or from desire: fear of expropriation, torture, execution, and desire for whatever consumer goodies the State can offer its loyal servants. Our predecessors would have called this slavish: only 'natural slaves' would permit themselves to be governed so (a point to which I shall return).

One answer to this problem is rampant nationalism. If all the people we need to mind about on a daily basis are 'of one stock' then we have less reason to distrust them. Their imagined consanguinity is of more force than their opinions, or professions, or personal priorities—or else all those occasions for distrust are smoothed away by national pride. The ideal of the nation-state is of an independent political and legal unit, all or almost all of whose citizens believe and feel themselves to be a single people, with a common history and customs, and dominant within a particular, bounded region.

> The Stranger within my gate, he may be true or kind,
> But he does not talk my talk—I cannot feel his mind.
> I see the face and the eyes and the mouth, but not the soul behind.
> The men of my own stock, they may do ill or well,
> But they tell the lies I am wonted to, they are used to the lies I tell;
> And we do not need interpreters when we go to buy and sell.
> The Stranger within my gates, he may be evil or good,
> But I cannot tell what powers control—what reasons sway his mood;
> Nor when the Gods of his far-off land shall repossess his blood.
> The men of my own stock, bitter bad they may be,
> But, at least, they hear the things I hear, and see the things I see;
> And whatever I think of them and their likes they think of the likes of me.
> This was my father's belief and this is also mine:
> Let the corn be all one sheaf—and the grapes be all one vine,
> Ere our children's teeth are set on edge by bitter bread and wine.[51]

The citizens of such nation-states may be more easily persuaded to care for their fellow citizens, to allow them 'welfare-rights' as well as 'liberty-rights', and may resent having to care, even through layers of bureaucracy, for people of another stock. But hardly any

---

display almost an identical conceit in *their* reactions to disagreement, though usually via a weary contempt rather than abusive rage.

[51] Rudyard Kipling, 'The Stranger', *Rudyard Kipling's Verse* (Hodder & Stoughton: London, 1940), p. 549.

nation-state will nowadays be homogeneous—and probably very few ever were. As Gray has pointed out, neither Spain nor Britain, for example, are strictly *nation*-states: they are both artifacts of monarchy.[52] Even if the United Kingdom were to dissolve into its principal parts, the resulting states would not be purely 'national'.[53] We must all put up with peoples of another stock, whether they are long-term inhabitants of the very same land or recent immigrants. Chesterton was quite wrong to think that 'we in the West are very lucky in having our nations normally distributed into their native lands; so that good patriots can talk about themselves without perpetually annoying their neighbours, [whereas] the people of Jerusalem are doomed to have difference without division.'[54] No lands are inhabited and structured only by *one* nation. For many of us, it is this very diversity of custom, history and talent that is most attractive, but we may still wish to insist that *our* customs are pre-eminent. Maybe the other peoples can conduct themselves in private by their own rules, but the rules of public life are those *we* choose.[55] And who are 'we'?

Most modern states, and especially those with an imperial past, contain many distinct constituencies. Jonathan Sacks, Chief Rabbi of the United Hebrew Congregations of the Commonwealth, offered one summary of the present British scene:

> We have 1. communities like the Hindu community, the Sikh community feeling extremely vulnerable. 2. We have a Muslim community wrestling with internal conflicts as to construe British identity. We have 3. the Christian community—different kinds but very much feeling marginalised, on the defensive against an increasingly aggressive secular culture. You have a lot

---

[52] John Gray, *The Two Faces of Liberalism* (Polity Press: Cambridge, 2000), p. 124.

[53] The Scottish Islands, Highlands and Lowlands have historically been at odds, and have very different styles. So also Northern and Southern England and the West. Wales could easily dissolve into separate valley-kingdoms. See D.H. Fischer, *Albion's Seed: Four British Folkways in America* (Oxford Universiy Press: New York, 1991) for an engaging analysis of some of the very different, notionally English, peoples who settled different parts of North America. See Stephen Oppenheimer, *The Origins of the British* (Constable & Robinson: London, 2006) for further speculation about past invasions of these islands (and an incidental rebuttal of the notion that the Irish, Welsh and Scots are 'Celts', to be distinguished from the boringly Anglo-Saxon English).

[54] G.K. Chesterton, *The New Jerusalem* (Hodder & Stoughton: London, 1920), pp. 111f.

[55] See Hendrik Spruyt, *The Sovereign State and its Competitors* (Princeton University Press: New Jersey, 1994)

> of people in middle England, not necessarily urban but rural populations feeling that somehow or other the country they were born in is not the country they see today—whether that takes the basis of a very tiny little issue like fox hunting or a big issue like immigration—feeling somehow or other they can't make sense of this. 4. Then we have a secular liberal intelligentsia that feels quite threatened by a revival of strong religious passions and 5. lastly we have from my own community, the Jewish community, which is feeling very bruised and embattled in the face of rising anti-semitism and anti-Zionism.[56]

Sacks went on to sketch John Gray's distinction between two sorts of liberal or secular society: 'Rawlsian Liberalism', in which no-one brings their personal or sectarian commitments to the public sphere, and 'Modus Vivendi Liberalism', in which people may openly live and speak as Jews, Sikhs, Muslims, or even atheists.[57] But Sacks's chief concern was how we might accommodate those many groups within a unit to which we could feel loyalty. The original British model, for immigrants, was that the Kingdom was, as it were, an enormous country house, in which immigrants were welcome as guests, to live by the host's rules. Once they had become properly British, they could welcome others to this particular vision of the good. A later model, the one (he says) that Rawlsian liberalism promotes, is of a grand hotel: we pay for the services we individually select, without any need to share a vision, and are accommodated as long as we don't upset the other inmates. The third is the house we build together:

> Society, not as a country house, not as a hotel but as the home we build together. It's not a hotel. It's a home. It's somewhere we belong but it's not a country house because a country house is where the owner feels at home but I feel like a guest. If you help build something, you're not a guest. If I can say to my children: I helped build that—then that is mine. And that is a third model—society as the home we build together.[58]

---

[56] Jonathan Sacks, 'How to build a culture of respect', http://www.pm.gov.uk/output/Page10556.asp (accessed 1st March 2008). This was a lecture delivered at King's, and provided as a background paper when the then Prime Minister, Tony Blair, was speaking on multiculturalism. Fox-hunting is not, of course, a 'tiny issue' to those who mind about it.

[57] See Gray, op. cit. My own sympathies, as must be evident, are with the latter kind.

[58] Sacks, op. cit. He amplified the argument in *The Dignity of Difference*, op. cit.

As far as I know the Chief Rabbi was not pilloried for the suggestion, as the unfortunate Archbishop of Canterbury was when he, in turn, addressed the issue: how can the ethnic and sectarian communities who live among us be accommodated in the established culture? 'Even when some of the more dramatic fears are set aside', he pointed out, 'there remains a great deal of uncertainty about what degree of accommodation the law of the land can and should give to minority communities with their own strongly entrenched legal and moral codes.'[59] His reward was to be vilified, first by those who imagined—without troubling to read what he had said—that he was endorsing all such customs as most frighten both non-Muslims and would-be Muslim reformers, and second by critics who pretended to believe—also without attempting actually to read his words—that he was being obscure. 'If we are to think intelligently about the relations between Islam and British law, we need a fair amount of "deconstruction" of crude oppositions and mythologies, whether of the nature of *Shari'a* or the nature of the Enlightenment'.[60] We need, that is to say, to *think*.

Different communities, obviously, differ in their priorities, in their conception of good pedagogic practice, in their conception of what 'success' amounts to. Any tolerant Empire will likely leave such communities to run their own affairs, within whatever limits are decreed for 'the public good' or the security of the Empire. The Ottoman Empire, for example, recognized distinct religious communities, *millets*, though it did not give an equal status to non-Muslims or non-monotheistic religions. Nor did it acknowledge any rights of exit from those communities (and especially not to Muslims).[61] Despite the scorn heaped on the Archbishop it is a simple fact that the United Kingdom also allows considerable powers of self-determination to such communities, though—unlike the Ottomans—it seeks to preserve a right of exit. Such exits are easier partly because most such communities (religious or non-religious) now overlap. Only a few require a pure allegiance from their members: we may simultaneously be Anglicans, academics, vegetarians, Anglo-Welsh, science fiction fans and sometime members of the Labour

---

[59] Rowan Williams, 'Civil and Religious Law in England: a Religious Perspective', lecture at the Royal Courts of Justice 7 February 2008: http://www.archbishopofcanterbury.org/1575 (accessed 1 March 2008).

[60] *Ibid.*

[61] Gray, op. cit., p. 109, after Bernard Lewis, *The Middle East* (Weidenfeld & Nicolson: London, 1995), pp. 321–3.

Party, and handle such tensions as this may involve at a personal or family level. Political Parties insist that no-one be a member of more than one such party (though the parties are themselves constructed out of many different elements), and some self-consciously 'ethnic' groups are likewise adamant that no-one can be, for example, both 'black' and 'white' (even if, in biological fact, they are). The Christian Churches, though their stated rules are usually rigorous, will often quietly accept the existence of boundary-crossers, and welcome any who choose to come.

Religious communities exist, and run their own affairs. One version of secular doctrine regards this as a failing. In effect, we should all give our allegiance entirely and absolutely to the State, and the laws it makes for all. Not all such secularists are 'liberal' in any recognizable sense, but some would claim to be so, distinguishing the actual laws of a particular State from those that a 'rational' State would enact. The laws that we *should* live by are the ones that *everyone* would or must accept: in Rawls's version they are the ones we would accept behind a 'veil of ignorance', if we did not know what status we would have in the society we conspire to make, nor what we would regard as a good life. These are the minimal laws that, it is imagined, *everyone* would accept in order to be able to get on with their lives, according to their own conception of what is good. Unfortunately, it is not clear that there are such laws, nor that they have any authority. Why should we (who?) all agree to be treated as merely independent individuals, bargaining our way around the world? Why should only such individuals be reckoned to have 'property rights'? Who is to be allowed a primary say in any particular stretch of land? The man who has built a fence around it? The man who has a piece of paper from his government (and a promise of military help)? The man—or more likely the family—whose ancestors have walked that land and sung about it for centuries? Who has 'parental authority' (if anyone)? Why are 'human beings' assumed to be the only ones who matter (and who are they)?

There is nonetheless some content in the more *liberal* form of the secular demand: liberals wish that people, individual human people, have room to live the lives they choose, and are not debarred from this except for 'serious' reasons (relating to the public good or 'national security'). Unfortunately, not everyone will think the reasons they give are serious. Consider what happens when a group of Hindus wish to keep a sacred bull alive, when the bureaucracy, playing its most powerful card, requires that the bull be killed (as being infected with bovine tuberculosis), even though he would never enter the human food-chain, nor associate with any other cattle. They are compelled to play 'by the same rules as everyone', even though these are rules they had no part in shaping, and would have roundly rejected if offered the opportunity.

Can liberals find some consistent principle of action? It may be reasonable to tolerate male circumcision for ceremonial reasons, although it is, technically, an assault, since it is, relatively, a minor excision (and even has some medical advantages). It may be reasonable to tolerate the techniques of animal-slaughter required by *kosher* and *hallal* rules, on the plea that they are not very much less humane than the techniques demanded in all merely secular slaughter-houses, and the rules about what may properly be eaten are central to the relevant communities' identities. It may be reasonable to allow Sikh male motorcyclists to wear turbans rather than the helmets others have to wear. Banks now routinely organize their loans to Islamic customers according to some interpretation of the ancient ban on usury. Schools attempt some compromise about the proper sort of clothing (especially their female pupils' clothing), and hesitate about the wearing of special symbols. Doctors' and nurses' rights of conscience are acknowledged when someone seeks an abortion, even if this may make the abortion more difficult to secure (and so, in contemporary-speak, violate the woman's supposed right to that abortion[62]).

On the other hand, we (that is, the mainstream culture) do not tolerate clitoridectomy, nor forced marriages, nor 'honour killings', nor the death penalty for apostasy.[63] The children of Jehovah's Witnesses will be made wards of court at once if their medical advisers suppose that they will need a blood transfusion (which their parents cannot personally allow). There are definite limits to the 'rights of conscience', which we mostly rationalize by referring to the 'harm' done to 'others'. There is no 'right' of suicide (or else anyone who saved another from suicide would be guilty of assault). There is no right even to consent to damagingly masochistic sex (and those who do will probably be found guilty of a mutual assault). No doubt that

---

[62] In the US there is, at present, such a legal right. There is no such legal right in the United Kingdom, nor in most other States which *permit* abortions, under some conditions, for 'the public good'.

[63] Only the fourth of these is strictly a 'religious' requirement (for Islam). Some Muslim scholars argue that the penalty (which is analogous to the penalty for treason) is not appropriate in a modern context.

we mean well: but 'harm' is a contentious concept, and so also is 'other'. They depend on assumptions (often religious assumptions) that not all reasonable people make (unless we identify such rationality with exactly those assumptions). Even we, the mainstream culture, although supposedly 'medical' reasons always seem to trump every other value, do not always hold that there is no fate worse than death: permanent exclusion from the society of our family and sometime friends may be at least as serious. 'Our' decision to tolerate some harms, not others, is, exactly *our* decision, and so is our insistence that each human individual is to be offered the largest possible range of options, and to make the choice herself—unless her choices prove (to us) that she is not to be trusted to make the 'right' choice. And do we have evidence that having 'the largest possible range of options' is actually helpful?[64]

So what determines 'right choices', and why do 'we' ever claim the right to interfere with the judgements made by other groups? In the international order the ruling assumption is that there should be no interference across 'State Borders' (and even the acknowledged exception, that any State may or must intervene to prevent genocide, is given rather little weight). Why do we not practice just such reserve towards self-governing communities *within* those borders? One answer is the managerial. We *need* there to be individuals who are alienated from all family ties and customary inhibitions, willing to rule their lives by the clock and the secular calendar, and convinced that the greatest harms are those that can be averted by judicious use of wealth. People who believe otherwise, and whose primary loyalties are to their kin, their ancestors, their co-religionists will not be so amenable.

In one version of secularism, 'religious' reasons and behaviour should not intrude at all on the public space: not only proselytizing is forbidden (as it is in Singapore), but any public display of difference.[65] It is difficult to see how this is not a restriction on personal lib-

---

[64] Suddenly afflicted with hay-fever, I approached a pharmacist with streaming eyes and requested some alleviation: her initial response was to offer me a wide range of medications, eye-drops and pills, leaving me to 'make my own decision'. This was not helpful!

[65] It has even been argued—by Robert Audi amongst others—not only that the religious should not invoke religious reasons in the public realm, but should not even act on their own religious motives in advocating any public measure (even if they do so with non-religious arguments): see Robert Audi, *Religious Commitment and Secular Reason* (Cambridge University Press: Cambridge, 2000). Roger Trigg, *Religion in Public Life: Must Faith be Privatized?* (Oxford University Press: Oxford,

erty, and incidentally a violation of the United Nations Declaration that all be free to practise their religion. It also requires a distinction between 'the public' and 'the private' that is difficult to define—and a distinction that for other reasons many feminists dislike. Presumably, to be consistent, children should not be informed of any parental convictions that are not to be made public, nor brought up in conformity with them if they are different (in the eyes of bureaucrats) from publicly acceptable norms. How do 'religious' reasons and motives differ from 'non-religious' reasons and motives? Many—but not all—vegetarians, for example, acknowledge what they would consider a 'religious' dimension to their practice, whether or not they advocate any sort of 'supernatural' religion, or are members of some recognized denomination. Is it OK to be vegetarian on broadly hygienic principles, or as a matter of 'moral taste', but not in obedience to an objective moral norm or the presumed will of God? Couples who wish to adopt orphan children must, it seems, be willing to mouth acceptable opinions, and not be supposed to be 'eccentric'. Even *natural* parents ought to consider themselves as State employees, and expect to be dismissed (that is, their children will be removed from them) if they misbehave (that is, if they dissent). Some militant atheists apparently agree, believing that all religion—without any clear attempt to define their terms—amounts to child-abuse, but they should perhaps be loath to encourage such a vast increase in State control: it is unwise, after all, to create social mechanisms that may fall into their own enemies' hands someday. One of the strangest features of many would-be reformers, as Chesterton pointed out, is that they combine extreme distrust of 'the Establishment' with an apparent wish to give it far more power.

> I am one of those who believe that the cure for centralization is decentralization. It has been described as a paradox. There is apparently something elvish and fantastic about saying that when capital [or any other instrument of power] has come to be too much in the hands of the few, the right thing is to restore it to the hands of the many. The Socialist would put it in the hands of

2007) is more alert to the absurdities and injustice of this proposal, which would presumably have barred civil rights activists from speaking of the Fatherhood of God, the Brotherhood of Man, and the Beloved Community. See Charles Marsh, *The Beloved Community: How Faith shapes Social Justice from the Civil Rights Movement to Today* (Perseus Books: New York, 2005) for a historical and theologically alert account of the American civil rights movement.

> even fewer people; but those people would be politicians, who (as we know) always administer it in the interests of the many.[66]

At the other extreme of secular opinion are the libertarians, who do indeed accept the parallel with international order: for them, the only bearable State authority would be the *minimal* state, enforcing only such laws as are required to defend us all from violence or fraud. The State, on this account, should make no larger claim to foster virtue, or defend 'welfare rights'. It would be something like the 'economic leagues' described by Aristotle: how people behave 'in private' would be none of the State's business, as long as they did no violence to another, and kept their particular contracts. But this system is just as prejudicial as the more authoritarian one I sketched before. What will count as harm? What as an acceptable contract that is worth defending? Whose contracts will these be? What constitutes the 'private' as against the 'public' realm? These questions can only be answered in some particular historical, social context. Nor can we expect that anyone would willingly make any contracts with people whose life-style and beliefs they thoroughly detested, nor willingly refrain from seeking their conversion or reform. Those who think they could have simply forgotten what sort of lives other people sometimes lead (and what those others think of theirs).

Any society that has any hope of being stable must somehow steer between the authoritarian and libertarian mode: the problem is no different for secularists than for the openly 'religious'. Remember Chesterton:

> The average agnostic of recent times has really had no notion of what he meant by religious liberty and equality. He took his own ethics as self-evident and enforced them; such as decency or the error of the Adamite heresy. Then he was horribly shocked if he heard of anybody else, Moslem or Christian, taking *his* ethics as self-evident and enforcing them; such as reverence or the error of the Atheist heresy.[67]

---

[66] G.K. Chesterton, *The Outline of Sanity* (1926): *Collected Works*, vol. 5 (Ignatius Press: San Francisco, 1987), p. 42 (my addition in square brackets); see also G.K. Chesterton, *The New Jerusalem* (Hodder & Stoughton: London, 1920), p. 6 'The mob howls before the palace gates, "Hateful tyrant, we demand that you assume more despotic powers"; and the tyrant thunders from the balcony, "Vile rebels, do you dare to suggest that my powers should be extended?" There seems to be a little misunderstanding somewhere.'

[67] Chesterton, *St Francis*, op. cit., p. 144f.

Muslim countries forbid the use and sale of alcohol. Secular democracies usually forbid the use and sale of ganja. How much can 'we', in a particular historical and social community, enforce? What shall we allow and what approve? Pretending that everything we approve is what *anyone* would approve, that what we forbid is what *anyone* would forbid, if only—in both cases—they were *sensible* (like us), is self-deceit. Immigrants may, not quite unreasonably, be urged to 'respect the angels' (that is, the customs of their hosts),[68] but they may also expect, like all of us, some day 'to judge angels',[69] and to play some part in shaping a new age (as Jonathan Sacks imagined). Politics, by Aristotle's account, is an 'architectonic' craft, concerned with right priorities. Without some such craft, we have no way of saying even what 'liberties' matter most to us, nor whose opinion matters.

[68] See *1 Corinthians* 11.10.

[69] See *1 Corinthians* 6.3.

10

More Local Problems

Honour, 'Indoctrination' and Faith Schools

Honour has a bad name in the mainstream British community. We associate it with such hideous notions as 'honour killings' of disobedient daughters or defaulting crooks, and consider it a device for compelling obedience through fear—exactly the sort of slavishness that our predecessors scorned. Mainstream reaction, especially among secularists, is to try and break down the walls of such communities as prate of 'honour'. We want every individual person to be *free* (that is, no longer to be subject to any authority but the Law's—that is, *our* Law's) and hope to encourage this by a progressive alienation from their 'life-denying' origins. We may then occasionally be perturbed that such alienated individuals don't see much reason to look after others, whether those others are infants or the elderly or the disabled. Rather than acknowledge personal obligations which it would be *dishonourable* to refuse we try to invent *impersonal* institutions that will do such necessary jobs for us ('necessary' just in that it would be inconvenient to have too many starving bodies on the streets, and alarming, sometimes, to consider our own future state). The rule of the impersonal or mechanical, in which things are done (or not done) according to some explicit rule, without any attention to motive, character or goal, itself provides an image of the sort of universe that atheistic materialists believe exists.

> Remember, please, the Law by which we live,
> We are not built to comprehend a lie,
> We can neither love nor pity nor forgive.
> If you make a slip in handling us you die![1]

---

[1] Rudyard Kipling, 'The Secret of the Machines': *Rudyard Kipling's Verse* (Hodder & Stoughton: London, 1940), pp. 729–30. Kipling continues: 'Though our smoke may hide the Heavens from your eyes, /it will vanish and the stars will shine again, /because, for all our power and weight and size, /we are nothing more than children of your brain!'

But of course such impersonal institutions still need to be staffed by people—and where shall we acquire staff of the requisite quality and virtue? The more we insist that there are no natural obligations and correspondingly no dishonour, the less we can trust the officials that we need, whether these are in 'the caring professions' or in 'the civil service'. *Obviously*, they will be in it for their own satisfactions, and act—if given the opportunity—for their own sake or their children's. That, after all, is what they will all have been taught to believe is the inevitable result of 'evolution'.

At the moment, fortunately, there are still some people who have been brought up otherwise, or found their own source of honour. Unfortunately, we both despise and need them. We need them for the reasons hinted at before (as insurance against our own incapability as well as the inconvenience of seeing dead bodies everywhere). We despise them because they are exiled from the happy round, and must be freaks to be willingly exploited. That combination of contempt and need is a familiar syndrome, most obviously in Hindu culture, where Untouchables (Harijan, Dalits) are needed to deal with excrement, dead bodies, leather.[2] At least in Hindu culture the 'higher' castes acknowledge that they have duties of their own, and can conceive that they, as individual souls, might someday be Untouchables themselves. Modern mainstream Western culture has an equal need for willing and reliable servitors, and also a lurking doubt that anyone could really be like that. Either our servitors are hypocrites, or they are fools, or they are suffering from an irrational infection, a mental microbe, requiring them to serve.[3]

There are at least two possible responses to our problem. The first is the more brutal: if fools are what we need, then let us create them, by whatever genetic, biochemical and educational corruption that we can. 'The rich man may come to be breeding a tribe of dwarfs to be his jockeys, and a tribe of giants to be his hall-porters'[4]—and a tribe of willing slaves to be his carers. 'The Law of Manu', dedicated

[2] See Kancha Ilaiah, *Why I Am Not a Hindu: A Sudra Critique of Hindutva Philosophy, Culture and Political Economy* (Bhatkal & Sen: Calcutta, 2001).

[3] The incidence of anorexia amongst the caring professions is reputed to be higher than in the normal population: those who believe that they have no personal *right* to exist are compelled to care for others (and the stress of regular failure makes a further anorexic turn more likely).

[4] Chesterton, *What's Wrong*, op. cit., p. 259.

to breeding four races of human being (so Nietzsche said[5]), may be the Law of the future (though we may need more than four). Amongst the tribes that will be created will be scientists, scholars, librarians: biomechanical servants, organic or electronic brains, to secure the information necessary for the being of less knowledgeable drones. They too may be instrumentally useful for those with power—but the powerful themselves will have much simpler goals than knowledge. This too is an implication of modern mainstream culture: 'education' itself is instrumentally useful, for those who need it. It may get them better pay. If we want more *dedicated* scholars, who don't care about the pay, we'd better engineer them. And they too will be despised.

There is at least one other response, which is to reject Western mainstream culture, but without thereby falling back into traditional, murderous cultures of the sort that countenance 'honour' killings, clitoridectomies, beatings, and the rest.[6] All communities within the larger, controlling State, must seek some way of bringing their children up, of educating them, that permits the proper unfolding of their faiths, learning from others but not abandoning their own. In other words, we need an expansion of 'faith schools'. The immediate response that this will be, or is, 'divisive', misses the actual reality: we are already very much divided, and we should all have serious qualms about any uniformitarian system to eliminate those divisions. On the available evidence, most 'faith schools'—though probably not all—are concerned to encourage a deep respect for those of other 'faiths', even the most avowedly materialist.

Michael Hand offers an influential argument *against* 'faith schools', on the plea that they are bound to be 'indoctrinating' their pupils (which is axiomatically bad).[7] Perhaps he has in mind such declarations of intent as the following:

---

[5] F. Nietzsche, *Twilight of the Idols, & The Anti-Christ*, trans. R.J. Hollingdale (Penguin: Harmondsworth, 1968), p. 56.

[6] The habit of assuming that if one is against That one must therefore be in favour of This (that is, that all oppositions are binary) is one that we ought all to strive against! We should also be aware that This and That are often very similar in their assumptions: in this case, in their denial that each individual soul is worth the saving.

[7] Hand, 'A Philosophical Objection to Faith Schools' op. cit, following too uncritically the judgement of I.A. Snook: 'Christian teachers of all persuasions are expected to teach for belief [sic] in certain propositions, the propositions varying from sect to sect. It is clear that such teaching is indoctrination because whatever

> The aim of the [Islamia Primary] School is to produce total Muslim personalities through the training of children's spirits, intellect, feelings and bodily senses. Education at Islamia caters for the growth of students in all their spiritual, intellectual, imaginative, physical, scientific and linguistic aspects, both individually and collectively, motivating all these aspects towards goodness. The ultimate aim of Islamic education is the realisation of complete submission to Allah on the level of the individual, the community and humanity at large.[8]

The declaration (which is more wide-ranging than corresponding statements by Jewish, Sikh, Catholic or Church of England schools) is indeed likely to be widely misunderstood: 'submission to Allah' does not necessarily mean agreement with particular would-be authorities on earth![9] But any school's Mission Statement will offer some conception of a fulfilled and proper life—as I shall observe below. Hand has a larger target, though, than Muslims, and offers what is meant to be a conclusive argument against *all* 'faith schools'. In that argument he unthinkingly equates 'passing on religious beliefs', providing an 'education that includes religious nurture' and 'teaching a religious faith'. He is also far too certain that it is false to say that 'passing on religious beliefs to children is not a matter of convincing them that certain propositions are true, but of equipping them with a vocabulary for the expression of feelings or the declara-

---

the particular proposition, the evidence for it is inconclusive: it is rejected by other competent authorities. That all religious propositions are doubtful in this sense is sufficient to indicate that teaching for belief in them is always indoctrination' (I.A. Snook, *Indoctrination and Education*. (Routledge and Kegan Paul: London, 1972), p. 74).

[8] http://www. islamia-pri. brent. sch. uk/admissions. html (accessed 7th April 2008). The related, independent, secondary school, Brondesbury College, has an even firmer mission statement: 'The aim of Islamic education lies beyond the borders of this world; it is to gain Paradise in the everlasting life and, ultimately, to learn the pleasure of Allah, the Lord of the Worlds. A College of moral excellence, therefore, is our primary objective where the complete personal development of the student is paramount. ' But its actual curriculum is straightforward: it 'offers essential aspects of Arabic and Islamic Studies in conjunction with a broad range of Sciences, Physical Education and National Curriculum disciplines, ... [and] aims to produce mature young men with leadership qualities and the ability to contribute, as responsible citizens, to the well being of the pluralistic society as a whole' (see http://bcbcollege.com/content/view/13/27/: accessed 7th April 2008). At least such concepts as 'well-being' have rather more content in this context than, as I shall observe below, they do in the National Curriculum!

[9] Rather, the reverse.

tion of intentions'.[10] Oddly, though he acknowledges that religious believers, in every major tradition, have arguments for their conclusions (even if those arguments are not absolutely conclusive), he claims that *persuading* pupils of those conclusions must always be by non-rational means, apparently on the assumption that we are never *rationally* persuaded by less-than-conclusive arguments.[11] In order to 'pass on religious beliefs', he supposes, the schools must make an attempt to induce their pupils to believe by other methods than rational argument, since no merely rational but inconclusive argument *ought* to persuade them. Doing this, he claims, destroys or damages their judgement, since they have internalized beliefs without rational warrant, and acquired a fatal habit of so doing. But this, as I have pointed out before, is the product of a false epistemology. Not all arguments are 'absolutely convincing' in the sense that Hand requires (that every reasonable person, confronted with the evidence, would agree to the conclusion—unless 'reasonable' is defined tendentiously as one who agrees with Michael Hand). Indeed, very few arguments are: and yet we may be rationally persuaded that a conclusion is well supported, and adopt it as our own. This teaching may indeed implicitly deny the claim that we ought only to believe what everyone would agree was proved, but that claim is itself absurd (since we should believe it only if everyone agrees it's true—and William James[12] and I believe it's not). There are rational and well-informed people who are not convinced—however foolish I may suppose they are—that the events of '9/11' (that is, of 11th September 2001) were what the rest of us suppose: in that sense the evidence for those events is not rationally conclusive. Must the rest of us be agnostic, and complain if our children's teachers repeat the usual story? What exactly does 'rationality' involve? Some 'rational and well-informed' philosophers have concluded, for example, that neither non-human animals nor human infants have any feelings at all that the rest of us need worry about. Are we to conclude that teachers should offer no judgement

[10] *Ibid.*, p. 94.

[11] It would seem to follow that barristers must be 'indoctrinating' the juries whom they would persuade, those applying for research funds hope to 'indoctrinate' their funders, and those who write articles about 'faith schools' must hope for similarly malleable readers. There are, after all, no absolutely compelling arguments (that no-one rational could possibly dispute) for anyone's guilt or innocence, for the value of a project, or for the conclusions that Michael Hand proposes!

[12] See James, *Will to Believe*, op. cit., p. 25.

on these matters, and that it would be wrong of parents to enquire exactly what *ethical* views were part of a school's mission so long as pupils passed the appropriate exams? May I, as a parent, not choose—if I can—a school whose *ethical* practices I can commend: one, for example, that is founded on vegetarian principles?[13] Or at least, if that is unobtainable, one founded on *humane* or simply *decent* principles?[14]

Faith schools, *pace* Hand, do *not* exist to persuade pupils of particular 'religious propositions', not even in the case I cited a moment ago, of the Islamia Primary School. In most cases the pupils will already have absorbed such propositions as are required in any particular faith (just as the children of avowed materialists will presuppose that the 'material world' is all that really exists, and that 'religious faith' is a folly). All that believing parents will be seeking is a school that does not openly or secretly seek to subvert the faith that is important to their families. This may result in many different sorts of 'faith school'. Some exist as part of their home community's normal civil life, as a way of keeping the community together. Jewish 'faith schools', for example, may operate on Jewish principles, but not see their task as teaching *propositions* about the object of Jewish worship. It is after all axiomatic in Orthodox Judaism that we cannot say anything positively and truly about God, but must be content with following the Mosaic Law that has defined the Jewish Community for millennia. Sikh schools, such as the Guru Nanak Sikh schools, ensure that 'students learn their mother tongue and are aware of the principles of Sikhism. More importantly they are encouraged to act within these principles which include doing the Nitnem daily [that is, praying], showing respect for adults, showing respect for other religions, caring for the elderly and underprivi-

[13] Such as the Krishna-Avanti school in north-west London (see http://www.krishna-avanti. org.uk/assets/files/Admissions%20Policy.pdf; though the school backed off its initial, more rigorous, admissions policy: http://www.timesonline.co.uk/tol/comment/faith/ article3047838.ece), or St. Christopher's Primary School in Norwich (see http: //www.stchristophers norwich.co.uk/index2.html).

[14] The philosopher Erazim Kohak (personal communication) remarked to me some years ago that his daughter, teaching at an American public school, had been rebuked by her headmaster for commending a pupil who had handed in to the office a lost wallet containing a large sum of money. Such commendations, apparently, were inappropriate behaviour.

leged, showing humility'[15]. The school's Aims are that students 'will have a sound knowledge of the life of the Gurus and the practical examples they gave; will have a sound knowledge of the principals [sic] of the Sikh faith; will acknowledge the Guru Granth Sahib as the living Guru and will learn the Gurmukhi; will understand important prayers such as the Mool Mantar, Japji Sahib, Asa Di War, Sukhmani Sahib and Anand Sahib; will explore the way of life and history in the Punjab before and after the Guru era; will understand the functions of Gurdwaras and other historical sites in the world today; will understand the concept of family and current societal perspectives'.[16] Of these aims, only one (to *acknowledge* the Guru Granth Sahib [the Sikh scriptures] as the living Guru [the final authority in Sikh affairs]) can be said to require 'belief' over and above the sort of learning that even non-Sikhs interested in Sikh thought and history would welcome.[17] Students are *encouraged* to pray (as they would not be in a fully secular establishment), but also to display such virtues as even secularists would mostly wish (though secularists of the more militant kind would not wish students to respect *any* religions at all, but rather to consider all their votaries knaves or fools).

Some—but certainly not all—*Muslim* schools may have a more specific remit: to educate the next generation of imams in traditional ways, ensuring that they have the Koran by heart, and at least an elementary grasp of Muslim law. Non-Muslims may be suspicious of such schools, as once Protestants were of *Catholic* schools: perhaps they are teaching some supposedly 'extreme' form of Islam, requiring their pupils to put aside their 'critical faculties' and the worthless opinions of mainstream society, in favour of 'jihad', an unending war against all 'unbelievers'. Non-Muslims may be especially indignant (have been especially indignant) if they suppose that such 'faith schools' are being supported by 'tax-payers' money'. No doubt there could be such schools, both here and elsewhere in the world, but it is worth noting, as Cristina Odone says, that 'not one of the 72 British citizens convicted under the Terrorism Act of 2000 attended a faith

[15] http://www.gurunanakschools.org.uk/secondary/ourschool.asp (accessed 6th April 2008).

[16] http://www.gurunanakschools.org.uk/secondary/page.asp?page=90 (accessed 6th April 2008).

[17] And even that is compatible with a fairly relaxed attitude to the scriptures: I too may 'acknowledge' the Guru Granth Sahib as the final authority *for Sikhs* (apart from God Himself), without acknowledging that authority for myself.

school'.[18] No doubt (once upon a time not long ago) *Catholic* schools were also, with some justice, seen as propagandist institutions, preaching the illegitimacy of Anglican orders and of the British Crown. And not so long ago nor very far away all *Christian* schools in general were thought subversive of the established order (as indeed they often are). The rest of us may legitimately demand that the minority communities within our borders *not* advocate armed rebellion, murder or flat disobedience—and most such communities would agree at once that the civil peace which permits their peaceful practices and protects their interests against crooks is worth maintaining, as long as the cost is not too high. Such communities, however, are also entitled to preserve themselves against erosion or dissipation: why else could it be *wrong* (as most of us now suppose) to steal Aboriginal children from their homes in order to break down those ancient ways judged incompatible with mainstream Western practice? There *ought* to be schools in Aboriginal communities that help their students to understand their origins and share their families' lives, as well as allowing their 'free' and fortunate development. The teachers in those schools *ought* to have at the very least respect for the Aboriginal ethos, while also being wary of its dangers: not all the ancient ways were right, any more than all the 'modern' ways. If God exists, we all live under judgement.

The moral would seem to be that 'faith schools' are a check against the deliberate or unthinking destruction of minority communities within a broadly liberal state. If Muslim States, correspondingly, are to be true either to traditional Islam (that requires respect for the Peoples of the Book, and for Humanity) as well as to the international order that we are all trying to create, they too must permit 'faith schools' that don't entirely accord with Muslim precepts (whether these are Christian, Jewish or mere materialist)—though we must expect there to be limits to that tolerance, as there also must be in the West. Quite how such 'faith schools' are to work, and what limits might legitimately be placed on the teaching that goes on in them, are matters for careful thought, by 'host' communities and 'minority' communities alike.

And of course the 'host' communities themselves are not as unanimous as some commentators have supposed. Not all schools, and not all the communities they serve, are persuaded, for example, that the proper route to adulthood lies through a University, or espe-

[18] See Cristina Odone, *In Bad Faith: the new betrayal of faith schools* (Centre for Policy Studies: London, 2008), p. 40. On the contrary, they were state-educated.

cially an 'Academic' University. As an academic myself, of course, I may be easily persuaded that such schools and such communities are mistaken, and hope very much that individual pupils fitted for such a life will find a way. But the mass of the British population plainly disagrees, and far more readily accepts suggestions that schools should specialize in Sport, or Art, or Business than in properly 'academic' excellence (which is reckoned to be elitist). One reason that the older 'selective' system has been rejected in the United Kingdom was that children admitted to the 'Grammar Schools' or given a bursary to attend an 'Independent School' (although they were thereby granted opportunities for growth and knowledge) were alienated from their home communities, and came to have different values, different beliefs, conveyed to them not only in clearly argued propositions but also in the style and manners of the schools. In the days when those fresh values were, in a way, still shared, at a distance, by the whole population, this was acceptable: nowadays, apparently, it isn't. How shall we educate *other people's* young in the ways that seem best to 'us' without our thereby destroying or diminishing their necessary ties to family and childhood friends? How shall we allow all the 'lesser' communities within our islands to contribute to the building of the larger community?

One answer is to pretend that there are some goals that everybody shares, some talents and beliefs that everybody needs, whatever else they want, and restrict our public schooling to those supposedly universal aims. Anything beyond those aims must be a matter for private schooling, in the evenings or at weekends. The same rationale can perhaps be used to defend a 'national curriculum' which reckons many disciplines are only optional—or frivolous. The flaws in the current syllabus—which make it unlikely that any ordinary student will ever be anything but monolingual—don't *necessarily* make this project foolish (though it is unlikely that any syllabus will satisfy all rational and well-informed observers). The present curriculum, we are told, should 'enable all young people to become *successful* learners who enjoy learning, *make progress* and *achieve*; *confident* individuals who are able to live *safe, healthy* and *fulfilling* lives; *responsible* citizens who make a *positive* contribution to *society*'.[19] What any of the terms I have italicized actually mean remains, to me, unclear, to say nothing of how the curriculum is supposed to enable young people to evade road accidents, cancer, crime, disappointment and

[19] http://curriculum.qca.org.uk/aims/index.aspx (accessed 6th April 2008): my italics.

depression. What will they *achieve*? What counts as a *positive* contribution? To achieve these aims (with a sudden descent into banality),

> the statutory subjects that all pupils must study [at stage 3] are art and design, citizenship, design and technology, English, geography, history, information and communication technology, mathematics, modern foreign languages, music, physical education and science. The teaching of careers education, sex education and religious education is also statutory. [At stage 4] the statutory subjects that all pupils must study are citizenship, English, information and communication technology, mathematics, physical education and science. The teaching of careers education, sex education, work-related learning and religious education is also statutory.[20]

All this embodies some unclear notion of what counts as a 'good life', and of what is needed, at whatever elementary level, if this is ever to be achieved. 'Rational and well-informed' citizens may well have different views, and prefer schools with clearer goals, and clearer notions of what those goals require. Notice, merely for example, that 'careers education' (whatever that is) remains mandatory, but not any 'modern foreign language'; 'science', but not 'history'; 'physical education' but not 'music'.

'Religious education', according to the Curriculum, provides some knowledge of Christianity and other belief-systems, and an opportunity to reflect on 'the ultimate meaning and purpose of life, beliefs about God, the self and the nature of reality, issues of right and wrong and what it means to be human'. These are worthy goals, no doubt, but whether they will be achieved depends a lot on the quality of the teachers, the school and the local environment. Parents may reasonably doubt that just *any* teacher, school and locality will do. They may wonder whether these goals can be maintained if the whole ethos of the educational system is as pragmatic as it appears to be, or what they can amount to when the stated aims of the whole curriculum are so obscure, and when particular subjects may embody, without clear argument, contentious morals.

Even (especially?) schools dedicated to 'Science and Technology' have severely *practical* aims. When secularists insist that schools

---

[20] http://curriculum.qca.org.uk/subjects/index.aspx (accessed 7th April 2008). The curriculum also includes 'non-statutory programmes, such as 'religious education, based on the Framework for Religious Education; personal wellbeing, which includes the requirements for sex and relationship and drugs education; economic wellbeing and financial capability, which includes the requirements for careers education.' These too are very poorly defined.

should not refer to any supposedly objective values, or to metaphysics (that is, to any religious possibility), they are in effect, if not intention, saying that everything that pupils learn should be judged entirely on what it might contribute to their *material* success (and that anyone who does not desire that success is automatically a failure). Science is not to be valued—as once it was—as revealing the glory of God, nor Art for adding to it: all that can matter is how much money can be made from some appropriate skill. Some secularists may respond that it is 'the good of humanity' that all schools should consider. But this too is a sectarian ideal, or rather many disparate ideals concealed under a single head. What is *humanity*, and what is *good* for it? Can anyone seriously suppose that there is no rational dispute about either term? Or even that the dispute can be settled by entirely 'rational' means (in the sense that Hand and others have preferred)? What good schools, as most of us ordinarily understand that concept, mostly hope is that their students are given the opportunity to *see* something honourable, something beautiful, something honest in the studies they enjoy or endure. In this they are closer to a sane epistemology: we don't always need to be persuaded by compelling external evidence. Sometimes, with help, we simply see a truth.

One further—very strange—criticism of 'faith schools' is that, being in receipt of public funding, they should not discriminate in their admissions policy, despite existing in the service of whatever 'faith community'. In fact, the admissions policies of such 'faith schools' as I have located seem a reasonable balance. The Guru Nanak Singh schools, for example, rank their applicants as follows:[21]

1. Children living with parents, legal guardians, or carers, who demonstrate a deep commitment to the Sikh faith. Evidence of this commitment will be required such as a statement from the Priest of the local Gurdwara and commitment to the five Ks.

2. Children living with parents, legal guardians, or carers, at least one of whom attends worship at least three times a month in a Gurdwara, and has done so far for at least three years.

3. Children living with parents, legal guardians, or carers, at least one of whom attends worship monthly in the tradition

[21] http://www.gurunanakschools.org.uk/secondary/admissions.asp (accessed 7th April 2008).

of any faith other than Sikh. The frequency of worship must be certified by the appropriate authorities. This certification will be used to establish priority within this criterion.

4. Children of families who live in the vicinity of the School.
5. Within each category, priority will be given to children in the following order:
   1. Children in Public Care/Looked After.
   2. Children with well documented acute medical needs whom the Governors believe would benefit from a place at the School.
   3. Children with brothers or sisters in the school who were admitted prior to Year 12. They should have at least one brother or sister attending the school at the time of admission.
   4. Distance from home to school (Note: Distance is measured by the LEA in a straight line from the School main office to the child's permanent home).

Jewish schools, for example those supported by the King David Foundation, have a similar system of priorities.[22] What would be the *point* of a 'faith school', a 'community school' that didn't? What indeed would be the point of *any* specialist school? It is now reckoned reasonable for schools to advertise themselves as geared to Art or Sport or Business or Technology. Obviously those who apply to such schools, especially if there is competition for the places, must give some indication of their sincerity and the likely quality of their performance. Children who are seeking a place at a ballet school must demonstrate that this is not a waste of space, as it would be if the home environment, the attitude of their parents, or their own physical incapacity made ballet practice impossible. An early convert to Islam, say, might possibly be welcome in a Muslim school, even if her family were not themselves Muslim: the admissions policy of Islamia Primary School in London, for example, although it follows much the same form as Sikh or Jewish schools in its priorities, seems not quite so strict in its criteria.[23] An early convert to Judaism or the Sikh religion would have a more difficult project, since both those faiths are largely *family* faiths (in fact, though not in

[22] See, for example, the King David Primary School in Liverpool: http://www.kdpsliverpool.co.uk/2007/Prospectus%2007%20-%2008%2003120.pdf.

[23] http://www. islamia-pri.brent. sch.uk/admissions.html (accessed 7th April 2008).

principle), and conversion amounts to being adopted into a new family.

By recognizing, funding and even partly regulating 'faith' or 'community' schools the State allows its subjects a proper say in how their children are to be taught, and to what ends. Denying them recognition, denying them a share in the common wealth, amounts to saying that they can contribute nothing of any value to the State we're building up together. That may, sometimes, be the inevitable moral, just as it is true that *some* family practices cannot be tolerated. But just as it does not follow from the latter truism that all children should be taken away and 'cared for' by professionals in State-licensed crèches, so also it does not follow that because some real or imagined faiths are vile that no faith except a State-licensed ideology (which is to say, the ideology of its actual ruling classes) deserves a voice.

Two Sorts of Slavishness

One of the charges against 'the religious' is that they are 'heteronomous', substituting the opinion of others or the commandments of an imagined God for their own judgement and responsibility. They are supposed to be willingly enslaved. The converse claim is that it is 'the religious' who are liberated from obedience to any earthly master, and that it is 'secularists' who are really slaves.

What would make this latter suggestion plausible? Actually, it's fairly easy.

In the first place, there is something very odd about someone who acts *only* on his own conscience and judgement, just as there would be something odd, even absurd, about someone who took his own unaided and uninterrogated memory as gospel.[24] We know we are often wrong about what has happened, even to ourselves, and we know that our own judgement is often partial, biased, ignorant. To think *morally* at all is to place ourselves and our favourite fantasies under authority. The real question is: whose authority?

If our only real reason for obedience is fear of material punishment or desire for material success, we show ourselves to be slaves, and specifically State-slaves. This is the sort of slavishness that many outsiders detect in 'Western' ideology, and which was identified by that Greek philosopher who has some claim to be called 'the Father

---

[24] G.E.M. Anscombe, 'Authority in Morals' (1962): *Faith in a Hard Ground,* op. cit., pp. 92–100.

of the West'.[25] By Aristotle's account 'natural slaves', who are slaves in fact, whatever their legal status,[26] can be identified in two ways—the physical and the ethical. In the physical sense, they are able to labour, but not to look ahead, to use their bodies and nothing better.[27] 'Nature would like to distinguish between the bodies of freemen and slaves, making the one strong for servile (*anankaion*) labour, the other upright and although useless for such services, useful for political life in the arts both of war and peace'.[28] In general, the relation of master to slave is like that of soul to body. Qua slaves, they do not even have 'a life'.[29] They are no more than organic tools.

If this is all that natural slaves were it would be easy to agree that there almost certainly are none, any more than there are zombies or humanoid robots (yet). So it would be more helpful to consider the 'ethical' discrimination: that natural slaves are instruments is true, but not because they have no feelings of their own. They share enough in *logos* to perceive it, but not to have it.[30] They cannot form a *polis*—a civil community of those prepared to work things out together—because they have no share in *eudaimonia,* nor in living *kata prohairesin,* according to a principled decision.[31] They do not *deliberate,* in the strict sense.[32] Asian barbarians, he reckoned, show their servility in their lack of spirit,[33] not any lack of wits. It is slavish to use indecent speech;[34] slavish to enjoy only the 'common' parts of music rather than 'noble melodies and rhythms';[35] slavish to put up

---

[25] I have examined Aristotelian ideas of slavery in 'Slaves and Citizens' in *Philosophy,* 60 (1985), pp. 27–46, and 'Slaves, Servility and Noble Deeds' in *Philosophical Inquiry* (Thessaloniki) 25 (2003), no. 3–4, pp. 165–76. Some of the following material was also used in the latter paper.

[26] Aristotle, *Politics,* 1.1255a31f. As D.B. Davis, *Slavery and Human Progress* (Oxford University Press: New York ,1984), p. 19, remarks 'it would be a mistake to think that Philo of Alexandria, for example, was merely employing figurative language when he insisted that a great king might be a slave, and a man in chains a freeman'.

[27] *Politics,* 1.1252a31f

[28] *Politics,* 1.1254b26f

[29] *Nicomachean Ethics,* 10.1177a8f

[30] *Politics,* 1.1254b22

[31] *Politics,* 3.1280a32

[32] *Politics,* 1.1260a12

[33] *Politics,* 7.1327b27f

[34] *Politics,* 7.1336b11f

[35] *Politics,* 8.1341a15

with insults,[36] and slavish not to seek revenge;[37] slavish to depend on anyone but a friend.[38] A freeman, by contrast, is one who is 'for himself'.[39]

In brief: slaves take their cue from others and have no thought of honour or the right. Humankind alone, so Aristotle thought, has any sense of good and evil, just and unjust, and the like,[40] but slaves are human by another's nature.[41] What does this claim amount to? It is less incredible than the notion that natural slaves are zombies, but may still be criticized (and often is) for being false or at least misleading. Isn't it obvious that we all depend on others for our first principles? Isn't it obvious, conversely, that even the most downtrodden slave can calculate the prudent way to live, and pine for the unattainable? We surely don't want to endorse the judgements of American eugenicists in their war against those they imagined to be 'feeble-minded'.[42]

Deliberation in the strict Aristotelian sense culminates in *prohairesis*, which is a particular deliberate attempt at living well.[43] Beasts don't do things for the sake of doing right, nor even—so Aristotle thought—rejoice in any beauty.[44] The pleasures of beasts—and slaves—are those of simple touch and taste. Does it follow that slaves are held to be like beasts in this, moved only by desire or fear? Perhaps, but even people with some grasp of reason are not always acting for what they conceive the best. Bad tempered people respond to the merest hint of insult 'as it were reckoning that one must fight back',[45] but without deliberate choice. In this case, it is an excess of spirit that preempts a principled decision, but a defect of spirit would have the same effect. Animals, children and slaves may all do things willingly, or unwillingly, but none act for the sake of beauty or nobility, which is the goal of virtue.

---

[36] *Nicomachean Ethics*, 4.1126a8; see *Politics* 4.1291a8

[37] *Nicomachean Ethics*, 5.1133a1

[38] *pros allon zen all'e philon*: *Nicomachean Ethics*, 4.1124b31.

[39] *Metaphysics*, 1.982b25

[40] *Politics*, 1.1253a16f

[41] *Politics*, 1.1254a11: I acknowledge that the phrase is more usually translated, perhaps correctly, as 'slaves are people who are naturally another's, not their own'.

[42] See Black, *War against the Weak*, op. cit.

[43] *Nicomachean Ethics*, 6.1139b3

[44] see *Nicomachean Ethics*, 3.1118a18f

[45] *Nicomachean Ethics*, 7.1149a33

Ordinarily kidnapped and conquered aliens are held by force from doing anything they think is noble—though perhaps they may discover even then some way of being beautiful. 'Natural slaves' really are what slave-owners usually believe all slaves to be: without any sense of honour, and with no wish for noble deeds or a life of which they need not be ashamed. Honour is to shame as freedom is to slavery.[46] One further gloss: barbarians show their slavishness by treating women as slaves,[47] and Persians in particular by treating their sons as slaves.[48] In brief—and perhaps beyond Aristotle's own intention—it is slavish not to recognize non-slaves when we see them.

Why should it only be *natural* slaves, as distinct from whatever captives or easy victims that can be found, that should be enslaved? The prudent answer is just that the 'naturally free' won't put up with it. To be thus free is not simply to be self-willed (on the contrary, such self-will may be slavish), but rather to live for beauty, as that can be embodied in ourselves, our friends, our *polis* and our chosen sect. It is *dishonour* that the free won't bear.[49] But whether it were prudent or not, Aristotle also reckons it *unjust* to enslave anyone who is 'born to be free'. It might not follow, of course, that we should always seek to release all those who have been wronged. Only a very powerful state—or a very religious one—could dare to proclaim a general jubilee: less powerful states who offered sanctuary to slaves would be regarded by their neighbours as more dangerous pirates precisely because a state composed of former slaves would have no common culture beyond the pursuit of 'necessary' goals. But the Aristotelian (and later philosophical) analysis did give some reason to be sorry about the institution, and to disbelieve the merely prejudiced conviction that everyone who was in fact a slave deserved to be.

Aristotle seems indeed to have believed that a supply of 'natural slaves' could best be found amongst servile barbarians—and anyway, that's where it *would* be found, since 'slavish populations' are exactly ones that cannot prevent or do not care to prevent their mem-

[46] See R. Just, 'Freedom, Slavery and the Female Psyche' in P. Cartledge & F.D. Harvey (eds.), *Crux: essays in honour of Geoffrey de St. Croix* (Imprint Academic: Exeter, 1985), pp. 169–88.

[47] *Politics*, 1.1252b5f.

[48] *Nicomachean Ethics*, 8.1160b28f.

[49] See Orlando Patterson, *Slavery and Social Death* (Harvard University Press: Princeton, N.J., 1982), p. 13: 'slavery is the permanent, violent domination of natally alienated and generally dishonoured persons'.

bers' being kidnapped. It would be unjust (it would be banditry) to seek to conquer people who don't deserve to be slaves (and really aren't). It is our right to provide against our being enslaved ourselves, and to control those who lack the power of *self*-control. 'But we should seek to be masters only over those who deserve to be slaves'.[50] Did he thereby license an enslaving war against particular peoples, as Juan Ginés de Sepulveda was to argue in the case of Amerindians?[51] It might equally be argued that, in practice, he banned the enterprise. So are there any 'natural slaves', people who are indefinitely manipulable by fear or greed, without their own conception of nobility, or any capacity for collaboration in the worthy ends for which a *polis* exists? The first answer is one that I implied before: namely, minor crooks. Maybe even some psychopaths of the kind described by Aristotle as 'bestial'[52] might be best served as slaves. But the mass of natural slaves have fewer or more tractable desires: they simply lack the capacity to internalize the law on which good citizenship relies, or even the capacity to look far enough ahead to have the right priorities. There are those who need good masters. Does it matter whether they are owned by individuals or by the State? Might they not prefer, if they could contemplate their whole lives for a moment, to live in a household rather than a prison? Do we imprison rather than enslave them out of proper respect for them—or rather out of unwillingness to take responsibility for them? In practice, we go on jailing recidivists until they are too old to be a nuisance, or still longer.

The second and more wide-ranging answer is 'ourselves'. It is of course a philosophical truism that we ourselves are slaves—to greed, fear, falsehood and the like.[53] St Croix makes a good point in observing that 'such austere philosophical notions are of greater assistance in the endurance of liberty, riches and peace than of slavery, poverty and war'.[54] The free and simple life, as it is conceived by millionaires burdened with responsibility and a weak digestion, will seem to the oppressed the height of luxury. Telling the poor that they

---

[50] *Politics*, 7.1333b39f.

[51] Against the substance of Papal declarations, eyewitness reports and the dictates of the Spanish crown: see L. Hanke, *Aristotle and the American Indians* (Hollis & Carter: London, 1959).

[52] *Nicomachean Ethics*, 7.1148b19ff.

[53] see T. Wiedemann, *Greek and Roman Slavery* (Routledge: London, 1988), p. 235

[54] G. de St. Croix, 'Slavery and Other Forms of Unfree Labor' in *Slavery and Other Forms of Unfree Labor*, ed. L.J. Archer (Routledge: London, 1988), pp. 19–32: p. 29

are 'really' rich is usually a pretext for oppression. My observation is a slightly different one.

Slaves, characteristically, weren't labourers in the ancient world (leaving mines and *latifundia* or factory farms aside). They were office boys, memory men, pedagogues, barbers, librarians, speech-writers, concubines and so on—in brief, the writer and most readers of this volume: white-collar workers. What are *our* goals? The goal of Aristotelian—and most other philosophical—virtue is *to kalon*, the beautiful or fine or noble. The virtuous aim to contemplate and to perform the beautiful. For them, some things are 'sacred', not for sale or purchase or surrender. For this, they are willing to endure physical hardship and social disapproval. It is enough, in the end, that they are doing right, whatever the ordinary cost of their nobility. Those who would live on any terms, or judge the quality of life by the amount of pleasure, wealth, applause or trivial information it contains are at least not virtuous. To treat even a slave as if she were only a slave (that is, *hybrizein*) is to fail in dignity.[55] To let oneself be treated as a slave (that is, in an older rhetoric, to 'forswear one's manhood') is to become a slave. Dignity, nobility, beauty are the central concepts of an Aristotelian ethic—but apparently not of a self-consciously modern, secular ethics. What can *we* rely on but immediate sensation (which is, pain and pleasure)?

Even clever and well-educated people nowadays find it difficult to say what it is to act *ethically*: any 'ethical constraints' on their possible actions, so they say, merely consist in the social disapproval that they fear would attend on them. They will sometimes even suggest that nothing can be 'wrong' which is not explicitly 'against the law', and add, with odd complacency, that laws differ in different states and ages. If this were really what they believed and felt it is difficult not to conclude that they really should be slaves: that is, their actions should be controlled, by whatever threat or bribery affects them, by people better able to understand what's right.

When an alternative, substantive, ethic is proposed, it often seems to be crudely hedonistic. All of us, on modern terms, it seems, are to be hedonists: life is not worth living, nor preserving, without an acceptable stock of passing pleasures. Those who put aside such pleasures or endure the related pains in the name of some transcendent norm must be freaks or hypocrites. Nothing at all is shameful—except being ashamed. The only acceptable reason for choosing one's own death is that one's life would otherwise be too painful to

[55] see Wiedemann, op. cit., p. 172

endure. Even the few remaining relics of an older ethic—as it might be, respect for children—may draw some of its present strength from admiration of those who do not look before or after, and whose pleasures and pains (we think) are transient. What once were virtues (courage, temperance, courtesy) are now called vices.

'It is beautiful to die instead of being degraded as a slave'.[56] But if nothing is worth dying for—and so nothing worth defending to the death—and the value of a life is reckoned solely by its weight of pleasure, how can we avoid the threat of literal enslavement? If our ethic is that of stereotypical slaves, can we be surprised if some more traditional people eventually seek to enslave us? What else could they do with servile populations that have forgotten honour, who will betray any bond and accept any degradation to preserve their pleasures?

To escape this fate, perhaps we should reconsider our lost ethic, our belief in order, beauty, honour, however much those concepts have been degraded or abused by sinners. Perhaps what we need, after all, is faith, the attempt to live in beauty. Perhaps this is closer to our actual motivations than modern secularists suppose—and militant atheists may themselves be seeking it. But there is also another way of understanding slaves, and what 'slavery' has gifted us.[57] On one account, the more traditional, the life of slaves (and also merchants) is exactly what the 'liberal' ideal entails. No one can count on her connections; everything is up for sale; no one is dishonoured by the acts of friends or family; only animal passions keep us all together. In the older view order is achieved when everyone knows their place. Clerics and smiths and farmers and farmers' wives and servants all have their own responsibilities, and need particular virtues to complete them. Good dogs do what dogs are required to do, and do it well. And most of us no more *chose* what we should be than dogs (hounds, mastiffs, sheepdogs, poodles) did. But times have changed.

> Subordination is sadly broken down in this age. No man, now, has the same authority which his father had,—except a gaoler. … There are many causes, the chief of which is … the great increase of money. No man now depends upon the Lord of a Manour, when he can send to another country, and fetch provisions. The

[56] Publilius Syrus (a freed Syrian slave, and writer of pithy sayings, in the first century BC): Wiedemann, op. cit., p. 76

[57] A way I partly explored in 'Deference, Degree and Selfhood' in *Philosophy*, 80 (2005), pp. 249–60.

> shoe-black at the entry of my court does not depend on me. I can deprive him but of a penny a day, which he hopes someone else will bring him; and that penny I must carry to another shoe-black, so the trade suffers nothing. ... But besides there is a general relaxation of reverence. No son now depends upon his father as in former times.[58]

Members of more traditional civilizations, as well as Social Darwinists and Nietzscheans, despise egalitarian ideologies: proper order, they say, requires us to believe in the rule of the best and brightest. More traditional societies at least supposed that there was some chance of 'dropping out' of the order imposed by birth and social duty, but only for those who pursued a higher calling. Slaves foster the illusion that we could all be radically rootless individuals, having none to rely on but ourselves. Merchants create, by their existence, the fantasy that everything is, potentially, for sale. Both groups, of course, may manufacture hierarchies for themselves, and recreate a social bond of deference. Both may find or invent strange deities to defend, in thought at least, their own self-respect. Merchants may hope that Hermes is on their side, and slaves that there is some God who willingly takes on their rôle and nature.[59] Nietzsche was perhaps not wrong to think that Christianity and Judaism were both, in origin, religions made for slaves, profoundly anti-aristocratic. The claim was meant to denigrate those faiths, and to exalt instead such breeding experiments as are dictated by the Law of Manu. Egalitarian ideologies, which include most Abrahamic and most Buddhist sects, have learnt the most serious lesson of historic slavery: to realize that there is a difference between who and what I am. Our predecessors could, without much effort, realize that they *might* themselves be slaves, that they might lose their rôles and given natures, and yet still live. Those who believed, like Plato and Pythagoras, that they *might* be tramps, leopards, lords or spiders, discovered a resilient Selfhood. We don't need to believe metempsychosis true, as long as we believe it *possible.* Without that possibility the very foundations of a liberal morality must crumble. In acting on another, I must be willing to conceive myself being acted on in just

[58] Samuel Johnson (10 April 1778), in James Boswell, *Life of Johnson* (London: Oxford University Press, 1953), p. 796

[59] See *Philippians* 2.5–8.

that manner, and so to treat others as I would wish to be treated.[60] But I could only be in that other's place if I am something more than my station and its duties. *My* actual present duties cannot be the same as yours, since I could not be you (this middle-aged male academic could not instead be, for example, a young, female dancer, or whatever else 'you', at present, are). Aristotle drew a similar moral from examining 'resident aliens', barred from any formal rôle in the life of the 'political' community, the *polis.* In elevating the contemplative life above the political, he explicitly affirmed the superiority of resident aliens, metics.[61] 'Contemplation' is the realization that we are alive in a way that transcends our social status and particular horrid history.

On the one hand, thinking of myself and others just as 'slavish', motivated only by present desire and fear, is an enormous loss. On the other, realizing my self as a slave must do, stripped of all honour, social status, duty, is to discover, to uncover, something very strange. There is a god in each of us, owing nothing to our current standing or our particular abilities: a fallen or a broken god, perhaps, but one still owed our worship. It may be 'slavish' by Aristotelian standards not to seek revenge: another way of expressing the same truth is that, being slaves, we must forego revenge. We must instead forgive. Especially, we must forgive all those that we have injured.

'Dr. Johnson', in Chesterton's imagination, identified the better way:

> When your parliaments grow more corrupt and your wars more cruel, do not dream that you can breed a Houyhnhnm like a race-horse, or summon monsters from the moon, or cry out in your madness for something beyond the stature of man. Do you in that day of disillusion still have the strength to say: these are no Yahoos; these are men; these are fallen men; these are they for whom their Omnipotent Creator did not disdain to die.[62]

Awakening from Aristotelian slavery is to discover, in ourselves and others, the image of divinity, the power to create, to start again.

If we are to do what is right, because it is right, we must submit ourselves to judgement. Those who act 'against their conscience' out of fear, desire, or social embarrassment, are slaves. Those who

[60] See also Geoffrey Madell, *The Identity of the Self* (Edinburgh University Press: Edinburgh, 1981).

[61] *Politics*, 7.1324a16ff.

[62] G.K. Chesterton, *The Judgement of Dr. Johnson* (1927): *Collected Works*, vol. 11, ed. D.J. Conlon (San Francisco: Ignatius Press, 1989), p. 294.

acknowledge that even their own conscience needs to be educated, reformed or balanced by the considered judgement of their betters, begin to walk in freedom.

Sex and Sacred Violence

Another of the charges constantly rehearsed against the Abrahamic faiths, and especially the Christian Churches, is that they are hung up on sex. It seems incredible to many moderns that anyone could ever suppose that sex is dangerous. We are programmed to find both sexual desire and sexual sensation yummy, whether it is focused and obtained by masturbation, sodomy or heterosexual coitus. Those who concentrate on the *sensations,* we may admit, run some risk of anti-Kantian behaviour, *using* some other for their own delight, but mutually engrossing sex must be, we suppose, delightful. We easily believe—on the basis of an anthropologist's brief survey—that South Sea Islanders were happily promiscuous until the missionaries came.[63] We are comforted to notice Indian temples (for example, at Khajuraho) covered with erotic carvings, and tell ourselves that successful sex is worshipful. How could anyone disagree, unless afflicted by self-loathing, body hatred or misogyny? Sometimes St.Paul is blamed for this, sometimes St.Augustine—though rarely by anyone who has actually read their works, or noticed that even the happy Greeks were not so happy. Aphrodite is an Olympian, but so is Ares: Sex and War both bring delight to many, and both are very dangerous.

The problem that this poses for contemporary society is that self-consciously *modern* Westerners are sure that there should be no restrictions placed on adult and consensual sex, and often seem to concentrate on this as the central difference between 'modern' and 'traditional' societies. Rape and deceit are wrong, of course, and it is also wrong, unspeakably wrong, to have sex with minors (especially when this involves some breach of trust). We are 'grossed out' by incest (though when the partners meet in adult life it's difficult to rationalize this feeling), and most of us are queasy about sado-masochistic violence, even when that is indeed consensual. What adults do in bed, to whom and with what intention, so we say, is for them to decide, and it would be 'judgmental' to interfere. Most traditional believers, on the other hand, are sure that sex should be confined to

---

[63] Margaret Mead, *Coming of Age in Samoa* (Cape: London, 1929); cf. David Freeman *Margaret Mead and Samoa: the making and unmaking of an anthropological myth* (Harvard University Press: Cambridge, MA, 1983).

heterosexual marriage (though they may be fairly tolerant of some pre-marital playfulness within their own communities, and may not seek to legislate against those who disagree[64]), and that some sorts of sexual enjoyment are debased. The sexual act is a *social* act, performed for the sake of procreation and the tribe. Traditionalists and modern eugenicists agree: individuals have no business stealing their tribe's future. Notoriously, and obviously, people have always sought for sex outside those bonds (and rationalized their willfulness). In patriarchal societies, wives, concubines and mistresses may have some social standing, some acknowledged rights, while prostitutes, call-girls and catamites are outside the law. All attempts to legislate are tainted, so we moderns think, by violence and by hypocrisy. Ashamed of their own desires, the (male) legislators project that shame on others, 'fallen' women and 'sodomites', and get respectable thrills by 'punishing' the victims of their own desire.

For 'moderns' it is often the sight of 'adulterous' women—including victims of rape—being stoned to death, or 'sodomites' being hanged, that reinforces their own hatred of 'religion'. Such practices, of course, are not endemic in the Abrahamic faiths. Nor are atheistical regimes entirely guiltless: eugenicist oppression was not founded on *religious* principles, and the idea that if it were not for 'religion' we'd all be happily having any sort of sex with anyone is obviously ridiculous. But it must be admitted that the Mosaic Law, and the early acts of Israel, embody radical, lethal, disapproval of all deviant sexual practices. Adulterers, both male and female, are to be stoned to death. Sodomy is an abomination to the Lord on a par with child-murder, bestiality and insulting one's parents.[65] The invading Israelites, as recorded in the Torah, were forbidden to mix with the tribes of Canaan, and offenders were brusquely killed.

> When the Israelites were in Shittim, the people began to have intercourse with Moabite women, who invited them to the sacrifices offered to their gods; and they ate the sacrificial food and prostrated themselves before the gods of Moab. The Israelites joined in the worship of the Baal of Peor, and the Lord was angry

[64] For the record, it was such traditionalists as G.K. Chesterton who were vehement against the abuse of power, often by eugenicist professionals: 'A little while ago the family of a young lady attempted to shut her up in an asylum because she believed in Free Love. This atrocious injustice was stopped' (Chesterton, *William Blake* (Duckworth: London, 1910), p. 78. See also his *Eugenics and Other Evils:* http://www.dur.ac.uk/martin.ward/gkc/ books/Eugenics.html, ch. 2. Unfortunately, it was not always stopped.

[65] *Leviticus* 20.1–17.

> with them. He said to Moses, 'Take all the leaders of the people and hurl them down to their death before the Lord in the full light of day, that the fury of his anger may turn away from Israel.' So Moses said to the judges of Israel, 'Put to death, each one of you, those of his tribe who have joined in the worship of the Baal of Peor'. One of the Israelites brought a Midianite woman into his family in open defiance of Moses and all the community of Israel, while they were weeping by the entrance of the Tent of the Presence. Phinehas son of Eleazar, son of Aaron the priest, saw him. He stepped out from the crowd and took up a spear, and he went into the inner room after the Israelite and transfixed the two of them, the Israelite and the woman, pinning them together. Thus the plague which had attacked the Israelites was brought to a stop; but twenty-four thousand had already died.[66]

The Lord, it is said, approved, and granted the priesthood 'for all time' to Phinehas and his descendants. A little later the Israelites attacked Midian, killing all the men, every male dependant, and every woman who was not a virgin. It is not said that the Lord approved, but neither is any condemnation expressly stated.[67]

It would be wrong to describe these acts as 'genocidal' or as 'ethnic cleansing'. The very same chapters that decree such grievous penalties for fraternizing insist that 'when an alien settles among you, you shall not oppress him. He shall be treated as a native born among you, and you shall love him as a man like yourself, because you were aliens in Egypt'.[68] Moses' wife was a Midianite, and David, Israel's favourite king, was the great-grandson of a Moabite.[69] But whatever their description they remain, to us, abominable.

> The violence of *Numbers* 25 has the following characteristics. First, it is ordered and justified in terms of an exclusive loyalty to a single deity. Secondly, it expresses a religious xenophobia. This xenophobia is religious, cultural, and sexual. The transgression

[66] *Numbers* 25.1–9.

[67] *Numbers* 31.1–18 (Phinehas led the assault). The Midianites were descendants of Abraham by his second wife, Keturah (*Genesis* 25), and Moses had dwelt among them during his exile from Egypt, marrying their priest's daughter. They continued a major power until the time of Gideon (see *Judges* 6–8), so the slaughter was perhaps not quite as extensive as it at first appears. Indeed there seems to be no *archaeological* evidence for the mass slaughter (see below). According to *Judges* 20. 28 it was Phinehas who in later life encouraged the general assault on the tribe of Benjamin for the atrocious rape and murder of the Levite's concubine (*Judges* 19.16–30).

[68] *Leviticus* 19.33–4.

[69] *Ruth* 4.13–22; see also *Matthew* 1.6.

> of the loyalty to God is attributed to the presence of foreign women. In short, the text is chauvinist and misogynist.[70]

How could we conceive that the Lord of the Earth should countenance such murders (especially as He had forbidden murder)?[71] And if He didn't, how could we ever trust the community which believed He did?

One response may be to treat the stories as allegorical—very much as we now read the Psalmist's pleas to cast his enemies into the pit,[72] or his gloating fantasy of dashing Babylon's children against the rocks.[73] What must be driven out is sin, and there is a penalty for failure. But 'it is all very well to say that the Canaanites that we should root out are vice and sinfulness, but we still have texts that speak rather clearly of slaughtering human beings'.[74]

> They did not destroy the peoples round about,
> As the Lord had commanded them to do,
> But they mingled with the nations,
> Learning their ways;
> They worshipped their idols
> And were ensnared by them.
> Their sons and their daughters
> They sacrificed to foreign demons;
> They shed innocent blood,
> The blood of sons and daughters
> Offered to the gods of Canaan,
> And the land was polluted with blood.

[70] David Lochhead, 'Monotheistic Violence' in *Buddhist-Christian Studies*, 21 (2001), pp. 3–12.

[71] Though later Rabbis did not doubt that Phinehas was in the right, they were disturbed that 'due process' had not been followed, and were cautious in the morals they drew from the story. Philo preferred to allegorize it entirely, seeing Phinehas as that Reason which refuses the wiles of Pleasure: see Louis H. Feldman 'The Portrayal of Phinehas by Philo, Pseudo-Philo, and Josephus' in *Jewish Quarterly Review*, 92 (2002), pp. 315–45. Ps-Philo even identifies Phinehas with the prophet Elijah, and suggests that he will live on till the Last Day.

[72] *Psalm* 55.23.

[73] *Psalm* 137.9—the verse is now usually omitted when the psalm is read in church. Perhaps it shouldn't be: it is an abrupt and terrible end to one of the most moving of the psalms of exile: 'By the rivers of Babylon we sat down and wept when we remembered Zion. ' We need to remember what our hearts desire.

[74] Collins, op. cit., p. 19.

> Thus they defiled themselves by their conduct
> And they followed their lusts and broke faith with God.[75]

It may also be that the stories don't record the *actual* incursion into Palestine, but are rather 'ideological fictions', warnings, centuries later, to such Israelites as were tempted by the alien gods.[76] Phinehas's (imagined?) example helped to fire up Mattathias, father of Judas Maccabaeus, to the murder of an Israelite traitor in the days when Antiochus Epiphanes was seeking to demolish Israel, and so led on to the Maccabaean revolt.[77]. These memories or fables, sadly, still provide the mind-set whereby Palestinians have been robbed and demonized by the twentieth-century 'Return'.[78] There must be a better way—as of course both Hebrew and Christian teaching say there is. We are not to condemn,[79] nor *judge* lest we be judged.[80] Pacifism, quietism, even if it is a distant ideal for most of us, must surely have the moral edge over homicidal zealotry?

But before we finally disown those earlier passages as demonstrating a merely xenophobic, pathologically doctrinaire attitude, it is as well to set them in context. The Israelites were not alone in practicing (or imagining) the total eradication of alien populations, their 'dedication' to the god of their devotion.

> A famous parallel is provided by the Moabite Stone, erected by the ninth-century king Mesha: 'And Chemosh said to me, "Go, take Nebo from Israel". So I went by night and fought against it from the break of dawn until noon, taking it and slaying all, seven thousand men, boys, women, girls, and maid-servants, for I had devoted them to destruction for (the god) Ashtar-Chemosh.' [81]

---

[75] *Psalm* 106.34–39. See also *Ecclesiasticus* 45. 23, which names Phinehas as 'third in renown' after Moses and Aaron.

[76] See Collins, op. cit., pp. 10ff. Whitelam op. cit., argues, with many examples, that modern histories of Israel are similarly inclined to *invent* a history that will validate contemporary Israel.

[77] *I Maccabees* 2.23–8.

[78] See Edward W. Said, 'Invention, Memory, and Place' in *Critical Inquiry*, 26 (2000), pp. 175–192.

[79] See *John* 7.53–8. 11.

[80] *Luke* 6.37–38, 41–2.

[81] Collins, op. cit., p. 5. See also Philip D. Stern *The Biblical Herem: a Window on Israel's Religious Experience* (Scholars Press: Atlanta, 1991).

A few centuries later the Athenians were only a little less destructive, when they slaughtered all the *adult* males of Melos, and enslaved the rest.[82]

At least the Biblical story offers a slightly better reason for this fierce intolerance: that the Canaanites (allegedly) killed children,[83] and by implication also served their gods or demons by promiscuous sex. The plague that was killing thousands, it is reasonable to suppose, was sexually transmitted.[84] The rules that Israel accepted were required if the people were to live. Seduction, under the circumstances, was an act of war, and a desperate population chose the only way they could see to survive. That we now have other ways, perhaps, is because they *did* survive, somehow maintaining the sense to see that ethnic origin was not the issue, and that there was a path to justice.

Is there a moral for us now? The primary moral drawn in traditional religion is that the pursuit of sexual pleasure is destructive. Most obviously, it may lead us to betray our friends and family, the people for whom we are responsible, the cause to which we are pledged. It is not the only passion with this effect, but probably the one that is most familiar to most people. Societies given over to that passion—openly or secretly—create an industry for its satisfaction, at whatever cost: child-sacrifice and temple prostitution were entwined. Such societies are also vulnerable to plague—a penalty that may be mercifully delayed, but not forever. We may all prefer a world in which we can say cheerfully 'let copulation thrive',[85] where mutual fancy rules and not repressive laws. We may even recognize, like St.Paul, that the Law itself begets iniquity: *hidden* bodies are as much the object of sexual fantasy as are naked ones. As a child myself of the sixties I can only agree that Aphrodite is Olympian—but not the *only* Olympian. She may help us through the early stages of a mature companionship, alleviating minor irritations from partner or from child, but we must move on—and can do only if we pledge our faith.

---

[82] Thucydides, *History of the Peloponnesian War,* 5.116.

[83] See also *Deuteronomy* 12.31, 18.10; *Micah* 6.7; *Jeremiah* 19.4–5. But see below: it is all too natural for conquerors to 'demonize' the people they oppress.

[84] My thanks to Martha Sherwood of Oregon for pointing out the possibility that strict sexual rules were required to counter endemic venereal disease.

[85] William Shakespeare, *King Lear,* Act. 4, scene 6 (Lear speaks): "Thou shalt not die: die for adultery! No: The wren goes to't, and the small gilded fly Does lecher in my sight. Let copulation thrive.'

Marriage as it has been understood is the public declaration that two people, man and woman, are undertaking the task of making a new household, with the intention (even if that is not always fulfilled) of procreating persons. There are other sorts of household, and even other sorts of marriage, but all depend on the partners' not being distracted from their central task. The rest of us offer applause, support and sanctions because we recognize that children are best brought up by their connected adults, not by clerks or nursemaids or transient bed-mates. It is very easy to be convinced that just any sort of partnership, any sort of willing marriage, is as good as any other. It is easy to be convinced—it has after all been the main theme of romantic fiction—that 'marriage' so easily turns sour because we are *compelled* to a pretence of love even when the passion of love has gone. It is easy to be convinced, but hardly rational: what other partnership would be promptly dissolved merely because one partner fancied a new beginning and no longer cared for the duties s/he'd undertaken? Divorce may sometimes be the least worst evil in a fallen world: it is not therefore good, for the children of the relationship, for friends or family or the married pair themselves. Our descendants—if they have any sense—will wonder how we could so easily and self-deceivingly pay for our sexual pleasures with the lives of children (whether they are aborted, or infected, or neglected, or compelled heart-brokenly to choose between their parents).

There is one other moral or implication or suggestion that we ought to face. The Israelites' campaign in Canaan strikes us as horrific, even when we can begin to see what reasons there might have been for it. But almost all the generations of humanity and almost all its cultures have been violent (and ours is too). Modern moralists condemn the Israelites' campaign, but very few such moralists are pacifists. Many of them, indeed, will offer speciously utilitarian arguments for killing off 'the unfit' or the inconvenient. What exactly is wrong with violence? Ares, remember, is an Olympian too. Many more peoples than the Israelites have 'cleansed' some land they have invaded, denouncing foreign custom and establishing their own in blood. It isn't true that every religion spread by violence, as some atheists now suggest: conversion by the sword is no conversion, and even those empires (the Islamic, the Spanish, or the British) that thought to embody a sacred trust did mostly acknowledge that such spiritual changes could not come by violence. States having a monopoly of violence may enforce a truce, but not the peace that comes from mutual respect and caring. But violence remains a fact, and one that is all too easily rationalized as 'the will of God', or 'a necessary step towards the just society', or 'a demonstration of our will to power'. Civilization, even a civilization that is, somewhat, peaceful, just and kind, depends on violence: historically, we have all been violent; even at present, we retain the option.

The problem here is not simply whether or when it can be right to go to war. The use of military violence might be conceived as a last resort to deal with obvious injustice, or we might instead decide that all such violence can only make injustice worse. What we need to face is that violence, however it is directed, makes us feel good. That is to say, it is indeed 'a god'. We may demand that its votaries sign up to obey some military code, but we must be aware that such codes are often no more successful than a marriage vow! The Army, like Marriage, is ordained as a remedy for sin. Is this comparison offensive? We all 'know', we 'liberals', here in the settled West, that Sex is good and Violence is bad. We all 'know' that sexual desire may lead, contingently, to calamity, and ruefully acknowledge that it must somehow be channeled into less damaging paths, but still hope that individuals can find their own route to their satisfactions. We 'know' on the other hand that no-one can really enjoy violence, or else they're sick, and that a decent social order will prevent all internal violence (and permit all *consensual adult* sex—unless it's violent). We 'know' that only 'fanatics' think it right to kill in the name of God (or of whatever other ideal they cherish). Perhaps we're right. But why are we right, and how can we deal with the unpleasantly obvious truth that violence is endemic, that we seek out victims and enjoy our triumphs?

Violence makes us—the perpetrators of violence that is—feel good. Unfortunately it also makes us feel Good (at least if we succeed). The very fact of attacking, hurting and humiliating someone else confirms us in our judgement that she *deserves* it. Violence (successful violence) is not only yummy, but justified in the very fact of its success. Weirdly, we dispose of our own sin (of violence) by imputing it to our victims.[86] We punish them for our own fault (and incidentally teach them—if they survive—to do the same in turn). There is a further complication: our wish is to be on the winning side, and we therefore, even more weirdly, hate those who do us good as well as those we've injured.

---

[86] This is not to say, by the way, that *Phinehas* got sensual or moral pleasure from his act, which may have been driven by desperation: that judgement had better be left to novelists, or best of all to God.

How are we to defuse all this? René Girard has proposed that the Bible itself is a record of its gradual rejection. We are to see violence from the *victim's* point of view 'from Abel to Zechariah son of Berachiah, whom you murdered between the sanctuary and the altar',[87] and culminating, for the Christian churches, in the crucifixion, whereby God made an end of sacrifice. Girard's anthropological speculation is that all human communities were founded on the act of scape-goating, uniting in the condemnation and killing of some one selected victim (and so displacing all our particular hatreds onto a single 'enemy'). The Bible, he suggests, compels us to acknowledge the *innocence* of that victim, and to begin to see the divine in those we persecute. Our enemy is our neighbour (as the story of the 'Good Samaritan' makes clear).[88] The *theological* story at least is plausible: when Jesus spoke of the coming of the Son of Man to divide, as it were, 'the sheep' from 'the goats' (as only a shepherd's eye could manage), he declared that 'the king will say to those on his right hand, "You have my Father's blessing; come, enter and possess the kingdom that has been ready for you since the world was made. For when I was hungry, you gave me food; when thirsty, you gave me drink; when I was a stranger you took me into your home, when naked you clothed me; when I was ill you came to my help, when in prison you visited me."'[89] This is something more, and something stranger and more shocking, than just endorsing general altruism or charity as a duty. Those that the favoured 'sheep' have cared for are the wretched of the earth, those on whom we ordinarily heap our hatred, who carry the weight of the world.

[87] See *Matthew* 23.35. The Zechariah that is intended is probably the one described as the son of *Jehoiada*, killed by King Joash's men according to *2 Chronicles* 24.20–2 (see also *Isaiah* 8.2), not the minor prophet Zechariah son of Berachiah. Either there is a scribal error (*Luke* 11.51 speaks only of 'Zechariah'), or he had two patronymics. A story in the *Protoevangelion of James* 16.9–24 suggests that the one intended was the father of John the Baptist, Zechariah son of Baruch, who was murdered on Herod's orders perhaps by the very people whom Jesus is addressing. The Orthodox Church includes this story in its liturgy, without appealing to the apocryphon: see http://www.anastasis.org.uk/05sep.htm (accessed 11 May 2008). My thanks to 'Christopher' of http://orrologion. blogspot. com/ for the reference.

[88] *Luke* 10.29–37.

[89] *Matthew* 25.34–37.

But that's not the end of the story. Occasional Canaanites are given some honour, but the mass of them are mentioned only as victims—and ones that *deserve* to be.[90]

> We can emphasize the concern for slaves and aliens in *Deuteronomy*, or the model of the suffering servant, or the NT teaching on love of one's enemies. It is not unusual for Christian interpreters to claim that 'the biblical witness to the innocent victim and the God of victims demystifies and demythologizes this sacred social order' in which violence is grounded. Such a selective reading, privileging the death of Jesus, or the model of the suffering servant, is certainly possible, and even commendable, but it does not negate the force of the biblical endorsements of violence that we have been considering. The full canonical shape of the Christian Bible, for what it is worth, still concludes with the judgement scene in *Revelation*, in which the Lamb that was slain returns as the heavenly warrior with a sword for striking down the nations.[91]

And the Son of Man, in judging 'sheep' and 'goats', sends the latter away to punishment. It is because that Day is expected that there is no point, no value, in seeking to disentangle wheat from weeds just yet,[92] nor any need to exact vengeance for wrong-doing. 'Zeal for the Lord' may be—originally—a virtue, but if it leads us to *anticipate* the Day it has become a vice. 'Thou shalt not take the name of the Lord thy God in vain':[93] do not, that is, be easily persuaded to act in the name of the Lord, and against the considered judgement of your peers. Phinehas may have done so, but that should not be a

[90] See Edward W. Said, 'Michael Walzer's *Exodus and Revolution*: A Canaanite Reading' in *Grand Street* 5. 1986, pp. 86–106; Robert Allen Warrior 'Canaanites, Cowboys, and Indians: Deliverance, Conquest, and Liberation Theology Today' in *Christianity and Crisis*, 49 (1989), pp. 261–66; Whitelam, op. cit., pp. 71–121.

[91] Collins, op. cit., p. 19, citing James G. Williams, *The Bible, Violence, and the Sacred: Liberation from the Myth of Sanctioned Violence* (Harper: San Francisco 1991), p. 243.

[92] *Matthew* 13.24ff.

[93] *Exodus* 20.7; *Deuteronomy* 5.11. See also *Matthew* 15.9: 'in vain do they worship me, teaching for doctrines the commandments of men' (after *Isaiah* 29.13).

precedent for us.[94] Or to put it another way, 'immanentizing the eschaton'[95] is an easy error.

Our anger is usually a vice—but maybe it is still an image of something better. In the words of a later, Neo-Platonically inspired witness: before Adam fell 'what is now gall in him sparkled like crystal, and bore the taste of good works, and what is now melancholy in man shone in him like the dawn and contained in itself the wisdom and perfection of good works; but when Adam broke the law, the sparkle of innocence was dulled in him, and his eyes, which had formerly beheld heaven, were blinded, and his gall was changed to bitterness, and his melancholy to blackness'.[96] So also anger: 'the Celestial Intelligences' fury of anger represents an intellectual power of resistance of which anger is the last and faintest echo'.[97] Ares, the real Ares, is an Olympian after all.

Pleonexia, Health and Achievement

In matters biomedical Human Health has become the one trump card that is played to defeat all disagreement, as though all of us were agreed both that Health (or at least Avoiding Illness) was the only serious goal we had, and also that Anything at All is instantly justified by the possibility that it will help someone attain that goal. Neither claim stands up to clear inspection. Most of us are entirely willing to take risks with our health, whether for trivial reasons (watching television, smoking cigarettes) or for grand (climbing mountains, working late at the office, testing dangerous treatments on oneself). Someone seriously obsessed with Being Healthy (and how much does that imply?) would be recognizably sick, and a

---

[94] Augustine, *De Doctrina Christiana* 3. 32 (http://ccat.sas.upenn.edu/jod/augustine/ ddc3.html): 'Although all, or nearly all, the transactions recorded in the Old Testament are to be taken not literally only, but figuratively as well, nevertheless even in the case of those which the reader has taken literally, and which, though the authors of them are praised, are repugnant to the habits of the good men who since our Lord's advent are the custodians of the divine commands, let him refer the figure to its interpretation, but let him not transfer the act to his habits of life. For many things which were done as duties at that time, cannot now be done except through lust.'

[95] A phrase coined by Eric Voegelin in *The New Science of Politics* (University of Chicago Press: Chicago, 1952) which has achieved a strange notoriety amongst utopians and neo-conservatives.

[96] R. Klibansky, E. Panofsky, & F. Saxl, op. cit., p. 80, citing Hildegard of Bingen: Kaiser ed., *Hildegardis Causae et Curae* (Leipzig, 1903), p. 43.

[97] Ps. Dionysius, *Celestial Hierarchy*, ch. 15, p. 197 (http://www.esoteric.msu.edu/VolumeII/CelestialHierarchy.html, accessed 10th September 2008).

dreadful bore as well. We may be less willing to take risks with our *children's* health—but even there, we are often well reminded that risk and excitement are a part of life, and that we should not aim to protect our children from all imagined ills. Health and Avoiding Illness are somewhat desirable, but they plainly aren't what we actually wholeheartedly pursue, nor do we ordinarily think they should be. 'Health' is standing in for a conception of Living Well, what our predecessors called *eudaimonia*. Because we dare not admit that some things matter more to us than bodily satisfaction, more than 'life' itself, we must pretend, when deciding matters of policy, that we worship bodily health above all things—though we plainly don't. Remember the extraordinary confidence with which the National Curriculum website speaks of the Curriculum's enabling pupils to lead 'safe, healthy and fulfilling lives'.

The one other goal that is admitted is Achievement (especially Sporting Achievement), sometimes concealed in the pretence that athletes must, by hypothesis, be 'healthy' (even if their bones are regularly broken, their tendons twisted and their immune systems unreliable). Interestingly, though it is taken for granted that 'ordinary health' must be supported by careful medication, the public, as interpreted by the media, are squeamish about the use of 'drugs' to maintain or improve 'performance'. This is, perhaps, the effect of a residual respect for individual virtue: it is important that the performances are the athletes' own, that they are showing what (almost) unaided human powers can do if harnessed by the human will, and also enjoying what is, after all, a gift.[98] It is easy enough for bioethicists of a particular, utilitarian, sort to demonstrate that we are inconsistent, superstitious, utterly absurd. After all, we expect our athletes to be trained, dieted, massaged and carefully advised: even a mediocre performance nowadays will probably far surpass the achievements of past sportsmen, since expectations have risen along with physiological knowledge. What difference would it make if sportsmen were also bred or medicated into a new perfection? The perfection they display is pointless, having little to do with ordinary survival needs or elementary enjoyments, but here at least we get an occasional glimpse of beauty, physical perfection enhanced by moral virtue. 'Taking drugs'—or so most of us suppose—diminishes the virtue, but not necessarily the physical perfection. Maybe the sportsmen of the future will routinely dose

[98] See Michael J. Sandel, *The Case against Perfection: ethics in the age of genetic engineering* (Harvard University Press: Cambridge, MA., 2007)

themselves before the event, and be suspected of cowardice or indolence if they don't.

The bioethical suggestion can be parodied: if all that really mattered was that the athlete runs faster, jumps longer, or kicks the ball more accurately, it would also be appropriate to equip them with mechanical prostheses and computer-guidance. Why bother inserting a person into the apparatus at all? The contest will then simply be between engineering teams, not athletes, as it almost already is in the case of motor-sports—except that there is still someone in the machine to risk his life and health. Would we still be interested in the outcomes, and the characters of the contestants without that risk?

Visible success, perfect performance, courage, are admittedly desirable, and most of us will resist the seemingly convenient, but really quite irrational, suggestion that we should use all available techniques (genetic engineering, training from early childhood, mechanical enhancement, medication) to 'improve' performances. Such things *don't* improve performance, but make it, gradually, absurd. We retain some sense of beauty and of human dignity. But although this is indeed a more traditional value than mere 'health' or 'freedom from disease' it is still (as above) distorted by the greed for *more*, and the mirage of 'perfection'.

> If the many become the same as the few when possess'd, More! More! is the cry of a mistaken soul; less than All cannot satisfy Man.[99]

What lies behind this demand is, at least in part, a refusal to accept what's given, an insistence on having things 'our way', and properly under control. The problem—or one problem amongst many—is that the more we control, the more we *must* control; the more we demand something *other* than the given the less we can enjoy even what is then provided. Oddly, the Darwinian synthesis which is, in many respects, a dangerous delusion at least gives us the opportunity to realize that *diversity* of talent and achievement, norm and form and physiology, is what the world requires of us. As long as we conceive ourselves as fighting a war with nature or our rivals, we shall lose. As long as we seek always to exaggerate some one particular talent or device we know already, refusing the gifts that God and nature send, we lose.

---

[99] William Blake, 'There is no Natural Religion', second series (1788) $5: Keynes, op. cit., p. 97.

'Health' and honourable achievement are familiar from the ancient set of lives—and the third life identified by Pythagoras and his philosophical followers is the life of vision: to receive the world with gratitude and joy. Thanks are the highest form of thinking, and it is there that we can intuit God, the final synthesis.

11

Considering the End

If our faith is vain, and there is indeed no God, no final vindication, no possibility that everything will 'one day' be straightened out or the rough places planed, we have no choice except to make such deals as we can bear, and can imagine being kept. Some atheists (whether they have been explicitly atheistical or covertly so) have concluded that we therefore have no choice except to *fight* (by whatever means) for family and friends and fantasies. Such fights need not always be open, or openly violent: indeed, there might be a case for arguing that 'violence is the last refuge of the incompetent'.[1] It would usually be better to conceal our victories, to get ahead by indirection and by guile. We may win by making ourselves (our friends and families and fantasies) indispensable even to those who would prefer to be our enemies. Such victories, of course, will always be only transient: we cannot guarantee our line against natural disaster, nor against the possibility that some *other* line will learn exactly the same lessons, and overmaster ours. Amongst the silliest of 'post-Christian' fantasies is the proud delusion that 'our' line will eventually rule and remake the cosmos, that Humanity can claim the powers we once attributed to God:[2] it is vanishingly unlikely, in a naturalistic context, that any natural being will ever do this much, and absurd beyond belief to imagine that, if any does, it will certainly be a descendant of 'our' line, or even remotely sympathetic to 'our' values.

---

[1] As Isaac Asimov claimed, through the mouth of Salvor Hardin, in *Foundation* (Doubleday: New York 1951; originally published in *Astounding* 1942).

[2] A notion derived from Ludwig Feuerbach *The Essence of Christianity*, trans. Marian Evans, aka George Eliot (George Chapman: London 1853); see Pannenberg *Apostle's Creed*, op. cit., p. 18f.

This is, of course, no real surprise. 'Cities and thrones and powers stand, in Time's eye, almost as long as flowers, which daily die.'[3] Kipling, like most traditionalists, could still suppose that 'the Cities rise again', also like flowers. Individuals die, whether they be individual creatures or individual institutions, and yet the world continues. It is of the essence of modernity, however, to understand that all things perish—and also Everything (that is, the temporal universe). The ancient dream that Everything will be dissolved, and then be formed anew, still has enormous power. So strong is it indeed that even speculative cosmologists, compelled to recognize that the whole cosmos is at once decaying and expanding, fruitlessly, forever, instinctively propose that *this* world is only one of indefinitely many in an imagined multiverse. They may even hope that creatures very much like us will appear again, indefinitely many times, even though we (they) can never learn from the experience.[4] Alternatively, they may suggest that the end-days of the universe can be stretched out 'forever', and that practically all the living creatures who will ever exist are congregated at 'the end of time', feasting off the Hawking radiation of black holes or the energy of gravitational collapse—or whatever other incomprehensible source of energy survives by then.[5] It is in that context that the worry I have addressed before becomes most pressing: if that is when the huge majority of living creatures live (and amuse themselves with whatever dreams they please) must we not assume that that is when *we* live?[6] It becomes overwhelmingly likely that we are virtual inhabitants of the last days' dreaming.

---

[3] Rudyard Kipling, *Definitive Edition of Rudyard Kipling's Verse* (Hodder & Stoughton: London, 1940), p. 487 (from *Puck of Pook's Hill* (Macmillan: London, 1906)). See also G.K. Chesterton, in *The Napoleon of Notting Hill* (Penguin: Harmondsworth, 1946; 1st published 1904), p. 25: 'Can you tell me, in a world that is flagrant with the failure of civilization, what there is particularly immortal about yours?'

[4] We can't learn, because the slate, as it were, must be wiped clean as each new universe buds forth. Otherwise the accumulated heat will, infinitely long ago, have reached an unimaginable maximum. See Stanley Jaki, *Science and Creation: From Eternal Cycles to an Oscillating Universe* (Scottish Academic Press: Edinburgh, 1974).

[5] On which see the seminal article by Freeman Dyson, 'Time without end: physics and biology in an open universe', in *Review of Modern Physics,* 51 (1979), p. 447.

[6] On what has been called the Doomsday Argument, originally proposed by Brandon Carter in 1983, that we are at least more likely to be in the largest generation of humankind than in any other (and so most probably nearly the last) see John Leslie, *The End of the World: Science and Ethics of Human Extinction* (Routledge: London, 1996), and Bostrom, op. cit.

There is an imaginable, humane moral to this fable, indicated by John C. Wright in one of the few space operas to be essentially philosophical. His speakers, themselves inhabitants of an immensely distant future, imagine that there will one day be a 'Universal Mind' or Civilized Society in which they may hope to participate, living in the long last days:

> You must realize what is at stake here: if the Universal Mind consists of entities willing to use force against innocents in order to survive, then the last period of the universe, which embraces the vast majority of universal time, will be a period of cannibalistic and unimaginable war, rather than a time of gentle contemplation filled, despite all melancholy, with unregretful joy. No entity willing to initiate the use of force against another can be permitted to join or influence the Universal Mind or the lesser entities, such as the Earthmind, who may one day form the core constituencies.[7]

The allegorical intent is obvious—though in the Christian universe the Universal Mind will be (and is) forever, and not melancholic. The meek—that is to say, the deliberately non-violent—will inherit all things (possibly).[8]

But of course there is a likelier alternative, if the natural world is all. There will be no such congregation, and our future, the future of all living things like us, is actually quite short.[9]

It is the essence of modernity that time is linear, not cyclical. It has been easy to suppose that it is also progressive—and one of the standard misunderstandings of Darwinian Theory, remember, is that though our ancestors were apes, our children shall be angels.[10] Darwinian Theory, as I have observed before, actually has no such impli-

---

[7] John C. Wright, *The Golden Age, vol2: The Phoenix Exultant* (Tom Doherty: New York, 2003), p. 156 (Eveningstar speaks). This is an intelligent gloss on Olaf Stapledon's imaginings, and also well worth reading in its own right.

[8] This is not wholly to endorse Tipler's suggestion (op. cit., pp. 45–100) that God identically *is* the ultimate Cosmic Singularity predicted by his version of quantum mechanics: I remain dubious that any such physical theory uncovers *God*, am definitely unpersuaded by 'the multiverse', and doubtful that the whole duty of man is to halt the expansion of the universe by utilizing baryon-annihilation for interstellar travel (*ibid.*, pp. 67–9). But all that is another story. At least these fantasies offer amusing and even helpful analogues of the real doctrine (that is, they are myths).

[9] See my 'Deep Time: does it matter?' in George Ellis (ed.), *The Far-Future Universe* (Templeton Foundation Press: Radnor, PA, 2002), pp. 177–95.

[10] See Harry W. Paul, *The Edge of Contingency: French Catholic reaction to scientific change from Darwin to Duhem* (University Presses of Florida: Gainesville, 1979), p. 79,

cation (though some Darwinians and maybe Darwin himself have believed that our species *could* be gradually improved—by incarcerating or exiling criminals, and sterilizing or killing 'imbeciles'). Whatever changes occur in the various populations that make up the present living world will probably owe far more to the *bacterial* population than to the human!

I wrote a moment ago that, if there is no God (in the sense intended), then *we* have no choice but to make what deals we can. But who are 'we'? If there is no God, there are also no strict norms, no fixed boundaries, no proper assumption that there is 'a congregation' which comprises all 'human' organisms, or all mammals, or all living creatures. Neither should we suppose that there are even clear 'individuals': everyone who is reading this is compounded of indefinitely many modules, memes and passing fancies; everyone who is reading this is as much a fragment of a larger somewhat as a bee is of a hive. Even hives exist as segments of a larger system (but the system itself, remember, has no clear edges, nor any final cause). The merely virtual realities which you and I, in a way, inhabit are constructed for us (if our ordinary, modern theories are correct) by the passage of electro-chemical signals between neurons, in accordance (no doubt) with settled habits that have, in the past, had some material success in propagating the seeds, the genes, of other similar constructs. 'We' (that is, you and I) believe in individual identities, in the freedom of our wills, in moral and intellectual demands—in short, in all the maxims of a sane humanity as described by Chesterton. Yet, if there is no God, not one of these maxims is reliable or likely to be correct. The little lighted area of our lives is set within a swarming darkness of which we have (we imagine) only the barest intellectual knowledge. It might as well be true that everything 'we' experience is a fiction devised in the end-time that I described before, since what we experience is a fiction anyway.

When story tellers imagine the end-time, and its fictioneers, they fall, inevitably, into speaking of it as if it were a civilized assembly of creatures very much like 'us' (at least in being individual identities, with plans and purposes and recognizable 'human' motives), even if they are equipped with a reliable Grand Unified Theory of everything from quarks to *Finnegan's Wake,* and a reliable Grand Unified

---

quoting a nineteenth century Catholic layman, Denys Cochin; also my *Biology and Christian Ethics* (Cambridge University Press: Cambridge, 2000), p. 36.

History of all things against which to try the Theory.[11] In this contemporary story the tellers are no different from myth-makers of the past, and casual believers everywhere, in imagining that gods and heaven are no more than an enlarged imperial court. Serious theologians and visionaries were better advised, and regularly insisted that God must of His nature be incomprehensible, and 'known' only in His energies, His acts. Within the Christian tradition it has been orthodox to insist that He is, in a way, more like a society than like an individual, but that even this metaphor should not be used as an excuse for costume drama.

Consider then the options.

A fully materialist and Darwinian understanding of 'our' situation makes it vanishingly unlikely that even this terrestrial globe, even the human lineage, let alone the cosmos as a whole, will ever be united, or that 'our values', whether they are ethical or epistemological, will be vindicated. The optimistic notions that a Grand Unified Theory is just around the corner, or that we shall soon 'know the Mind of God',[12] or that our lineage is guaranteed to last as long as dinosaurs, or our civilization even as long as Ancient Egypt, are all entirely without warrant. Fantasists may imagine a cosmos bound together by transluminal connections, quantum entanglements, wormholes, and shortcuts through folded space, and maybe some of these imaginings are possible. But on the available evidence they are at least as unlikely as such older fantasies as the World Aloft, where stars and constellations represent immortal hunters across the plains of Heaven. Such fantasies have their place in a story-telling species, but materialists at least can hardly rely on them.

Although the grander fantasies of our future are indeed fantastic, we may still hope, perhaps, for a *global* unity, a peaceful resolution of our differences, and solutions for environmental problems. Unfortunately, these hopes are hardly less fantastic: dreams that we must, perhaps, retain, but without any certain evidence that they can be fulfilled. On the contrary, it seems much likelier that they *won't* be. We know (if we know anything) that the San Andreas Fault will one day swallow San Francisco. We know that there will one day be a

---

[11] See, for example, Robert Charles Wilson, *Darwinia* (Tor Books: New York, 1998).

[12] As Stephen Hawking put it in *A Brief History of Time* (Bantam: London, 1988); he has since abandoned the idea, having noticed that Gödel proved it impossible some years ago. That having the Mind of God is just being a well-informed physicist is, in any case, not quite what St. Paul supposed: see *Philippians* 2.5–7, cited on pp. 194, 246 above.

pandemic plague to exceed the effect of HIV/AIDS. We know that we are living through a Great Extinction to rival the disasters of the Triassic or Cretaceous (maybe even the Permian) end-times. We know that we will continue to disagree—and that, in any case, it would be disastrous if we didn't! Maybe some other trends (for example, the steady increase in computing power) will somehow save us before the worst befalls, but we don't know how. One easy solution to the Fermi Paradox is that all technological civilizations of the kind that might, with luck, explore the universe, inevitably self-destruct before they can: so the very fact (if it is one) that our technology is almost good enough to send out von Neumann probes is another sign that we are near the end.[13] How then shall we live, in the little time we have? In the past the shortness of our individual lives could be ignored by thinking of ourselves instead as family, representatives of an abiding unity such as a nation or a church, or simply as cells within that vaster thing, the earth. We might also expect to wake at our death to life eternal. When *everything* is mortal we seem to have no recourse but fantasy, or else despair.

Perhaps we should live entirely in the present moment (of which alone we are sure)? That moment of course is hard to notice: hardly existent at all between our fantasies of past and future. Really to live in it, putting aside all aspects of our experience that reach out one way or the other, is a difficult discipline, except perhaps when it is granted to us 'by the presence of a god' (sex, or sudden discovery—or, less agreeably, pain). Oddly, this would coincide with one strand of orthodox religion: to take no thought for tomorrow.[14] But maybe it is also a little too close to an attitude we already indulge too much: a belief that nothing matters except our immediate circumstances, that the future can go hang. Here in the continuing darkness of our days we may worship, cautiously, the little gods of sex, good food and friendship, work and games and music. Any of these may become obsessions—and of course there are other gods indistinguishable from demons. Atheism, as the conscious rejection of their claims, is often a useful, even a vital, discipline: we should not always be afraid to identify some gods as dangerous and disgusting

---

[13] See Stephen Webb, *If the Universe Is Teeming with Aliens … Where Is Everybody? Fifty Solutions to Fermi's Paradox and the Problem of Extraterrestrial Life* (Copernicus Books: New York, 2002).

[14] *Matthew* 6.34; see also *Luke* 12.20ff.

'thieves and rebels'.[15] Unfortunately, any wholesale and global atheism leaves us without discipline, without any way of lightening our path.

> Atheists have been with us for a long time—long enough to notice that they have not in fact given us much evidence to suppose that the godless heart is capable of a more generous hope than the religious. In reality, liberal ironists, sullen postmoderns, and Nietzschean self-creators do not create soup kitchens, tutorial programs, AIDS hospices, health clinics, or hunger coalitions.[16]

'Religion is the opium of the people': perhaps Marx was—almost—right. 'Faith is the substance of things hoped for, the evidence of things not seen'.[17] The Stoics were wrong to think that everything is perfect as it is. The Epicureans were wrong to think that there was no pattern to be seen in time. 'What we must completely get away from is the notion that the world as it now exists is a rational whole; we must think of its unity not by the analogy of a picture of which all the parts exist at once but by the analogy of a drama where, if it is good enough, the full meaning of the first scene only becomes apparent with the final curtain; and we are in the middle of this.'[18] The Kingdom is to come.[19]

And also, the Kingdom is at hand; it is 'upon us'.[20]

'Belief in God' is the belief that Justice will be done, that 'God's Will' will prevail. This is not a comfortable belief (since most of us are uneasily aware that we aren't just). Neither is it an easy one (since all of us can see that Justice is not being done right now). 'Now the judgement of God is upon us, and we must learn to live together as brothers or we are all going to perish together as fools.'[21] One

---

[15] Blake, 'A Descriptive Catalogue' (1809): op. cit., p. 571.

[16] Marsh, op. cit., p. 135, commenting on Richard Rorty's forlorn hope of a merely 'secular' social reform.

[17] *Hebrews* 11.1.

[18] William Temple, cited by F.A. Iremonger, *Life of William Temple* (Clarendon Press: Oxford, 1948), p. 537f. According to Sacks *The Dignity of Difference,* op. cit., p. 96, the Rabbi Akiva taught in the second century A.D. that God 'left the world unfinished so that it could be completed by the work of human beings'.

[19] See W. Pannenberg, *Theology and the Kingdom of God*, ed. R.J. Neuhaus (Westminster Press: Philadelphia, PA, 1969), p. 56.

[20] *Matthew* 3.2, 10.7, 12.28; *Mark* 1. 14 see also *Matthew* 24.14.

[21] Martin Luther King, cited by Marsh, op. cit., p. 149.

response is unbelief: maybe there is no Justice, nor any reason to expect a change of life. Another, which may also be couched in atheistic terms, is to denounce What Is in the name of What Should Be. The denunciation is heart-felt, but also in the end absurd. As Plotinus told the Gnostics of his day, 'If God is not in the world, He is not in you'.[22] If 'What Should Be' has no part to play in bringing about 'What Is', there is no basis for our denunciation of What Is.[23] Believing in oneself alone is a superstition.

In other words, militant atheists, precisely in their passion to denounce 'the God of this World', as they imagine Him, reveal their own allegiance to a greater God, but (like Plotinus's Gnostics) so separate their God from this world here as to make their own convictions vain. The better course, and the one that the openly religious have pursued, is to place their trust in the God 'who brought Jesus Christ from the dead'[24] and who will make all things new.[25] Believing in God is taking sides, specifically the side of the oppressed. 'Heal the sick, raise the dead, cleanse lepers, cast out devils. You received without cost; give without charge.'[26]

In the end, we wake.

---

[22] Plotinus, *Ennead.* II.9 [33].16, 26ff.

[23] I sought to explore the paradox in 'God, good and evil': *Proceedings of the Aristotelian Society,* 77 (1977), pp. 247ff, reprinted in J. Houston, ed., *Is it reasonable to believe in God?* (Handsel Press: Edinburgh, 1984).

[24] *Hebrews* 13.20

[25] *Revelation* 21.5

[26] *Matthew* 10.8

Index

Aboriginals 212, 234
Abortion 80, 222
Abraham 24, 25, 29, 81, 155, 178, 186, 195, 213, 250
Abrahamic faith 1, 20, 23, 28, 31-2, 110, 173, 174, 185, 186, 195, 202, 246, 248, 249
Achievement 16, 22, 23, 38, 89, 155, 161, 181, 200, 235-6, 258-61; see Success
Acorns 89, 93, 148
Acts of the Apostles 174
Aestheticism 196, 198
Albright, W.A. 43
Aletheia 108, 178; see Truth
Alexander, Denis 120, 121, 142, 152, 155,
Al-Ghazali 32, 166, 189
Al-Qaeda 161
Altruism 107, 182, 256
Amazon 1, 2, 133, 155
Ammonius Saccas 66
Anatta 22, 93-4; see Buddhism
Ancestral spirits 56-7, 178, 213, 221, 223; see 9, 82-3, 169
Anderson, Bernard W. 72, 187
Angels 21, 65, 77, 83-4, 123, 170, 173, 177, 178, 189, 194, 204, 208, 226, 264
Animal Experimentation 33, 104
Animal Procedures Act 112
Animals 2, 17, 33, 63, 67, 92, 96, 110-24, 145, 201, 209, 213, 231, 241
Annunciation 173
Anorexia 21, 228
Anscombe, G.E.M. 108, 194, 239
Anthropocentrism 88-92, 97, 100-3, 156, 166-7
Aphrodite 248, 253; see Olympians, Sex
Apuleius 67
Ares 248, 254, 258; see Olympians, Violence
Aristotle 35, 52, 108, 113-5, 119, 179, 225, 226, 240-3, 247
Armstrong, A.H. see Plotinus
Armstrong, A.H. & Markus, R.A. 192
Articles of Religion 8, 204
Ashurnasirpal II 86
Asimov, Isaac 262
Assman, J. 6
Athanasian Creed 190
Atheism as heresy 1, 84
Auden, W.H. 180-1
Audhumla 72
Audi, Robert 223
Augustine 63, 70, 100, 108, 118, 119, 174, 184, 248, 258
Aurelius, Marcus 26, 158
Authority 3, 18, 21, 29, 30-4, 36, 44, 45, 63, 65, 67, 78, 84, 102, 107, 157, 182, 198-9, 204, 208, 209, 221, 225, 227, 233, 239, 345
Awe 45-6, 51, 124, 182-3, 185, 216
Aztecs 207

Baboons 114, 116, 117,
Babylon 67, 72, 196, 211, 251
Bacteria 2, 21, 121, 135, 144, 152, 197, 200, 210, 265

Barbarians 240, 242
Barfield, Owen 118
Beauty 3, 29, 50-5, 78, 94, 97-8, 108, 115, 124, 137-8, 153, 161, 163, 167, 182, 185, 186, 241, 242, 244, 245, 259-60
Bees 106, 113, 148, 156, 265
Begbie, Jeremy 49
Behe, Michael J. 145, 157
Bekoff, Marc 115
Belshazzar 196
Berger, Peter 83
Bergman, Ingmar 38
Berkeley, George 5, 40-1, 86, 105, 152, 188, 205
Bhagavad-Gitá 178
Bhakti 55, 190
Black, Edwin 80, 133-4, 137, 209, 241
Blake, William 44, 45, 48, 72, 85, 176, 177, 260, 268
Blasphemy 24, 213
Boethius 73, 170
Bogey 24, 40, 50, 160; see Nobodaddy
Book of Common Prayer 142
Book of James 173, 256
Borges, J.L. 68, 71
Bostrom, Nick 27, 263
Bowler, Peter J. 35
Boyer, Pascal 25
Brights 19-22, 199
British Humanist Association 9
Brondesbury College 230
Brosnan, Sarah F. 117
Brunner, John 149
Bryan, William Jennings 126, 131
Buchan, John 186
Buddhism 2, 5, 24, 28, 29, 31, 32, 61, 93-4, 163, 173, 174, 178, 196, 199, 202, 203, 213, 214, 246
Burrell, D.A. 8
Butterflies 112, 164
Buziszewksi, J. 105

Caldecott, Stratford 123-4
Calderon, Pedro 158-9
Calvin, John 205
Cambridge Platonists 99, 101
Canaanites 41, 82, 249-54, 257
Cancer 3, 35, 235
Canovan, M. 131
Capitalism 127, 140, 206; see 222
Carter, Brandon 263
Carthage 81, 83; see Canaanites
Cary, Philip 100
Casaubon, Isaac 65-6
Caste 55, 178, 202, 210,
Catastrophism 63-4, 140-5; see 96, 180
Catholics 45, 47, 195, 213, 216, 230, 233-4,
Cats 80, 111, 113-5, 122
Cattle see Cows
Chastity 41-2, 126; see Sex
Cherryh, C.J. 200
Chesterton, G.K. 4, 10-11, 13, 17, 25, 26, 36, 40, 45-6, 61, 80, 82, 83, 98, 99, 100, 104, 108, 122, 123, 125-57, 158, 161, 170, 171, 184, 189, 191, 192, 193, 199, 210, 215, 216, 218, 224, 225, 228, 247, 249, 263. 265
Children 17, 18, 24, 40, 48, 56, 79-82, 104, 106, 112, 127, 130, 131, 133, 136, 160, 183, 198, 205, 206, 219, 222, 224, 227-39, 241, 245, 253-4, 259, 264
Chimpanzees 81, 112, 116
Chinese 56-7, 147
Choice 3, 11, 21, 26, 28, 47, 141, 151, 152, 223, 241, 262, 265
Christmas 30-1, 38, 49, 85, 175
Chronicles 256
Chrysippus 91, 92; see 89
Cichlids 120
Circumcision 18, 222
Cladists 135
Clarfield, A.Mark 56
Clitoridectomy 18, 222
Cloning 123
Cohn, Norman 63, 64, 140, 141, 176
Collins, John D. 86, 251, 252, 257

Colossians 84,
Common descent 2, 64, 121, 126, 141, 157, 197
Common sense 54, 79, 95, 112, 114, 115, 177, 178, 204
Complexity 50, 71, 135, 150, 153-4, 189, 191, 268
Consistency 13, 19, 20, 35, 64-5, 70, 73, 95, 138, 149, 165, 168, 207, 222, 224, 259
Contemplation 51, 55, 58, 171, 179, 247, 264; see Prayer
Continental drift 35
Control experiments 58-9
Convergence 120, 156-7, 165, 196, 197
Cook, A.B. 176
Copernicus 35, 166
Corinthians 84, 160, 226
Cornwell, John 39, 80, 85, 108, 182,
Cosmic unity 58; see The One, Complexity
Couliano, Iouan P. 92
Cows 17, 72, 93, 95, 101, 111, 137, 222
Crick, Francis 32-3
Cronos 176
Culverwell, Nathaniel 101

Dance of Immortal Love 119, 179, 192
Daniel 196
Dante Alighieri 40, 205
Darrow, Clarence 126
Darwin, Charles 12, 41, 42, 106, 112, 126, 128, 131, 135, 136, 140, 141, 145, 166, 197, 265
Darwinian Theory 35, 106, 125-57, 182, 188; see Social Darwinism, Neo-Darwinian theory
Darwin's Doubt 12, 145-8, 156, 167
Davis, D.B. 240
Dawkins, Richard 18, 21, 26, 39, 70, 79-81, 83, 85, 86, 108, 121, 135, 139, 140, 148, 154, 156, 188, 215
Day, John 81
Death 23, 38, 39, 41, 42, 47-9, 58, 108, 112, 114, 140, 152, 159-66, 170, 173, 174, 180-1, 214, 222, 244-5, 249, 267
Defensor Fidei 7, 9; see 14
Dembski, William K. 105, 125, 135
Demons 19, 21, 25, 40, 44, 72-9, 83-4. 176, 178, 214, 251, 253, 267
Dennett, Daniel 19, 21, 146, 208
Denton, Michael J. 150
Depression 3, 11, 40, 52, 236, 258
Descartes, René 32, 97, 166, 190
Deuteronomy 162, 253, 257
Devils 3, 5-29, 65, 77, 78, 81, 269
De Waal, Frans 117
Dinosaurs 74, 173, 266
Diogenes Laertius 16, 48, 108, 181
Diogenes of Sinope (the Cynic) 94, 181
Dionysus 178
Disease see Sickness
Divine Commands 29, 70, 76, 78, 107, 177, 188, 239, 251, 257, 258
Dogs 54, 95, 101, 110-5, 119, 121-2, 245
Doomsday Argument 263
Dossey, Larry 60, 79
Dostoyevsky, F.M. 182
Downing, F.Gerald 181
Dragon 24-5, 40, 72
Dreaming 10, 14-5, 24, 26, 27, 43, 46, 52, 74, 107, 133, 141-2, 143, 158-71, 176, 178, 211-3, 247, 263, 266
Drunkenness 51-2, 124, 177, 190
Ducks 169
Duffy, Eamon 46-7, 49, 181
Dukkha 178
Dyson, Freeman 121-2, 263

Ecclesiasticus 252
Egypt 65-6, 70, 72-5, 86, 178, 199, 250, 266
Eliade, Mircea 194
Elijah 82, 251
Elysia viridis 197
Empedocles 148, 150

Empires 7, 206, 215, 220,
End-Times 158, 164, 169, 262-9; see 27
Engels, F. 89
Enlightenment 22, 24, 29, 126, 165, 220
Environmentalism 96, 100-3, 144, 201, 266
Epictetus 89; see Stoics
Epicureans 48, 93-6, 100-1, 119, 148-9, 154, 160, 178, 188, 268
Esdras 178
Eudaimonia 240, 259
Eugenics 42, 58, 80, 133-4, 138, 155, 209, 249, 265
Excommunication 32; see Heresy
Exodus 29, 257
Exorcism 76-9, 211
Explanations 72-9, 149-50
Eyes 156-7

Facts and Values 87; see Objectivity, Reality
Fairies 38, 151, 159, 171, 173, 176, 178, 185
Fairy tales 24-5, 40, 159, 176
Faith schools 227-39
Father Brown 61, 127, 148, 162, 171
Feldman, Louis H. 251
Ferguson, Kennan 114
Fermi Paradox 267
Feuerbach, Ludwig 262
Feyerabend, Paul 35
Ficino, Marsilio 65
Final causes 33, 92, 126, 156, 213, 265
Findlay, J.S. 208
Fine tuning 27, 149-50; see multiverse
First People 39, 75,139
Fischer, D.H. 218
Flaubert, Gustave 83
Flood 63-4, 67, 140, 141, 144, 176, 214
Folk psychology 73
Food 56, 63, 77, 90, 95, 113, 120, 222, 249, 256, 267
Forgiveness 47, 79, 107, 116, 204, 227, 247,
Foxe, J. 6
Freedom 11, 28
Freeman, David 248
Fried, G. 62, 162
Friendship 15, 43, 94, 96, 101, 110-24, 158, 171, 186, 192, 197, 202, 223, 235, 241, 242, 245, 253, 254, 262, 267
Frisbie, Charlotte J. 78
Frye, Northrop 51
Fuller, Steve 22

Gaisser, Julia Haig 67
Galactic Empire 7, 19, 20, 85; see 33
Galileo 32, 166
Galton, Frederick 57-9
Gandhi, Mahatma 195
Gardner, Robert & Heider, Karl G. 207
Gasman, D. 133
Gee, Henry 135
Gefter, Amanda 71, 156
Genes 26, 37, 64, 80, 105, 107, 117, 121, 122, 131, 138, 167, 168, 210, 265
Genesis 62, 63, 64, 67, 68, 72, 81, 96-100, 102, 250
Genetic engineering 104, 120, 121, 122, 200, 259, 260
Genocide 81, 203, 207, 223, 250
Geology 63-4, 140, 145, 155
Ghiselin, M.H. 105
Girard, René 20, 256
Glamour 53-4, 176, 185; see 26
Gnostics 161, 269
Gödel, K. 214-5, 266
Golden Rule 107, 213, 246-7
Good Life 221, 236, 240, 259
Gosse, Philip 155
Gould, Stephen Jay 126, 153, 156
Graham, Gordon 107
Gray, John 218, 219, 220
Gunkel, Herman 72
Guru Granth Sahib 233
Guru Nanak Sikh Schools 232, 237

Gyges' Ring 105

Hadith 29, 207
Haeckel, Ernst 133
Haldane, J.B.S. 148
Halder, G. 157
Halevi, Shira 68
Hand, Michael 12, 229-32, 237
Hanke, Lewis 243
Harpending, Henry 129
Harrison, Victoria S. 31
Hartung, John 85, 86
Hasid 77, 194, 203
Hauerwas, Stanley 45
Hawking, Stephen 70-1, 154, 156, 164, 263, 266
Health 133, 137, 201, 258-61, 268
Hebrews 23, 268, 269
Hedonism 94, 115, 118, 244,
Heidegger, M. 4, 61
Hengel, Martin 194
Heracles 181
Herbert, George 29
Heresy 1, 5, 17, 84, 85, 127, 188, 225
Hermetic Corpus 65-7
Herrick, James A. 136
Hertog, Thomas 70-1
Hick, John 152, 163
Hildegard of Bingen 258
Hinde, R.A. 114
Hinduism 5, 20, 24, 55, 61, 178, 199, 202, 214, 218, 221, 228
History 37, 42, 51, 64-5, 75, 81, 86, 98, 126, 136, 140, 167-8, 187, 194, 197, 202, 204, 210, 214, 217, 218, 236, 247, 252, 266
Hitler, Adolf 11, 137; see 42
Hocking, W.E. 197, 208
Holmes, Oliver Wendell 209
Holocaust 133; see 8
Honour 16, 22, 24, 105-6, 112, 222, 227-9, 237, 241-2, 245, 247, 261
Houyhnhnm 247
Howard, Michael 212
Humanism 9, 17, 85, 102, 201, 234, 262
Hume, David 189
Humphrey, Nicholas 79
Humphreys, Colin J. 30
Hunter, Cornelius G. 20, 152, 155
Hunter, George William 131
Huntingon, Samuel 203-9, 212, 213, 214
Hutton, F.W. 120
Huxley, T.H. 140

Iblis 177; see Satan
Idolatry 5, 28, 43, 57, 185, 186, 210, 213, 251
Iliad 69
Illuminati 7, 33
Imbeciles 118, 133, 200, 209, 265
Immortality 158-65
Incas 79-80
Incest 95, 248
Inconsistency see Consistency
Individualism 206, 246
Infanticide 80-3, 198, 249, 251, 253-4
Innocent IV 83
Inquisition 5, 83
Intellect 51, 164-5, 171
Intelligent Design Theory 32, 34, 151-3, 155
Iremonger, F.A. 268
Isaiah 6, 26, 28, 38, 48, 212, 256, 257
Isis 67, 181
Islam 2, 6, 7, 29, 32, 36, 97, 161, 195, 199, 203, 205-7, 213, 218, 220-2, 226, 230, 233-4, 238
Islamia Primary School 230, 232, 238
Israelites 43, 69, 70, 80, 81, 82, 84, 86, 102, 178, 185, 187-8, 249-54; see 186-7

Jaki, Stanley 32, 263
James 29
James, William 12, 79, 148, 231; see 15
Jefferson, Thomas 131, 216
Jeremiah 26, 253

Jesus 22, 31, 32, 44, 46-7, 68, 76, 84, 85, 86, 102, 174, 181, 193, 194, 256, 257, 258, 269
Jews 8, 23, 68, 83, 85, 86, 133, 160, 194, 199, 203, 204, 213, 219, 230, 232, 238
Jihad 161, 233
Jñana 55, 190
Job 92, 187
John Apostle 49, 55, 161, 179, 203, 252
John Paul II 102, 118, 145
Johnson, Samuel 245-6, 247
Jones, Jim 161
Josaphat 195
Joyce, James 168; see 265
Judah, Rabbi 111
Judas Maccabaeus 252
Judgement 37, 40, 45, 54, 82, 87-109, 112, 116, 143, 144, 187, 194, 198, 213, 216, 231, 234, 239, 247, 252, 255, 257
Judgement Day 38, 45, 143-4, 198, 216, 257, 262, 268; see Flood
Judges 250
Julian, Emperor 204
Julian of Norwich 170
Just, R. 242
Justice 3, 11, 18, 24, 28, 38-9, 41-3, 55, 80, 89, 105, 111, 116-7, 126, 128, 130, 131, 140, 157, 177, 184, 191-4, 207, 213, 242, 249, 253, 255, 268-9

Kant, Immanuel 27-8, 50, 147, 191-2, 196; see 199, 248
Karma 55
Keats, John 163
Keith, Arthur 96, 129
Khajuraho 248
Kierkegaard, Soren 81
King David Foundation 238
King, Martin Luther 268
Kings 14, 57, 86, 90, 102, 159, 161, 181, 191, 193, 196, 199, 204, 240, 250, 252, 256
Kingsley, Charles 56
Kipling, Rudyard 217, 227, 263
Klibansky, R.. Panofsky, E. & Saxl, F. 52, 258
Kohak, Erazim 232
Koran 29, 36, 162, 166, 177, 207, 233
Krishna-Avanti School 232

Lamb of God 72, 257
Language 15, 73, 76, 111, 115, 118, 120, 124, 178, 193, 236
Larson, Edward J. 126
Larson, Frederick A. 30
Lash, Nicholas 5, 19, 118, 173, 188, 196, 200
Lecercle, J.J. 214-5
Leslie, John 263
Leviticus 70, 81, 249, 250
Lewis, Bernard 220
Lewis, C.S. 20, 21, 103, 168-9, 184,
Liberty of conscience 8, 15, 17, 68, 191, 206, 214-26, 227, 243, 247
Lichtenberger, Henri 42
Lion King 90
Literal readings 24, 29, 31, 37, 38, 61-5, 68, 126, 174, 258
Lizards 7, 19, 34, 122, 214
Lodge, Oliver 34
Logic 8, 10, 12, 13, 25, 70, 73, 106, 145, 153, 175
Long, A.A. & Sedley, D. 89, 91, 93
Love 8, 28, 40, 46-7, 49, 51, 53-4, 70, 105, 107, 114, 123, 124, 161, 167, 179, 183, 186, 190-1, 215, 250
Lovejoy, A.O. 14
Lovelock, James 144
Loyalty 15, 105, 113, 169, 182, 188, 204-6, 219, 250-1
Lucretius 93, 178
Luke 70, 71, 102, 173, 252, 256, 267
Luther, Martin 7, 21, 36, 186

Maccabees 252
Macintyre, Alastair 114-5
Mackey, James P. 194
Mackie, John 87-8; see 119
Macrobes 20-1; see mental microbes, devils

Macrobius 170
Madell, Geoffrey 247
Magic/magicians 14, 54, 57, 60, 65, 76, 77, 92, 126, 160, 176
Mahoney, Michael J. 34
Maimonides, Moses 5
Malachi 38, 198
Malin, Shimon 73
Malthusians 42, 128
Manu, Laws of 228-9, 246
Marcion 85, 86
Margulis, Lynn & Sagan, Dorion 197
Mark 22, 84, 268
Marriage 46, 142, 249, 254, 255
Marsh, Charles 224, 268
Marx, Karl 14-15, 158, 268; see 195
Mary 173
Masturbation 94, 184, 248
Mathematics 13, 88, 116, 150, 175, 214-5, 236
Matthew 22, 29, 40, 70, 79, 84, 143, 159, 193, 207, 250, 256, 257, 267, 268, 269
Matrix 163
Maximus Confessor 58, 62, 154
McCartney, Paul 52
McDonald, Kevin 85, 86
McEvilley, Thomas 94, 184
Mead, Margaret 248
Melancholia see Depression
Memes 6, 19, 20, 21, 22, 26, 28, 265
Ménard, Pierre 67
Mental disorders 78
Mental microbes 3, 5-29, 40; see memes, devils, demons
Mephistopheles 59
Metempsychosis 110-1, 119, 160, 228, 246
Micah 29, 253
Millian Principle 18
Missionaries 6-7, 24, 181, 202, 248
Mitochondria 64, 143, 197
Moabites 249, 250, 252
Mohammed 202, 203, 206
Molech 81, 82
Monkeys 17, 117
Monkey Trials 126, 131
Moral realism 3, 87-109; see 49
More, Thomas 21
Mormon, Book of 69
Morris, Simon Conway 157
Moses 65-6, 250, 252; see 6
Multiverse 27, 263-4
Murdoch, Iris 43

Nagasena 93
Nagel, Thomas 111
National Curriculum 230, 235-6, 259
National spirits 9, 208, 216
Natural kinds 120, 139, 156
Natural Slaves 18, 113, 217, 240-3
Navaho 78
Needham, Joseph 147
Neo-Darwinian theory 2, 3, 13, 36, 125-57, 144, 146, 147, 156, 157, 216-7
Newman, John Henry 33
Newton, Isaac 128, 214
Nicomachean Ethics 179, 240, 241, 242, 243
Nietzsche, F. 13, 16, 42, 136, 157, 167, 213, 229, 246
Nihilism 88, 105, 211
Nirvana 94, 174
Noah 63-5, 143, 153, 213
Noble, Denis 139, 152, 153,
Nobodaddy 85, 86, 186, 187; see Bogey
Non-contradiction see consistency, logic
Norms 33, 91, 93, 95, 130, 148-57, 224, 265
Numbers 41, 249-51

Oberon 98
Objectivity 43, 45, 51, 54, 67, 87-109, 112-3, 115-6, 184, 224, 237
Obligations 10, 16, 55, 95, 96, 104, 113, 119, 227, 228; see moral realism
Octopus 111, 112

Odone, Cristina 233-4
Olbers' Paradox 75, 160
Olympians 24, 44, 248, 253, 254, 258
Omnipotence 23, 172, 174, 175, 193, 247
Omnipresence 154, 175, 179
Omniscience 151, 172, 174, 175, 193
Ontologism 100
Opium of the people 14-15, 38, 268
Oppenheimer, Stephen 218
Orestes 70
Orwell, George 55, 65, 88, 209, 214
Other/Otherness 98-100, 124, 213
Ottomans 220

Pain 6, 9, 16, 41, 83, 94, 96, 99, 116, 118, 161, 172, 181, 183-4, 187, 244-5, 267
Palestinians 43, 252
Paley, William 153
Palmerston, Viscount (H.J. Temple) 56
Pannenberg, Wolfhart 186, 262, 268
Panpsychism 111
Panspermia 33
Parents 18, 56, 105-6, 131, 133, 160, 222, 224, 232, 236, 249, 254
Parthenogenesis 30, 136
Passover 75
Patterson, Orlando 242
Paul 77, 86, 160, 181, 201, 248, 253, 266; see *Colossians, Corinthians, Philippians, Romans, Titus*
Paul, Harry W. 264
Pearson, Helen 138
Pedagogy 5, 18-19, 78, 104-6, 112, 131, 133, 220, 222, 227-39, 244, 254; see children, faith schools
Perry, T.D. 95
Peter 143
Pharaoh 74, 199
Philia 114-6; see Friendship
Philippians 194, 246, 266
Philo of Alexandria 62, 97, 240, 251
Phinehas 86, 250-2, 255, 257
Pigs 89, 90, 92, 99, 112, 137,
Pike, Nelson 62
Pindar 176
Pitman, Walter 64
Plamenatz, John 23,
Plantinga, A. 12, 69, 135, 145, 154, 215
Plato 16, 43, 50, 65, 66, 96, 97, 103, 105, 159, 160, 163, 164, 167, 170, 180, 199, 204, 210, 246
Playing God 107
Pleasure 16, 18, 94-6, 101, 114-5, 118, 142, 183-4, 230, 241, 244-5, 251, 253-5
Pleonexia 18, 100, 258-61
Plotinus 11, 22, 27, 51, 53, 54, 56, 66, 76, 124, 148, 154, 159, 161-2, 165, 171, 179, 180, 181, 184, 185, 190, 192, 199, 269
Plutarch 52, 91
Pois, Robert A. 201
Politics 240, 241, 242, 247
Polytheism 25, 175-6, 185, 198; see Olympians
Poverty 48, 127, 130, 132, 133, 134, 243
Pratchett, Terry 38-9
Prayer 28, 55-60, 78-9, 233
Preece, Rod 119
Primatt, Humphrey 102
Prince of Wales 7, 10
Procreation 94-5, 127, 129, 133, 142, 147, 150-1, 183, 249, 254
Prohibition 43, 177, 213, 253
Property 17, 104, 192, 207, 211, 221
Prophecies 7, 19, 29, 49, 55, 66, 68, 82, 194, 203, 251, 256; see 199
Prostitution 18, 249, 253
Protestants 2, 7, 8, 29, 34, 36, 61, 144, 174, 195, 204, 213, 216, 233
Protoevangelium see Book of James
Provan, Iain W. 69
Psalms 175, 193, 251, 252
Ps-Dionysius 258
Psychopaths 19, 116, 183, 243
Publilius Syrus 245

Punishment 96, 133, 190, 208, 239, 249, 255, 257
Purification 5, 24, 58, 99-100, 109
Pythagoreans 16, 33, 35, 110-12, 124, 246, 261

Quasi-realism 95-6, 99-100
Questions of King Milinda 93

Races 33, 41, 42, 120, 130, 133, 221, 229
Radhakrishnan, S. & Moore, C. 94
Rae, Murray A. 69
Rahab 72
Ramsey, William 12
Rawls, John 219, 221
Regis, Ed 200
Renaissance 65, 66, 92
Revelation of John Divine 84, 198, 210-11, 214, 257, 275
Reality 13, 27-8, 39, 46-7, 49-55, 58, 92, 123, 124, 146-7, 150, 154-5, 158-71, 184-6, 209, 236; see Truth
Rhodes, Cecil 127-8
Ricci, Matteo 56-7
Ricoeur, Paul 74
Ritchie, D.G. 6
Rituals 7, 14, 24, 28, 56, 58, 75-6, 77, 80, 82, 84, 86, 175, 178, 196, 197, 200, 202
Rives, J.B. 81
Robots 37, 240
Rochester, Earl of see Wilmot
Rokeah, D. 204
Romans 174, 201
Rorty, Richard 14, 99, 182, 209, 268
Royalty see Kings
Russell, Bertrand 23, 187
Russell, Eric Frank 20, 21
Ruth 250
Ryan, William 64

Sacks, Jonathan 15, 204, 213, 218, 219, 226, 268
Sacred 67, 69,81, 84, 196, 200, 206, 207, 208, 212, 221, 244, 254, 257
Sacrifice 28, 44, 72, 79-83, 112, 181, 207, 249, 251-3, 256
Said, Edward W. 89, 252, 257
Salam, Abdus 32
Salt, Henry 195
Samuel 102
Samuelson, Norbert M. 55, 185
Sandel, Michael J. 259
Sanity 10-11, 14, 26, 158, 214, 237, 265; see 225
Santa Claus 31
Satan 2, 18, 40, 91, 187; see Devils, Iblis
Saussure, Ferdinand de 214
Scapegoating 16, 20. 256; see Girard, Sacrifice
Schleiermacher, Friedrich 49, 85, 175-6
Schools 18; see Pedagogy
Schopenhauer, A. 53-4
Schwartz, Regina M. 41, 71
Schwartz, Richard H. 111
Science 3, 10, 12, 14, 20, 28, 30-60, 72-4, 107, 119, 128, 130-1, 146, 147, 156, 166, 190, 201, 212, 213, 236, 237,
Science Fiction 21, 46, 85, 136, 141, 162, 164, 167, 170, 200, 211
Scopes Trial 131
Scripture, Reading 3, 20, 29, 31, 44, 61-86, 97, 172, 174, 187, 194,
Self 11, 15, 20-2, 27, 36, 40, 51, 85, 101, 110-2, 122, 162-3, 165, 180, 190, 199, 208, 236; see 242
Self-confidence 35
Sepulveda, Juan Ginés de 243
SETI 34
Sex 23, 24, 53-4, 94-5, 176, 248-56
Shadows 13, 36, 58, 163, 176
Shakespeare, William 28, 128, 253
Shame 11, 159, 169, 180, 242, 244, 249
Shari'a 207, 220
Shelley, Percy Bysshe 163
Sherwood, Martha 253
Shestov, Lev 53-4

Sickness 21, 48, 56, 76-8, 93, 127, 129-30, 131, 132, 166, 253, 260
Sikhs 218, 222, 232-3, 237-8
Silk, Joan B. 116
Simonides 52
Simon the Just 55
Sky 50, 73, 186; see Zeus
Slaves/slavery 17, 23, 48, 75, 101, 113, 129, 131, 159, 187, 192, 217, 228, 239-48, 253, 257; see Natural Slaves
Slavishness 32, 36, 114, 217, 227, 239-48
Smith, John 99
Smith, Joseph 69
Smith, Wilfred Cantwell 32, 195
Smuts, Barbara B. 114, 117
Snook, I.A. 229
Social constructions 19, 103
Social Darwinism 18, 35, 41, 125-57, 246
Socrates 40, 85, 160, 163, 170, 182
Sodomy 94, 248, 249; see 133
Song of Songs 62
Sorcery 59; see Demons
Southcott, Joanna 36, 199
Speciation 120, 142
Species 17, 115, 116, 119-23, 130, 139, 142, 144, 156-7, 195-7, 200, 265
Spengler, Oswald 202
Spinoza, Benedict 25, 91-2, 101
Sprat, Thomas 98
Sprigge, T.L.S. 110, 111
Spruyt, Hendrik 218
Star of Bethlehem 30-1
Stars 9, 67, 74, 75, 93, 98, 99, 149, 170, 210, 228, 266
Star Trek 38, 46, 74
St.Croix, Geoffrey de 242, 243
Stern, Philip D. 252
Stoczkowski, Wiktor 129
Stoics 25, 26, 88-101, 108, 118, 119, 171, 186, 187, 188, 268
Stone, Dan 42, 133,
Stories 6, 14, 16, 21-2, 24-5, 28, 37-50, 65-71, 72-6, 108, 110, 141, 147, 159, 162-3, 173-4, 181, 194, 202, 251-2
Stout, J. 182
Stove, David 105
Sturluson, Snorri 72
Success 59, 86, 146, 151, 176, 181, 205, 212, 220, 235, 237, 239, 255, 260, 265
Suicide 161, 222, 244-5
Sun 27, 34, 41, 45-6, 52, 67, 72-4, 75, 80, 139, 148, 157, 170, 210
Supernatural 19, 25, 26-7, 68-9, 83, 84, 123, 210-1, 224
Superstring Theory 35, 36
Sykes, Brian 143
Symmachus 8-9, 204

Targum 68
Taliban 198
Taylor, Thomas 67
Teilhard de Chardin, Pierre 122, 200
Temple, William 268
Thankfulness 4, 47, 56, 261
Themistius 204
The One 50, 154, 163, 172, 179, 185, 192
Theoria 179
Thirty-nine Articles see *Articles of Religion*
Three Lives 16, 258-9, 261
Thucydides 253
Tiamat 72
Time 24, 37, 39, 100, 139, 170, 171, 172, 194, 202, 209, 263-4, 268
Tipler, Frank J. 21, 32, 125, 145, 201
Titus 28-9
Toleration 7, 9, 16-18, 28, 52, 81, 204, 220, 222-3, 239, 249; see Liberty of conscience
Tolkien, J.R.R. 211
Tolstoy, N. 195
Torah 55, 249
Tortoises 113
Torture 43, 83, 132, 180, 181, 182, 217
Toynbee, Arnold 203
Traffic accidents 82

Treason 61, 96, 204, 222, 252
Trigg, Robert 223
Trinity 179, 189, 190, 191
Truman Show 46
Truth, worth of 2, 5-6, 9-10, 13-6, 19, 22, 29, 31, 37-8, 44-50, 54, 55, 58, 62, 65, 68-9, 73, 87-8, 95, 99, 100, 102, 108, 124, 146-7, 157, 160, 165, 178, 182, 184-5, 190, 193, 203, 209, 214, 237; see Reality
Turkeys 95, 123, 138, 189,
Turkle, Sherry 112
Turner, S.M. 56

Ummah 204, 205
Unamuno, Miguel di 160
Universities 234-5
Untouchables 228; see Caste
Upton, Charles 178

VanderWilt, Jeffrey 176
Van Vogt, A.E. 173
Vegetarianism 110, 220, 224, 232
Violence 23, 207, 209, 225, 248-58, 262, 264
Virgin Birth 30-1, 181; see 173
Virtual Realities 27-8, 55, 59, 157, 158, 211, 263, 265; see Dreaming
Voegelin, Eric 258
Von Balthasar, Hans Urs 62, 123-4
Von Rad, Gerhard 187
Von Wright, G.H. 74

Waddington, W.G. 30
Waking Up 3, 10, 26, 27, 52, 53, 91, 98, 158-71, 211, 267, 269
Ward, Maisie 126
Ward, Martin 10
Ward, Michael 184
Watson, James 33
Webb, Stephen 267
Weikart, Richard 42
Weisman, Avery D. 114
Wells, H.G. 41-2, 126-33, 137, 139, 146, 183
Whitelam, Keith W. 43, 252, 257
Whitman, Walt 70
Wiedemann, Thomas 243, 244
Wigner, Eugen 13, 150
Wilderness 90
Williams, Charles 181, 184, 193
Williams, Mark 11
Williams, Paul 110
Williams, Rowan 220
Wills, Garry 63
Wilmot, John 13
Wilson, E.O. 167, 168
Wilson, John A. 73
Wilson, Robert Charles 266
Wink, Walter 21, 40, 77, 208, 216
Wisdom of Solomon 97
Witchcraft 44, 99; see Magic, Objectivity
Wittfogel, Karl 208
Wittgenstein, Ludwig 98, 208
Woese, Carl 121
Wollstonecraft, Mary 67
Women 17, 67, 143, 206, 242, 248, 249, 251, 252
Word of God 69, 174, 215
World-hive 122, 209; see 130, 200, 265
World State 197, 208-214
Worms 112, 157
Worship 5-6, 9, 23, 26, 61, 66, 81, 82, 84-5, 100, 101, 108, 173, 176, 178, 186-7, 201, 232, 237, 247-50, 257, 259, 267
Wow Factor 175-82
Wright, John C. 264

Yahoos 247
Yang Xiao 57
Yeats, W.B. 177
Yourgrau, P. 215
Yuk Factor 104
Yum Factor 104, 248, 255

Zechariah 256
Zee, A. 150
Zeus 23-4, 176-7, 199; see Olympians
Zizek, Slavoj 61-2
Zombies 240, 241